Dust from our Eyes

Books by Joan Baxter

The Hermit of Gully Lake — the life and times
of Willard Kitchener MacDonald

A serious pair of shoes: an African journal

Strangers are like children: stories of Africa

Graveyard for dreamers: one woman's odyssey in Africa

Benin, The Congo, Burkina Faso:
Politics, Economics and Society
Contributing author

Dust
from our
Eyes

An unblinkered look at Africa

by Joan Baxter

Wolsak and Wynn

Cover photograph: Joan Baxter
Cover design: Rachel Rosen
Author's photograph: Wes Baxter
Typeset in Goudy, printed by Ball Media, Brantford, Canada
Book design: Julie McNeill, McNeill Design Arts

The publishers gratefully acknowledge the
support of the Canada Council for the Arts,
the Ontario Arts Council and the Book
Publishing Industry Development Program
(BPIDP) for their financial assistance.

The Canada Council   Le Conseil des Arts
for the Arts   du Canada

ONTARIO ARTS COUNCIL
CONSEIL DES ARTS DE L'ONTARIO

The author gratefully acknowledges
the support of the Canada Council.

Canadian   Patrimoine
Heritage   canadien

Wolsak and Wynn Publishers Ltd.
#102 69 Hughson Street North
Hamilton, ON
Canada L8R 1G5

Library and Archives Canada Cataloguing in Publication

Baxter, Joan
    Dust from our eyes : an unblinkered look at Africa / Joan Baxter.

Includes bibliographical references and index.
ISBN 978-1-894987-30-1

    1. Baxter, Joan. 2. Western countries–Relations–Africa.
3. Africa–Relations–Western countries. 4. Women journalists–Canada–
Biography. 5. Women journalists–Africa–Biography. I. Title.

PN4913.B28A3 2008   070.92   C2008-905815-1

Printed in Canada

Contents

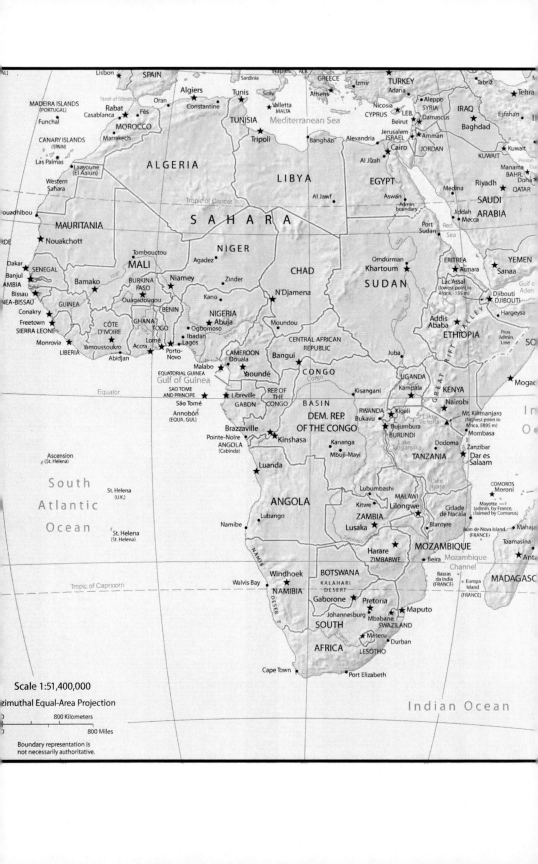

Introduction

Among your characters you must always include The Starving African, who wanders the refugee camp nearly naked, and waits for the benevolence of the West.

Taboo subjects: ordinary domestic scenes, love between Africans (unless a death is involved), references to African writers or intellectuals, mention of school-going children who are not suffering from yaws or Ebola fever or female genital mutilation ...

Binyavanga Wainana[1]

A West African proverb warns that before you rush in to help clean the straw out of your neighbour's eye, you should pause long enough to remove the dust from your own. There are many scenarios that might spring from this bit of African wisdom and how it could play out today. Most are not particularly good news for the heart-shaped continent.

At a recent talk to mark International Development Week at Saint Mary's University in Halifax, Nova Scotia, I spoke about the great wealth of knowledge in Africa, and how it was so often ignored or denigrated by outsiders busy trying to develop the continent in their own image. I illustrated this point with photographs of Africans in many walks of life, many of them able and able-bodied farmers beaming at the camera, or pointing with pride to their harvest. The presentation highlighted Africa's under-touted historical accomplishments, as well as its wealth and agricultural wisdom, with a backdrop medley of wonderful music from Africa.

Afterwards a middle-aged man in blue jeans approached me. The exchange went something like this. "Your pictures," he began, hesitantly. "I mean, they were different. Were those in a special part of Africa?"

"No," I said. The photographs had been taken quite randomly on farms, in villages, and in cities in six different countries on the continent.

"But was that a special group of people?"

"Oh no," I said. "Those were ordinary everyday scenes of African farmers and in many different places in Africa. They were probably quite typical."

He nodded slowly. "I never saw pictures of Africans who looked good like that," he said finally, as he turned and walked away.

In May 2000, *The Economist* blasted the words "The hopeless continent" across its cover, and no reader would have had to look inside to see which continent that issue of the magazine was devoting its attention to. The media have helped perpetuate the racist stereotype of Africans as savages, and the persistent – ridiculous – notion of the continent as "dark."[2] Africa's former BBC correspondent, George Aligiah, put it this way: "For most people who get their view of the world from TV, Africa is a faraway place where good people go hungry, bad people run government, and chaos and anarchy are the norm."[3]

The major North American networks tend to carry little news from Africa, so when they do, it is almost inevitably limited to the worst of the worst. Most stories will hint that there is something inherently brutal about a particular group of African people. They probably won't ask or answer the question: Why did this happen? It is also highly unlikely that someone watching prime time television in North American will see many reports on positive things Africa and her people have to share with the world.

The good intentions of outsiders garner more media interest than good acts by Africans themselves. I recall listening to a radio interview with a man leading a team of well-heeled Canadians setting off on an adventure to climb Mount Kilimanjaro. But that wasn't quite how the Tanzania safari was presented. Apparently, this was an altruistic act; the travellers had linked up with a group that organizes spectacular climbs to raise funds for charity. The proceeds of their trip to Africa, which they would get from donations, would go to charities. I waited to hear his answer to some of the questions that sprang to my mind – admittedly a bit jaded after all my years in Africa. I wanted to know, for example, how much the trip would cost per person; I guessed around 5,000 US dollars (or more). I wanted to hear how much would be left for charity after the costs of their adventure, for which charities and for which purpose. I wanted to know what the Canadian travellers knew of Africa and her people. And, perhaps unreasonably, I also would have liked to hear a calculation of the environmental costs of such a long air trip and climb up a mountain already suffering the effects of climate change, visible in fact on the top of Mount Kilimanjaro where the glacier is melting. But the interview ended with those questions not answered. Ornery as I am, I question the ethics of such expensive ventures cloaked in charitable clothing, even if the destination of the travellers is Africa and the funds they raise are for Africans. The proceeds of this particular African expedition were for Canadian charities.

Another kind of media story that makes it out of Africa is the one that zeroes in on the efforts being made by dedicated development and emergency workers who are in Africa trying to ease the plight of the people there. But the aid workers – or at least their organizations – are generally not African in origin. The hero or heroes portrayed by such reports are usually people from Western countries.

There's nothing inherently wrong with reports that applaud good works by outsiders in Africa. But they offer a skewed view. Far more Africans are doing good work on their continent than are foreigners. I'm a journalist with an interest in Africa, so I would like to see a lot more media coverage from the continent because it is incredibly complex, fascinating and diverse. More and better coverage would help the outside world understand the continent, her triumphs and her problems, and perhaps encourage people to do more to support African efforts to solve their own problems and scrutinize their own country's policies at home and abroad. We could use another few – or few hundred – books like Stephanie Nolen's *28: stories of AIDS in Africa*. These books bring African voices and realities to people off the continent. They transform the meaningless statistics that are the mainstay of newscasts into three-dimensional human beings courageously confronting the great odds stacked against them.[4]

The world's major media – especially ones feeding stories to North America – are short on African correspondents. They are equally short on African editors and on publishers who have an in-depth knowledge of the real issues on the continent. Some of those issues are historical – the past wrongs that Africa has suffered at the hands of the slave-traders, the colonists and neo-colonial 'friends' and 'helpers.' Some of these latter-day helpers intervene with good intentions. But sometimes these *blind* good intentions have paved the road to more dependence, trouble and still bigger problems. "Africa has become a 'comfort zone' used by the West to calm down its masses," writes Baffour Ankomah, editor of *New African* magazine. If any African cities were ever shown in full flower, he observes, Westerners might see that their cities are not the only nice places on earth, and that 'comfort zone' would whittle away.[5]

Others in the business of helping Africa are not so well intentioned. They may disguise their interventions as charitable and helpful and play on public goodwill, when they are actually motivated by self-interest. These groups are much more concerned with creating policies orchestrated to re-chain Africa, to reshape it to fit rigid and unhelpful economic and political doctrines – with increased profits at home.

The effort to push feminine hygiene products on Africa is a fine example of such 'charity.' The Proctor & Gamble companies, Always Canada, Tampax and Being Girl, have a project called "Protecting Futures" with a "Pad Program" to provide African women with sanitary pads.[6] Well-meaning consumers in the wealthy world are encouraged to contribute to this venture because, chimes the Always Canada website: "It's amazing to think that a small thing like a pad might have such a dramatic effect on someone's future." Exaggeration certainly, but also misleading to Western consumers whose goodwill is being lassoed by companies claiming that purchases (of tampons and pads) will somehow secure a girl's future in Africa. Indeed there will be "dramatic effects." There will be increased profits for these companies carving out new markets, and a new dependency on imported, costly and environmentally unfriendly consumer products in Africa, while the perfectly good traditional methods (pieces of cloth) will be made to look suddenly old-fashioned and inferior. A concocted problem with a lucrative (for Western companies) solution. Straw and dust.

Europe and North America have never felt the need to hold any "truth and reconciliation" commissions, which would allow the ordinary citizens to know more about their own foreign policies, past and present. Neither the ills imposed on the world both during the centuries that European countries were stealing and settling new continents nor those of the more recent neo-colonial interventions that spread "disaster capitalism," as described in Naomi Klein's book, *The Shock Doctrine*, are open for discussion.[7] Klein documents the imposition around the world of unpopular Milton Friedman-style economic reforms, reforms which benefit the rich and powerful. Enacting these reforms requires heavy-handed political oppression to contain any opposition from the ordinary people adversely affected by the economic dogma. Given that most of the world views sub-Sahara Africa as a never-ending disaster, and given the region's weak and impoverished states with presidents who toe the economic reform line (or else), Africa has been an easy mark for disaster capitalists from the World Bank, International Monetary Fund (IMF), the Western donors that control them, and other lenders cum creditors. The pillars of this disaster capitalism, which Klein calls the "free market trinity," are privatization, deregulation and cuts to social spending. These neo-liberal or market fundamentalist policies have been the prevailing economic dogma applied in Africa – and around the world – for almost three decades, resulting in an increased disparity between rich and poor. By 2006, two percent of the world's population owned one half of the world's wealth.[8]

Economic reforms don't come in isolation. As elsewhere, in Africa they require compliant leaders to enforce them, so long as they are not compliant or soft when their people take to the streets to protest rising prices, unemployment and growing poverty. Some of these African leaders are not very good leaders at all, and they probably wouldn't be able to stay in power very long without their friends in the West. In fact some might never have made it to power without their friends in the West, some of whom haven't been stellar leaders either.

The situation in Africa today is not all that different from the one created at the end of the 19th century by Belgium's King Leopold, which was detailed so graphically and powerfully by Adam Hochschild.[9] Leopold managed to convince his backers in Europe and the United States that his brutal plundering of the Congo was not plundering at all, but a humane effort to fight the slave trade and 'civilize' the natives.

Paradoxically, Africa is crippled with debt to the West, when in fact the West owes Africa so much. Gerald Caplan passionately articulates this: "We should give back what we've plundered and looted and stolen. Until we think about the West's relationship with Africa honestly, until we face up to the real record, until we acknowledge our vast culpability and complicity in the African mess, until then we'll continue – in our caring and compassionate way – to impose policies that actually make the mess even worse."[10]

"In April this year [2008], I caught a replay of *Idol Gives Back*, an offshoot of the reality TV singing competition called *American Idol*," writes journalist and musician Khadija Sharife. "In under an hour, the show managed to raise $18 million for disadvantaged African and North American children and families. The visual images of Africa were potent, tattered clothing, starving babies, machetes, guns, rape and famine – they did not mention that Africa is still the place where multinationals derive their coltan, oil, gas, uranium, gold, diamonds, copper and other strategic minerals. They did not say that Africa is a rich continent whose people interestingly 'are poor', and why they are poor!"[11]

In this book I take a look at this question and at some of the ways the West is both culpable and complicit in Africa. I examine some Western interventions – often covert or at least 'quiet' – that favour one leader or political/ethnic group over another. Interventions that arm and enrich those who promote Western interests, meddle in African political and economic affairs, and create dependence, despair, disaccord and pain.

Africa is rife with pain. Much of it is self-inflicted and by not focussing here on the self-inflicted pain I have no intention of diminishing those tragedies caused by it. The tragedies of ethnic hatred that can lead to genocide, of greed and corruption that drive African elites to perpetuate the crimes of the colonial era on their own peoples, or the heartbreak of lives thwarted or lost because of the lack of a few dollars to pay for schooling or medical care, and the great disaster of HIV/AIDS, with the suffering and hardship that brings.[12]

Over almost a quarter century of living and working in Africa, I've seen many social ills and crimes of which Africans were the authors. I've picked my way through villages where the stench of death was like the breath of hell burning my lungs, around dismembered corpses of children after warfare in northern Ghana and over bodies tossed into mass graves and water wells in Côte d'Ivoire. Young men in fatigues, weighed down by grenades and guns and good luck charms, told me they were invincible because of their magic charms and that they had "not yet killed enough."

I've also met with and interviewed African leaders who made my skin crawl. Among them, former Rwandan Prime Minister Jean Kambanda serving a life sentence in a Malian prison for genocide and crimes against humanity in his country. A special wing had been built on the otherwise dismal prison for the six convicted Rwandan *genocidaires*, which cost 40,000 US dollars and offers them comfort and privileges not accorded to Malian prisoners guilty of petty theft – or even to the majority of Malians. When I interviewed Kambanda, he refused to acknowledge his crimes. Instead, while he fingered a gold cross around his neck, he complained bitterly about the food and heat in the Bamako prison.

Another was the smug and sinister Liberian president, Charles Taylor, who replied to my questions while sitting on a throne-like chair of cane, as women acolytes knelt fawning at his feet. Taylor is now on trial for war crimes by the United Nations-backed Special Court for Sierra Leone.

There is also Blaise Compaoré, president of Burkina Faso, who was implicated in the assassination of his predecessor, the dynamic young president Thomas Sankara, and in arms trafficking and diamond dealing that perpetuated conflicts in Liberia, Angola and Sierra Leone. In the eerie silence of a high-security compound in the Burkinabé capital of Ouagadougou, just weeks after the death of Sankara in 1987, Compaoré dismissed his bodyguards and greeted me with a chilling attempt at seduction, grabbing my arm and stroking it, telling me it had been too long since I had come to interview him. Another female journalist from a major French newspaper suffered a more grievous encounter with him and headed, still sobbing, straight to the airport to board a flight back to France. Compaoré, the man his own people once called the "snake in the grass," allegedly involved in assassination, illicit weapons and illegal dealing in conflict diamonds, and countless human rights abuses, is still in power today, one of Washington's new allies and better 'friends' on the continent.

There were countless days in Africa that I despaired over the corruption, unnecessary famine, disease, and conflicts that solved absolutely nothing and pitted despairing Africans against each other. But these are the stories that sell easily; these are the tales of tragedy that fill our screens and dominate our media coverage from Africa. I've sold a lot of them myself. They have produced a seriously distorted view of the continent and they rarely tell the whole story of *how* a tragedy came to be, what factors led to it.

Africa has been drowning in crocodile tears wept by politicians and leaders for years. They were flowing like hyperbolic rain when President George W. Bush, whose popularity at home was bottoming out in early 2008, took a trip to Africa – a "mission of mercy" – and announced that it broke his heart to see children dying of malaria. Has George W. Bush or his speech writer ever seen a child die of malaria?[13]

Many citizens in Western countries think their development aid is charity and believe that the rich north is 'helping' the poor south. It's not their fault. This is a convenient myth created by Western governments and lending agencies to make their kind and good citizens happy, even if it's not really true. Aid resources that flow from north to south are a mere fraction of what flows in the other direction through "unfair trade agreements, abusive transfer pricing and capital flight," not to mention the cost of all those technical experts sent out from the wealthy world who can consume a major percentage – sometimes all – of the official aid budget that tax-payers may have thought was intended to help poor people in Africa.[14]

I examine quite a few myths in this book, and ask a lot of questions that sometimes do not have logical or satisfying answers. How, for example, can Western benefactors help solve Africa's problems when, as I learned over years of reporting on those problems, so many of them have their roots in the capitals of the world's major economic powers, many of them in the West? What is Africa losing in the way of wealth and wisdom, and why? What will be the fate of people in Africa in this century as their water resources dwindle because of climate change, a global calamity for which Africa has almost no responsibility? How can Western countries call themselves donors when they are the very creditors that have taken out far more out of Africa in debt servicing, unfair trade, natural resources and cheap commodities than they ever give back?[15]

In the 1990s, when I was working at an international agricultural research centre in Kenya, I was shown a press release prepared by an expensive public relations firm in New York to convince the American government to continue financial support for the network of international agricultural research centres, many of which shared Board members with multinational agrochemical companies. The headline announced that for every dollar the US donated to this international agricultural research network that claimed to be improving agricultural output in the tropics, it received two dollars in return. I suggested to my boss that this was not something to brag about. He said it was; this would keep the funds flowing in for agricultural research. Yet the stated mandate of the research centre was to "put money in farmers' pockets."

As I write, a new scramble for Africa is raging, with the US and her Western allies (and especially their multinational corporations) squaring off with China in a fierce battle for African oil and other resources and the political alliances that provide access to them. The competition between the West and China – one as rapacious as the other – manifests itself as a new version of the Cold War on the continent, with India also moving in on Africa in search of oil, gas and other natural resources.[16] All this undermines the efforts by indigenous and international human rights groups, and social justice movements, to help Africans build peace and improve their governance, human rights, health, education and natural resource management on their own continent.

At the same time, an increasing number of concerned and caring people in the wealthy world are anxious to "do something good" or "make a difference" in the lives of people in Africa. This is a heartening trend. But doing something good and making a difference starts with learning about the continent, its past, its present and what its people say they need. Do people in Africa really need containers filled with second-hand teddy bears or more cast-offs from the rich world undermining local efforts by Africans to produce what they consume, consume what they produce? No matter how good the intentions behind many aid projects, they may be useless – or worse – if they are not based on a deep understanding of the problems in Africa, and the source of those problems.

Some development workers head off to the continent armed with loads of goodwill but not much in the way of knowledge of its geography, political boundaries, history, ethnic make-up, cultural diversity, political leadership, or of Africa's own knowledge base and its real needs. Many Africans are glued to their radios all day, listening to international broadcasters, UN radio where it's available, and their own local stations. They are always thirsty for more knowledge, political news and understanding of African and world affairs. Many of them wonder just what kind of help that ill-informed outsiders can possibly offer. People who head to Africa to listen *and to learn* are sure to find their mission rewarding. Many have done so, finding it hard to leave and returning home richer for their experiences.

Much can be learned from Africa and its philosophies and cultures that might ease some of the less attractive aspects of modern societies where material things can seem more important than living things, such as human beings. Africa is rich in spirit, though the continent is rapidly losing its own identity, its pride, its forests, its waterways, its natural resources and its cultural wealth in the headlong push to develop economically – which unfortunately has yet to pay off economically. It is now drowning not just in crocodile tears but also in plastic and rubbish, and suffocating under toxic clouds from burning garbage.

If I may be so bold, I would also request that the experts pause – put down their spreadsheets, their reports, and tuck their economic dogma out of sight for just a few moments – to take a hard, unblinkered look at the unsustainable path that the wealthy industrialized world has followed, despite all the evidence of environmental devastation and climate change it is causing. If they refuse, which they well may, then the export of our mistakes (along with a good deal of our junk and toxins) to Africa will continue. The world's impoverished majority are the most vulnerable to the changing climate, but they haven't enjoyed the sumptuous lifestyles that caused it.

This book is my own attempt to make some sense of the contradictions that plague many of the development schemes in Africa, with stated intentions and actions often not jiving with real intentions and actions. It has emerged slowly, forming over the many years that I lived, raised children, worked in, reported from Africa and ever-so-slowly began to grasp the two realities that have so adversely affected the continent. First is the enormity of the injustice Africa suffered in the face of European colonization and then neo-colonization. Second is the danger of the Western mindset that seems condemned to judge other cultures and continents from the road it has decided is the high one, the only path to take, the one-way street to its own definition of progress.

Without a major shift in the modern mindset and approach to the planet that sustains us, I believe that we could all be condemning Africa – already suffering from changing rainfall patterns that affect their subsistence crops and their water supplies – and ultimately everyone on this planet to a bleak future. Escalating food and fuel prices, hunger and unrest among the world's poor are just the tip of the melting icebergs.

Africa knows best how to live without all the modern energy-guzzling amenities that are generally equated with progress. Perhaps it is time we tried to learn from the wisdom on the continent, before that wisdom is lost completely. Time to make sure that those off the continent who have the power to shape Africa's future and propose solutions for the continent's problems have a little more knowledge and understanding in their minds – and no dust in their own eyes.

PART I

Breaking the heart-shaped continent

1

Who's crazy?

Could a greater miracle take place than for us to look through each other's eyes for an instant? We should live in all the ages of the world in an hour; ay, in all the worlds of the ages.

Henry David Thoreau[17]

I travel to discover other states of mind.

V.S. Naipaul[18]

It was March 2003, and I'd come to Niafunké in northern Mali to do a story about an award-winning African blues man. I'd just suggested to him – not very diplomatically or politely – that some people might think him crazy, *"fou."*

"Fou?" he said, offering me a puzzled look before turning his back and striding away. His blue and pink cotton robe billowed around him as he moved over the dried, fractured mud flats that he had informed me were his "irrigated rice fields." I chased after him. On this windy and extremely hot day in late dry season, with the sands of the Sahara sweeping across the cracked earth under our feet, Ali Farka Touré was taking me on a tour of his farm. I'd just returned to Mali from Côte d'Ivoire, where I'd been covering the on-going civil war that had divided that nation in half, with rebels in control of the north and the government of Laurent Gbagbo in control of the south. It was a great relief to be back in peaceful Mali after the horror of war south of the border. Even the long drive – two days on road, or in the

sand *searching* for the road north of the River Niger that would get us to Timbuktu – was a pleasure after travelling through a war zone where everyone, from teenage girls to elderly men, seemed to be dressed and primed for combat.

Here, by contrast, Ali Farka was working away at a peaceful enterprise. His ambition, he said, was to transform the desert-like landscape on the banks of the River Niger into lush, green fields and bountiful orchards. He talked almost non-stop about his dreams to turn the inland waterway into Mali's bread – or rather rice – basket, to feed the people of the country's vast desert north. It sounded as if he were talking more to himself than to me, trying hard to convince himself that he could revive his sorry rice fields and create an oasis where his ailing orchard now stood. Half of the 3,800 fruit trees he had planted had shrivelled and died in the relentless desert wind.

A decade earlier, Ali Farka Touré had been touring the globe as one of Africa's most celebrated musicians, living it up in five-star hotels in world capitals. He had all the success of an American Idol, without any of the burning desire for fame that has been sweeping much of the world like an epidemic of vanity and idiocy. Without even trying very hard for success, Touré had won a Grammy award, America's top musical honour for the album he did with Ry Cooder, called *Talking Timbuktu*.[19]

Today, however, he was not talking Timbuktu; all he wanted to talk about was farming. At the age of about 62, after five round-the-world musical tours, this Malian blues man had come home to stay in the destitute desert town of Niafunké to farm.[20] He said he was producing the food needed to support his two wives, nine children, ten grand-children and the 50 other people he now fed in his native town. He thanked Allah that he was able to do so.

With a smile that suggested he wasn't particularly worried about it, he told me his money was gone. He had poured a lot of it into the farm, for cement that had been shipped down the River Niger from the Malian capital Bamako on enormous barges for constructing the now empty irrigation canals and for the expensive fruit seedlings. More of his money had gone into urban development projects in Niafunké; he paid for road repair and ditching along some of the narrow sandy alleyways in the town. He had opened a small hotel, hoping to put his neglected little town on the tourist map. When fuel ran short for the town generator, he paid for that too, bringing it downriver from Bamako by boat. And of course, being a traditional man in a traditional corner of a relatively traditional African country, Ali Farka's door was always open and there were always huge, communal bowls of rice and sauce for anyone who happened by his home.

With his own financial resources as parched as his orchard, in an unforgiving climate in a desert outpost of mud homes with thatch or hot tin roofs, surely, I thought, his decision to move back home to a sea of human need that stretched as far as the eye could see in all directions, just *might* be construed as crazy?

I said as much as I squatted beside him while he dug up the first of his potato crop. Typically, I was clutching my microphone as if my life depended on it, waving it impertinently in his face, hammering out questions and thinking – not for the first time – how impolite is the profession of journalism, how overbearing are we intruders in Africa with our endless questions and our cameras. But I had to get the story out of him because editors and producers back in the UK and Canada were waiting for it. I'd been trying all day to get him to tell me why he had given up the touring and jet-setting to return to Niafunké to become Benefactor General.

And all he wanted to talk about was how his potatoes were growing.

I tried again. "You had it all, Ali Farka. You had fame. You had a fortune. You toured the world, you won the Grammy Award, you had fans everywhere; you had international recording contracts. You could have lived in the lap of luxury anywhere you wanted. This is the American Dream. But you gave it all up and came back to hardship and hard work here. Why?"

He didn't reply because he had plunged his hands into the sand, pulled out a couple of reasonably healthy potatoes, and was grunting in satisfaction. Beside him, his younger brother and his seven-year-old granddaughter helped him dig more. But now they were pulling up clump after clump of pathetic and limp little brown things that looked more like dead mice than potatoes. Termites had devoured most of his crop.

I made some sympathetic noises about the fate of his potatoes then tackled him again.

"What I meant, Ali Farka, is that some people just might say it's crazy to try to farm here, to try to feed half the town of Niafunké. You are a famous musician and farming doesn't have quite the same cachet or glamour."

But he was still preoccupied with those potatoes, working with his brother and his granddaughter to harvest what little the termites had left of the crop, pulling up the plants and salvaging any healthy tubers that went into a jute sack. For dinner, he said.

Then, before I could get my microphone back in the range of his mouth, he was off on another tangent, loping off over dried fields with his shotgun over his shoulder, calling back that he had spied a bird that might be good for dinner. He lifted his shotgun, aimed, fired, and then stared across the brown wasteland of the field where the wind was whipping up dust devils and bits of dried vegetation. He broke into huge guffaws and when he saw the confusion on our faces, explained that he had been shooting at a lump of donkey dung, not a bird at all. I laughed too, finally, and did what I should have done much earlier; I stuck the microphone back in my bag.

I had been doing exactly what I promised myself all the time that I would not do as a foreign journalist working in Africa. I had been forcing my questions and my idea of what the story *should* be on someone when the time and the mood were not yet ripe. I'd been doing too much talking when I should have been listening, watching and just absorbing to learn and figure out what the story really was.

Things work differently in rural parts, especially the rural parts of the world that are still beyond the reach of power lines, easily accessible satellite television, paved roads and major thoroughfares, all the rapid social change they bring. In much of West Africa, people still live by ancient dictates that govern good manners, morals, and how to behave with others – although this too is changing rapidly with the advent of international television and films, and the increasing mobility of young people in search of paying work.

In traditional life, time is not something to be calculated, squeezed and hurried along, with something tangible to show for each hour or minute that passes. Time is wealth but it is not money. It is something to be savoured, enjoyed, respected. Time rules, takes its own course, just like the River Niger that carves its own illogical and audacious path across West Africa, from its birthplace in the Fouta Djallon hills of Guinea and then across Mali, where it veers northwards to form an inland oasis and to play chicken with the Sahara Desert near Timbuktu, before heading south again through neighbouring Niger and into Nigeria to form an oil-rich delta, emptying at last into the Atlantic Ocean. It may not be the best way for water to get from point A to point B. It certainly isn't the most direct, the quickest, or the most *logical*. But a river – like a human life without the relatively recent belief that it should or could be planned every step of the way – is not really about a destination. It's the journey. It's just the way the river runs.

For the first time all day, I shut up and went with the flow. I followed Ali Farka as he led us through more fields, past more dry irrigation canals, and then back to his low-slung riverboat, the *pirogue* that would ferry us away from the farm, across the river and back to his home in Niafunké. We clambered aboard and Ali Farka indicated that I should sit beside him on the strut in the middle of the boat for the ride home. When I was no longer brandishing my microphone and asking questions, I found I could finally absorb the subtle beauty of the place. I could finally reflect on some of the things Ali Farka had already told me, starting with the importance of family and destiny. His mother called him "Farka," which means donkey in his mother tongue Songhay, because she had given birth to and then lost nine babies before him. She hoped that by calling her tenth child donkey, she would outsmart the spirits that took human babies from their mothers, and spare her tenth child the same fate. As Ali Farka said with a smile, the deception had worked and he had survived his birth to tell the tale, and so had his younger siblings.

Ali Farka had never set foot in a formal school; he told me could neither read nor write. This certainly didn't seem to restrict his ability to philosophize, ponder life's mysteries or summon ancient historical accounts like a scholar. He said his education came not from schools but from his parents and elders in the community. Griots are West Africa's bards – their oral historians and praise singers – and they taught him the history of his people and the region. He had never studied music and could not write a note. His talents were God-given, but they had been nourished by traditions of sharing, where music and the culture are integral to life itself, not for hire or for sale.

As we approached the northern bank of the river, Ali Farka's younger brother turned off the motor, allowing the river canoe to drift the remaining 50 metres to the grassy shore. Ali Farka took up his guitar and began to pluck the opening chords of the hauntingly beautiful ballad, "Hawa Dolo." The late afternoon sun was glinting off the white sand dunes that lined the river. The sultry breeze stirred up tiny, white-capped ripples in the milky-green water that lapped at the gunwales and something stirred deep inside me that defied any logical description or definition. I felt the magic of the place, of the music that springs from it like a hymn to the majesty of the desert, the river that runs through it and the people for whom this is home. I took out the microphone, but asked no questions, allowing the microphone to absorb the sounds that belonged to that setting, of which my voice was not one.

As if reading my thoughts – or the fuzzy feelings of well-being for which I had no words – Ali Farka broke into his trademark huge and irrepressible grin. "This river is our gold, our diamonds," he said. "It's my mentor, teacher, protector and my power."

He said that the music that the rest of the world calls the blues did not spring from the waters of the Mississippi River in the United States as is commonly claimed on that side of the great ocean separating Africa from North America. Africans took it there from its source, right here in northern Mali – the river the Songhay people call the Jimbala, the southern Malians know as the Djoliba and Europeans decided to call the Niger – or black in Latin. The river can be blue or green or grey, depending on weather and the time of year, and after a heavy rain it turns a little brown with muddy runoff. But it is never, ever black.

These days, said Ali Farka, the Jimbala – the spirit of the river – was ill. He said human beings had abused and ignored its totems. They no longer observed sacrifices and taboos that always safeguarded the river on its long course through the Sahel of West Africa, a dry band of land south of the Sahara Desert that stretches from Chad in the east right across to Senegal in the west.

"I have huge fears for this river," he said. "It's the advance of the desert. Just look at the dunes."

He pointed to the white banks of sand that rose on both sides of the river like cresting waves poised to crash into the very slim blue strip of water. "If a solution isn't found for this river, we're really finished," he said.

He told me there were once taboos about what could go into the river and what could be taken out; these unwritten laws had protected it for centuries. In modern times, the River Niger has become a repository for garbage churned out by the mega-tonne in rapidly growing cities along its shores. Its waters absorb the toxins of the modern world – lindane and countless other pesticides used in abundance on farms along the river, the effluent from battery factories and dyeing operations in Bamako. There are almost no crocodiles and hippos left in the river because, he said, hunters came from all over the world to slaughter them in the mid-20th century when shoes, belts and purses made of exotic animal skins were in high fashion in Europe, Asia and North America. So now, Ali Farka said, these species had "sought refuge elsewhere."

There had also been rules about who could cross the river, and where and when. He said it disturbed him enormously when he saw foreigners "play" in the river, which many expatriates did near Bamako on their noisy Sea-Doos.

He said he could not accept the lack of respect for and intrusions into the river; these were dangerous: "They offend the river spirit." There were secrets about the spirit Jimbala that should not have been told to just anyone. Great empires grew up along this river and they understood the river's language. "Because we've abandoned the taboos, disrespected the river's spirit, the rain doesn't fall and fishing is poor," he concluded.

The boat slid onto the shallow sandy bank, but he remained seated, picking out more Malian blues. He ended the melody with a flourish of chords and stared out at the once-great river that inspired his music and which now, quite literally, gave him the blues. "Without this river," he said to no one in particular, "I would be deaf, I would have no voice. If the river ceased to exist, then I would cease to be."

Then without warning or prompting he turned to me and spoke directly into the microphone, finally replying to the question with which I'd been pestering him all day.

"I'm more farmer than I am musician. I prefer life here. That other life [of musical stardom] was – if you'll excuse my language – like dried crap; you step it in and it just doesn't stick. If God gave me big buildings in the United States or Canada or Japan or Germany or Australia, could I put them in my pocket and bring them home? No, that's impossible."

He said he wasn't going to stop making music, but he wasn't going on any more tours – if people wanted to hear him play live all they had to do was come to Niafunké. He grew up by the river, working the fields and learning from his people, and all he was doing was following his destiny. "I know what I left behind me [when I gave up touring and came home]. But my philosophy is to work to make life better here and to share it. What I eat, others will eat. When I drink they will drink, what I wear they can wear. And I live with the river all the time."

Three years after that, in March 2006, Ali Farka Touré passed away. Malian friends phoned me in tears to tell me the sad news and to let me know that state radio in their country had interrupted regular broadcasting to play Ali Farka's blues. Their country was in mourning. Sitting snowbound in Canada that winter, I pulled out my own notes and recordings of those magical days I spent in Niafunké, visiting with him and his family.

I realized that the visit with Ali Farka Touré had given me more infinitely more than insignificant radio features about his music and his decision to turn his back on all that was his for the taking in richer parts of the world, and to return to his roots and to the river spirit that had inspired him and his people near Timbuktu. Unwittingly, he helped crystallize many of the ideas in this book, ideas that had been collecting and developing in my mind and notebooks over many years in Africa.

As a Westerner born and bred, I might find it amazing that an African who had attained what many of us in the industrialized countries spend our lives striving for, would give up the life of an international star and go back home. From another perspective, it wasn't the least bit amazing. There were no paparazzi in Niafunké; nor was Ali Farka embroiled in any messy mental breakdown or divorce scandals while the whole world looked on with *schadenfreude*. When he died, he died with dignity and was mourned by many great musicians and people not just in his native Mali but all over the world. His son, Vieux Farka Touré, has now taken up where his father's music left off.

What Ali Farka showed me that afternoon confirmed what thousands of encounters with insightful Africans had shown me over the years. There is a lot more to a good life than easy access to shopping malls and fast-food joints, better homes and gardens and a head full of retirement plans.

Friends in Africa who have heard or seen it for themselves, express surprise and shock at the way elderly people tend to be treated in the rich world, put away in homes where their wisdom may be lost and their minds and final years allowed to waste away in neglected isolation. They comment on the lack of manners and respect among young people in their own rapidly changing societies, where youth are turning their backs on everything from simple good manners to respect for their elders.

Mali's former Minister of Education the late Mohamed Lamine Traoré, a philosophy professor, suggested to me that the students fortunate enough to receive a formal, primarily Western-style education in schools, can be the most ignorant and poorly behaved. He maintained that this was because they no longer receive crucial education at home, which instils a sense of respect for others and teaches the social responsibility that has kept people in his country going, through thick and through very thin in one of the world's monetarily poorest countries.[21] When a Malian comments that so-and-so is *"mal eduqué,"* they do not mean that person hasn't been to school. They mean that person has been raised poorly, to have no respect for others and for their own heritage.

In Bamanakan, the language spoken by the Bamana people of Mali and a lingua franca for much of the nation, the standard greetings involve the words in Bamanankan for good morning, good midday, good afternoon or good evening. The standard response for a man is "*n ba*," which translates literally as "my mother" but which means "Thanks to my mother who raised me I am fine." The standard response from a woman is "*nse*," which translates literally as "my power" but which means, "Thanks to my power as a woman I am fine."

This simple linguistic example casts great doubt on Western misconceptions about the universal suppression of women's rights and powers in Africa, on stereotypes of African woman as meek and hapless victims. Women have led major protests that led to major political change in West Africa, leading street demonstrations in Mali and in Ghana, as just two examples.

Misconceptions, of course, go two ways. Strange notions about people and life in the wealthy West also abound in Africa. In a village in Cameroon where I was visiting a friend's family, I was treated as if I were a VIP throughout my stay. My friend's father vacated his room and bed for me. On the first Sunday morning I was there, much to my chagrin I discovered he had killed the family's one duck and it was now cooked and in the pot sitting on the small table that had been set up and also set for me in the middle of the small living room. I was informed that I should sit down to eat, while many members of the extended family gathered around to watch. As ludicrous as I felt sitting there like an impostor pretending to be an important guest, I felt even more so when I was told I mustn't take a bite until they had found some red wine to accompany my Sunday morning meal. I told them I didn't need wine, refraining from telling them I also didn't want any; that would have been impolite. There was much discussion, and then his father told me that I must wait because wine was on its way and it was well known that, "White man cannot eat without drinking red wine." A few minutes later a young emissary arrived from the home of the elderly chief, who had managed to find an old bottle of sweet Sangria with about one glassful remaining, which was poured for me with great enthusiasm and pride.

In Kenya, when we returned from a holiday in Canada, Dalmas, who worked for us as a watchman, informed me that he had two sad events to relate that happened during our absence. He began by saying that one of our cats had been run over and killed. Then he told us that the gardener who had been working at the house for years and who lived with us had passed away suddenly after a small operation to remove a lump on his neck. When I asked Dalmas why he had offered me these sad bits of news in that order, why he had told us about the death of a cat before he told us of Peter's death, he solemnly informed me that, "Whites prefer animals to people."

In several African countries I've been stopped from even carrying my own handbag or from picking up a shovel to dig in a garden because it is well-known that white people do not perform physical labour. When I tell people that white men and women work very hard – farming, fishing, building – all the time, there are often looks of disbelief.

But some of the widespread thoughts about Western society, especially about modern urban life among those who have lived, studied and worked in the West, are better informed and can be quite telling. In a dozen countries on the continent I listened for countless hours to Africans bemoan the growing disrespect for and denigration of the elderly in their own societies, something they attribute to imported values from wealthy lands where the quest for eternal youth and beauty are becoming obsessions and creating multi-billion-dollar industries. They worry about the sterility of life in new and "modern" neighbourhoods – increasingly gated communities – in African cities, where it is possible for people to live side-by-side for years and not even know each others' names, never exchange a word of greeting. Others worry about the growing disparity between extreme rich, the miniscule minority, and the extreme poor, the vast majority. The latter may live in hovels cobbled together from scraps of tarpaulins, roofing sheets, old car bodies and anything else they can scrounge from garbage heaps, while next door, inside the high walls topped with razor wire, their obscenely rich brethren construct enormous palatial homes.

Maybe the crazy treadmill of modern life, driven by money, property, possessions and attention to cosmetic beauty and self – a life that Ali Farka had said didn't "stick" to his shoes – isn't an enviable universal goal that should drive development and define a civilization. You don't have to be crazy just because you reject the North American Dream, especially the latter-day version that has now gone global, fuelled by vanity, intolerance and greed, a model that George W. Bush described in 2002 as "the single surviving model of human progress."[22]

Sometimes I wonder if you have to be crazy to ignore the fact that the model Bush and some major economists of our times both endorse and promote, which Naomi Klein describes as disaster capitalism, is the one that is driving our species to ecological catastrophe – or extinction.

Sometimes the most basic tenets of life and reason can be forgotten in the mad rush for progress, and in the dangerous assumption that any one cultural experiment in civilization is going to last eternally. As Jared Diamond[23] and Ronald Wright[24] have written so eloquently and forcefully, the more 'successful' a civilization under a powerful elite orchestrating the unsustainable exploitation of natural resources, the more impetus for it to collapse in on itself, despite the tendency of that civilization to view itself as being on the right path, invincible and superior to all others.

In recent centuries, dominated as it has been by European civilizers, Africa has not developed much of this hubris. Anything African has been denigrated for so long that many Africans have come to believe in the inherent superiority of everything non-African. In much of Africa, it is almost impossible to find any local dishes or food (even locally grown rice or chicken) on the menus in hotels or restaurants catering to the well-heeled.

The idea that Africa has much to teach the world, that Africa is rich with knowledge of its own and traditions of which it can be proud, is one that has been largely overlooked – first by outsiders and now increasingly by Africans themselves.

Many people in Africa are trying very hard to hold on to their own cherished values and traditions and find their own development path. There are African writers, artists, musicians and thinkers desperately trying to remind their people to stick to their belief that people matter more than do things.

One Cameroonian friend and journalist colleague periodically chose his most cherished *boubou* (robe) or any material possession to which he felt he was becoming too attached, and gave it away randomly to someone needy in the Malian capital. There were plenty of those to choose from. He said this was an important reminder not to become too attached to material possessions. I was happy he never challenged me to do the same, and asked me to part with something that I really, really liked owning – a piece of jewellery, a piece of technology, a favourite dress. I would surely fail the test.

2

No longer ourselves

*I am convinced that a French man deprived of the correct
vintage red wine at his meal suffers just as much as a Burkinabé
who has no water to drink with his.*

Thomas Sankara[25]

*Money is what they like most, money is what they like.
And people who have plenty of money belong to high society.
But if you could go and see how they live, a shame, a shame,
Then you'd discover how savage they are, boy, so much wilder
than we.*

The late Cameroonian writer/musician/philosopher,

Francis Bebey.[26]

The puzzle of what keeps Africa ticking despite all the missing basic
necessities we rely on in the West had been turning circles in my
mind since I first landed on the continent in 1982. It plagued me
even more each time I returned to my homeland – which now seems
to me the land of much too much. It would be dishonest to say I ever
solved the puzzle.

Eventually, I came to the conclusion that the question that had
been plaguing me – what keeps Africa ticking despite all the missing
'basic necessities' – is downright silly. It is interesting only because it
reveals the troubling truth that despite almost a quarter of a century

of living in and breathing Africa, I remain a victim of my own Western thoughts on what constitutes basic and necessity.

Human beings have been kicking about this planet for between 250 and 400 thousand years. But it is only in the past few decades that a very few of them in a very few monetarily and materially rich countries discovered the list of what they need to survive growing by leaps and bounds – indoor plumbing, first sterilized and then bottled drinking water, electricity, telephones, paved roads and cars to drive on them. New items are being added every day to the list of must-haves: Internet, credit cards, cell phones, Blackberries, I-pods and I-phones, enormous screen Plasma TV screens, total climate control inside our homes and vehicles. And then, when the sedentary lifestyle these promote starts to show up on thighs, tummies and hips, we need home gyms full of machines on which we sweat and grunt – walking, rowing, cycling, lifting heavy weights – as we mimic all the hard work we've saved ourselves from doing. Is it just me, or is there something slightly mad in that logic?

Since the things the moneyed people on the planet call needs are beyond the wildest imaginations or dreams of the majority of people in Africa, it's fortunate that the majority of people in Africa don't spend all their time worrying that they don't have them and don't let that the long list of what they don't have get them down too much.

I recently heard a Ghanaian suggest that depression – as we know it and treat it in the West with antidepressant drugs and therapy – is a symptom of a society in which people don't talk to each other enough. She pointed out that the large extended family has been lost, and so has the emotional support it can offer.

The majority of people in Africa go about their lives, celebrating births and weddings, toiling away at farm chores and essential tasks related to their own welfare and survival. They sometimes do the work of draught animals behind push-carts, sell whatever they can grow or get their hands on and live on amounts of money each month that some children in North America would sneer at if offered as a daily allowance. A good many people in Africa dream, strive, work hard and make do, keeping the faith that this is what God or Allah or other deities intended for them, and praying while they just get on with their lives. And that's as close as I've ever come to answering that futile question about what keeps Africa going. It's really very simple: life does.

Development insider and author, Giles Bolton, puts it this way: "Most of Africa gets on with day-to-day life without crisis ... the continent may not be one large bed of roses, but nor is it an arid pit of despair."[27]

It has been far more useful to open up my mind to allow people in Africa to fill it with all sorts of new ideas and points of view than to ask rhetorical questions comparing material lives on and off the continent. In this way, I also found out that much of what made African societies tick along was far too complex for words, particularly not the feeble English translations of words for concepts, social beliefs and behaviours that simply don't exist in our language.

Why did it take me so long to stop dwelling on squalor and monetary poverty and start trying to unravel the rich and complex social fabric that was all around me in every country I lived in on the continent? I have no answers, but I have theories.

One, I was often working as a journalist, searching for headlines and stories that constituted news, and I was rarely living in a country deemed newsworthy in the West. I have spent most of my adult life in Africa and most of that in towns or cities – even countries – that never make the evening news, or the morning news, or the headlines, not even in major newspapers in North America. Burkina Faso, Cameroon, Mali and Niger are hardly household words outside Africa. Ghana, Kenya and Sierra Leone are better known, but a rather surprising number of people in North America think Africa is a single country.

The planet Mars makes news in major media far more often than does the West African nation of Mali, not to be mistaken for Maui in Hawaii, or Bali in Indonesia, or Male the capital of the Maldives, or Somalia in the Horn of Africa, or Malawi that is a very different African nation a few thousand kilometres to the east and south of the huge, land-locked, sand-swept Mali – once the seat of a wondrously wealthy empire that covered much of West Africa.

In 1998, I had a phone call from CBS radio in Chicago, asking me to speak about then US Secretary of State Madeleine Albright's visit to Sierra Leone. The producer in Chicago seemed surprised when I said Bamako was a good long way from Sierra Leone, and that Albright wouldn't be coming to Mali for another day. No, I explained, Freetown wasn't in Mali; it was the capital of Sierra Leone.

The man at the other end of the line went silent for a moment, before asking me where on earth Mali was then, and what on earth Madeleine Albright was doing visiting such a place. I mentioned that it was once the seat of a great empire that had covered much of West Africa, with its religious heart in Timbuktu, a fascinating country with much to show the world. More silence on the other end. I went on to explain that Mali was of strategic importance to the US, a moderate Muslim country that the US very much wanted to keep and cultivate within its diplomatic and military sphere of influence, bordering as it did on Algeria, Mauritania and within listening range of Libya, which was still considered a terrorist state back then. This information clinched it. The CBS producer decided to do an interview with me, not about Mali, but about its strategic interest to the US. Mali, per se, didn't interest him in the slightest. How could it when he had never heard of it?

In some ways, I suppose African countries such as Mali and another two or three dozen of the 53 nations on the continent can feel very proud of never having made the major network news in North America the way Rwanda, Liberia, Ethiopia, Sierra Leone, South Africa, Sudan and Zimbabwe have. That means they have not suffered tragedies big enough to make news or be the subject of blockbuster films in America – Apartheid, genocide or atrocious civil wars, or a famine massive enough to catch the eye of the Western media. Although the conflict that has killed the most people since World War II, in the Democratic Republic of Congo, somehow managed to escape much coverage in the West.

Because I was working as reporter in Mali, and constantly looking for stories that would be considered news to BBC and Associated Press, or just might pique the interest of editors in North America, I tended to overlook the real story of Mali that was all around me. So I was slow in starting to try and penetrate the complex and puzzling world of its culture and everyday life. And even when I started trying, progress was painful.

The reason for that was simple: I had to stop always thinking and seeing like the Westerner I was, raised in a neat little city in a cozy corner one of the world's wealthiest nations. That is, I was still distracted by and focusing far too much on the obvious, the squalor and the real lack of money that kept children out of schools or in schools so ill-equipped and understaffed they were not worth attending. That kept whole families away from health care facilities and sentenced them to lives of extremely hard labour. All the above are real and unavoidable truths. But they do not define Mali or even Africa. Far from it.

To appreciate Africa, and especially a country as hot, dry and monetarily poor as Mali, with its unwritten but highly developed and sophisticated social rules, it helps if the outsider can go through a kind of mental cleansing to remove cultural biases. Or, as Malian sociologist and author Aminata Dramane Traoré put it, I would need to learn to "see with the heart." That meant ridding myself of the tendency to judge a country by what I could see with my outsider's eyes and to try to feel, to comprehend the incredible organization and structure that underlies the erroneous impression of chaos and the very real lack of modern infrastructure, which I might see at home. Paved roads, gleaming office towers, covered sewers, golden arches, that sort of thing.

In 1999, during her short term as Mali's Minister of Culture, Aminata Traoré issued an invitation to people all over the world to come to Mali and travel down the River Niger to Timbuktu to observe the dawning of the new millennium, even though, according to the Islamic calendar, the year was not 1999 but 1421. Nevertheless, since the rest of the world seemed to be preparing for a huge party to welcome in their new millennium, Traoré decided to throw a party in Mali as well, a cultural festival of art, beauty and poetry in one of the world's poorest countries.

She called the festival *Tombouctou 2000: Voir avec le Coeur*. "To see with the Heart," she said, was her invitation to outsiders – and to all Africans busy rejecting their own values and culture – to take a journey down the River Niger through Mali and try to perceive things a little differently as they did so. She said they needed to see past the obvious monetary poverty to the subtle beauties of the Sahelian landscape and the marvellous wealth of human relationships and humanity in homes and on mud roads in neighbourhoods or villages of mud huts in Mali.

My Western upbringing made me want to dismiss it all as a lot of dirt-poor people living in misery in a dirt-poor country – which is how some foreign media portrayed Mali and other countries in the region. A German man, living high on the hog in the Kenyan highlands, once described to me his feelings about the Sahel: "It's hot and dirty and I hate it." Traoré wanted to dispense with the rigid mindset still so prevalent in some development circles, despite the United Nations Human Development Index that offers a more holistic picture. The idea that a country that is least developed physically and economically is therefore least developed socially and culturally, or worse, somehow inferior and backward, and sitting there helplessly waiting for help from the West.

What she tried to convey to me, at great length and with emotion that made her voice crack, was that there were other stories to tell and ways of seeing, not just in Africa but in life itself. While the media focused on conflict in a war-torn country, elsewhere on the continent Africans were living in peace and harmony, maintained by their own deep traditions of and belief in tolerance, dialogue and consensus.

She and other friends on the continent pointed out to me that Africa hasn't received the attention and credit it deserves for its own great discoveries and laudable traditions and contributions to the world. The herbal medicines stolen from its forest dwellers, the minerals and gems extracted from its soils, musical idioms that have shaped much modern music, the cash crops such as cocoa, coffee, rubber, tea and cotton that farmers toil to produce often at the expense of their own food crops, from Kenya across to Senegal.

Nor has Africa received compensation for the complete disruption of its own cultural and economic development when tens of millions of its most able-bodied youth and adults were chained and shipped off as slaves to Arab countries and to the Americas, where those who survived the journey would help the US develop its agricultural economy and eventually become the super-rich superpower it is today.

Every child in the West learns about the holocaust perpetrated against Jews in Germany, but few school curricula delve into the holocaust in the Congo during the period it was the main source for rubber and ivory for Europe and North America and was the personal fiefdom of the Belgian King, Leopold II. An estimated ten million people died during that period of colonial plunder in the Congo, roughly half the population.[28]

The heart of darkness immortalized in Joseph Conrad's writing, with its "taint of imbecile rapacity" was not an African heart; it was the "rapacious and pitiless folly" of "civilized" white men like Mr. Kurtz, turned monsters by their greed.[29]

Aminata Traoré said she did not want the world to see her country or Africa with a *bleeding* heart. Africa has had far too much pity and condescension. What Africa needs – what it hasn't had, she told me – is justice in the political and financial arenas, respect and acknowledgement that its people knew how to live with each other and get by, down through the millennia, without any Western aid at all.

"Another Africa is possible," was her mantra.

Mali may officially be one of the world's least developed countries when it comes to amenities, income levels and early childhood morbidity rates, but it is not when it comes to its culture and heritage and even how its people get along with each other.[30]

Among the many joys of living and working in much of West Africa is the informal repartee that is considered perfectly normal – expected – between strangers who happen to find themselves face-to-face.

Just as most Africans living in Europe or North America refer to fellow Africans as their brothers or sisters, no Malian abroad or at home considers another Malian a "stranger." No matter what the occasion, people greet each other. This means that modern activities – scheduled meetings, interviews, political gatherings – can be incredibly time-consuming. For the foreign journalist, ever-pressed to meet a deadline just hours or even minutes away, it can all be a terrific headache and exercise in patience.

Greetings are not a simple grunt or a "hi" tossed over the shoulder as you pass someone. In any of the multitude of languages in West Africa, a round of greetings usually goes something like this. "How are you? The family? The house? The work? Did you sleep in peace?" To which the reply is always something like, "fine, no problem, good, peace-filled, thank you, thanks be to God, praise be to God, Peace be with you, thanks be to God or Allah."

In Mali and other countries in the region, that is sometimes followed by an exchange of names, and often of native villages or regions where the family name comes from. There will inevitably be some tracing of ancestry to see whose forefather might have been related, somehow, to yours. And then the joking begins. Cutting right through any stiff formality and breaking any social ice that just can't last long in the social and physical heat of the region.

"Oh, Keita are you? Then you're my slave." (Unlikely, given that Keita is the name of a noble family among the Bamana in Mali).

Or, from a Bamana to a Fula: "You, Diallo, you are my small cow."[31]

Or, from a Fula to a Bamana: "You, Kante, your father (grandfather, great grandfather) was my slave. You must show me respect. Walk behind me."

All this with loads of laughter, which I admit left me, at first, completely perplexed, especially when I watched my friend and colleague, Sadio Kante, march up to the much-feared head of Malian state security, tackling him with taunts about he should bow to her as he was, in name, her slave. They bantered back and forth, laughing as if they were long-lost kissing cousins. Well, fact is, they usually found out that at some level, they were 'cousins,' linked by ancient *sinankunya* alliances made by their ancestors to forever join and keep peace among extended families, clans and ethnic groups.

Then there were the social categories into which peoples with Mandé heritage in West Africa, no matter which ethnic group, could be placed – the inherited status as a 'noble' or people of 'caste,' which included griot praise-singers, cobblers, weavers, blacksmiths.[32] If you were born to parents who belonged to one of these groups, you inherited their trade or profession, and were considered a person of 'caste.'

For the outsider, this can be highly confusing, even alarming, given the stigma of the word caste in English and French. In spite of my resolution to go at this objectively, I could not rid myself of a premature and dogmatic judgement that any society that separates its people into clear groups depending on inherited trades and social roles – noble, caste and slave – must be mired in the some kind of dark age.

I found lots of agreement among friends from other parts of Africa. A Nigerian journalist friend summed up my own initial thoughts on Mali's caste system.

"The issue of castes in Mali is a very complicated question. It's something that one cannot condemn outright, but for a person who's not part of the system, it's difficult to understand. It's difficult for somebody, not just Westerners, but other Africans who come from countries where such things do not exist, to understand how a person who has been considered a praise-singer – or griot – for centuries, is considered superior or inferior to another who has been an iron-smith or a blacksmith for centuries. In modern times you have maybe a blacksmith, an iron-smith, who has gone to school, to the best universities in the whole world, but when he gets back to his own country he is considered as a nothing. It is his family background, his ancestral background that counts. It's a form of marginalization. It's detrimental to the progress of Africa as a whole."

A very thoughtful and knowledgeable Cameroonian journalist who deplores the caste system in Mali, saying it contravenes human rights and brings shame to Africa, has produced a detailed film on the subject. He also maintains such ancient systems must change and conform to modern values of equality.

Malians who spoke to me about caste, however, disagree. One of the first of these was Issa. Issa is a former student leader, a graduate of the country's school of administration, who pushed hard for student rights and the need for a university in his country back in 1991, the year Mali was making the transition from dictatorship to multiparty democracy. He has taken only one wife, and has pledged himself to monogamy although polygamy is the norm among Mali's Muslim majority. He has so far had only one child, a daughter whom he spoils and carries about and dotes upon like no other Malian father I know; no other father I know anywhere.

He is politically active and was highly critical of the foreign intrusion in Mali's democratic process throughout the 1990s. This was a time when Western powers were busy cementing 'friendship' with African leaders elected in the era of democracy that came, not coincidentally, right after the Cold War ended and the West suddenly decided it no longer wanted friendly and beholden dictators on the continent. It now wanted friendly and beholden *elected* leaders.

Issa happily discussed geopolitics and world events for hours on end. To me, he sounded and looked like a thoroughly radical and modern young man.

Then one day he started to speak of his ancestry and his 'noble' status. He said he was not just of noble birth, a *horon* in *Bamanankan*; he was a *horon des horons*, a 'noble of nobles.' So, he said, was his wife, Bintu, also a university graduate. He went on to say that his daughter would also have to marry a noble of nobles, and that if she chose to defy tradition and marry someone from a caste – belonging to a class of griots or blacksmiths or weavers or cobblers – it would be over his "dead body."

I imagine that my face betrayed all the shock I felt when Issa said this. As a Canadian baby boomer, I grew up naïvely believing that one's social class played no role in one's life and prospects in life. I thought, again naïvely, that the whole notion of class was something passé, that those born into the upper class were not more likely to succeed in life than those born on the middle rungs of the social ladder, and that those born anywhere on the social ladder could easily climb right to the top without any resistance from the established nobility. Perhaps because I thought social snobs were ridiculous, I made the very silly mistake of believing snobbery based on birthright and the money it might bring was inconsequential in the scheme of life in my country.

I was blithely unaware that the notion of class, and all it meant for success, was alive and well, being purchased and growing ever more sleek and glamorous in private clubs and schools, in fraternities and sororities and other elite invitation-only groups, and on exclusive golf courses across Canada. I thought – mistakenly – that in our modern times with universal access to public education that made social mobility possible, class was irrelevant, a distasteful relic of the stale old world of European royalty and titles. Nor did I take into consideration the snobbery that can develop among the nouveau riche.

And so, given the many lapses in my own logic and knowledge at that point about how materialism, greed and *laissez-faire* economics drive wedges through society to produce social strata in the wealthy world,[33] I reacted instantly and negatively to Issa's words about his daughter having to marry a noble; my face froze and I could see that he saw my shock.

He was quick to respond. "Why do you look surprised? The same thing exists in the West," he said. "The British still have their royal families and all their noblemen and women. And it exists here too. There are social classes, people of caste are there to look out for us nobles, but in exchange, they are allowed more freedom and leeway in how they behave. We are expected to live up to our status as nobles, speaking little and maintaining dignity at all times. And we are obliged to look after them, support them."

"So the difference is in the behaviour of nobles and people of caste?" I asked slowly, struggling very hard to keep my mind *open*.

"No," he replied without hesitation. "It's in the blood. The lineage. My genealogy is noble. I studied at university, but that doesn't mean I have to reject traditional values. My daughter will also go to school, but she will never marry a man of caste. Money is starting to ruin our social system and the balance there was. The West is imposing its values on us, and we have to fight to retain what is good for us."

"Yes, but then would you defend the old system of slaves as well?"

"No," he said. "In the north, among the Tuareg, there is still slavery. The Bella people are the slaves to the Tuareg, but not to be bought and sold as they were during the slave trade from Africa. Slavery is a dangerous word. And here in the south of Mali, former slaves have been adopted by their noble families; they share their names. There are people descended from slaves who share my family's noble name; they live in freedom like all Malians."

"But Issa, still, this is …"

"In the West, everyone talks about freedom," he interjected. "Everyone does what he wants. We don't have so much of that kind of freedom in Mali. You marry the person your family approves of, the person who will make you happy and make those around you happy. These are marriages of reason. They are more solid than marriages of love. Look at the divorces in the West. Divorce here was impossible because it brought shame to the family. Those who did divorce did so not in public in town, but under a tree in the bush. That tree would then die. I think we should come back to these things. Western civilization has dominated the world, but it's not the best civilization. There are African civilizations and Asian civilizations and it is Western civilization that has brought us so many catastrophes, the world wars that Africans had to go and fight in Europe. Western civilization is science and technology. Can those bring us happiness? That's my question. We want a cultural revolution in Mali to bring back our own values that we are losing because of all the imported ones. Western social organization has completely disorganized our society. We have become like bats, you know? Bats are not birds and they are not mammals, they're something in between. We are no longer ourselves. We haven't become White but we're no longer Black either. We need to come back to our traditions."

After that lecture, I felt censured and deeply unsettled. He had set me thinking about my prejudices, but I was not convinced; his arguments reminded me too much of ones I'd heard in many fundamentalist religious or utopian circles, which zero in on a particular historical tradition and elevate it to a holy status it had never had or even deserved. Nor had he convinced me that he represented the young people of Mali who were just starting to enjoy some of the modern freedoms I grew up cherishing, at least the one that allows you to choose your own partner in life. The word freedom – like civilization, development, advanced and poverty – was starting to squirm, twist and mutate in the raging heat of a Malian May.

Next, I headed downtown to talk to some girls in one of the country's more respected high schools, that is, the young people who graduate from this *lycée* are at least able to read and write correctly in the country's official language, French. It is a Catholic institution attended by mostly Muslim Malian teenage girls, where I reasoned that tradition might get a little shaken up. Surely, I surmised, they would be radically opposed to traditions that bound them to marry within a particular social group?

Wrong. Again.

Of the 20 young women I ambushed randomly as they sauntered out of the *Lycée Notre-Dame* in the old, treed *Quartier du Fleuve* of the Malian capital, only three said they would go against tradition and marry a man of caste. Even among those three, they did not say they would go against tradition because they found the old taboos abhorrent or unjust. No, they would choose their own mates from whatever social category they wished just because, as 16-year-old Alimata Togo put it, "times are changing in Mali."

"Before, griots didn't marry nobles," she said. "But now they do. I think it's okay that way because we can choose whom we want to marry. Before, if a noble fell in love with a griot they couldn't marry, and if a griot fell in love with a noble, they couldn't marry because tradition forbade it. Now, with mixed marriage, everyone can marry everyone."

Seventeen of the young women who spoke to me were far more adamant in their responses, insisting that they would marry men of noble status only, who would probably be selected for them by their parents and grandparents. Interestingly enough, all claimed to be of noble birth, perhaps an indication of just which segment of Mali's population could afford or was choosing to educate their daughters.

Flummoxed by the young women's lack of, well, feminist fervour, I trotted off again to see my instructor in all things cultural: sociologist Aminata Traoré who had tried so hard to teach me to perceive things with my heart and not my Western eyes. I wanted to know how Malian intellectuals – including some human rights lawyers – could justify inbuilt social hierarchies in their society that, to me, seemed like recipes for discrimination.

"You must try to understand that so-called 'people of caste' are not lower socially than nobles," Traoré said slowly, measuring her words carefully, as if terribly conscious of the pitfalls of trying to explain the complexities of her own culture to a foreigner ready to pounce in premature judgement. After centuries of condemning other cultures and religions around the world, we Westerners have developed a reputation that makes many people in Africa afraid to reveal to us the intricate secrets of their own societies and countries.

"People of caste have a special role because of their creativity," she continued. "They have a mastery of the spoken word and their music, or other talents they inherit. Each family has its own griot, and the griot helps to solve conflicts, helps negotiate good marriages, inform you if you are doing bad things and remind you of our values. This enables Malians to stay together in peace, despite the poverty and the difficulties."

Aminata Traoré, like Issa – felt that 'progress' itself was eroding the very foundation of the system of complementary roles within the society. She insisted that the different groups – nobles, the trades-people and praise-singers who constitute the people of caste, and even former 'slaves' – are not arranged top-down, as are social classes in Western society, but horizontally, as different components rather than as strata. They are closer to trade guilds than social classes.

Another who spoke to me on the subject was Pierre Claver Hien, a history professor at the University of Ouagadougou in neighbouring Burkina Faso. He told me that Mali has managed to protect its own culture far better than has his own country, far better than most other countries in Africa. He said that Westerners who criticize Mali's ancient social classes of nobles and people of caste, or call the country backward, are hypocritical.

"Mali's social classes are complementary and mutually dependent; they look out for each other," he said. "They create a balance, stability and give each person a strong sense of identity and a strong social obligation to behave in a way that benefits the whole society. There is little crime, fighting is taboo and the country is peaceful. These are classes people are born into and in which they are happy. Would you prefer that they adopt the Western class structure that is now taking over Africa? Today, in America and Europe, a person's class is defined by how much money they have. Money gives people power to abuse those who have less money, who are in lower classes. Is that a fairer system? The West is not well-placed to lecture Africa about social hierarchies. Not at all."

I heard a similar take on this from Abdoul Aziz Ly, a scientist from Senegal living and working in Mali. Senegal shares several of the same ethnic groups and traditions as its neighbour, Mali, and Aziz Ly is of noble birth and of Fula ethnicity. He maintained that outsiders never understand the intricacies or the importance of the traditional social system of nobility, caste and even former slaves. Nor, he said, do they realize what problems arise when this ancient social balance is upset and its structure destroyed by imported ideas and values. Aziz Ly, like all my tutors, was very patient, laying it all out for me slowly and clearly.

It isn't just people from Europe and North America who don't understand, he said. It is also progressive intellectuals from other parts of Africa, who have been schooled in the West and have adopted what he called "Western paradigms." As a scientist with a West African research institute that focuses on problems peculiar to the West African countries already suffering from climate change and the southward progress of sand from the Sahara Desert, Aziz Ly worked with colleagues from many different countries. Not all of them were familiar with the social structure bequeathed to his country by the great empires that had flourished in the region.

"One day a very top level political scientist came into my office," he told me. "He was from Nigeria, and when he entered, an uncle of mine was there and we were making our usual joke. My uncle was sitting there, and the Nigerian professor asked me, 'Who is this guy?' and I replied, 'Oh, this is one of my slaves.' He was shocked. So he called all the others in the offices around and said, 'Come, come, Aziz has slaves now'."

Aziz Ly laughed, shook his head. "So then everyone gathered around to discuss this. They were condemning me, and so I told them to ask my 'slave' if he wanted to be freed. So the Nigerian asked him that, and he said he didn't want to be freed. Then they asked him why. And he told them he gains from this, because if I am his nobleman, then I am obliged to feed him. Of course this isn't really the case any more; it's just our tradition and it helps us know how we fit together. There is an inner logic and unless you take this into account, you will misinterpret what you are criticizing. You should not take this out of context or you will turn something very positive into something very negative."

He went on to say that much of the problem lies in semantics – there are simply no translations in French or English for the words that West African groups use to describe nobles, castes and so-called slaves. These are dangerously loaded words in English and French, and they function as poor translations of concepts that are foreign to native speakers of these European languages.

Yet despite its importance in maintaining the social peace and cohesion that allow so many impoverished people in West Africa to survive and enjoy fulfilling lives, this ancient system is now breaking down, turning topsy-turvy, according to Aziz Ly. And what cultural jackhammer was causing all this damage?

"Money," he said.

3

The case there for God

"Ah, there is a story to tell, because people are moving everywhere nowadays. All young people are now moving to make ends meet. If you move from one place you don't get any satisfactory there, then you have to move to another place. But by moving around, you drop totally, you don't have any single penny, you see. Outside world today they can't imagine that African people moves up and down like that. But we the Africans, we knows that this will go on as long as this economic and political crisis is going on every now and then killing one another. But as you know, your own time hasn't reached for you to die, so then God will just give you the option to move out. That's why African youths are just moving up and down. If you ask any other one, I think they will give you similar answer like this."

Ahmed Jalloh, of Sierra Leone, stranded in the desert
outpost of Nara, Mali, on the edge of the Sahara Desert.

Money – the lack of it and its inequitable distribution, as well as its abuse and misuse as a catalyst for corruption and political power struggles – is the cause of great hardship and disenchantment in Africa. Yet the bitterness of many young Africans unable to afford a formal education or to find employment and income on their own continent amazingly does not transform them into instant terrorists, eager to take up arms and confront the powerful people, corporations and institutions abroad that have some responsibility for their sorry fates. I've seen people in Canada get more angry over the suggestion that drive-thrus be banned to reduce carbon emissions, than young Africans do who are deprived of just about everything – schooling, paying work, safe drinking water, transport other than their own two feet.

Sadly, however, frustrated young men with no way to earn the money that they desperately need to support their families, or to even afford the costs of marrying and starting a family, are easy marks for people calling themselves rebels. Some can be drawn effortlessly into local and regional conflicts, turning on each other rather than on a global order that has failed them.

Assassinated African leaders who dared to challenge that global order, such as Thomas Sankara, Amilcar Cabral, Patrice Lumumba and (probably assassinated) Samora Machel are still mourned on the continent, as are many other potential leaders who died in prisons belonging to dictators who were friends of the Western powers. Their deaths have helped erase hope among Africa's youth that their countries can ever achieve economic and political independence. Hundreds of years of European domination have torn at the fabric of their societies, their traditional faiths and perhaps worst of all, their faith in themselves.

Africans have become their own biggest critics. Many of them have started to judge themselves through European eyes, describing anything authentically African – be it religion, a cultural practice, ways of dressing and eating, traditional rites of passage, even architecture well-suited to the climate and landscape – as primitive, backward or uncivilized.

Robbed of their self-confidence and led to believe that their cultures, traditions and ways of life are out of date in this modern world, but blocked from the formal education and opportunities that would allow them a fulfilling paying career to enjoy modern benefits, the youth of Africa are succumbing to despair. Their despair makes them vulnerable to anyone and anything that looks like an escape from poverty, a rebel leader, a miracle-making pastor, or crime.[34]

Unable to carve a decent life for themselves in their countries, many of the young people I knew in West Africa spent nearly all their time dwelling on one thing: how to get to Europe or North America or to anywhere that they could earn a little money honestly. They would be willing to do anything: clean toilets, drive a taxi, labour in a factory, clean homes, baby-sit, wash dishes, pick fruit, load trucks, sweep airports. If only they could obtain an entry visa for Europe or Canada or the United States. Failing that, they were willing to walk across the Sahara Desert or climb into a leaking boat and try to sneak their way into Fortress Europe as illegal migrants.[35]

During the seven years I lived in Mali, I spent countless hours enjoying the weak shade of a small neem tree in front of the home of Hawa Soumanou, an elderly woman friend. Hers is a crumbling structure. There is no indoor plumbing. A tiny cluttered courtyard on the edge of an open sewer doubles as a kitchen and living room. This sewer flanks a mud path cum road in one of Bamako's oldest and least physically endowed neighbourhoods. I greatly enjoyed sitting there in the heart of the city, listening and watching. I eventually learned to tune out the things that at first offended my overly sensitive senses: open sewers, rubbish heaps, livestock roaming about and blowing dust. Instead, I came to notice all the things that made life rich in that poor neighbourhood: the chattering and infectious giggles of small children playing with whatever came their way; the happy news of a marriage, or a festival, or a baptism for a healthy newborn; the laughter that erupted when people discussed the shenanigans of their politicians; and even their woes. I loved the familiarity of the community of that road, the time people took to greet each other and to exchange stories as they passed on foot.

But even as I learned not to worry (at least not *too* much) about the unpleasant smells and the mounds of garbage and the physical squalor as I sat under the neem tree watching life go by, there was one thing that bothered me more and more. There was a constant parade of young people who approached and asked for my help in getting a visa for Great Britain, Canada, the US or France.

Their impressions of these places are inevitably vague, shaped in part by soap operas on their televisions that lead them to believe that most white people live in huge palaces, do no work at all, and spend their days meeting their illicit lovers in their private vineyards. Roads are paved with gold, money grows on trees and life is very easy indeed. White people, it is often believed, are always rich, cannot move without a vehicle and do not know how to walk or work physically.[36]

Africans returning from the wealthy world often perpetuate these myths that life there is easy and money very easy to come by. They may not wish to divulge that they earned their salaries by cleaning bathrooms, suffered humiliating insults, and that they did not live like kings while abroad. Few in Africa have any idea of just what squats and slums and hardship really await the unskilled or the *sans papiers* (illegal) immigrants in Europe or North America. Some are shocked when they learn that in major European and North American cities there are homeless people living on the streets. Few people seeking visas seemed to want to listen to me list the constraints they would have to adapt to in the wealthy world, where competition is extreme, taxes must be paid and where time is money and thus king, ruling every minute of the day. From their perspective, these issues were all irrelevant. The important thing was a steady income that would provide funds to help support the family back home and could be saved towards a more secure future. A minimum wage job in Europe or North America could bring in more than a teacher or even a doctor earns in much of Africa.

Many young people I met assumed that because I was Canadian and a journalist, I must be a powerful person with lots of strings to pull. They thought I would know my way around in the maze of immigration bureaucracies and that I could easily get them a visa for any Western country.

Nothing could be further from the truth. Cameroonian and Malian friends with full-time jobs as journalists were turned down for visas to visit my family in Canada, despite my letters of invitation. They were told they could not prove they were not planning to stay. Many Africans have suggested to me over the years that Canada is even more restrictive and unfair in its visa practises than are other Western nations.[37]

On landing in Sierra Leone in November 2006, I was met at immigration by a smiling and congenial official who looked up at me and said affably, as he stamped my passport without hesitation or a single question, "You are from Canada. Your country has horrible immigration policies."

Disinterested in my repeated reminders that I was Canadian, a Malian woman friend in her early seventies urged me to go to the American embassy on her behalf and get her a visa for the United States. She knew a woman her age that had made her way to the US and was working as a nanny, making more money in a year there than she could earn in a lifetime in Mali, or so she had been told. Couldn't I get her a visa so she could go to the US for one year to do the same? She would work very hard, she assured me. She didn't want to stay in the United States; she just wanted to go for a year and earn some money to bring home. She had a lot of inherited children from her extended family to support, their education to pay for, food to put on the table – or, to be precise – the mat on which communal bowls of rice were spread on the floor of her compound to feed the extended family and anyone else who happened by at meal times.[38]

I knew she didn't believe me when I said I could not help her get a visa to the US. She was not impressed when I suggested that she was better off staying right where she was, in her home, surrounded by people who loved, respected and understood her, right there in the crumbling neighbourhood of Dravela, Bamako.

Law students or young women finishing up their high school and even people who could not read and write, would bring me magazine advertisements that said "Immigrate to America" or "Canada Seeks Immigrants" and offered the post office box numbers for legal or immigration experts with African names and North American addresses. They showed me amateur brochures from schools and colleges in Canada and the United States that I suspected didn't even exist. The brochures promised that for a few hundred more dollars sent to a post office box in Toronto or Pittsburgh, the African applicants were assured admission and student visas.

All smack of 419 scams, the same kind of letters that land from cyberspace in our Inboxes, sent by con artists in Nigeria or Russia or wherever they may be in the real world, asking for bank details in exchange for a share of some huge fund they have allegedly managed to obtain from obscure sources.[39] If many educated and forewarned people in the rich world succumb to temptation and fall for these scams, as they do by the thousands, it is hardly surprising that Africans with no bank accounts or money to put in them are also victims.

Many are desperate, and have little formal education and almost no knowledge of how things work in the developed world. In the West, rules are more rigid than they are in Africa, where charm and ancient family or ethnic connections can often work as magic potions that unlock bureaucratic doors and render official rules or laws immaterial.

Surely, the visa-seekers reasoned out loud to me, if the Western nations sent out all those development workers to "help Africa," then their governments and populations must care about the plight of Africans. They would surely open their borders to those who wanted to earn an honest living, even if it were doing menial work in the developed world?

Visas for the Promised Lands of the West, however, are extremely difficult to obtain for the average West African. At the same time, the West is quick to grant visas, and immigrant status, to Africans with professional degrees and training and will even organize job fairs· to recruit them. This has led to a tragic brain drain from the continent. More African doctors and nurses now work abroad, primarily in the UK and North America, than work at home.[40] More Ghanaian doctors work in New York than there are Ghanaian doctors in Ghana itself. In 2008, the medical journal, Lancet, suggested that active recruiting – poaching – of Africa's health professionals by rich countries is a "crime" and, "a violation of the human rights of the people of Africa." Shoppers Drug Mart and the province of Alberta came under particular criticism for this poaching of Africa's health professionals. [41]

Many Africans have told me that if only they were able to find work and a decent income on their own continent, they would far prefer to stay at home.

Then again, the remittances that expatriate Africans send home to their families and communities often account for a major, incalculable, percentage of the country's Gross Domestic Product (GDP). Pushed by then French President Jacques Chirac in 2003 to crack down on illegal immigrants leaving Mali to try to make their way to Europe, Mali's President Amadou Toumani Touré replied, "Our countrymen [abroad] contribute decisively to the development of their country. Every year they send the equivalent of the total develop-ment aid that Mali receives from France."

Illegal immigration for the average Malian – or youth from almost any West or Central African country without academic credentials or political pull – is often seen as the only option.[42] Immigration proce-dures in the West have always been complex, and after 9/11 they became even more complex and opaque as European and North American nations tightened the screws on border controls and secu-rity clearances. So the process of obtaining even a tourist visa for Western countries became an unlikely dream for young Africans. Even applying for one can be a costly nightmare.

The best vantage point in Bamako for witnessing the frustration and drama of the desperate search for visas was, I discovered, at the French embassy. France was the preferred gateway to Europe because there were daily flights to Paris and also because, as Mali's former colo-nial power, France was the European country that Malians knew the best. I spent several nights at the French embassy observing first-hand the plight of visa-seekers. People would line up for weeks on end; eld-erly women would camp out on the roadside enduring mosquitoes and teargas, awaiting their turn to obtain *an application* for a visa.

It was a sorry spectacle. First, it was depressing to see so many Malians so desperate to try to go abroad to work, proof that despite all the economic reforms Mali had been doggedly pursuing at the behest of Western donor countries, the economy was worse than ever. Second, it was depressing to see so many other Malians exploiting the despair and need of their countrymen. On the boulevard that housed the embassy, a local mafia sold places in the long queues in front of the visa office. Local young men, enterprising sharks who needed no lessons in exploiting market potential and the economic principle of supply and demand, worked in cahoots with the police, who would show up around midnight. While Bamako slept, in front of the French embassy there were almost nightly altercations when the police arrived to teargas and bludgeon people out of their places in the queue, and offer those places near the front of the line to those who were willing and able to pay them.

It was an embarrassing situation for the French diplomats, especially after some of their own nationals working within the embassy were sent home, reportedly for accepting large bribes in return for visas. Eventually, a new visa office was opened beside the French embassy. To obtain an appointment there, to obtain an application form and submit it or to receive a visa that had been granted, applicants now had to do so via cell phone, using one of only two telephone numbers. Because of the great numbers of people seeking visas, it was next to impossible to get through by phone. So the local mafia simply changed their mode and place of operation. Malian visa-seekers now hired them to spend their days dialling those numbers, and there were rumours of complicity of employees inside the phone company that housed the visa offices numbers.

An offshoot industry that has arisen from the quest for visas is the renting out to applicants of healthy bank statements, which some foreign embassies require as part of the application process. Such bank statements can be fabricated by people working within the banks and visa applicants pay to use them, until such time as their visa is granted and they are erased.

Even those who manage, despite all the obstacles, to acquire a legitimate visa to France, are still not assured entry to their former colonial power. They may have the requisite documents in place, have gone through the incredibly difficult process of obtaining a visa, undergone the strict scrutiny of French immigration and security personnel who screen passengers leaving Bamako with Air France, landed safely in Paris, and then find themselves pulled aside, whisked off in a police van, and sent back home again on the next Air France flight. Some deportees who make a fuss are shackled, and I witnessed on several flights their abuse and humiliation at the hands of burly, beer-swilling French policemen in civilian dress, who flew with them as official escorts back to Mali.

One evening when I got word that an Air France flight was bringing home a group of deportees, I raced to the airport to interview them on their arrival. They were fearful of giving me their names, afraid, they said, that those who had loaned them money to get their papers and air ticket to France, would hear them on the radio and know they were back in the country, and come expecting a pay back, which of course they didn't have.

One young man, disillusioned and despondent, told me his grandfather, like many thousands of African men in former British and French colonies, had been summoned to Europe to fight for the liberation of Europe during World War II. His grandfather had been injured there, and as the bitter young man said to me, now France was repaying its debt to the descendants of Malian veterans by treating them "like animals" and refusing them entry to "Europe that Africans helped to free."[43]

The next day, in my usual sitting place on the dusty roadside in downtown Bamako, a group of young university students approached my BBC colleague, Saïd Penda, and me, asking us to help them fill out the application forms and come up with the money to send to a college in the US that promised them visas and "professional" education. The brochure for the college looked as if it had been printed up on a typewriter and then photocopied in a back alley in Timbuktu.

Saïd, impatient and frustrated, advised them to stop sending off money to con-men and fake colleges, to stop dreaming impossible dreams, and to put their energy and creativity to better use at home. Then he turned to me and put into words the unfolding tragic drama of the continent.

"Africa has become a prison for its youth," he said. "Just like people behind bars, they spend all their time dreaming up ways to escape. That's the biggest tragedy of all."

Escape, however, is not easy, not in this new world where the West claims to be championing freedom and fighting terrorism. Freedom does not extend to the average African seeking a visa for Canada, the US, or any country in Europe. That kind of freedom is something that requires money. Africans must have enough money to buy their way into the 'free world' with their technical skills and solid bank accounts, either that or be one of the extremely few people living in a refugee camp who manages to obtain refugee status and a sponsor to get them to the West, having already survived war or other tragedy in their own country.

Still, it seems to me that the ultimate tragedy is not that the average African cannot get out of the prison of poverty on their continent. It is the fact that their own continent has become a prison for
so many of its inhabitants, especially the youth. Its borders have been
thrown open by economic reform policies to permit the influx of
cheap consumer goods from abroad, increasingly from China. Free
market policies from the University of Chicago School, which
African leaders reject only at their own political peril, have also
cranked African borders wide open for the wholesale outflow of the
continent's natural resources. But the so-called free trade, when it
comes to rich and poor countries, is a "one-way street."[44] Alas, the
borders of the wealthy countries that demand Africa open up its
doors for the free exchange of goods and commodities are also sealed
to keep out the average African wishing to go there to work, even just
to visit.

With the help of sophisticated rings of human traffickers, many
Africans are able to find hidden passages to get past the immigration
controls. Many are subsequently caught and deported; many others
fail to get out of Africa; untold numbers perish while trying to make
their way to Europe.

Their deaths rarely make headlines in the West, and often go all
but unnoticed. In Canadian newspapers, on occasions when news of
such a tragedy is carried at all, you are likely to find the wire service
stories of drowned would-be migrants on their way to Europe
squeezed into a few lines as a news brief up one narrow side of the
international news page. I have often found such horrific stories,
reduced to a few lines of print, dwarfed by advertisements for elaborate prom dresses or southern holidays for people from cold northern
countries. The death of 45 African migrants in pirogues off the coast
of Mauritania in March 2006, earned only an AP brief of two sen-
tences in a Canadian newspaper, not even a word on the major television or radio networks on the continent. And that was just one I
happened to catch; such tragedies have become regular occurrences
and often aren't reported at all.

Whether they are young men willing to climb into the wheel
wells of passenger jets heading to Europe and freeze to death, or
young people willing to climb into a leaking canoe or freighter and

59

perish in the sea, surely the desperation that drives them to their deaths should catch the attention of the public in the West, and spur editors to ask why the despair, what is causing it?

Howard W. French, senior writer and former correspondent in Africa for *The New York Times*, puts it this way: "Africa is the stage of mankind's greatest tragedies, and yet we remain largely inured to them, all but blind to the deprivation and suffering of one-ninth of humanity. We awaken to the place mostly in fits of coarse self-interest and outright greed."[45]

The victims of brutal deportation or of ruthless human traffickers who live to tell their tales have powerful and sad stories. I met so many of them over the years I would need to dedicate a whole series of books to telling their stories. But I can recount a few fairly typical tales of woe.

One came from Chernor Kabia, a young Sierra Leonean who had fled the horrific war in his country. His parents had both been killed in the conflict and he lived in fear of rebels, on whom he had informed in his own country. He showed me his school records and birth certificate, as well as a dog-eared newspaper clipping that identified him as a student activist for peace in his country.

He and a friend had obtained a visa for Algeria, he told me, and flown to Algiers, where they went to the United Nations High Commission for Refugees (UNHCR) and were granted official refugee status, a paper valid for one month.

"On the way from that office," he said, "the Algerian police stopped the bus, say[ing] they are looking for Blacks and [they] told the driver to drive off. They put me on their truck direct to a police station."

"Did you show them your attestation from UNHCR?" I asked.

"I do show them, they reply me 'no problem.' They say they are not arresting me; they want to separate legal Blacks from illegal ones. I even show them the [UNHCR] attestation. One of their boss saw it, they say, 'Oh God, this boy is legal. Why do you arrest this boy?' So the other boss say they are working on order to arrest all Blacks, legal or illegal."

After that, Kabia told me he spent two days in the prison, and the boss there told him he would be freed, as he was legal and his papers were okay. "They tell me everything will be okay. They type some paper, up to now they are using the manual typewriters, in Arabic, they force me to sign. I refuse because I say I don't know what is in the paper."

Then, he said, he was "beaten mercilessly" for refusing to sign. The next day he was taken, along with 50 other young people from Sub-Sahara Africa, to court. There they were told to remain silent and informed they had 24 hours to leave the country.

According to Kabia, the next day hundreds of fellow Africans – Nigerians, Cameroonians, Malians and Congolese among others, were "packed up like animals, in four trailers, each containing about 150 Blacks. Whether you are genuine or not, they say every Black should leave Algeria."

He used a tiny notebook he kept in a pocket to detail the events of that journey, from the Algerian capital south into the desert, from Blida to Medea, Djelfa, In Salah.

"Some guys, two Malians try to escape in In Salah," he said. "They [were] shot in the throat. After they shot them, they took them and call all of us generally and they say 'if any of you dare to do this [try to escape] you will be shot; you better not try this'. Plenty of Nigerians died; their parents will never know."

"There was one Nigerian lady," Kabia said. "She was six months pregnant. She died on the trailer, so we stop and dig some sand and bury her. Her mother, her parents will never know; she dead in the desert." He said another young woman, from the Democratic Republic of Congo, who was travelling with her one-year-old baby that had been born in Algiers and carried an Algerian birth certificate, eventually died along with her baby in a town called Tizawazi.

He consulted his little black book when I asked him how many deaths there were among the deportees during the journey through the desert of Algeria.

"Before we left Tamanrasset [Algeria], the death figure was 31 Nigerians, 6 from Niger, 2 Ghanaians, 20 Cameroonians and 2 Malians. Some die of hunger, some of them jumped off, sustain injuries, no medical facilities, they will stop trailer and place you on the sand. Some died of these injuries."

He said the survivors were eventually dumped unceremoniously in the Algerian desert near the border with Mali. From there, they had to make their way on foot to the border, about 20 kilometres over rock and sand dunes. There was little traffic on the desert tracks, and they had no money to pay their fare in the rare vehicle that passed with passengers headed to the desert outpost of Kidal in Mali. Some of the girls, however, were able to sell their female services to Algerian gendarmes in exchange for the fare, or even for some bread or water.

"They know that the place they dump you is a killing field," Kabia said. "If you die in the desert and go to eternity, you will tell your story there."

"Why should we believe you?" I asked, finally. "You could be making all this up."

"I have so many evidences. In Mali, there are still plenty young Nigerians dying. Also in that desert by Abeïbara, let them fly in helicopter they will find human bones and graves of the people everywhere."

What he told me was corroborated by countless young Africans I met in subsequent years, and countless more reports came of such suffering in the Sahara Desert. To my knowledge, no rescue efforts or investigations were ever carried out into this major human tragedy.

Contrast this with the disappearance of 32 European adventure tourists in 2003 in the same desert, kidnapped by Salafists.[46] They had chosen to travel south across the Sahara without a guide and against the advice of their own governments. After six months, all of the hostages were released and returned home safely, except for one German woman who died during the ordeal, reportedly from heat prostration. The international press corps flocked to Mali to cover the story. From the disappearance of the tourists through to their release, this story made headline news around the world.

Then there was the 17-year-old Nigerian girl I'll call Blessing. She was shy, so soft-spoken that I was hardly able to make out her heavily accented English as she recounted how she had wound up battered, bruised and penniless, in Bamako.

"I there fo' Nigeria. My mother die. My father die," she said. Desperate for some income to help raise her younger sister, she entrusted herself to a Nigerian woman who promised to take her to Benin and then to Europe for a job. Instead, the woman shipped her to Mali, where she informed her she was "to work fo' man, finish." She was told that if she wanted to go to Europe, she would have to "work fo' man" to earn money to pay for the fake passport, visa and the fare to get her across the desert to Europe.

In Mali, the woman handed her over to a Nigerian man. He took her to a miserable little brothel that called itself a hotel, and put her to work to earn her keep, which he took from her and kept himself. One of her clients was a man named Chris. "Chris carry rope, he tie me for my hand, for my back," said Blessing. "Then he hold me leg and he wound me all my body. The case there for God."

Fortunately for Blessing, she was saved by other Nigerian girls caught in the same racket who found her bleeding and bruised after the violent rape. They took her to the office of the Anti-Slavery Committee, comprising Nigerians and Malians who were struggling with Malian human rights activists to stop the human trafficking. The Anti-Slavery Committee cared for her, paid her medical bills and then brought her to the attention of the authorities in Mali to highlight the problem young African migrants were facing. A member of the Anti-Slavery Committee, Michael Destiny Oraka, alleged that in Mali there were police officers, immigration officials and even diplomatic personnel who were involved in the black market trade in human beings.

Mamadou Dembélé, national director of judicial affairs in Mali, told me that the phenomenon of human trafficking and sex trade had become, "a cancer, gangrene in our society."

Nowhere was the gangrene more evident than in the desert town of Gao, about 1,200 kilometres northeast of Mali's capital. A place more difficult and desolate than Gao is hard to imagine. Bisected by the Greenwich Meridian that runs right through the centre of the sandy 'downtown,' with the Sahara already burying its roads and homes and dunes encircling it, Gao felt to me far more like the proverbial end of the world than did Timbuktu. Just to get to Gao from just about anywhere was a long, hot and trying journey. Many of the thousands of young Africans who arrived there were from Nigeria, but they also came from many other West and Central African countries. Many were young girls trapped into prostitution even before they arrived, unable to leave until their traffickers felt they had paid their dues for the voyage from their own country and then onwards to Europe. It was a human disaster of enormous dimensions, an epidemic of despair that was also a factor in the HIV/AIDS tragedy on the continent.

With the help of a local journalist in Gao, I set out to track down the Nigerian man alleged to run the show. His name was Austin, and we found him in a dark, bare room adjacent to a notorious brothel appropriately called The Grotto, where the girls were put to work for a few months or years to pay off their travel debts to the traffickers. I asked Austin how many young Africans passed through Gao each year, hoping to make their way north to colder but more lucrative pastures in Europe.

"It's uncountable," he said. "It's like sand, thousands of people. I cannot tell you exactly ... but it's thousands of people." Austin, with a vested interest in the traffic, refused to admit to me that the desert crossing was difficult or dangerous. "We are Africans, it's easy for us."

"Crossing the desert isn't easy for anyone," I said.

"There's many people living in the desert," he countered.

"Yes, but you come from Nigeria," I said. "Nigerians are not desert-dwellers. If an inexperienced and ill-equipped person heads out, they die."

"Yeah, well we want to experience Africa ..."

"Oh come on, the people you send across the desert only want to get to Europe. Let's be honest ..." I said, angered by his reptilian regard.

"Yeah but if you don't have money, how are you going to get there? Whites, I'm sorry to say, doesn't give Africans visa. That's why you see Africans going through desert, that's why. You can't blame us."

"Yes, but so many of them die in the desert."

"Yeah, people die, even by air crash, people die."

That was about as far as I was going to get with Austin. He claimed he earned his daily bread by 'barbing' at his little barbershop in Gao. He denied that he had anything to do with trafficking of the desperate young people who landed there.

The police chief in Gao confirmed that Austin was one of the local kingpins. But Austin was a small player in a mafia that, according to the police, extended from Europe, through Mali and then branched out into the countries across West and Central Africa. Its epicentre is in populous Nigeria, a country that remains impoverished despite all the oil that has been taken out of it. When the traffickers in Europe needed a new shipment, say two dozen new girls, they simply tell their people on the ground in any one of the countries they covered, and two dozen new girls would be 'recruited' with promises of respectable paying work and free passage to Europe. The deputy governor of the region of Gao, Abdoullaye Mamadou Diarra, said that their routes took them through Mauritania and up through Morocco, and occasionally through Algeria, although that country was full of military and, as Chernor Kabia had learned the hard way, unsympathetic to illegal and legal African migrants. The ultimate destination was Europe, and the clandestine African emigrants generally hoped to enter it via Spain and occasionally Italy. The officials in Gao spoke of the hardship endured by the young people, shipped off in pick-ups or dump trucks into the desert, where they were often abandoned by ruthless and unscrupulous drivers, or where they died of starvation and dehydration if the vehicle broke down. There were wrenching reports by *Agence France Presse* the previous year of one truckload of would-be migrants being stranded in the desert resorting to cannibalism to survive. The Nigerian ambassador to Mali called me up and asked to do an interview so he could make a plea on the BBC for young people in his country to stay home and avoid the perils of illegal migration and human trafficking.

The gendarmes in Gao were more than willing to talk about the crisis. They said that the Western Union money transfer outlet in Gao reportedly had the highest turnover of any Western Union office in Mali. They pulled out piles of false Malian and Guinean passports and ID cards they had seized in recent months from young migrants from Nigeria, Cameroon, Democratic Republic of Congo, Sierra Leone, Liberia and Ghana, all of whom they had intercepted before they started out on deadly journeys into the desert. Off the record, the authorities in Gao felt that there was complicity of some immigration individuals.

Canadian funds had recently paid for the construction of a new passport office in Mali that produced digitized passports, intended to prevent the trade in fraudulent ones. But somehow, individuals were still finding ways to falsify passports and ID cards. One police officer said he had caught Nigerian and Ghanaians, who could neither read nor write nor speak a word of any Malian language or the official one, French, carrying Malian passports and university papers proclaiming them holders of doctorates.

The officials in Gao suggested that if I wished to talk to some of the young women caught in the traffickers' web, I would find them in the brothel called The Ghetto. When I arrived there, I realized I had been followed by two burly Nigerians on a motorcycle. A Malian man emerged from inside and met me at the gate with his strong arms folded across his chest, and all three confronted me. They asked me what I thought I was looking for and then without waiting for an answer, informed me that whatever it was, I had no business looking for it there.

In the market, I did find one young Nigerian man who reluctantly agreed to speak to me and admitted that he was heading out soon through the Sahara.

"It is because I don't have money that I am willing to take the risk," he said.

"Yes, but is it worth losing your life in the desert for the money you might make in Europe?"

"You see me here," he said. "I'm hustling, always hustling, to see I have my daily bread. If I go to Europe I will also hustle. A lazy man have no food.

"A dead man has no food," I replied. "What good is daily bread if you're dead?"

"Nobody is praying to die," he replied. "If you make up your mind to travel, you pray, you give yourself to God."

4

Miracles, marabouts and magic

For the first time in my life, I have to say that my morale and hope are really finished. Things are so bad in Mali that I can no longer believe in anything any more.

Letter from Mahamoudou, a Malian student

It is not just to God that the desperate young Africans give themselves when they try to get to a country where they can find work. The despair has also led to an unreasonable faith in miracles, which makes young people extremely vulnerable to con-men promising all manner of supernatural powers to ensure safe passage to Europe or a fast-track to wealth. Given the difficulty of earning a decent living honestly in many countries in Africa, con-men and trafficking networks are multiplying and spreading out over the continent like the plague. Pastors and evangelists – African, American, European – spreading fundamentalist Christian dogma and promising miracles, are rapidly becoming wealthy while those who place their faith in them become poorer. Evangelical preachers and their Salvation or Flaming Bible or Spiritual Redemption churches are multiplying as fast as cell phone billboards, as the only two obvious and profitable growth sectors in West Africa. Islam and Christianity, however, continue to live side by side in many African countries, compatibly and with exemplary mutual acceptance and respect, at least where religious leaders are not deliberately trying to divide them.[47]

Traditionally, spiritual healers such as marabouts, the name given to Muslim mystics, hermits or holy men in North and West Africa, have been a part of the cultural picture in Africa. They were highly respected because they were not in the business of making a lot of money with their powers. In Mali, it is still common practice to visit women who specialize in reading cowry shells for insight, and then help their clients resolve difficulties they might be having with a spouse or children. The cowry-readers don't demand a lot of money for their services nor do they claim to be able to produce miracles. They read the cowries to assess your problems, offer good advice and maybe suggest the sacrifice of a chicken and perhaps some herbal remedies. They continue to play an important role as rather gentle mediums and mediators in their society. I found them to be soothing and wise.

But as traditions break down and desperation grows, people begin to seek mystics to help them overcome the problems associated with poverty. The late Mohamed Lamine Traoré, professor of philosophy and former Minister of Education in Mali, spoke to me about this phenomenon. He said the difficulty for Africans is that so many of them now have to work with a "double mind." Many attend formal schools with a secular Western education that usually focuses more on Europe than it does on Africa and the majority of Africans now follow Christianity or Islam, but when push comes to shove, some still have enormous faith in their own traditional mystics.

"In villages in Mali, people continue to believe in their tradition-al seers, people whom in Bambara[48] we call *soma*, which means 'some-one who knows,'" Professor Lamine told me. "These people use many spiritual arts and plants for their therapeutic work. Even today, a man might wake one morning in a village, and tell people he was going to visit with the *soma* today because his fields were not producing well or his wife could not get pregnant. Sometimes, these diviners, or *soma*, are their own neighbours, individuals in the village who prac-tice their ancient arts openly, without any shame or fear. And they do not charge for their services; the people who visit them take along a few Kola nuts or a tiny bit of money as a gift."

In the cities, however, Mohamed Lamine Traoré said that "schiz-ophrenia" exists, particularly among those who have attended formal schools, and consider themselves to be modern, *au courant* with European ways of doing things, such as praying in churches or mosques where ancient beliefs are frowned upon. These people don't like it known that they still believe or engage in traditional mysticism. Because they are in the city, they no longer know who is who, and keep their visits to mystics such as marabouts secret. And this makes them vulnerable to charlatans.

"A true diviner *never* solicits clients," Traoré said. "They respect ancient rules and don't promise great things. They speak in parables and they will tell you what they can and cannot do to solve problems you take to them." Traoré's doctorate came from the Sorbonne in France, but his dissertation had been researched entirely in Mali on the power and culture of authentic geomancy, which involves reading complex signs about a person and their surroundings and interpreting them. He had no doubt that the mystics possessed enormous wisdom and power. Indeed, he said, West African diviners drew heads of state from all over Africa and even from Europe to consult with them on their political careers.

"In Africa, that is part of an enduring culture; no religion or science or scholarship can remove it," he said. "I have a hypothesis that Africans were so traumatized by their history, first the slave-trade and then colonization, that when we see that history, we understand why Africans, and black Africans in general, are still so attached to these ancient beliefs and practices. They have had a tragic destiny, and when there is tragedy, there is fear. If you look at American Blacks, at Africans taken as slaves to Brazil and elsewhere, we see that their faith in the powers of voodoo and geomancy has endured. In the West, where science and technology have developed, there is a rationality and faith in physics and chemistry and biology and genetics. But psychoanalysis is far closer to the practices of our own traditional therapists, the role our traditional mystics played in Africa."

Alas, he said, authentic marabouts and mystics are now few and far between. Charlatans are taking over, taking advantage of the growing desperation and emotional trauma of people whose traditions have been denigrated and are disappearing, replaced by new values and modern desires that are impossible dreams.

Joseph, a Cameroonian, knows the dangers of placing one's faith in a marabout. Joseph is tall, lean, smart and worldly, passionately interested in current affairs and the workings of the world. He is good-natured, sincere, hard-working, and usually full of good cheer as well. Each Sunday he walks about seven kilometres to his church in downtown Bamako because he doesn't have the money, about 25 US cents, he would need to take public transit, a green *Sotrama* van. When he can find employment, he works as a painter, or as a labourer, moving anything that needs moved, or running errands, anything at all to earn his daily bread honestly. When that fails, he prays for a little bit of help from friends who might at that moment have a little income and a few dollars to spare.

In a rare good month he might earn 100 dollars. With this he buys food and pays his part of the rent for small rooms he shares with other young people facing the same problems. The rooms he rents in Bamako are dismal little chambers without electric lights. They are set in long rows of similar rooms within rambling, crumbling compounds, with no indoor plumbing or running water. His worldly belongings, after over a dozen years of effort and searching for work in Mali, fit into one small duffle bag. It's a Chinese-made bag bearing the logo of 'Abibas,' the type of knock-off guaranteed to tear shortly after purchase, particularly if any weight is put inside. Fortunately, Joseph has little to carry.

He originally left his home in Cameroon in 1990 at the age of 21, heading first to Abidjan in Côte d'Ivoire. At that time, before civil war had erupted in that country, Abidjan was a mecca for young migrants seeking jobs involving manual labour. Joseph had hoped Abidjan would be a stepping stone to Europe where he could find a job and income so that he could send money home to his elderly mother and his younger sisters. Today, he is stranded in Bamako, unemployed and unable to send more than a few dollars at a time back to his mother, who is seriously ill. He doesn't have enough money even for the return fare by bus to Cameroon. And he certainly doesn't have the means to get to Europe.

Before I met him in 1998, Joseph and a dozen other young Cameroonian men set off from Bamako for northern Mali, on their way to Europe. They had all been working in Abidjan and had saved up a few hundred dollars each to pay their fare across the Sahara Desert. They decided they could pose as a Cameroonian soccer team during their journey. But before they set out through Mauritania, they planned a stop in a fabled town called Nioro du Sahel to see a famous marabout.

The marabout in Nioro du Sahel was said to have helped many young migrants on their way to Europe, for a substantial fee.

"People in Bamako told us that he was a powerful marabout," Joseph said. "They said if we saw that marabout, we wouldn't have any problems with police or even need a visa to cross into Mauritania. He had a fetish that would make us invisible and we could easily walk to the Mauritanian capital [Nouakchott] without being seen."

Once they arrived in Nioro du Sahel, it took the young men almost a week to get in to consult with the marabout. His son welcomed them and then told them they would have to pay him money while they waited to see the great mystic. When the marabout finally received them and worked his magic, they had to pay him nearly all their remaining funds before he would render them invisible for the long trek through the Sahara.

I asked Joseph when, precisely, they realized that they were not invisible.

"To our great surprise," he replied, "not too long after we had crossed into Mauritania, we were intercepted by Mauritanian soldiers. They told us that Mauritania didn't need foreigners. We realized then that we had been duped by the marabout, and that we were not invisible at all. It was all lies."

But surely they must have known that they were not invisible before that; surely they must have seen each other? Yes, he said, but the marabout had led them to believe that the magic he provided would make them invisible not to each other but only to the authorities that might pose a threat to their passage along the way.

The Mauritanian officials manhandled them into the back of their truck and dumped them on the long brown unmarked border, telling them to march south out of Mauritania and into Mali. They wandered about in the desert in northern Mali for days, lost, with nothing to eat or drink, until they found themselves near the city of

Kayes in northwestern Mali, nearly dead of dehydration and sun-stroke. There, they begged for coins to pay for bush taxis back to Bamako.

"Would you go and see a marabout again?" I asked Joseph.

"No, what they do isn't real. The marabouts are crooks. They take your money and say they're doing magic and afterwards you realize it was fake."

Would he still like to make it to Europe? Yes, he told me, and still tells me each time he writes. He will never stop trying to get to a country where he can earn some money honestly. "Africa is a prison," he said. "I go to church and I pray and I pray. I would go anywhere I can get a visa. My mother is very ill, and I have nothing to send her. I don't know what I did to deserve this."

For every con-artist behind a computer keyboard in Africa, every would-be perpetrator of a scam to try to convince wealthy cyber-visitors to part with their bank details – and the money in their bank accounts – there are countless young people like Joseph. Honest as the sun is bright and determined to maintain their faith that one day their hard work might pay off. For that, deep religious faith is a useful asset. Africa has it in abundance.

The ingenuity and intellectual energy that goes into the trafficking of miracles and false hopes by con-men in Africa knows no bounds. One group of these crooks, called "Fe-men" in Cameroon, have developed elaborate and incredibly devious schemes to hoodwink even sceptics, combining a mastery of psychology with clever sleights of hand. One well-known scheme involves trunks full of blackened pieces of paper the size and shape of bank notes, and a "magic fluid" that can be bought by the unsuspecting victim of the scam. The victim is told that banks use a black dye to protect currency while it is being moved from mint to bank, and a special fluid is used to remove the dye once the bundles of bills are safely in the bank vaults. To erase any doubts the victim might harbour, the Fe-men rub charcoal on a couple of real dollar bills (or franc notes, or whatever currency they work with) and then use a bit of the 'magic fluid' – water – to wipe it off. Then, when the con-artists feel the victim has been adequately convinced, they offer to sell him (or her) an entire bottle of the fluid, along with the trunk full of blackened bits of paper. The Fe-men are so sophisticated that they adjust the price of the fluid to what they figure the chosen victim can obtain by begging and borrowing from friends and relatives, who might wish to be involved in the winnings. This could be hundreds or even thousands of dollars.

Once the victim has handed over the money, the con-artists simply disappear. When the truth finally dawns on the owners of the magic liquid and the trunk full of blackened bits of paper that they have been had, it is too late. Such is the vulnerability of people so chronically short of money, and who are confronted daily with visions from a world of plenty that play across television and video screens. They can only dream of attaining all they have learned to want from the West. Reality has failed them, so uncountable numbers of people in West Africa cave in to their desire for instant miracles. It's no different from the working poor in North America who fall victim to false hopes, and spend what little money they have on lottery tickets and at video lottery terminals. A ragged blue t-shirt I saw on a man in a dusty village in Sierra Leone bore the plea, "Dear God, please let me prove to you that winning the lottery will not spoil me." I think the wearer was unaware of the sad irony; he couldn't read.

It seems a problem too big to contemplate, let alone combat. But, this being Africa, it wasn't long before I found an antidote to my depression about the vulnerability of Africans seeking magical solutions to real problems.

His name is Momnougui Penda, a Cameroonian living in Bamako. In another part of the world, where genius can be lucrative and there is some public money spent on furthering the public good and those who struggle to protect it, Momnougui Penda might be well be on his way to a Nobel Prize or at least several honorary degrees. He would certainly be living a comfortable life with all of the things we in the rich world think of as normal amenities.

But Momnougui Penda lives in West Africa, where honesty doesn't usually pay off with financial dividends and where elected governments are more accountable to foreign creditors than to the people who elect them. So Penda's genius goes largely unnoticed and unrewarded.

I first met him at a modest exhibition of locally made 'appropriate technology' held in the immodest interior of the Congress Palace in Bamako. Most of the display booths bore the logos of international NGOs[49] or research organizations, and exhibited locally processed goods and foods. These had little hope of ever making it onto any shelves other than those at such UN- and NGO-sponsored fairs dedicated to good ideas and local initiative and potential. There were locally made soaps and shampoos made from shea nuts or *karité,* to which the value had been added right here in Africa.[50]

There were also locally designed and manufactured solar cookers and water heaters. Those too didn't have much chance of making it past the cottage industry stage, not without some serious investment and financing that just wasn't coming.

I've seen many such adapted technology exhibitions over the years in several African countries, and have yet to see much of that adapted technology in use by real people. Almost five decades of foreign development assistance in Africa has only made Africans more dependent on imported technology, much of it ill-adapted to local conditions or of substandard quality. Small trade fairs exhibiting locally made goods and consumer items always make me a little sad because the good intentions and good ideas on display seem doomed.

Such cynicism, however, does not afflict Momnougui Penda. There he was, all on his own, no funding from anyone, standing inside a neat perimeter of mud bricks, a trowel in his hand and stacking bricks with mortar. He explained to anyone who would listen the many advantages of building with mud in that hot part of the world. Mud is free but for the digging; it insulates against heat during the sweltering months that last from March right through to the onset of the annual rains in July, and against the dry, cold (okay, cool), dust-laden Harmattan winds that sweep from the Sahara Desert down across West Africa from November through January.

Cement is expensive and imported, he explained, and in the Sahel the interiors of homes made with concrete bricks are like ovens for half the year. The only problem with mud bricks is that they require firing if they are to withstand the elements. That means using firewood and the fragile, degraded Sahelian landscape cannot afford to lose its precious trees to fuel kilns to fire bricks. That would accelerate the southern advance of the desert. But unfired mud bricks are subject to erosion by the torrential rains that fall for three or four months each year.

Not one to let an eroding mud wall stump him, Momnougui Penda came up with a solution: 'improved' mud bricks that could be used for corners of the home and around windows and doors to increase the durability and strength of dwellings and buildings constructed in the almost-traditional way. For key structural parts of a house, Momnougui Penda reinforced the bricks with short lengths of steel rods, or rebar. This cost only pennies per brick; far cheaper than a building of concrete bricks.

I asked him why he was doing this, what was in it for him: did he produce such bricks and sell them? He said no, he didn't have the means to produce anything except the idea, which he hoped would be taken up by architects or perhaps one of the development agencies that helped put up health centres and rural schools in West Africa.

So far, he said, he wasn't having much luck promoting his idea. But he wasn't going to give up because he was an inventor, "among other things." What other things? Well, he had a small workshop on the outskirts of the city where he made furniture, and he was also an "investigator in parapsychology."

I asked what that involved. He said it had to do with the way Africans, in their desperation, had given up on hard, honest work to succeed in life and were squandering their hope, energy and precious resources on magic and miracles. We arranged to meet so he could tell me more.

I picked him up at his home, a small mud house without electricity or running water, and we went together to the container he had converted into a workshop, a few kilometres away. Here you could order the construction of a table or chair or door, or drop off a radio for repair. This is where Momnougui Penda told me he earned his "daily bread," by which he meant the income he needed to support his wife and two small children. I suspected his income from the workshop could probably be counted in coins that hardly added up to a dollar a day. But his real passion, he said, was investigating parapsychology and magic.

In this capacity, he had become known as "Maitre" Penda, a title normally reserved for teachers or lawyers in francophone West Africa. He moved about with a well-worn, black leather bag of tricks, exactly the kind of bag a North American physician might have carried back when doctors still made house calls. I guess he earned the title in recognition of his quiet sartorial elegance and his remarkable range of talents.

To become an investigator in parapsychology, Maitre Penda said he had taught himself how to perform a large repertoire of purportedly magical tricks, which he used to disprove magic. He was soft-spoken, thoughtful, and dressed in neat black trousers and white shirt, he looked more like a teacher than he did a magician. Speaking in excellent English, which was not his first, nor second, nor even his third language, but a fourth he picked up in school in Cameroon, he said, "I try to investigate African traditions and then see how these can help people."

I asked what on earth that meant. He told me to pay attention as he opened his magic bag and pulled out an egg. I was to touch it to make sure it really was a chicken's egg. I felt its weight, rolled it around in my hands and agreed that it was indeed a chicken's egg.

"Now I'm going to show you something else," he said, as he extracted a white cloth from his bag. "I put this egg on this cloth. Just look at this egg and count to ten."

I did as I was told.

He then asked me to hold out my left hand, and announced that he was going to break the egg on my hand. Before I could protest, he did just that. But instead of a yellow yoke, out came a note for 5,000 francs CFA (about ten US dollars).

Rather than charge me for the miracle or promise me he could help me become rich by producing more eggs filled with money, or ensure a safe trip across the desert and easy money in Europe, Maitre Penda explained to me how he pulled off the sleight of hand. He had distracted me with the white cloth while he deftly switched the real egg for another that he had prepared in advance by making a small hole through which he had extracted the yoke and white, and then inserted the money.

"You know that if I was able to produce a 5,000-CFA note in an egg, I should not even have to work," he said. "There are so many eggs; I just need 50 francs [ten US cents] to buy one and bring it home and change it into money. If I could really do that, I would be like Bill Gates, a very, very rich man who doesn't need to work to earn any money at all."

"Are these the same kinds of tricks that some of the rather crooked marabouts or juju-men are doing to get money out of people?" I asked.

"Yes, this is exactly what they do. For them it is just a means of making money and making people fear them and consider them as people with powers."

He had mastered dozens of different tricks that are used commonly by charlatans masquerading as marabouts or mystics, whose business is to make money from their tricks. His intention, however, was not to squeeze money out of a gullible paying public, but to perform the magic tricks to make the public *less gullible*. He had been hired to train police officers in neighbouring Burkina Faso to detect fraud and identify con artists, and even by a development project that felt his message was an important one to spread to the general population in northern Mali.

According to Maitre Penda, his fellow Africans, whom he called his "brothers and sisters," were wasting their lives. They were squandering their life savings and often those of their relatives as well, and wasting energy and initiative on the false hopes that magicians raise.

"People believe too much in miracles," he said. "And many people are cheating each other. I ask people to think about it. Someone tells you he can make you rich, and he himself is not rich. Or there will be a marabout who says he can help your children succeed at school, when he himself is illiterate and his children are not even at school. Or you'll find a con artist who says he can help you win the lottery, but surely if he can make you win, he could make himself win first. So what happens is these people take your small money to help them solve their problems, and your problem remains."

He concluded: "I know that it's very hard, very difficult to face certain problems when we think that others have the solution," he said. "But what happens very often is that if you put all your hope in someone who pretends he can solve your problems, you'll be disappointed. By the time you realize that he has disappointed you, it's already too late. I'm convinced that if the people – the youth, the governments – try to fight with their minds and their hands to solve these problems without thinking about marabouts, oracles, or even God, many problems will be solved. We have our intelligence, our strength; we have to think to study our own problems to work to solve them. I think that the power is in all of us."

5

Burying African hopes

We have to dare to invent the future … Everything that we are capable of imagining we are also capable of attaining.

President Thomas Sankara

Despite Momnougui Penda's optimism and belief that Africans have the power to improve things on their continent, there are external forces and factors at play in Africa that make it extremely difficult for any one person, or even any one nation, to change. Occasionally, however, one of those rare individuals comes along who appears to have the energy, ingenuity and creativity to turn the universe – or at least a small country in Africa – on its head.

Thomas Sankara was just such a person. He ruled Burkina Faso, one of the world's poorest and least-known countries, for four years. Its capital, Ouagadougou, is fodder in the West for quizzes and other trivial pursuits. Previously a colony in the French West African Federation, France officially granted the country political independence in 1960, as the new nation of Upper Volta.

Even its name was problematic, as if it were only half a country and the rest of it had floated off down the Volta River. By August 1983, the country had already seen four presidents come and the most recent one, military pharmacist Jean-Baptiste Ouédraogo, was about to go. On August fourth that year, four young military officers seized power in a coup to overthrow Ouédraogo's weak regime.

The four officers, Captains Thomas Sankara, Blaise Compaoré, Henri Zongo and Commander Jean-Baptiste Lingani, quickly formed their "National Revolutionary Council," with Thomas Sankara as head of state.

The coup was not bloodless; at least five people died in the cross-fire. But the overthrown president was not killed and he eventually resumed his work as a pharmacist. The physical elimination of predecessors was a sad tradition established in Togo in 1963, when President Sylvanus Olympio was killed in the coup that brought then Sergeant Gnassingbé Eyadéma to power. Eyadéma then proceeded to promote himself to General, and ruled his country with an iron fist stained with blood[51] and corruption until his death in 2005.[52]

In all that time, General Eyadéma had unflagging financial and military support from both France and Germany. The French built him a huge military airport and base in the north, near his native village of Pya, where General Eyadéma constructed a palace for himself. Twice France sent in troops to save Eyadéma's presidency during attempted overthrows. Western governments applauded him for the stability in Togo. Tourists from Europe could enjoy luxury resort hotels along the coast and take organized bus tours into the hinterland to watch Africans pound millet in wooden mortars in their villages for a few hours.

As in many countries in Africa and around the world, there were two distinct nations within the single country of Togo: one occupied by a tiny obscenely wealthy elite closely connected to the larger-than-life president, and the other inhabited by a huge majority with no political connections, benefits or money to speak of.

From the start, Thomas Sankara made it clear that he was not going to be just another corrupt, luxury-loving African president dancing to the tune of foreign masters. On the anniversary of his first year in power, Sankara changed the name of his country from Upper Volta to Burkina Faso, which combined two indigenous languages to describe this small, landlocked country as the "land of upright men" or "land of people with integrity."

He had no time for diplomatic niceties or even diplomacy as it is generally practised. Sankara openly challenged the powers that be in Washington and Paris, hobnobbing with Nicaragua's then-Marxist leader Daniel Ortega and Cuba's Fidel Castro. He also turned his back on Libya's Colonel Muammar Gaddafi who would ally himself with dissenters on the continent and cause a great deal of trouble for Western-backed regimes, but only if they deferred to him as their master.[53] This, Sankara refused to do.

He tried to demystify the African Big Man, the new breed of man on the continent whose wealth, traditional status or connections, and formal education afforded him every privilege that he wanted, legitimate or not. Sankara's actions were also an attack on the stereotype that many Western authors and journalists have drawn of African leaders: kleptomaniacs unable to restrain their own greed and ego once they are firmly ensconced in the golden presidential chair.

Thomas Sankara broke not just stereotypes but also the unwritten rules of how a president of a 'least developed' African country was supposed to govern. By the mid-1980s he was being heralded by many on and off the continent as leading a wave of promising second-generation leaders who would finally tackle some of the real problems plaguing Africa. Others who offered hope to Africa's youth at the time included Ghana's Jerry Rawlings before he and his revolution went flabby, Uganda's Yoweri Museveni before he decided to overstay his welcome at the helm of that country and involve himself in dirty wars in the region, and Mozambique's Samora Machel before he perished in a mysterious air crash over South Africa in 1986.[54]

Sankara shunned all luxury and imported goods. He dispensed with the custom-made Mercedes and Cadillacs that abounded in many presidential fleets in impoverished countries. He chose instead the tiny Renault 5, *Le Car*, as the official presidential and ministerial vehicles. Gone too were massive presidential convoys. Sankara could often be seen moving about the capital, Ouagadougou, in the front seat of his little black Renault, arm out the window and waiting like everyone else for traffic lights to change.

The more usual pattern I had witnessed during the 1980s in other African cities – Niamey, Yaoundé, Lomé, Cotonou, Kano[55] – was that major thoroughfares were simply shut down for the passage of the president, sometimes hours before the president came through in a cacophony of sirens and a blur of speeding BMW motorcycles, luxury sedans, jeeps and military vehicles. This caused major traffic blockages and long waits while motorists sat and waited, and *waited*, for the president's motorcade. Jaded and despairing Africans found humour their best, and only, weapon against leaders they had not chosen and had no power to remove from office. They would muse that their countries had plunged into poverty as the people waited in traffic, blocked while the president crossed town to urinate.

Sankara was a refreshing change.

A fitness fanatic, he liked to cycle. I saw him occasionally on his bicycle pedalling furiously around the man-made lake near the luxurious Hotel Silmande. One of his revolutionary acts was to have civil servants leave their offices at four o'clock on Tuesday and Thursday afternoons for two hours of mandatory physical activity – cycling, soccer, walking or running. He often joined in with staff from the presidency, jogging down Independence Boulevard.

He dispensed with all the pomp, props and palaces so popular among the Francophile presidents in francophone Africa. He also shunned imported goods and foods, believing it best to produce and consume locally. He promoted development that started at home, building on traditional knowledge and resources.

When French President François Mitterrand made a stop in Ouagadougou in November 1986, he was treated to a banquet of Burkinabé foods and drinks. There was no wine or champagne – French or otherwise. That was something simply *not done* in diplomatic circles in Africa or elsewhere either. Then, during an official toast that evening, Sankara dashed protocol altogether and perhaps wrote the script for the events of October 15, 1987.

"We, Burkinabé," he said to President Mitterrand, in front of the large corps of journalists who had accompanied him to Ouagadougou, "have never understood why criminals like Jonas Savimbi,[56] the head of UNITA, and murderers like Pieter Botha,[57] have the right to travel to France, which is so clean and beautiful. They stain the earth with their hands and their feet covered with blood."

In his reply that evening, after he patronizingly congratulated his Burkinabé host for his excellent mastery of the French language, President Mitterrand said that he admired Sankara's qualities but that "he went too far."

"Thomas Sankara makes it difficult to sleep," said President Mitterrand. "He asks so many questions that he leaves no one with a clear conscience." Then, as a nostalgic afterthought, he added, "He reminds me of myself when I was young, and full of energy and idealism."

Energy and idealism abounded in Burkina Faso during the Sankara years. The country crackled with it. Sankara's government ministers told me that he was a tough task-master, sleeping only a few hours a night. He opposed vices such as alcohol, tobacco and sloth. Head on, he confronted: ancient fears of the supernatural; female circumcision[58] and the way men treated women; filth in the cities; laziness and incompetence in the civil service; and environmental degradation with an official "three-pronged fight against desertification," which meant planting trees and banning both bushfires and uncontrolled grazing of livestock. Any marriage ceremony was not complete until the bride and groom had legally 'consummated' it by planting two trees.

At weekly cabinet meetings, Sankara's regime issued a host of decrees known as *kitis*. Nearly all were highly original policies intended to reduce the country's chronic dependence on foreign capital and imported ideas of what constituted development for the continent. There was often nothing inherently wrong with these decrees. Many were quite pointedly and brilliantly drawn up to wipe out Burkina's problems – overnight. And that was impossible. But Sankara liked to say that anything conceivable by the human brain is achievable by the human being. And for a time in that dusty little country, even the impossible did seem possible.

The *kitis* came hard and fast. The BBC African Service could hardly get enough reports from Burkina Faso, not a place one would usually associate with many reports for the international media. Thomas Sankara provided a bit of intriguing news from what was too often a morbidly depressing part of the world that filled newscasts with stories of famine, wars, corruption and political stagnation. I no longer had to pitch stories; the BBC called me up to see what was new in Ouagadougou.

There was something new under the African sun – a guitar-playing, humorous, passionate, athletic, articulate, driven and honest young president with a puritanical bent and a seemingly endless supply of novel and innovative ideas.

One of the decrees declared Burkinabé cotton the mandatory cloth for all government workers and for anyone wishing to enter the presidential office. This cotton, called *Faso Dan Fani*, was Burkinabé – grown, processed, woven, dyed and sewn in the country. The aim was to add value at home to what had previously been a cash crop, exported raw to France. Sankara also wanted to increase prestige for home-grown textiles to counter the devastating effects on tailors, weavers and farmers of the dumping of cheap second-hand clothing or ready-mades from abroad.[59] Fashion shows ensued, as Burkina's designers and tailors proved that home-made could be attractive and trend-setting. As Sankara pointed out, woollen suits and choking ties were wrong for the hot Sahelian climate. Such European apparel was extremely uncomfortable in offices that were not air-conditioned. Cotton was, though.

Sankara then banned the use of energy-guzzling air conditioners in government buildings except during the three very hottest months of the year, radically reducing state power bills.

That this dramatic measure, like many of his policies and his speeches, made him a lot of enemies did not appear to worry Thomas Sankara. At a diplomatic reception one evening, I asked the American ambassador to Burkina Faso if there was any truth in the rumour that one of his embassy drivers had been refused entry to the presidential offices because he was not wearing *Faso Dan Fani*. He avoided giving me a direct reply, but did say that he would never, ever allow American embassy staff to be dressed in those "potato sacks."

One of the more spectacular decrees was intended to eliminate prostitution and begging on the streets. Both social ills were to be wiped out with a slash of the pen and a few words of encouragement from the president himself. The decree specifying the new laws on begging coincided with the establishment of social centres set up in major towns and cities, where beggars could train as artisans. Donations from the public would be accepted to feed the beggars who moved to these social centres.

In charge of the program was the minister of social development, Josephine Ouédraogo. The country's first female ethnologist,

Ouédraogo commanded both respect and admiration among rural and urban Burkinabé, although she told me her greatest problems came from her male peers in the educated urban elite right there in Ouagadougou. She explained that the purpose of this *kiti* was to curtail the rapid increase in the number of beggars from Qur'anic schools. These boys, known as *garibouts*, throng roadsides throughout West Africa, begging for money they collect in empty tins, typically ones that once held imported tomato paste from Italy or France.[60] In theory, the money is for their schools and their upkeep, but more and more children are being exploited by their teachers, or marabouts. It is a tradition that began centuries ago to enable children to leave their homes to attend Qur'anic schools under respected marabouts, and learn humility by seeking community support. In recent times, the tradition has been perverted as the roadside Qur'anic schools proliferate in West African cities and their students have become beggars in the employ of some unscrupulous teachers.

Ouédraogo told me exemptions to the ban on begging had been made for disabled persons and women with twins, who would still be permitted to ask for alms, but only on Fridays and in front of mosques.

When I suggested that it was difficult not to give to young boys in rags who were clearly needy and who congregated on roadsides to ask passers-by for coins, she looked at me long and hard. "That's our problem. You Whites create these beggars. You are turning our country into a country of beggars." She went on to say that donations would be welcome in the shelters, and that giving money to anyone who was not handicapped was not a generous act.

As for the prostitution decree, Sankara followed that up with a conference for sex-workers in the Officers' Mess in the centre of Ouagadougou. Five hundred women – many mere girls – showed up to hear him speak, most of them Ghanaian, Nigerian, Nigerien (from Niger), Togolese or Ivorian; few Burkinabé girls could admit publicly to their work in the sex trade without intense social ostracism and rejection by their families. He told the assembled women that they were victims of "social injustice" and advised them to take up more "honourable professions" as hairdressers, seamstresses or waitresses. State-owned restaurants that had been opened in the newly designated 'green spaces' or neighbourhood parks in Ouagadougou (another *kiti*) were to employ these women immediately.

This was not entirely successful. Given the dearth of employment possibilities for young women with little or no formal education, many of the ones I found working in the state restaurants had not given up their extracurricular income-generating activities. They had simply moved from the bars and streets to state-owned restaurants, where their usual clients found them. Several who spoke to me were young Ghanaians, who had come to Burkina Faso to earn hard currency – the CFA franc was pegged to the French franc and not in freefall as was the Ghanaian cedi at the time.

A Ghanaian teenager named Rose told me that she worked in a bar, but that at the end of the month the bar owner paid her only 3,000 CFA (about 15 US dollars), never the 12,000 (about 60 dollars) that was her official salary. He always justified this by saying that some of her customers had left outstanding bills or she had broken some drinking glasses. To pay her rent, Rose told me she had no choice but to "follow some men" after the bar closed. But, she said, pounding her chest with a clenched fist, "I may sell my body, but I never sell *me*, Rose!"

The young foreign sex-workers I interviewed all greatly admired Thomas Sankara.

The revolutionary president had a propensity for revolutionary slogans, which drove many people mad. "Our homeland or death, we shall overcome!" was one that was chanted with a raised Che Guevara-style salute of the fist. "Down with imperialism!" and "Down with neo-colonialism!" were two more. And sometimes in the course of his long-winded but never predictable or dull speeches, he might come up with still more original slogans. "Down with inflated turkeys" he proclaimed one day, to denounce the African elite that would look down on their fellow Africans who were not acquiring wealth and becoming sub-Saharan Europeans.

No one, except perhaps the peasant farmers for whom a special ministry was created, was spared the sharp blade of his criticism. He said that Africa's educated elite had let the continent down. Students tended to come out of universities, often European ones he said, with top marks and then come home "to rest." He said their role was to share their knowledge and expertise with the "popular masses." He also expected them to contribute like everyone else to grassroots construction projects and tree-planting exercises.

In a speech on International Women's Day, he reminded Burkinabé men that they were all sons of mothers, yet still treated their own wives "worse than cattle." When I asked him in 1987 why he insisted on all the slogans that could be construed as deliberately provocative, Sankara replied that he had no choice but to "call a cancer what it is, a cancer."

An attaché from the German embassy said that Sankara was "simplistic and naïve." The American ambassador to Burkina Faso from 1984 to 1987, Leonardo Neher, was an amicable Texan with many diplomatic postings under his turquoise belt buckle. He told me that US President Ronald Reagan had pulled him out of retirement to "straighten out" Thomas Sankara. Then he admitted that he was surprised that he truly "liked the guy," and he also truly believed that Sankara's revolution was sincere in that he was overturning the "feudal system" and making real change in the country.

Just because Neher respected some of these changes didn't mean the US intended to sit back and just watch as Sankara's message spread and sparked revolutionary fervour among youth on the continent. In early 1987, I invited the ambassador to dinner to sound him out on official American plans about how to deal with Burkina's pistol-toting, red-beret-wearing president. After dinner, after he told me that he viewed Sankara almost as a son, the American ambassador pounded his fist on my table and proclaimed, "But we are not going to allow another Cuba in Africa!" These were exactly the same words used in cables from the CIA Kinshasa bureau to its Virginia headquarters in 1960, as plans were made to eliminate Congo's prime minister, Patrice Lumumba.[61]

Thomas Sankara was garnering followers and fans throughout Africa, although he was less popular in his own country where his reforms were being hammered through at a relentless pace and falling like cleavers on comforts and complacency to which many privileged and influential people had grown very accustomed in recent years. In early 1987, on one of his almost weekly forays into his country's hinterland, he delivered a speech about a new campaign to "produce and

consume Burkinabé." Sankara maintained that political independence was meaningless if African countries were still tied to the economic apron strings of their former colonial and other neo-colonial
powers. He told the nation that Burkina Faso had to produce and
consume a whole list of products, including its own fruit juices.
Despite the abundance of fruit grown in sub-Sahara Africa, it is
impossible in most countries to find any indigenously produced fruit
juice. Soft drinks such as Coca-Cola and Fanta, and now the new caffeinated 'energy' drinks made by the same companies, are to be found
everywhere. Yet local fruit such as watermelons, mangoes, oranges,
guavas, papayas, tamarind and a wide variety of indigenous fruits not
known on the world market, can often be found rotting in roadside
markets because of seasonal surpluses. As Sankara said, trees that
abounded in the Sahel produced delicious and nutritious fruits that
were often going to waste.

A "Day of the Tomato" was declared, which involved demonstrations of sun-drying and preserving techniques. This was intended to
curtail the consumption of expensive imported and ubiquitous
canned tomato paste from Europe, and to prevent Burkina's tomatoes
from rotting unsold under the Sahelian sun in roadside markets during periods of abundance.

Included in the campaign to consume what Burkina Faso produced were local liquors rather than imported French champagne and
wine, and beer made by French-owned companies brewed exclusively with imported (French-grown) hops and wheat. Sankara engaged
a German brew master who experimented successfully, so the
German ambassador told me, with locally grown maize added to the
beer. The brew master showed that the popular local brew, *dolo*, made
with sorghum, could be produced industrially and bottled, to replace
some of the beers imported from Europe. Unfortunately, the German
ambassador then had a visit from his French counterpart, who
informed him that Burkina Faso and Burkinabé beer were both part
of the French domain. The German brew master went home, and the
experiments ended.

In his speech that afternoon, as he explained the intent of the
"produce and consume Burkinabé" campaign, Sankara – who never
read from a prepared text – suddenly veered onto the subject of apples.

"Why do we import apples from France into our country that is overflowing with tropical fruit that we can't sell? One apple costs more than a dozen mangoes," he said. "The rich people buy apples because they are expensive. If an apple cost not 140 CFA [about 50 cents at the time], but 14,000 [about 50 US dollars], those people would still buy them. To them the apple is a symbol of their wealth, power and their superiority over the rest of their brothers and sisters in this country who can't afford to eat even their own local fruit. People buy them because they come from Europe and not from our trees here, because they can't resist the temptation to eat just like a French man."

I was listening to the speech live on state radio, with a group of friends from several European and African countries. There were some chuckles. There was some open-mouthed incredulity. Someone said Sankara had really gone crazy. Another said he was becoming a "banana republic dictator." Someone else said there was biblical significance in the speech.

"From this day forward," Sankara announced, "it is forbidden to import apples into Burkina Faso. Then there will be no more temptation." The nation was stunned. So were government departments supposed to enact the new decree. So were Sankara's advisors who told me they never know where one of his speeches would lead him.

"This is for our fruit-growers," said Sankara. "Let's produce and consume our own fruit. Let's feed ourselves. Let's not waste our precious currency on importing apples."

Unlike many other revolutionaries whose dogma and dreary rhetoric can be incredibly dull and depressing, Sankara infused almost everything he did and said with humour, plenty of dry wit and a spirit of spontaneous goodwill. He ruled with a pizzazz, energy and enthusiasm that was unrivalled in Africa, probably the world. He was full of mischief, and enjoyed tweaking the noses of the great and powerful, as he did to the amusement of many when he invited the Soviet and American ambassadors to the ground-laying ceremony for one of the community health posts and "peoples' pharmacies" that were going up all over the country. There, he had them each take turns laying a stone and applying mortar to the new building, and announced to the small press corps in attendance that in Burkina, the foundation had just been laid for the "wall of détente" between West and East in their Cold War.

Pranks like this did not endear Sankara to the powers that be in foreign capitals and in their embassies in Ouagadougou. Many Burkinabé also griped about the revolution. Some did not appreciate the rationale behind or the speed of the monumental changes Sankara was pushing on them. But many took up the challenge, and said they had been waiting for a president like this. "We complain about him because we can," said Halidou, a friend who worked at the post office. "It is important to know the difference. If we really hated him, we would be too afraid to complain."

The country was filled with stubborn courage and determination. "The limits of the human being are infinite," Sankara said to me during an interview in April 1987. "Mediocrity and laziness are not human. The human being is the most powerful machine there is."

For many years, there had been talk of finally completing the rail line that had originally been planned to go right across West Africa, linking Cotonou in Benin with Abidjan in Côte d'Ivoire. It had been started in colonial times, but the final rail link between Niamey and Ouagadougou that would close the loop had never been laid. Sankara's dream was to complete the railway, and have it sweep north of Ouagadougou to newly discovered deposits of manganese, before continuing on to Niger.

Speaking at an anti-Apartheid conference he hosted in early October 1987 in Ouagadougou (the very first anti-Apartheid conference held by and in an African country), he said that he had tried repeatedly to secure the financing for the missing rail link from the World Bank and the donor community. They had refused, offering instead financing for a road to the northern mining region. That is why, Sankara told an appreciative audience, he had launched the "Bataille du Rail," a grassroots 'battle' to construct the railway without foreign financing. Between 1985 and 1987, 62 kilometres of rail were laid by volunteers – students, civil servants and by foreign dignitaries who were invited out to the project to see what Burkinabé were doing for and by themselves, and in some cases, found themselves expected to heave a concrete block into place, in the blazing sun and blowing dust. The only foreign donation for the project was a few rails that Canada provided from a plant in Trenton, Nova Scotia.

One of the pillars of Sankara's revolution was to fight the scourge of corruption, long before this became a fashionable mantra for the World Bank, donors and African leaders. Many former government ministers with ill-got wealth, including my landlord in Ouagadougou, were fearful of being called up by the Popular Revolutionary Tribunals. They put their Mercedes literally under wraps while Sankara was in power, covering them with cloth and hiding them away in their compounds.

In mid-1987, Sankara's government launched its Anti-corruption Committee to vet members of the regime and to assess their wealth and assets after almost four years in power. Sankara was the first to appear before the committee. It would have been easy to scoff at the exercise, which at first glance looked like pure propaganda and more showy revolutionary theatre that made cynics laugh scornfully. After all, the government had appointed the committee that was vetting them. Certainly this was the view expressed to me by the Soviet correspondent from *Pravda*, and some derisive French journalists who came to Ouagadougou to attend the Pan-African film festival (FESPACO), an event that Sankara turned into a worldwide showcase of African cinematography and culture.

But those sceptics were not there to watch the proceedings of the first anti-corruption interrogation. It happened in the *Palais de la Justice*, where I took a bench in the back to watch Thomas Sankara as he faced the committee, while the proceedings were broadcast live on national state radio. Sankara stood with his red beret clutched in his hands clasped behind his back, facing the stony-faced committee as he listed his worldly belongings. The list included: two guitars that were cracked from the dry heat; two bicycles; three radios; one deep freezer that did not work and a refrigerator that did; a monthly income smaller than his wife's who worked for the state shipping company; and a 1978 Mitsubishi car (which often had to be pushed to get it started). There were also gifts from foreign dignitaries totalling millions of dollars, which he said he had turned over to the State Treasury.

Many people laughed this off. Some people listening on tiny battery-operated radios in villages of mud and thatch said they were shocked at how "wealthy" Sankara was, so naïve were they about how those who did not have to scrape their survival out of the soil really lived. In Ouagadougou, his detractors – and there were many of these – said it was all a hoax; he could take whatever he wanted, whenever he wanted, from the state.

But the message of the exercise was not lost on the vast majority of people in the country, that is: you could be a Big Man, a president, an honourable patriotic Burkinabé, you could be *somebody* without being wealthy, driving a new Mercedes and flying to Paris for weekend shopping trips.

He broke with tradition and refused to hand out favours to his family, not even his father. His family lived as they always had, in a typical mud home not far from the centre of town, a stone's throw from the presidential office, in fact. His mother still rose each day at dawn and headed to the market with a basket of greens on her head, to peddle them. His father, Joseph Sankara, who had fought for France and been imprisoned in Nazi Germany during World War II, was crippled by an injury he sustained in Europe. Thomas Sankara refused to send his father to France for treatment.[62] He said that he could not give his family anything that every single Burkinabé could not have. Culturally, this was simply unacceptable in Burkina Faso.

Later, people would say this was his biggest mistake, where he had gone wrong. They said he should have looked after his father, his family, himself. That, they would have understood. As it was, they understood little of what he was doing. Not then.

I once asked Sankara if he didn't think he was moving too fast. "No," he said, wringing his hands, his eyes alight. "Look around you. You see the children, all the children who are hungry, malnourished, illiterate. You see the desert moving in on us. If this were 20 or 30 years ago, we could afford to move slowly. We have no time left."[63]

In August 1987, Sankara relented a little, and admitted that "two steps without the people are not worth one step with the people" and agreed to make some compromises to take into account the negative reaction to the unrelenting pace of change.[64]

By then, it was already too late. By the time the sun set on the evening of October 15, 1987, Thomas Sankara was dead. He, along with six of his closest advisors and seven drivers and guards, were gunned down at the *Conseil de l'Entente*, a high-security complex for high-level security meetings of West African leaders. Sankara, wearing his red track suit in preparation for Thursday evening sport, was shot several times at point-blank range. One lone survivor escaped over the high walls of the complex, and went into exile where he identified some of those who had done the shooting, commandos led by Lieutenant Gilbert Guenguéré who fell under the command of Blaise Compaoré. But that survivor subsequently and mysteriously suffered mental problems and his accounts were then dismissed.

A curfew was imposed and national radio proclaimed that the "traitor" Thomas Sankara had been overthrown. Later that evening, a terse statement on the radio informed the nation that the Rectified Revolution had begun under the Popular Front, led by none other than Sankara's right-hand-man, Captain Blaise Compaoré.

The bodies of the fallen men were taken in the dark of night in the back of a Peugeot pick-up with no license plate to a bleak cemetery in a neighbourhood called Dagnoen on the outskirts of Ouagadougou. There, eye witnesses described how they had watched from afar as unidentified men dumped the corpses onto the ground and then covered them with a shallow layer of brown earth.

Until the rectified revolutionaries, led by the new president Blaise Compaoré, forbade visitors to the graveyard, Dagnoen drew tens of thousands of Burkinabé who came to toss onto the shallow graves flowers and notes of affection and grief addressed to "Toma." Older women and men stood there weeping. Younger people hurled insults at the armed commandos who stood watch, calling them "murderers" and "assassins."

If the world had been watching for a few moments on the days following the coup, it quickly lost interest in the drama unfolding in the Land of Upright Men. On October 19, 1987, the stock market crashed and the world's media, at least the few who had deemed the coup newsworthy enough to mention at all, quickly forgot Thomas Sankara.

Africans did not.

They knew why Sankara had been killed; he had defended Burkinabé and African interests and courageously, even recklessly, thumbed his nose at the world's rich and powerful while he did so. But they didn't know, exactly, who had killed him. Slowly, people began trying to piece together the pieces of the puzzle. In such exercises, especially when the man most likely to have handled the in-country preparations is still firmly in power, and foreign involvement is covert, it is extremely difficult to come by solid facts. But here are a few pieces for a puzzle that can never be completely solved, not without a confession from a few of the world's most secretive secret services.

Sankara's outspoken assault on neo-colonialism, imperialism and hypocrisy seriously rankled in circles of power from Washington to Paris, from Tripoli to Abidjan. Sankara had belittled President Félix Houphouët-Boigny, the so-called dean of African heads of state and the man that many called the Sage of Africa. Houphouët-Boigny had ruled Côte d'Ivoire since its independence and had amassed an untold fortune, only some of which he used to build a palace and basilica in his native village of Yamoussoukro, a building that rivalled the Vatican in size and splendour.

Blaise Compaoré had just married a woman with family connections to Houphouët-Boigny, and he had made several secret visits to Abidjan to visit the dean in the months before the coup. More compelling testimony that Houphouët-Boigny (and by proxy his allies in Paris) was eager to remove Sankara came from former Malian president, General Moussa Traoré, who had been overthrown in a coup in 1991. In the course of his 1999 trial for embezzlement, Moussa Traoré admitted that he had been given one million US dollars by Houphouët-Boigny to fight a border war against Burkina Faso in 1985, in an attempt to destabilize Sankara's regime.

There were also reports that Charles Taylor, the notorious warlord who spearheaded wars in both his native Liberia, in neighbouring Sierra Leone and led insurgencies also in Guinea in the 1990s, worked with Liberian exiles in Burkina Faso to help Compaoré stage the coup to overthrow and kill Sankara.[65]

One of Sankara's former government ministers told me that the late revolutionary had also flirted with danger by shunning an invitation to join the secretive and exclusive Masonic lodge known as the

Rose Croix that seemed to form an unbreakable bond of brotherhood among many of francophone Africa's presidents. French favourites Félix Houphouët-Boigny and Gabon's Omar Bongo were members of the Rose Croix, as was French President, François Mitterrand. Masonic Lodges that are now all over Africa work very much like Africa's secret societies, developing permanent and indestructible bonds among members.

The French government had never cared for Thomas Sankara. In May 1983, then President Jean-Baptiste Ouédraogo had appointed Thomas Sankara as his prime minister. Shortly thereafter, President Ouédraogo had his new prime minister arrested. Ouédraogo was on a very short leash from Paris, and Sankara's arrest came during an unofficial visit to Ouagadougou by French President Mitterrand's advisor on African affairs, Guy Penne, France's *eminence grise* in Africa.

In his short term as prime minister of Upper Volta, Sankara had been very outspoken about the continued French domination of internal affairs in former colonies in Africa. That, apparently, was not to be tolerated. Penne had been in Ouagadougou only a couple of hours when Sankara and two of his closest allies were put under house arrest. Massive street protests ensued. Some former student leaders told me that the demonstrations had been supported by Libya's Muammar Gaddafi, who at that time loved to support any anti-Western movement. Sankara was freed, thanks to Blaise Compaoré who had evaded arrest and was able to bring military support from the commando training camp in the southern town of Pô.

So Compaoré, the new man at the helm in Burkina Faso after Sankara's death in 1987, knew better than anyone else that Sankara could not simply be overthrown; his popular appeal could not be held behind bars. If he was to be removed, he had to be permanently eliminated. Predictably, Compaoré steadfastly denied having anything to do with the coup that brought him to power.

When I met with him on October 17, 1987 in the high-security zone of the *Conseil de l'Entente,* Compaoré insisted he had been in bed sick, "in my underwear" when the shooting started and that he had run outside with his own weapon thinking he himself was being attacked. He told me that the revolution had gone stale, that people were fed up, and that is why they were out on the streets celebrating on the day following the coup, which had been declared a holiday.

I told him that I had seen no one celebrating. Apart from a few unruly groups of drunken young men from the disbanded Committees for the Defence of the Revolution lurching about, the roads of Ouagadougou had been almost eerily deserted in the vacuum left by the assassination. The only crowds I had seen had been weeping and grieving at the graveyard in Dagnoen. He looked confused, then haltingly explained that this was because "the Burkinabé don't like bloodshed." And he said repeatedly that he never wished to be president.

I have to conclude that he was lying. Since 1987 he has clung to power, had opponents and dissenters imprisoned or executed, changed the constitution of the country to permit him to run in successive highly questionable elections, and is still president of Burkina Faso as of this writing.

Later, Compaoré would claim that Sankara had been plotting to eliminate him with a private militia. This too seemed preposterous. If Sankara had been plotting anything, he would have protected his own wife and two small sons, got them out of harm's way. In fact, it was Blaise Compaoré's wife Chantal who, conveniently, had travelled to Paris just before the coup.

And there were other problems with Compaoré's denials. First, some of those who invaded the *Conseil de l'Entente* and did the killing were his closest 'comrades.' Secondly, Sankara's widow Mariam said Compaoré was not sick the night before the coup. She said Compaoré had been with her husband until three in the morning, and that she had been relieved that the rift between the old friends had been healed. "They were laughing like schoolboys," she told me. She had no doubt who was behind the coup in Burkina Faso, and she eventually had to be evacuated from her own country along with her two boys after numerous late-night attacks and threats on their lives.[66]

Here's another disturbing truth. Africa finally had a president who was fighting corruption head-on and regularly making its debt payments and trying very hard to produce some boots and boot-straps with which it could pull itself up, exactly what Western donors constantly claim they want African presidents to do. And yet, throughout Sankara's short term in office, Western powers had been busy cutting development assistance to Burkina Faso.

Some African journalists preferred not to ask who was behind the coup, but to ask who wasn't. They fingered not just Blaise Compaoré and his commandos, but also France. A journalist from the Burkinabé presidential office told me that when the shooting was going on in the *Conseil de l'Entente,* there were celebrations with champagne inside the French embassy, just down the road. And Chantal Compaoré was reportedly drinking champagne in Paris at the Burkinabé embassy there.

Even with the curfew and shoot-to-kill order in place there was some unexplained night-time activity in Ouagadougou following the coup. First was the mysterious arrival at the Hotel Independence of a large van with no registration, out of which a band of tight-lipped, big-muscled American Special Ops men emerged and proceeded to unload large aluminum Halliburton cases. This was witnessed by Emmy-award-winning American journalist Marco Werman who repeatedly asked the men what they were doing in Burkina Faso. Through gritted teeth as they unloaded their luggage from the van, one of those burly thugs finally muttered, "We're here to work."[67]

There was also a late-night landing at the airport in Ouagadougou of a Libyan transport plane carrying at least two bullet-proof Alfa Romeo cars as a personal gift to Blaise Compaoré from his friend in Tripoli, Colonel Muammar Gaddafi.

It was impossible to get a quote from the American ambassador about the coup – he had left the country two weeks before it occurred, and his replacement had not yet arrived. In any case, there was a conspicuous absence of condemnations of the assassination from the normally sanctimonious Western diplomatic community.

On January 1, 1988, at the annual New Year's diplomatic get-together in Ouagadougou, the German ambassador to Burkina Faso – one of the few Western diplomats who greatly appreciated and respected Sankara – suggested a moment of silence be observed for "those who are no longer with us." He was ridiculed by his counterparts from other Western embassies.

Meanwhile, Compaoré and his henchmen in the Popular Front began the long process of trying to eliminate Sankara's name from the national vocabulary and psyche. It was clear from the very beginning that Compaoré was taking no chances and he did not leave the heavily fortified confines of the Conseil de l'Entente for almost two months. When I went to interview him a second time after the coup, in December 1987, he said he had no intention of answering any questions about the coup or Thomas Sankara.

It wasn't until January 11 that Blaise Compaoré first appeared in public at a public rally on Independence Boulevard. At that event, he shook hands publicly with the other two remaining members of the former four-man National Revolutionary Council, Henri Zongo and Jean-Baptiste Lingani. Both became part of his government, but they seemed to have lost their tongues and remained eerily silent, becoming almost invisible on the political scene.

Graffiti appeared on university buildings in Ouagadougou that said: "four minus one = zero."

Student protests criticizing Compaoré and his rectified revolution were met with vicious beatings and arrests. One medical student was left permanently blind from such a beating by the security service. When I asked the head of security about the 3,000 new young recruits acting as spies for the Popular Front, and about the beatings by the police, he replied, "The police are not angels. You must understand that these people were threatening the security of the country and the peace. If on occasion some of them get beaten, it's not surprising." When this quote went out on the BBC, my phone rang and I was summoned again to his office, informed that were I not pregnant, I would be spending some days in his special cells.

Compaoré clearly meant business – the business as usual among African leaders looking for long careers in office. Ruffle no feathers in foreign capitals, and rough up the people at home if need be to keep the 'peace.'

In 1989, Compaoré was the very first president to make an official visit to China after the massacre in Tiananmen Square of thousands of students demonstrating for democratic reform. While there, Compaoré made a widely quoted speech praising China's example of how to deal with dissent, which he said he would apply in his home country.

While his plane was on its descent to Ouagadougou for his home-coming, Compaoré's two remaining revolutionary comrades, Henri Zongo and Jean-Baptiste Lingani, were being secretly tried and exe-cuted for an alleged plot against him. Their bodies have never been found; no funeral has ever been permitted for them. Nor has one for Thomas Sankara. A death certificate issued to Mariam Sankara in January 1988, says that "Comrade Thomas Isidre Sankara," born on December 1, 1949 at Yako in Burkina Faso, had died on October 15, 1987 at 16:30 hours in Ouagadougou "of natural causes." The cam-paign by Aziz Fall and the International Justice Campaign for Sankara (IJCS) for those causes to be fully detailed and exposed has led to nothing tangible, except the decision by the United Nations Human Rights Committee (UNHRC) that they must be investigat-ed, and in death threats to Aziz Fall, who is living in Canada.[68]

Perhaps multiple gunshot wounds are indeed a "natural cause" of death for an African leader who defies the developed world and their friendly leaders in Africa itself.

In the end, I suppose what happened was inevitable. Reality had to be restored to the dream world in which, for a time, hope was blooming and self-confidence flowering. Such a revolution could start a dangerous precedent on the continent, where self-determina-tion might endanger all sorts of things: access to natural resources; reliable allies in the UN General Assembly where a president who was bought and paid for could be counted on to vote correctly; con-trol of a continent that European and other industrialized powers still viewed as a prize too great to lose.

Sankara's former Minister of Peasant Affairs, Jean Léonard Compaoré, had this to say about his fallen leader: "He wasn't a revo-lutionary or a politician. He was a preacher, a missionary." He paused and searched the night sky as if searching for explanation in the stars. "Maybe he was a kind of messiah. He was not down here with us. His inspiration came from above – somewhere beyond you or me."

I have tried over the years to look at the coup objectively. Sankara had come to power by the gun, had carried a gun, and was fated to go out by the gun, in a bloody coup. He had imprisoned opponents in the labour movement, and he had attacked the world's superpowers –

the Soviets and the West. He had stood up to giants, who eventually helped to eliminate him. He knew the rules and he knew that he had flouted them. He may well have known he was going to die too. As a martyr to the causes he believed in, he is probably far more effective in promoting them even today than he would ever have been trying to implement them in his own country.

Today, in many countries in Africa, there are journalists who continue to resurrect the hopes that Sankara inspired in Africa's youth, printing his quotations in their papers to keep his dreams alive. Children, political clubs and "Sankarist" parties bear his name.

This is the positive legacy he has left.

Unfortunately, the lessons of his death, clearly understood by Africans, are negative. First, Sankara's sad fate, along with that of other presidents who shared his belief that Africa must become truly independent, is a deterrent to any African leader who truly threatens foreign interests and the balance of power on the continent. Secondly, if you behave correctly and obediently after seizing power in a coup, you can rule for many years in astounding material comfort and with impunity. You can even rig elections, transform yourself into a democrat, and become fêted as a peacekeeper as Compaoré has done.[69] Providing, that is, you obey the unwritten rules for governing an African country.

6

Greasing the political gears

Corporations are like the feudal domains that evolved into nation-states; they are nothing less than the vanguard of a new Darwinian organization of politics.

Robert Kaplan[70]

One wonders if the West wants any more in Africa than the maintenance of dictatorships just sufficiently powerful to guarantee a fairly constant supply of cheap agricultural and mineral commodities that cannot be found elsewhere.

Andrew Buckoke[71]

A joke from Africa goes like this.

Joke-teller: Why has there never been a coup d'état in the United States of America?

Respondent: Because the US is a democratic country, with a tried and true electoral process.

Joke-teller: Wrong!

Respondent (me): Because the US has a mature democracy that doesn't operate like a banana republic?

Joke-teller: Wrong again, ha ha.

Exasperated respondent: Then tell me, for crying out loud!

Joke-teller: There's never been a coup in the US because *there is no US embassy there!"*

Pause. Then the exasperated respondent replies. "But that was before, during the Cold War, when the West and East were willing to do just about anything to maintain their spheres of influence in Africa. Democracy has come and the people of Africa are choosing their own leaders. Things have changed." Pause. "I hope."

Some journalists, writers and scholars give the impression that the mismanagement of resources and the problems on the continent are almost entirely the result of poor African leadership. Implicit in their works about the continent is a hypothesis that leads inescapably and very conveniently to the conclusion that many in the West want to hear: Africans are not capable of governing themselves.

That is certainly the theory Martin Meredith puts forth in his massive tome covering 50 years of independence in Africa.[72] Meredith gives short shrift to the accomplishments of Tanzania's former head of state, the late Julius Nyerere, who was modest, self-effacing and affectionately known as "the teacher." Nyerere was a believer in the socialist ideal, who until his death in 1999 was viewed as one of the great statesmen of the past century. Meredith also finds only negative and demeaning things to say about Ghana's first president, Kwame Nkrumah, ignoring completely his vision and his intellect. He seems to single out for harshest criticism presidents who stepped out of the Western sphere of influence and its economic models.

A similar thesis drives the writing and work of Ghanaian economist, George B.N. Ayittey.[73] Ayittey claims that the "externalist theory" that blames imperialists, colonists, neo-colonists and the World Bank for Africa's problems, which he sees as economic and political, is "kaput." Ayittey is also president of the Free Africa Foundation.[74] If you follow the dots, you will find the Free Africa Foundation is closely linked with and funded by policy think tanks in the US, such as the Heritage and John M. Olin Foundations and the CATO Institute, institutions leaning so far to the right it's surprising they haven't all fallen down. Ayittey acknowledges funding for his book from the

Lynde and Harry Bradley Foundation, which was founded on US military wealth. Not really surprising, then, that he absolves Western interference in Africa's politics and economics for Africa's current political and economic woes.

While Robert Calderisi, a former World Bank official with much African experience under his belt, appears to care deeply for Africa, I have enormous difficulty accepting his analysis of the problems and realities on the continent, starting with his statement: "… Africa has been making its own history since Independence and has been largely free of foreign domination since the end of the Cold War."[75]

The arguments of these authors assume that Africans truly have been governing themselves for decades; that they chose the bad leaders themselves and kept them there. There is little evidence to support these.

Many people off the continent sincerely believe that once the European colonial powers such as Belgium, the UK, France,[76] Portugal and Spain granted their colonies political independence, they stepped out completely and allowed African leaders to run African nations. There is also the widespread myth that when European countries or America intervened politically or militarily on the continent, their intervention was purely benevolent, to save Africans from themselves.

This is hardly the case. First, the colonial powers hand-picked the men who would head their former colonies at independence. Afterwards, individually and sometimes working covertly with each other and with other African leaders, outside powers removed or quietly helped to remove nationalist African leaders such as: Congo's Patrice Lumumba; Cap Verde's Amilcar Cabral; and Burkina Faso's Thomas Sankara.

Martin Meredith doesn't mention the latter two. On the subject of Patrice Lumumba's toppling and subsequent assassination, one of the more blatantly criminal acts of the US Central Intelligence Agency (CIA) and the Belgian authorities, Meredith merely repeats CIA and Belgian descriptions of Prime Minister Lumumba as a "mad dog" to justify the coup as a "public health measure." His description of President Mobutu, as a "the great plunderer," depicts a power-mad despotic kleptomaniac who destroyed his country almost single-handedly. Yet Mobutu was hand-picked by the US and Belgium to replace Lumumba. And Western governments stroked, supported, financed and praised him every step of his destructive way. In 1982, while visiting Kinshasa, US Vice President George Bush Senior told Mobutu that he respected his "dedication to fairness and reason. I have come to admire, Mr. President, your personal courage and leadership."[77]

My experiences in Africa must have been very different from those of writers who place all the blame for the continent's problems on African leaders.

One has only to look at the fate of Thomas Sankara to understand a lesson many in Africa learned a long time ago: African leaders who truly defend the interests of their own people at the expense of Western interests on the continent have rarely lasted – or lived – very long.

When the Cold War ended, for a time many people in Africa believed that the superpowers would pack up, go home, and stop playing risk, chess and other strategic war games on the continent. Freedom and democracy would then prevail and bring prosperity to all, not just a select few. Dictatorships would be replaced by leaders more accountable to Africans because they would be chosen by the people themselves at the ballot box.

My first, first-hand experience with this democratic dawn came in Ghana on November 2, 1992. In the town of Tamale in Ghana's Northern Region, it was hot and sunny, reflecting the mood in the country. Ghanaians were going to the polls for the first time in more than a decade. President Jerry John Rawlings had been ruling non-stop since 1981 as head of the Provisional National Defence Council (PNDC). Some people had been wondering out loud if the "provisional" in there really stood for "permanent."

Naïve as it seems with the advantage of hindsight, I was one of many in the country – and all over Africa – who really believed that the metamorphosis from dictatorship to democracy would be achieved by simply holding elections.

The Berlin Wall was down. Western powers no longer needed to coddle the dictators who had been their allies during the Cold War.

The Eastern Block was no more. The shards of the Soviet Empire had better things to do than to buy friends in Africa or to deliberately arm rebel movements on the continent – although they were happy to dispense with excess Kalashnikovs, landmines and other Cold War armaments to those who could pay for them.

Western democratic countries no longer had the Communist menace to rationalize their support for oppressive, anti-democratic regimes. Western nations and international institutions began to back away from many of the men they had either put in place or helped to retain power. Or they began to apply pressure on these regimes to hold elections and legitimize their rule. Suddenly, at the beginning of the 1990s, the Western democracies discovered the urgent need for good governance and the spreading of multi-party politics and democracy thoughout Africa.

There was lots of lofty rhetoric about the winds of change that were blowing in Africa. The excesses of the past in so many African countries – the media restrictions, the heavy arm of the security forces, the opaque nature of government dealings and finances, justice systems tied to the whims of a president and his entourage, the unbridled megalomania of despots – would all vanish. And all of this was just an election away. Well, that's how it looked. Before it became clear how tricky elections could be, how easy it was to trick in elections.

Since then, in many countries on the continent, voters have watched many fraudulent elections return corrupt and unpopular presidents to power, and they are growing very tired of it. In 1997 and 2002, elections held in Mali were seriously flawed, and the people were well aware that they were deeply flawed. But on both occasions the international community congratulated the victors, and the people simply accepted the verdict, deciding that peace mattered more than good suffrage.[78]

But election-riggers are playing with fire. After the presidential elections in Kenya in 2007, the press reported widely that early results tallied showed opposition leader, Raila Odinga, well in the lead, with his party winning more than twice as many seats as the ruling party. Without reason or warning, the vote counting was halted and when it began again, it showed incumbent Mwai Kibaki suddenly in the lead. Within hours, the election commission declared Kibaki the winner and he had himself sworn in for a second term as president. Violence ensued, more than a thousand people were killed, homes were destroyed and people displaced.[79] Rebuffing initial international efforts to negotiate peace and find a solution after what was clearly a fraudulent counting process, Kibaki went ahead and named a cabinet. He forbade opposition rallies, permitting police to brutally suppress unrest by opening fire and killing protesters. Politicians on both sides spurred the people on to unprecedented ethnic violence in the country. It took the concerted efforts of former UN Secretary-General Kofi Annan to broker a power-sharing deal between the two factions, allowing Kibaki to remain president and with opposition leader Raila Odinga as his prime minister.

While Kibaki and his inner circle, dubbed the "Mount Kenya Mafia" by the opposition, are ultimately to blame for the electoral fraud, the question remains as to whether he and his powerful supporters would have behaved in such a reprehensible way, risking war and even genocide in the country by fiddling election results, had Kibaki not figured out in advance that he had powerful friends abroad. Almost immediately after he had himself sworn in for a second term as president, he received congratulations from the American ambassador to Kenya.

During his first term, President Kibaki had been extremely cooperative in allowing the US rendition of suspected al-Qaeda members from Kenya, rendition being that interesting exercise in double standards that allows the Central Intelligence Agency to go about the planet cherry-picking people it suspects of terrorist inclinations and flying them in unmarked executive jets to "black sites" where they can be interrogated, gloves off and no pesky public oversight. President Kibaki had also cooperated with the US as it built up a strong strategic military presence in his country. This had helped the US orchestrate via Ethiopia (also a good ally of the American administration) a proxy war in Somalia.

The US ambassador eventually reversed his position on Kibaki, acknowledging publicly what European and other observers had already noted about "serious irregularities" in the vote-tallying after the elections. But by then, Kibaki had dug in his heels, people had died and latent ethnic tensions had risen to the surface in horrendous attacks based on ethnicity, a dangerous card that politicians had used for years to garner support in multi-party elections.

But all this was still many years down the road.

Back in 1992 in Ghana, after initially resisting the Western pressure to transform himself into a democrat, the one-time revolutionary Jerry Rawlings acquiesced. He announced the advent of multi-party politics, legalized political parties, appointed an independent election commission and set the election date. International election observers, notably the Commonwealth observers group, flew in on the eve of the poll.[80] One was a Cypriot who seemed preoccupied not by the elections he was there to observe but by the "damn Turks" who he moaned to me on the eve of voting day, had "no right" to be on his island. Another was an Australian who could easily have had a starring role in *Crocodile Dundee,* and whose main goal in Ghana seemed to be finding cold beer. The Commonwealth observers in Ghana's Northern Region were led by a Tanzanian in a finely tailored suit who was outspoken about the discomforts in the north of the country. He said he would not return for second round of voting that was required if Rawlings did not obtain the requisite majority in the first poll.

Perhaps the head of the Commonwealth observers' team in the capital Accra felt the same way; anxious to wrap the whole thing up so he could go home and not come back. That would help explain why he spoke live on the BBC World Service halfway through election day to make the stunning declaration that Ghana's elections had been free and fair. I was dumbfounded, as were many Ghanaians. I had spent the morning moving through Tamale and villages in the region witnessing the vote and had logged a litany of problems. There were underage voters lined up at polls and telling me they were voting for Rawlings, dubious voters' lists, violent intimidation of opposition supporters at some polling stations, and stuffed ballot boxes carted around and planted with the use of Canadian and German aid vehicles. These examples of fraud merely compounded the complete monopoly that Rawlings had had in the run-up to the polling in using state monies, state television and military aircraft that got him around the country to campaign for himself and his party.

I filed a report for BBC about the irregularities I had seen. Later, as I headed out to watch more voting, the Tanzanian Commonwealth observer cornered me – he was on his way into a private clubhouse for a beer. He asked what kind of nonsense I had been reporting about irregularities. I started to repeat the long list.

He waved his arms about and said, "Irregularities? Those aren't irregularities. What do you expect? This is Africa."

Later on, I would see he had a point. The daytime irregularities were trivial compared with the evidence that poured in during the hours and days following the election, after the observers had gone to bed or boarded their planes and left the country. Throughout the night after the poll, I stood in the central square, known as the Police Park in Tamale, taking notes as men climbed ladders to rub out the vote tallies written on the giant chalkboard that was serving as official scoreboard for the poll in the Northern Region, replacing them with ones more favourable to Rawlings' party. Next day I asked the head of the Independent Electoral Commission in the Northern Region about the midnight changes to the numbers on that giant blackboard. He told me that mistakes had been made and that those had been corrected.

Rawlings won on the first round. Since the election observers had decided hours before the actual voting was even over that the election was "free and fair," opposition complaints to the contrary were ignored in Western diplomatic circles. This rapidly entered the local and colourful slang lexicon in northern Ghana. At the market and the fuel pumps, rising prices were said to be "free and fair" and eventually this was shortened to "Ah well, it's just F and F," as a closing line in any conversation about the ever-growing difficulties people faced in their lives.

By the time the next set of elections rolled around, perhaps the Western world might have chosen another favourite, whose election would be declared free and fair. He (or she) might be a reasonable person, a good politician and even a good leader for his or her people. But could a good leader of an African nation look out for his or her people's interests and foreign ones at the same time? And would Western donors sit back and allow a leader who threatened their interests to remain in power even if he or she had won elections?

They hadn't in Algeria in 1991, when the first multi-party elections were held in that country since 1963. In the post-Cold War poll of 1991, the Islamic Salvation Front (FIS) won 188 seats outright, despite – or perhaps partly because of – a clampdown on the party in the run-up to the elections and the arrest and imprisonment of two FIS leaders. The results of the first round of polling suggested the FIS was almost certainly going to win an absolute majority in the second round. That second round was never held. The military took over, and in January 1992, the civilian president resigned, probably under pressure from the military. The conflict that ensued became know as the Dirty War, in which excluded Islamic elements confronted brutal security forces that were responsible for six thousand disappearances.[81] More than 150,000 died in the seven years following the military take-over. European countries such as France and Germany not only failed to condemn the aborted elections and the military coup of December 1991, but generously supplied Algeria's military regime with military and financial support throughout the Dirty War.

In 1992, in the Republic of Congo (the smaller of the two Congos, with its capital Brazzaville, distinct from the Democratic Republic of Congo with its capital Kinshasa), Professor Pascal Lissouba became the country's first democratically elected president, after 13 years of heavy-handed rule under Marxist – then no-longer Marxist – President Denis Sassou-Nguesso. In his short time in office, President Pascal Lissouba along with his Prime Minister Bernard Kolelas had challenged the unofficial monopoly of the giant French oil company Elf (now Total) that controlled 75 percent of production in Congo. Lissouba had opened negotiations with US-based oil companies including, according to Bernard Kolelas, Mobil (now ExxonMobil). And this, Kolelas said to me when I met him during his exile spent in a hotel in Mali's capital Bamako in 2001, was what led to the derailing of the Republic of Congo's fledging democracy.

Global Witness described Elf's operations in the Republic of Congo this way: "Elf treated Congo as a colony, buying off the ruling elite and helping it to mortgage the country's future oil income in exchange for expensive loans. The company even financed both sides of the civil war, as it also did in Angola."[82] Some former Elf officials did wind up in prison for their "misuse" of their company's funds, but that did not change the political situation or corruption and influence peddling in Congo.[83]

Before the next set of elections could be held in 1997, the Republic of Congo's former (unelected) leader, Denis Sassou-Nguesso, put together his own private army. Lissouba made the fatal mistake of sending out official security forces to surround Sassou-Nguesso's house, and a vicious conflict ensued. Sassou-Nguesso's forces, aided overtly by Angola and allegedly covertly by France (and Elf), took over the capital Brazzaville, or what was left of the once splendid tropical city flush with oil wealth. Lissouba and Kolelas fled; Denis Sassou-Nguesso declared himself president. To make it all official, give himself the democratic seal of approval, in 2002 he organized and won elections with 90 percent of the votes. Bernard Kolelas and Pascal Lissouba were not allowed to run; both had been sentenced to death in their absence and remained in exile.

Officially, France didn't make a whimper about the non-democratic state of affairs in the Republic of Congo. In December 1997, when he was challenged at a press conference about covert French support for Sassou-Nguesso before and during the war that led to the overthrow of a democratically elected leader, then French Prime Minister Lionel Jospin replied that France didn't do those things any more. "Those days are gone," he told journalists in Bamako. But Pascal Lissouba and Bernard Kolelas openly accused France of supporting their rival, and few could help but remark how warmly French President Jacques Chirac welcomed President Sassou-Nguesso after his election victory in 2002.[84]

In October 2004, Cameroon held its third set of 'democratic' presidential elections since 1992. For the third time, President Paul Biya was in the running, although he had been running the country in his own fashion – sometimes from a golf club in France – since 1982. That was the year his predecessor and Cameroon's first president, the late Ahmadou Ahidjo, ceded power to his hand-picked prime minister, Paul Biya, and headed off to retirement in a chateau in France. Ahidjo had been told by his French physicians that he had serious heart disease and that he needed to step down and take up residence in France where he could benefit from the necessary medical care.

According to Cameroonian "common knowledge," it was only after he had settled in France that he learned there was nothing seriously wrong with his health and that he had been duped by the French physicians (presumably in the employ of the French authorities).[85] By then it was too late.

Paul Biya had settled comfortably into the presidential seat and the 70-million US dollar presidential palace in the capital, Yaoundé, which his predecessor had been having constructed. Designed by a Swedish architect, it came with artificial waterfalls and a zoo, an underground bomb shelter and escape tunnels. Even an armed insurrection in 1984 by the Presidential Guard still loyal to Ahidjo and acting on his behalf could not unseat President Biya, who spent several days camped out in the palace bomb shelter while the military bombarded the city and rounded up northerners suspected of supporting the insurgency.

I was in Yaoundé to witness this battle, and later learned from a military commander in the west of the country that he had waited three days to come and save Biya's regime because it took him that long to make up his mind that he wanted to.

With a sleight of hand, the French government had neatly manoeuvred Ahidjo out of the way. He had a nationalistic streak, and had been setting aside Cameroon's oil revenue in an account he managed, saying it was for the future of all Cameroonians. Paul Biya displayed none of the nationalistic tendencies of his predecessor.

It was a mutually satisfying arrangement between master and privileged butler. Paul Biya could give carte blanche to French petroleum corporations and logging concerns in deals brokered by the son of the French president in the 1980s, Jean-Christophe Mitterrand, known disparagingly by some French journalists as *"Papamadit"* or "Daddy told me to."[86] In return, President Biya (and his inner circle) could benefit from all the perks of being a chosen leader in an African country full of resources the master wanted – untold amounts of money in foreign bank accounts, palaces and luxury galore, a very high life indeed of jetting about to golf courses abroad.

Paul Biya continued along his merry way, abusing human rights, imprisoning journalists and doing what he pleased with his country's resources. African journalists frequently referred to him as France's "poodle."

Two elections later and Biya was still in power, even though his country still ranked consistently near the top or at the very top of the list of the world's most corrupt countries, as compiled by the international watchdog group, Transparency International. Both those elections were seriously flawed, in the terminology of the international monitors, downright fraudulent according to just about everyone else with functioning eyes in their heads. But that didn't diminish Paul Biya's popularity in Paris. There he was a popular fellow. Then came some good reasons for Washington to take an interest in the stability of Cameroon under President Biya.

Had Paul Biya suddenly reformed himself, turned over a new leaf, morphed into a wonderfully engaged leader looking out for the welfare of his people and ended the thieving of state monies and oil revenues?

No, not exactly.

But he was guardian angel for the largest foreign investment project on the African continent at the time – an oil pipeline that ExxonMobil and a few other giant petroleum corporations had driven right through Cameroon's precious rainforests. And so it follows that Washington had an interest in seeing that Paul Biya, who championed the pipeline, stayed firmly in power in Cameroon to defend that investment on behalf of American oil corporations.

In October 2003, ExxonMobil, Chevron and PETRONAS began pumping oil from fields in Cameroon's northern neighbour, Chad – another desperately poor and poorly run country. From Chad, the oil flows south through Cameroon in a pipeline 1,070 kilometres long, which cost 3.7 billion US dollars to construct.

In the late 1990s, there had been a good deal of opposition to the construction of the pipeline that was to go right through the world's second largest remaining rainforest, the last refuge for both the endangered Baka pygmy groups and for immense floral and faunal riches, some not yet even documented and named.

A coalition of non-governmental organizations campaigned hard against the project, raising serious concerns about the social, cultural and environmental impacts of the pipeline.

In calling for a stop to the pipeline project before it got going, South African Archbishop and Nobel Peace Prize laureate, Desmond Tutu said, "Africa cannot afford the environmental devastation of such a project. We need to help construct, not destroy." He continued, "The Chad/Cameroon project is not the help we asked for or needed. In the absence of rule of law and respect for human rights and the environment, financing of large-scale development is destroying the environment and us."[87]

In 1997, in the face of environmental concerns about the effect of the pipeline, then chairman of ExxonMobil was quoted by the *Wall Street Journal*, saying that developing countries ought to avoid environmental controls because otherwise they risked losing foreign investment. In July 1998, 86 NGOs from 28 countries wrote a letter to the president of the World Bank, James Wolfensohn, detailing the human rights abuses in southern Chad, and the inadequacy of the environmental impact assessment and environmental management plan for the project submitted to the Bank by ExxonMobil.[88]

Despite such efforts and the pleas of Desmond Tutu and the coalition, the pipeline project went ahead full steam, with a few cosmetic changes to silence the critics. The many protest letters to president of the World Bank were to no avail.

Not only did it give its blessing to the pipeline, the World Bank liked the project so much that it offered the needy little corporation, ExxonMobil, 200 million dollars in financing for the construction.[89]

In 19 weighty volumes, the World Bank extols the virtues of the pipeline and the oil sector development that it can bring to Cameroon and Chad, and to Africa as a whole. Dissenting Cameroonians and social justice groups do not have the means or manpower to compete with such an impressive body of Bank literature and argue with all those extensive and expensive studies.

In his staunch defence of the pipeline project, Robert Calderisi – who was World Bank spokesman for Africa at the time – notes that the idea of compensating small-scale farmers for fruit trees cut down to make way for the pipeline was "rather original" because, he says, they were mostly subsistence farmers who "consumed the fruit themselves."[90] This reasoning confounds me; I would have thought it precisely because the farm families depended on the fruit trees for their own subsistence, and would continue to do so for the long life span of the trees, that they should be well compensated for this tremendous loss.

It's hardly surprising that there is so much cynicism in Africa about the real interests of foreign investors on their continent, given the track record of multinational oil companies in oil-rich African countries. Those that have for many years opened their oil fields to powerful petroleum corporations – Nigeria, Congo (Brazzaville), Angola, Chad, Cameroon and Sudan to name just a few – remain desperately poor and can hardly be said to have developed because of the oil revenues. The only development that has come with the oil revenues is that of a tiny, extremely rich elite working hand in hand with the foreign politicians and investors, along with an increase in corruption and the rapid deterioration of African social values, and in some cases civil conflict. As author and journalist Nicholas Shaxson puts it, "For those people who did notice that the citizens of these oil zones seemed to be getting poorer and angrier, the answer was to send a few dollops of aid to tide the natives over until the oil money kick-started their economies."[91] Trouble is, the oil money generally kick-starts corruption, injustice and unrest.

The World Bank and all the proponents of the pipeline project also failed to worry much when the almost 20 million US dollars that were handed over to Chad's president, Idriss Déby, that was supposed to be channelled into education and fighting poverty in that country, instead was transformed into arms for his army and security forces.

In an interview in 2004, World Bank Country Director for Chad, Ali Mahmoud Khadr, said, "The premise that underlies this project and the associated oil revenue management program was not that the World Bank Group or any other donors would come in and take oil money and manage it on behalf of the Chadians. The premise was always, we're not going to fish for them; we're going to teach them how to fish."[92]

Fish? How did fishing come into the picture? African fishermen and women have been fishing happily for millennia without any need of instruction from anyone. It's only very recently that they have had any trouble as Africa's waterways suffer the ills of development – silting caused by deforestation, pollution caused by industry and agricultural toxins or a lack of fish caused by small-mesh nets and offshore factory trawlers from Europe and Asia. The most recent issue has been vast losses of water resources due to climate change. The once huge Lake Chad is drying up.

The issue at hand was not fish, but Chad's oil and the fact that the country's eight million inhabitants, among the poorest in the world, were supposed to benefit from petro-dollars. The World Bank was supposed to be ensuring this with a scheme it had set up that stipulated 10 percent of Chad's share of the revenue (which was just over 12 percent, with the ExxonMobil consortium taking the rest) would be held in trust and 80 percent should be used for social, health and education programs.

In the words of a Western diplomat quoted by IRIN news service in late 2004, "The scheme is good on paper. But we are not there yet."[93]

In December 2005, the Chadian government approved legislation to access more of its oil revenues, saying it needed the money immediately to pay its civil servants and cover costs incurred by 240,000 refugees from the neighbouring Central African Republic and the Darfur crisis in Sudan. The World Bank reacted swiftly. On January 6 it suspended all new loans to Chad, and 124 million US dollars already earmarked for the country. Then World Bank president Paul Wolfowitz said the dialogue should continue. There was no consideration given to stopping oil production, which would have been perhaps the most effective way of ensuring the government of Chad respected the agreement.

A year after the oil began flowing, Chad – a country the size of France – still had just 650 kilometres of paved roads. Only one percent of the population had access to electricity. The remaining 99 percent had no electric light, lived on about 70 US cents a day and could expect to live to the age of 45. And those vital statistics were not changing for the better.

"A stone's throw from the small village [Kome]," says IRIN, "the US oil giant ExxonMobil generates seven times as much electricity to power its 40-km-wide enclave as the state-run utility STEE produces from imported diesel in the rest of this poor landlocked country."

Meanwhile, the pipeline was transporting 225,000 barrels of crude oil per day from the Doda Basin in Chad to the Cameroonian port of Kribi on the Gulf of Guinea. From there, it was shipped across the Atlantic to North America. All that African oil helped keep air conditioners, SUVs, Hummers – and whatever other gadget or device – humming away.

In August 2006, President Déby ordered both Chevron and PETRONAS out of Chad, saying they had refused to pay their taxes, leaving ExxonMobil the only consortium remaining in the country. Some observers were quoted by the BBC as saying this may have been a move to make room for Chinese oil companies, as it happened just three weeks after Chad resumed diplomatic relations with Beijing.[94] Two years later, in September 2008, the World Bank cancelled the pipeline deal, saying Chad had failed to use the revenues for health and education.

In early 2008, President Déby did manage, rather remarkably, to fend off an assault by rebels coming south from the troubled border area with Darfur who attacked the capital city. Chad's President Déby accused neighbouring Sudan of supporting the rebels and international pressure mounted on China to stop supporting the Sudanese government and arming it. Then two of Déby's political opponents disappeared. French President Nicolas Sarkozy jetted in, promising to demand an inquiry into their disappearance. But his mere presence tacitly confirmed French support for the Chadian president; Western leaders simply do not make state visits to leaders they consider pariahs or intend to depose. Imagine, for example, any Western leader flying in to visit President Mugabe after he had himself re-elected in Zimbabwe in 2008. Yet on the democracy, election freedom and human rights fronts, Idriss Déby's regime ranked about on par with Robert Mugabe's.[95]

Chad and Sudan – two African countries with foreign friends, two countries full of oil, and two countries full of poverty and trouble.

But long before that the pipeline through Cameroon had been laid, the oil was flowing and this brings us back – at long last – to the bogus elections in 2004. These were Cameroon's third elections since Biya became a democrat in 1992. Once again, Paul Biya won. A

Cameroonian journalist from the BBC World Service told me that she estimated only about one percent of the population was actually permitted to vote. She said that those who refused to proclaim themselves supporters of the ruling party, led by Paul Biya, could not get their names on the voters' lists. But the American government, like the French and all the other champions of democracy in the G8 club, seemed unwilling to say too much about the fraud that returned incumbent President Paul Biya to power in Cameroon.

I was in Cameroon in November 2004, just three weeks after the polling. All those who spoke to me – scientists, friends, people on the street, waiters in restaurants – told me the same story: the elections had been blatantly and shamelessly rigged.

All were indignant; some were downright furious. Their fury was not directed so much at their president, however, of whom they expected nothing more than cheating to wrangle himself another seven years in office. More telling was the rage they expressed about the foreign election observers, and those in foreign capitals that had sent those observers to Cameroon to monitor the poll. Cameroonians were outraged that they had failed to notice – or rather, failed to openly denounce – the extent to which the elections had been rigged. The only election monitors that did heavily criticize the poll were the 1,200 people from the Roman Catholic Church in Cameroon.

The others, international monitors, either closed their eyes or sealed their lips. A mission from the International Organisation of French-speaking Countries said voting took place peacefully and transparently in good conditions even though it expressed some muted reservations about how the election had been organized.

The Commonwealth observer team, led by former Canadian Prime Minister Joe Clark, was a little more critical, but in a wishy-washy way that fell far short of condemning the fraud. Joe Clark admitted that the election "lacked the necessary credibility" and that the electoral poll had been poorly managed and many people had been deprived of the right to vote. That didn't stop him from endorsing the final result. The Commonwealth report concluded that, "Even given the deficiency in the management of the register, we believe the intention of those who voted was reflected in the result."[96]

It made Cameroonians howl in frustrated rage – or with their usual laughter in the face of rather blatant Western hypocrisy. As a Canadian in their midst, and therefore a proxy for the long-since departed Joe Clark, I took a good deal of the flack they might have liked to vent on him. Had he been within hearing range of all those incredulous and unhappy Cameroonians, I wonder how Clark would have reacted. Would he have tried to tell them to their faces that really and truly, Canada and the Commonwealth wanted to promote true democracy in Cameroon?

In early 2008, violent demonstrations erupted in Cameroon because of high gasoline and food prices and then turned into protests against Biya's regime. They were met with violent force from the authorities; dozens of people died. The president blamed the violence on the opposition, which he labelled "the apprentice sorcerers in the shadows." In a richly ironic twist of reasoning, he stated that "people were trying to obtain through violence what they had failed to achieve through the ballot box."[97]

Shortly after that, Parliament amended the constitution, allowing Paul Biya to run in presidential elections in 2011 and offering him immunity for "errors" made as president, when or if he ever did relinquish power. Western governments and media didn't make a peep.

With the new tussle for African resources – as the US and other Western countries compete against China and other Asian nations for influence and access to those resources – the incentives for the kind of behind-the-scenes activities that ensured there were friendly regimes in place during the Cold War are back again in full force.

Yet there is evidence that the more a country depends on the export of natural resources, the lower its economic growth.[98] Many countries rich in natural resources that have exploited them for many years for export are still short of the funds they need to take care of essential human needs. These countries lack the true necessities – food and nutritional security, adequate water supply and shelter from the elements.

This raises a key question: who *has* been benefiting from Africa's natural wealth? Without doubt, many African presidents did amass vast fortunes from wholesaling their countries' resources, much of which was spirited out of their countries. But this only accounts for a fraction of the resource revenues that have been accrued in Africa.

About the only thing that can be said for sure is that the vast majority of people in sub-Sahara Africa have not benefited at all from the exploitation of their resources. In all ways – socially and monetarily – real poverty has been growing steadily on the continent. This is despite small, single-digit GDP growth figures trotted out from time to time by the World Bank to show economic progress in a particular country or region in Africa, figures with no mention of how that growing wealth is being distributed.

Sub-Sahara Africa is the only part of the world where the absolute number and percentage of the extreme poor rose between 1981 and 2001.[99]

The names of the countries and the names of the precious resources found there are interchangeable. The essential question remains the same: How can (insert name of African country) have an annual production of X (barrels, carats, tonnes, truckloads, shiploads) of Y (oil, gold, platinum, diamonds and other gems, tropical timber, base metals, strategic minerals, medicinal products) and still remain so poor or be growing poorer?

How could it be, for instance, that Mali was producing more than 60 tonnes of gold a year (and more cotton than any other country in sub-Sahara Africa) and still be coming out at the bottom of the United Nations' Human Development Index, usually ranking among the five least developed countries on earth?

And how could it be that Nigeria, Angola, Cameroon, Gabon and the Republic of Congo (capital Brazzaville) and more recently Mauritania, and Equatorial Guinea could be such important oil producers and still suffer such crushing monetary poverty and dismal statistics on access to basic education and health care, life expectancy and other key indicators on human development?

Sierra Leone is working very hard to heal itself after a decade of brutal civil war that lasted from 1991 until 2002. On the annual Human Development Index prepared by the United Nations Development Program (UNDP), in 2007 it ranked dead last on the list of least developed countries. Yet billions of dollars worth of diamonds have come from its soils. Other major diamond-producing countries in Africa – Angola, the Democratic Republic of Congo (former Zaire) and the Central African Republic – are not exactly glittering examples of prosperity and peace either.

Cameroon, Gabon, Liberia, the Democratic Republic of Congo and the Republic of Congo have exported vast amounts of tropical timber; all still remain poor and indebted.

Cameroonians, who have watched their real income plummet by more than half in the past decade, must at the same time watch the daily destruction of their bio-diverse tropical forests in the steady flow of timber on trucks heading to the coast for export to distant lands.

The pattern is disturbing – only the resource, the name of the African country and its leader changes. This, in turn, raises the all-important and double-edged question of why, since independence, so few African leaders have defended the interests of their people and why their people have accepted the leadership of those who do not defend them.

7

You are a good friend and we welcome you

Although good with slogans, the makers of American foreign policy don't have much talent for fostering the construction of exemplary democracies; drawn to dictators whom we hire to represent our freedom-loving commercial interests.

Lewis H. Lapham[100]

The major purpose of the dirty money structure that we in the West have created and expanded is the movement of money from poor to rich – out of the hands of the poor, into the hands of the rich; out of the countries where 80 percent of the world's population lives, into the countries where 20 percent of the world's population lives.

Raymond Baker.[101]

Some African presidents have called the Western bluff on democracy repeatedly, adjusted to the post-Cold War game and then again to the post-9/11 rulebook, and now are rapidly warming up to the new bargaining powers they have in playing China and Western nations off each other.

The rules of the bluffing game have evolved over the years to accommodate the changes in the identity and relative influence of the outside kingmakers, but much remains the same. Greatly simplified and slightly satirized – and my apologies in advance to the exceptional African leaders who have defied and who continue to defy the

rules and to Western leaders who have tried to end the hypocrisy –
they might be boiled down to something like this:

One: African leaders must say the right things about cherishing
and promoting democracy. What they do – in terms of human rights,
rigging elections, suppressing freedom of the press and other internal
issues that don't impinge on foreign interests – doesn't really matter,
as long as they don't draw too much attention to themselves, as in *real*
attention on CNN and prime time. (The usual damning reports from
organizations such as Amnesty International, Human Rights Watch,
ActionAid, Global Witness, Oxfam, Kairos and other caring NGOs
interested in social justice and environmental costs of development
are expected, are to be denied hotly and not worried about.) But the
leaders will probably have to be removed if they start eating their citizens or doing something horrific that *will* transform neglected and
little-known countries in Africa into headlines in the Western media
and embarrass the Western companies and governments that are
active there. (Uganda's Idi Amin and Central Africa's Jean-Bédel
Bokassa[102] would have done well to learn this unwritten rule).

Two: African leaders must remain 'friendly,' which translates as
reasonably subservient allies that serve foreign interests first. They
should promise Washington and London et al. that they're Free
Market converts and keen to wage war on terror (and maybe use new
anti-terrorism legislation to crack down on political opponents), and
only then turn their attention to their own personal profits, which
must not exceed or diminish those of foreign investors. It is risky, but
sometimes useful, to play one major Western power off the other.
This may be necessary to calm the odd trouble-making diplomat
(who has not learned these rules) that makes threatening noises
about cutting aid or loans because of human rights abuses. France, for
example, might promise to become a friend if the British or
Americans start harping about corruption or human rights, and vice
versa.[103] Currently, China is an alternative friend, and one that does-
n't yet have annoying indigenous watchdog and human rights groups
monitoring its business and political alliances in Africa. (Sudan's
president chose the China Option alternative, so did Zimbabwe
under President Robert Mugabe, and others are either working on or
considering it).

Three: African leaders must follow all the free-market, Structural Adjustment Programs and Poverty Reduction Strategies prescribed for them by the World Bank and IMF. This includes privatizing everything in their country while inviting in multinationals, squeezing out the public sector and opening their borders to dumped, inferior or out-dated environmentally unfriendly foreign goods. Words to be avoided at all cost are: nationalization, labour rights, environmental protection or higher resource royalties. Anti-corruption Committees are to be set up, and can be useful tools for prosecuting would-be rivals if used correctly. They are free to call themselves socialists so long as they bust trade unions and send all their ill-got capital out of the country to Western banks and tax havens and put down 'rebels' who oppose any of the above. They must be extremely welcoming to foreign investors and happily join the Multilateral Investment Guarantee Agency of the World Bank Group, MIGA, to improve the investment climate in their country and "enhance investor confidence in the safety of investments."[104]

Four: African leaders must go through the motions and hold elections of some sort to legitimize their rule. International observers will come and must be admitted (unless the China Option is in place and working). Among the observer groups sure to show up are from the Commonwealth or *La Francophonie*, the Carter Center, the National Democratic Institute (NDI) that seems to represent the US Democratic Party, and the National Endowment for Democracy (NED) that was inaugurated by President Ronald Reagan in 1984 and seems to represent the US Republican Party. None of these observers is likely to outright *condemn* the polls, providing that Rules One to Three have been obeyed. There is likely to be far less outcry (internationally) over constitutional changes that allow African leaders to remain in power for third, fourth and even fifth terms, as long as they have played by these rules.

Five: All of the above may be ignored if your country happens to sit on enormous oil reserves, have particular strategic import to Western powers and might also have the capacity to develop a nuclear arsenal and other weapons of mass destruction. (Born-again friend to the West, Muammar Gaddafi, is in the enviable position to opt for this rule).

Presidents in Africa who play the game like good sports are generally assured long and happy lives in the marble and gold corridors of power, sometimes until they die. This will be called democracy and the National Endowment for Democracy in the United States, along with its friends at the Project for the New American Century (PNAC),[105] will say they are helping to bring freedom to the peoples of the world.

To quote from PNAC's statement of principles, which seem to define US foreign policy under Republican governments, "we need to strengthen our ties to democratic allies and to challenge regimes hostile to our interests and values." In other words, if a government is hostile to US interests, it will be challenged – democratically elected or not, and vice versa.

Compare, for a moment, the complacency and complicity of Western observers about fraudulent 2004 elections in Cameroon with what happened just weeks later in another part of the world. In November 2004, people in the Ukraine went to the polls. The incumbent, pro-Russia candidate, Viktor Yanukovych, declared victory over his rival, pro-Western opposition candidate, Viktor Yushchenko. Without further ado, the US, Canada and the European Union (EU) all loudly cried foul and denounced the electoral fraud.

A popular uprising by Yushchenko supporters was given a great moral boost by Western diplomats, politicians and media that feted the mass demonstrations of protest in Kiev, heralding them as the "Orange Revolution" and a great step forward for freedom and democracy all over the world. In the end, new elections were called and Canada helped pay for those too, just at it had the first flawed poll. Indeed, it has since then been shown that Canada helped fund the leaders of the "Orange Revolution" itself.[106]

Second time around, Western favourite Victor Yushchenko won the elections and not surprisingly, his first declaration made to the Council of Europe in Strasbourg was that his reform plan was geared towards the "strategic foreign policy goal of EU membership."[107]

The moral of these two apparently unconnected – but contrasting tales, one in Europe and one in Africa – is that what's unacceptable fraud in one place may not be unacceptable elsewhere. Double standards apply.

Human Rights Watch denounces the charade of democracy not just in Africa but around the world, noting that the West accepts the results of flawed elections if the winner is an ally. "Such divorcing of democracy from the international standards that give it meaning helps to convince autocrats that mere elections, regardless of the circumstances, are sufficient to warrant the democrat label," says the Human Rights Watch report. "As such unworthy claimants as the leaders of Egypt, Ethiopia, Kazakhstan, and Nigeria wrap themselves in the democracy mantle with scant international objection, the concept of democracy gets cheapened, its human rights component cast aside."[108]

More than a few Africans I've met in recent years also suggested that the administration of George W. Bush was never very well positioned to lecture anyone on democracy, good governance and human rights. When I asked for clarification, they recalled for me the questionable elections in 2000 that put George W. Bush in power, and noted all the international agreements and institutions the US has refused to sign or pulled out of – the Kyoto Accord, the Ottawa Landmine Treaty, the International Criminal Court, the Convention of Biodiversity. And they asked if an administration that condoned torture had the right to speak about what constituted good or bad governance in Africa and respect for international law.

Increasingly people in West Africa are starting to say the same to me about Canada, whose credibility as an international role model and global citizen is eroded as it opposes or tries to scuttle global agreements and treaties.[109]

This sabotaging of international agreements for the global good does not prevent the governments of Canada or the US from taking sanctimonious stands against anti-democratic African leaders who break the rules, while remaining silent about those who heed them.

The starkest example of this is the criticism that they have directed over the past decade at Zimbabwe's Robert Mugabe, one of those African leaders that the West now loves to hate, loudly and openly. "But there was a time, not very long ago," writes Ankomah Baffour, when he [Mugabe] was the "darling of Western governments and their media reported him like a saint. The British Queen even gave him a knighthood."[110] But then Mugabe broke the rules of the game. In 1998, he sent troops to the Democratic Republic of Congo, ostensibly to protect against invasion by Rwandan and Ugandan forces, which were believed to be fronting for foreign (Western) interests.[111] He cozied up to China. He loudly criticized the West, accusing it of hypocrisy. Mugabe also brutally suppressed opposition and freedom of expression, committed atrocious abuses of human rights and democratic process, brought in land reform that led to the collapse of agricultural exports and the previously flourishing economy. His land reform took tracts land from white farmers and handed them out to many of his wealthy black friends (although some argue that 80 per cent of the arable land still remains in the hands of a few thousand foreign families).[112] He deliberately perpetuated the rift between Black and White, established first by British colonists and later institutionalized under Ian Smith's White minority rule, after Smith unilaterally declared Rhodesia's independence. Mugabe took a leaf from the colonists' handbook, using race and ethnicity to divide and rule. He played on the racism that white settlers planted and nurtured in his country, and reversed it to entrench and perpetuate his hold on power. He deserved criticism, political isolation and international pressure to reform or step down.

He blatantly hijacked the electoral process in 2008, fomented violence and then went ahead with a run-off presidential poll that the opposition MDC party boycotted, making Mugabe the default victor. In a rare show of interest in internal African affairs and elections, the world's mainstream media brought daily reports of Zimbabwe's poll and its aftermath, offering proof of rigging as if this were something new on the continent. Sanctions were announced along with stern warnings from Washington and Ottawa to Mugabe, and then to other African leaders who refused to condemn him. At the annual meeting of the world's industrial powers in Japan in 2008, the G8 leaders warned that their aid to African countries would be tied to good governance and to the willingness of African governments to criticize and isolate Robert Mugabe. This strident criticism from the West created some backlash. I heard a few people in Sierra Leone, inundated with BBC's unrelenting criticism of Mugabe during the election period, say they had come to like Mugabe because of his "courage" in standing up to the West. *New African* magazine described the "feral nature" of the Western media onslaught as "the Zimbabwe treatment," as if "Zimbabwe was the greatest crisis the world had seen in the new millennium."[113]

If Western governments wish to play the referee and ostracize one "odious tyrant," which is how one CBC reporter described Robert Mugabe in July 2008, then they need to do the same with other tyrannical leaders – and there are quite a few of those on the planet, some quite friendly with Washington, Paris, London and other Western capitals, such as Ottawa. I've heard some people in Africa quip that some Western capitals have not always been free themselves of tyrannical leaders. At a massive protest march in Bamako against the invasion of Iraq in 2003, the placards read *"Bush et Blair, terroristes."*

The problem with official Western condemnation of tyrants and flawed elections in Africa is that it is so selective. The British, Canadian and American criticism of President Mugabe rang hollow next to the loud silence in the West about 'friendly' tyrants on the continent. Some came to power in coups years ago, coups supported by the superpowers during the Cold War, and these presidents have since then transformed themselves into democratically elected leaders, fraudulent polls notwithstanding. Then with minor changes to their constitutions they remain in power long after they should have taken their millions of dollars – or billions – and retired to enjoy the spoils of their rule.

A host of other independent watchdog groups based in the West may protest and write detailed reports of atrocities, abuses and oppression in these African countries, but Western governments – and mainstream media – tend not to notice very much.

The examples of such anti-democratic or pseudo-democratic regimes in Africa that merit criticism and sometimes condemnation but don't receive much of it from Western leaders are numerous. Freedom House, a non-profit group that promotes and monitors democracy and freedom around the world, ranks Zimbabwe in its lowest category on the freedom scale, as "Not Free," when it comes to political and human rights and civil liberties. But down there with

Zimbabwe are also the African nations of Algeria, Angola, Cameroon, Chad, Côte d'Ivoire, Democratic Republic of Congo, Equatorial Guinea, Eritrea, Guinea, Libya, Mauritania, Republic of Congo, Rwanda, Somalia, Sudan, Togo, Tunisia.[114] When was the last time that major North American news corporations sent out correspondents to send daily reports on elections in the Democratic Republic of Congo, or Algeria or Egypt, all allies of the West? When was the last time Libya's leader, Muammar Gaddafi, a new friend to the West, even held an election? Answer: never.

Many regimes continue to rule with impunity, imprison journalists, rig elections, change constitutions to allow their presidents to stay on indefinitely, oppress their people and work away with Western governments and corporations. When they start to hobnob with China, welcome Chinese arms and investors, suddenly the West discovers that this is not good. Prominent figures such as Steven Spielberg make grand gestures against the Chinese – withdrawing his services from the Beijing's Olympics because of China's support for the regime in Sudan that is supporting groups committing atrocities in Darfur. There is nothing wrong with such gestures, except that they ignore all the past and current Western interference in and exploitation of the continent. They are conspicuously selective.

Uganda's President Yoweri Museveni doesn't state it quite this clearly – although he's unlikely to do so given that he is one of those African leaders who played by the rules of the political game on the continent and thus was happily (for him) re-elected in February 2006 as president of his country. But before that, he did put the contradictions in words: "Since the modern African state cannot be independent, it becomes easy prey to manipulation. If our states can be so manipulated, how can they expect to solve the problems of the people except with the permission of the former colonial rulers? A state which does not have the capacity to tell the colonial or neo-colonial rulers that it will act independently, in spite of what those rulers think, is completely handicapped."[115]

In 1998, Herman Cohen, the former US Assistant Secretary of State for Africa turned senior advisor at the World Bank-affiliated Global Coalition for Africa, visited Bamako to attend a workshop on good governance on the continent. He painted a rosy picture of how

Western pressure and support had helped democratization of the continent, saying that in the past decade, the number of democratic countries in Africa had quadrupled – gone from 5 to 20. I asked him how he defined a democracy. He said that it meant being able to criticize without being visited during the night by the secret police. I mentioned that right there in Mali, a country being applauded far and wide as a model democracy in Africa, eight days earlier 46 student leaders had been taken at night and thrown behind bars on no charges. They had been calling for a student strike over the reduction in bursaries for needy and deserving students who otherwise could not obtain a secondary education. The cutting of bursaries was a World Bank recommendation for the impoverished country.

Herman Cohen didn't respond to that, saying he preferred to look back five or ten years and compare the situation then and now in Africa. "For a good 15 or 20 countries," he said, "they are much better off in terms of freedom for the individual and also businesses, freedom to do business and engage in commerce without government interference."

I then asked him a question that many Africans had asked me, and for which I had no answer: "Why is it that the G8, particularly the US, which is pushing so hard for democracy on one hand, is also the country selling 70 percent of the world's arms? How do you as an American and an advisor to the Global Coalition for Africa reconcile that?"

He replied that America sold mostly very sophisticated and high-tech weapons, and mostly to "Saudi Arabia and Kuwait." The US was not selling weapons to Africa, he said. "This is the work of the Bulgarians and Romanians who want to get rid of surplus arms."

"Then why is the international community and the US not pushing the Middle East towards democracy the way they are Africa?" I asked.

He eyed me closely, paused, then said, "I can't answer that question. I'm not a Middle East specialist."[116] Things deteriorated from there.

Since that interview, the US, the UK and several of their allies have started spreading democracy to the Middle East. It's not quite as easy as it is in Africa; to get the friends they want in power in Afghanistan and Iraq it has proven to be extremely costly in human lives and as-yet-to-be-tallied billions – trillions – of dollars. By comparison, Africa is far easier to manipulate and dominate, and has been since colonial times. Countries are extremely fragmented and ethnically diverse, states are weak, borders are illogical and nonsensical, and few African nations have ever known anything other than foreign domination.

The West has its work cut out trying to counter ever-more pow-erful China. China declared 2006 the "Year of Africa." President Hu Jintao visited Nigeria, Kenya and Morocco and Chinese Premier Wen Jiabao toured Angola, Congo, Egypt, Ghana, South Africa, Tanzania and Uganda. The new China Option for African leaders offers regimes viewed as pariahs by the West support they could not otherwise obtain.

Many people in Africa are deeply concerned about China's grow-ing interest and involvement in their countries, concerned about the lack of transparency in agreements being signed to grant China access to the continent's resources.[117] Others applaud it.[118] China doesn't demand political or economic reform in return for gifts or investment in whatever form it may be, and doesn't make any pre-tence of caring for the environment, by offering the environment lip service before forests are felled, or the earth is blasted open by min-ing, as the West has tended to do.

At first glance, China might appear less intrusive and invasive than the West. The Western approach lays out a whole range of polit-ical and economic pre-conditions for loans, grants and sometimes also investments, "opening up the heart of the government to donor influence."[119] The Chinese may initially seem to impose fewer *overt* conditionalities. But perhaps that's just because they are less public about what they expect in return. Their 'gifts' are generally condi-tional on access to natural resources – oil, minerals, timber, fish and oil – with no regard at all for environmental damage or negative impacts on human rights or social justice.

China is just as ruthless as any other neo-colonial power in appro-priating – stealing – African knowledge, art, designs and products for mass reproduction in China, and then selling the cheap knock-offs back to Africa undermining local industry and crafts-people. Today,

the colourful prints stacked up in West Africa's markets bearing intricate African motifs are nearly all made in China. So are the colourful
woven baskets one finds in North American shops, the patterns and
designs of which have been stolen from the women of northern
Ghana and southern Burkina Faso. So too are the necklaces and beads
found in dollar stores and even in the hands of African vendors struggling to sell them as locally made souvenirs to European visitors. The
welcome mat being extended to the Chinese on the continent has
nothing to do with their having good intentions or better intentions
than Western nations. It may have something to do with Africa's
fatigue at Western hypocrisy and an African elite – set on enjoying
their wealth and privilege no matter how they have to get it – that is
well-schooled in the rules of the neo-colonial game.

At least there is a strong body of Western watchdog groups and
legislation to ensure some access to some information that does bring
to light abuses of human rights, social justice and the environment in
Africa. So far China – not being a democracy itself – does not.

African populations are once again at the mercy of wrestling elephants, and as they say in Africa, when elephants fight the grass gets
trampled. It's all about resource- and influence-hungry world powers
willing to fight proxy wars far from their shores. This bodes poorly for
future peace and for the progress of democracy on the continent.
Outside forces will likely choose to throw some support – financial or
strategic – behind potential leaders who will favour their access to
key natural resources in the new scramble for Africa.[120] This almost
eliminates the chance of the election of any leader who may wish to
regulate development of his or her nation's natural resources to
ensure they are used in ways that benefit their own people and protect their environments. This includes any potential president who
might not wish to sell off all the country's oil or other resources to
China or to Western-based multinationals or permit still more dese-
cration of the landscape and environment.

In 2005, Liberia held its first post-war presidential elections. It
came down to a race between two leading candidates. One was an Ivy
League economist, former World Bank official, former finance minister in the country. The other was an international soccer star with no

post-secondary education, a populist with enormous appeal among Liberian youth, many of whom were disenfranchised and marginalized after the long years of conflict in the country. It doesn't take a World Cup soccer referee to figure out which of the two would be the darling of the West. So it's hardly surprising that American observers of the vote, which the Ivy League economist won, declared it most "impressive." Irregularities in the poll that were detailed by the international soccer star candidate, George Weah, were ignored and he eventually stopped protesting for the sake of peace in the country. Two years after her victory, Liberian President Ellen Johnson-Sirleaf flew to Israel – by far the largest recipient of US aid and military support – and signed an agreement with the Israel Diamond Institute to conduct a survey of the Liberia's diamond resources. At the signing ceremony President Johnson-Sirleaf noted "the deep friendship between the two countries that goes back to the establishment of the State of Israel."[121]

The following year in next-door Sierra Leone, Ernest Bai Koroma, an insurance magnate who appeared business-friendly, won the presidential elections in his country. Again, this did not mean that he was either a good or a bad president but it did mean that he would likely feel he *should* follow the unwritten rules that were not necessarily in the interests of his nation, its people and its environment. Some members of the cabinet he appointed became known in the country as the "Maryland Mafia," because they had been living in the US for years and had close links to business interests there. Just two months after President Koroma was inaugurated, Eli Avidar, the head of the Israel Diamond Institute jetted in to Freetown to meet with him and with Vice President Samuel Sam-Somana, who then travelled to Israel to speak at the Third International Rough Diamond Conference, where he urged investors to come to Sierra Leone so that the country could fight poverty through the diamond industry.

There is nothing intrinsically wrong with such foreign investment and interest in another nation's precious resources. Yet these so-called investments in African nations as war-ravaged as Liberia and Sierra Leone – that have endured conflicts fuelled by smuggled diamonds – rarely benefit anyone except the foreign investor and a few people in strategic positions of power in the country where the resources are being exploited. And any president that truly wishes to alter the status quo has little chance of remaining in or coming to power.

This is especially the case in countries blessed – or cursed – with oil. Nigeria, the first major oil producing country in Africa, knows this curse better than most. In the 1990s, the Ogoni people of Nigeria's Niger Delta area tried to stand up and be heard on the international stage, lamenting the devastation of their farmland, fishery and their lives because of oil. Nigeria's military leader, General Sani Abacha, quickly had the leaders of the group, Movement for the Survival of Ogoni People (MOSOP), thrown in prison and condemned to death. Celebrated Nigerian playwright and environmentalist Ken Saro-Wiwa was one of those activists, and he focussed the world's attention on this travesty of justice in Nigeria. In 1995, heedless of the worldwide outcry and pleas for pardon from human rights groups and religious leaders (including the Pope), General Abacha went ahead with the execution of all ten Ogoni activists.

All the evidence was there to show that Abacha was a bloodthirsty thief who had stashed billions of dollars away in Swiss banks and in other tax havens around the world, among these other, far greater, crimes.

Then, mysteriously, the Nigerian president died suddenly in 1998, supposedly of a heart attack, surrounded by an unconfirmed number of prostitutes of unconfirmed nationalities. Nigerian diplomats in Bamako told me that the young women were Pakistani and that they had poisoned General Abacha. Some US intelligence reports also suggested there was evidence that he had been poisoned; others denied that such evidence existed.[122] Since his passing did not evoke a lot of mourning inside or outside the country – the Nigerian diplomats in Mali danced and sang when they heard the news – the issue of how he had died fizzled out quite quickly. It didn't seem to matter to many people whether he had been killed or if his heart had given out naturally in the heat of a small orgy; his body was buried immediately with no autopsy. Now that he was gone the path was open to return the country to civilian, elected, rule.

General Abacha had been a British- and American-trained soldier who had also been behind several coups in Nigeria. He was handed power in 1993 by an outgoing military ruler who had annulled the results of Nigerian elections, won by a civilian candidate, Moshood Abiola. Why did this not raise an outcry among Western governments? How was he able to stay in power and do as much damage to his country and its oil wealth as he did? Where did he get his support? It wasn't from ordinary Nigerians, who did not elect him. Why did US President Bill Clinton, just three months before Abacha's mysterious death, say that he "hoped" General Abacha would stand as a civilian candidate if presidential elections were held in Nigeria?[123] Why did the United States, Britain and the European Union not impose sanctions that might have dampened Sani Abacha's enthusiasm for repression and brutality, and perhaps saved the lives of Ken Saro-Wiwa and the Ogoni activists?

Here are a few of the answers: ExxonMobil, Chevron and Shell. The Shell Oil Company (British and Dutch) had already extracted about 32 billion US dollars worth of oil from the region and had a lot to lose if movements like MOSOP got a foothold in Nigeria. Shell also allegedly helped the Nigerian military under Sani Abacha to suppress opposition movements such as MOSOP. And like all multi-nationals working in dangerous or conflict zones, Shell has its own security forces to protect its investments in Nigeria.

Raymond Baker of the Brookings Institute summed it up this way at a Senate hearing, "Nigeria is one of the principal suppliers of oil to the United States, the most populous country in Africa and pivotally important to the stability of that continent. Yet, the biggest single thief in the world in the 1990s was almost certainly the late military dictator Sani Abacha, with $12 to $16 billion passing out of Nigeria in corrupt and tax-evading money during his murderous five year regime, most of this to the personal accounts of Abacha and his immediate family members."[124]

In 2006, another group of Nigerian militants calling themselves the Movement for the Emancipation of the Niger Delta began a campaign that they claimed was against the unfair exploitation of their oil and their environment. They regularly took hostages and threatened to shut down the oil pumps. Their campaign continues today and contributes to sudden rises in world oil prices.

According to Washington's international broadcaster, the Voice of America (VOA), Africa's Gulf of Guinea will soon account for up to a quarter of US oil imports. This is a region that has, till now, been dominated by former colonial interests. BP-Shell has done well for itself in Nigeria. France has certainly enjoyed helping itself to the oil abundant in Gabon, Cameroon, Republic of Congo and Angola (where China is now such a major player that in March 2007, Angola, flush with oil wealth, decided to send the International Monetary Fund packing, saying its services were no longer needed).[125]

Although almost invisible next to the enormous American-led drama playing itself out in the Middle East, America's new two new acquisitions in the Gulf of Guinea – the former Portuguese colony of São Tomé (and Principe) and the former Spanish colony of Equatorial Guinea – are extremely important to Washington, ExxonMobil and Chevron. The tiny nation, São Tomé and Principe, comprises just two tiny islands in the Gulf of Guinea, while Equatorial Guinea with its capital Malabo includes five inhabited islands and a chunk of the mainland, snuggled between Cameroon to the north and Gabon to the south.

In 2004, the Voice Of America, which has a powerful relay station in São Tomé and Principe, announced, "The tiny West African islands of São Tomé and Principe are interesting to the United States not only for their oil potential, but also for strategic positioning in the Gulf of Guinea."[126]

The Center for Strategic International Studies (CSIS), a right wing think tank closely tied to corporate and energy investment groups in Washington, kept busy producing reports on rising energy stakes, security and governance in Africa.[127] CSIS set up a task force on Gulf of Guinea security to examine whether US interests were at risk in the Gulf of Guinea, whether heightened US engagement was warranted, and if so, what US policy strategy "might best advance US interests."[128] The CSIS task force report states, "The Gulf of Guinea is a nexus of vital US foreign policy priorities. Every US foreign policy interest in Africa – democracy, respect for human rights, poverty alleviation, terrorism, HIV/AIDS, organized crime, energy security, strengthening regional peacekeeping capacities and regional political integration – is significantly at play there."[129]

The average observer might ask if a task force weighted down with oil industry heavy-weights can claim to be genuinely interested in democracy and respect for human rights and combating HIV/AIDS, particularly when it was formed explicitly to look at rising US energy stakes and security in the Gulf of Guinea, presumably to protect those rising stakes. The US Council on Foreign Relations, in a 2006 report, *More than Humanitarianism: a strategic U.S. approach toward Africa* (a project co-directed by the same Stephen Morrison who co-chaired the CSIS task force on security in the Gulf of Guinea for US oil investments there), laid out the new game and the high stakes this way: "Africa is of growing importance. By the end of the century, for example, sub-Sahara Africa is likely to become as important a source of US energy imports as the Middle East. China, India, Europe, and others are competing with each other and the United States for access to oil, natural gas, and other resources. The world's major powers are also becoming more active in seeking out investments, winning contracts, and *building political support* on the continent."[130] (emphasis added)

In early 2007, Washington announced that it would establish a new Pentagon command covering Africa, to be called Africom. No longer would the US exercise its hegemony over Africa from its Eurocom military base in Germany. The new Africom would help ensure US influence and control over Africa – her oil, her political movements (facilitating the Global War on Terror), and everything else of strategic importance to Washington.[131] To date, the only African president who has offered to host the US Africom base for Africa on her soil is Liberia's Ellen Sirleaf-Johnson. Some are warning that whichever country does agree to host it, risks repercussions and possible retaliation from groups opposed to Western, particularly American, expansionism.

But São Tomé is slated to become the site of a large new US naval facility. So perhaps it is no surprise that in 2003, President Fradique de Menezes of São Tomé benefited from American help in putting down an attempted coup d'état. Speaking with VOA in 2004, he said, "We would like to have this very close relationship with Americans. Of course, we talk about military [protection], and why because myself at a certain moment, due to the expectations created around this oil business and due to our weakness, this is a very small islands state … it's better to have good friends who really can care about us, and this is the response I had very positively from Washington."[132]

Starting in 2001, São Tomé became a prime destination for high-level American delegations, and not just the oil magnates jetting in and out. When General Charles Wald, deputy commander of the US European Command, made his way out to the islands from his headquarters in Germany, he suggested that the islands could become another Diego Garcia. That should not have sounded very promising to the local population, not if they were aware of what happened to the inhabitants of Diego Garcia when the British and US decided they wanted it as a military base – they were ferried out to sea and relocated on distant islands. The American military have dubbed this colonial military outpost on the stolen island of Diego Garcia the "Footprint of Freedom."[133]

In February 2005, the rights for oil exploration in a large block around São Tomé and Principe were awarded to a consortium of Chevron and ExxonMobil, with a nine percent share reserved for a Nigerian oil company, EER, to appease Nigeria that had disputed São Tomé's ownership of the offshore development zone.[134]

On VOA, US officials said São Tomé could become a "lillypad, a forwarding operating base with several hundred troops, not only to safeguard American interests in the islands' possible oil fields, but across West Africa." Securing new territories and oil reserves in what had been a region considered within the sphere of former colonial powers in Europe – France, Britain, Spain and Portugal – meant that the United States would have to pay less attention to genuine democracy than they would to leaders in these new oil republics in the Gulf who would protect their interests and on whom they could count.

In Equatorial Guinea, President Teodoro Obiang Nguema Mbasogo has been in power for more than a quarter of a century, having put himself there in 1979 by overthrowing his own uncle, Macias Nguema, described by some as not just a brutal but also a genocidal dictator.

Economist Robert Klitgaard, who headed a World Bank project in Equatorial Guinea in the 1980s and who met with President Obiang several times, entitled his 1990 book about the country and its regime *Tropical Gangsters* and portrayed him as a very clever, very charming and very, very ruthless man accused of widespread torture and other human rights abuses that hardly inspired confidence in him as a reliable friend to anyone but himself and his immediate family.[135]

For many years, as long as there was no real Western or other interest in the country, none of this really mattered much. So Western governments took the high road and openly criticized the regime in Equatorial Guinea. Then, in the 1990s, oil money began to flow.

In 2003, IRIN news spelled it out: "A few years ago, Equatorial Guinea was an international pariah state, a dictatorship accused of corruption, mismanagement, repression and torture on a scale unparalleled in Africa. But the discovery of abundant offshore oil and gas over the past decade has started to change official attitudes in Washington to this former Spanish colony of just over 500,000 people. The United States closed its embassy in the capital Malabo in 1995, when the small West African state still relied on modest exports of cocoa, coffee and timber to sustain the coffers of its non-democratic government. But Washington decided to reopen the diplomatic mission when three American oil giants, ExxonMobil, Amerada Hess and Marathon Oil, came to control most of Equatorial Guinea's rapidly increasing oil and gas production."[136]

The same IRIN report notes that within the country very little had changed. Little of the oil wealth had trickled anywhere but into the private accounts of the president and his men. According to the American Department of Energy, Equatorial Guinea is the fourth largest recipient of US investment in sub-Sahara Africa. The CIA describes Equatorial Guinea as a "nominal democracy," given that President Obiang did hold elections in 1991, 1996 and 2002, but notes that these were "flawed" and that most businesses in the country are owned by the president's family members.[137]

On 7 March 2004, seven months before the US would open its new embassy in Equatorial Guinea's capital, Malabo, across the continent in Zimbabwe 70 mercenaries were arrested when the authorities in

Harare impounded an airplane that had flown in from South Africa. The alleged mercenaries at first claimed they were on a completely innocent mission: headed to the Democratic Republic of Congo (another war-town, desperately poor and resource-rich country) to provide security at a diamond mine.

The next day, in Equatorial Guinea, 15 foreign mercenaries were arrested by security officials who claimed the men were in the country to prepare the ground for a coup against President Obiang. Five months later, in August 2004, 14 foreign mercenaries and five local men were put on trial in Malabo, charged with conspiring to murder the president. At this trial, Nick du Toit, leader of the group of mercenaries – mostly South African and Armenian – claimed that he was playing only a limited role in the plot and that he had been recruited by the British super-mercenary, officer and gentleman, Simon Mann, who had been arrested with the larger group of alleged mercenaries in Zimbabwe.

Simon Mann makes an interesting study. He's someone who seems to glide about in that opaque medium of swirling shadows and spooks; the grey area separating legitimate and legal military establishments and operations from covert operations that are illegal by any standard, but appear still to be sanctioned, if not planned, by Western powers.

A graduate of Eton, attended primarily by princes and the political elite, Mann had then moved on to the prestigious British military academy, Sandhurst. After that, he joined the Scots Guard, an army regiment also associated with royals and the upper crust of British society. From there, he graduated to the British special forces unit, the SAS, and became a commander. He left the British military in 1981, although he certainly didn't cut his public school ties with those at the pinnacle of Britain's military and political pyramid: during the first Gulf War he worked for Britain's commander there, General Sir Peter de la Billiere.[138]

In 1989, Mann was co-founder, along with wealthy British businessman Tony Buckingham, of the controversial mercenary firm, Executive Outcomes, employing many men who had got their boot-camp training in South Africa during Apartheid. Executive Outcomes built its reputation – some might say notoriety – by training African armies and putting down rebel movements for African governments or providing corporations working in dangerous or conflict zones with "armed guards."[139] Its specialty was conflicts in countries rich in precious resources such as Angola and Sierra Leone.

After helping to found the mercenary group with Buckingham, Mann then linked up with another former colleague from the British Scots Guard, Tim Spicer, and Executive Outcomes metamorphosed into a conglomerate of shady companies linked with security, oil, diamonds, and other mining interests. The names Mann, Spicer and Buckingham pop up all over Africa where there are valuable resources and conflict, and surface again later in this book.

While Buckingham continued his exploitation of minerals and oil across Africa, Simon Mann had gone on to other interesting pursuits. He had moved to South Africa and it was from there, with much coming and going to Spain and the UK, that he and his backers plotted the coup in Equatorial Guinea. In his book about this "Wonga Coup," Adam Roberts argues that Mann's plot was closely based on Frederick Forsyth's novel *Dogs of War*, which in turn was allegedly based on a coup plot that Forsyth himself financed back in 1973, to try to rid Equatorial Guinea of its first sadistic president.[140]

Mann's coup plot had no such altruistic intentions. The idea was to replace President Obiang with the opposition leader, Severo Moto Nsa, who would be little more than a puppet in their hands. Moto had been living in exile in Spain, in between trips home that inevitably saw him eventually imprisoned, and then released. The Spanish Prime Minister, José María Aznar, who would be defeated in elections in 2004 after the Madrid bombings, was widely thought to support any effort that would remove Obiang from power, and replace him with Moto. President Obiang was working closely with American oil companies and while he remained in power, Spain was excluded from the oil riches in its former colony in America's "New Gulf."

In the end, the coup failed, largely because Mann and his co-plotters made no effort to keep it completely secret, assuming perhaps that President Obiang was such a pariah both on and off the continent, that there would be open support from Spain and tacit support from South Africa, the UK and also the US for such a regime change.

Support was forthcoming from Spain, which was sending two warships to the Gulf to coincide with the planned arrival of opposition leader Moto on a plane from the Canary Islands. There was also substantial financial support from the Wachovia Bank in the US and from sources in Britain. One unnamed source said that there were "some serious American guys on the Canary Islands" implying that they "represented American intelligence, and thus some sort of American approval for the plot."[141]

On March 7, 2004, Mann, his crew and 60 mercenaries had taken from South Africa in an American-registered Boeing 727. Mann had arranged to purchase the plane from Dodson Aviation, an American company that specialized in selling planes for the US government. The South African authorities had already alerted their counterparts in Zimbabwe; President Nelson Mandela had banned mercenaries and mercenary activity on its soils and would not countenance such activities. So when the would-be coup-makers landed in Harare, they were arrested.

Mann was originally sentenced to prison in Harare, and then extradited to Equatorial Guinea in 2008 to face trial again. In response to Mann's sentencing, Michael Gove of *The Times* newspaper in London defended this British "hero" by saying Mann's security firms "have been scrupulous about operating in concert with Western policy goals while maintaining a discreet distance."[142] Gove went on to say that men like Mann were needed to strike blows "against barbarism and against kleptomaniac tyrants," which is how he described President Obiang. I wonder what words Gove uses for privateers in the business of shedding blood for profit, and of the shadowy men atop the tangled web of companies plundering Africa's natural wealth. Civilized, noble and peace-loving?

Sir Mark Thatcher, son of former British Prime Minister, Margaret Thatcher, was also implicated for financing an Alouette II helicopter that was to be used in the overthrow of President Obiang.[143]

The president of Equatorial Guinea alleged that those behind this coup plot were: multinational oil companies; foreign powers including the government of Spain (at the time); an opposition leader from Equatorial Guinea living in exile in Spain (Severo

Moto), a former British cabinet minister; and Elil Calil, an oil tycoon and London-based millionaire.

In July 2008 in Equatorial Guinea, Simon Mann was tried and sentenced to 34 years and four months in prison for his role in the 2004 coup plot. But it seemed unlikely he would have to serve it all in the notorious Black Beach Prison in Equatorial Guinea. Media reports hinted that he had struck up good relations with his captors and the authorities in the country, dining with one minister, to whom he loaned him a copy of *The Wonga Coup*, the book by Adam Roberts about the foiled coup plot. During his trial, Mann protested that he was not the most senior coup plotter. He also fingered Eli Calil and Mark Thatcher, and said that South Africa and Spain had given the green light for the plot. Both countries denied any involvement.[144]

Earlier, British Home Secretary Jack Straw had admitted to parliament that the UK government had known of the coup plot two months before the arrests of the would-be coup-makers in Zimbabwe. But in April 2005, a UK court on the Channel island of Guernsey blocked the release of papers naming alleged backers of the aborted coup in Equatorial Guinea. And in 2007, a South African magistrate dismissed charges against eight of those accused of plotting the coup. He threw the case out after a number of state witnesses claimed the botched putsch had been sanctioned by South Africa, British and American governments.[145]

President Obiang may be happy to get the affair – and his country with its thinly disguised dictatorship – out of the international spotlight lest his regime begin to attract more widespread international scrutiny.[146] An investigative story by the *Los Angeles Times* showed that President Obiang kept hundreds of millions in the Riggs Bank in Washington, DC. In 2004, a US Senate Report on banking regulations revealed that by 2003, Obiang had become the Riggs Bank's biggest client, opening his first account in the mid-1990s just after the extent of the oil reserves of his country had been discovered. There was loud condemnation of Riggs Bank and ample evidence that President Obiang was not merely corrupt, but also guilty of horrendous human rights abuses, including torture.

This, however, did not lead to his downfall, or to a cooling of relations with Washington. In April 2006, President Obiang visited

Washington, and met with Secretary of State, Condoleezza Rice, who welcomed the president of Equatorial Guinea with the words, "… thank you very much for your presence here. You are a good friend and we welcome you."[147]

A host of Western-based groups – Global Witness, Global Policy Forum, Oxfam, World Vision, One World, Worldwatch Institute, ActionAid and many others, including some dedicated people within the World Bank – continue to lobby for change and to delve into the issue of natural resources in Africa and how much local populations benefit, or suffer, as a result of them. Kairos, the Canadian Ecumenical Justice Initiatives, sums up what is known as the "paradox of plenty" this way: "Under neo-liberal economic conditions, resource extraction in Africa by transnational mining and oil companies occurs in conditions reminiscent of early colonialism … In fact, over time, the more a country depends on natural resources, the lower its economic growth."[148]

Yet the international donor community, the World Bank and the IMF have continue to push for and finance foreign investment for even more intensive and wide-scale exploitation of Africa's natural resources, claiming this will lead to economic growth. Perhaps their own?

At the World Summit on Sustainable Development held in Johannesburg in October 2002, then British Prime Minister Tony Blair announced the Extractive Industries Transparency Initiative (EITI), and its first plenary conference was held in the UK in June 2003. Its declared aim was to "increase transparency in transactions between governments and companies within extractive industries."[149] In plain English, this means dealing with the reality that oil wealth and other resource riches acquired in Africa rarely seem to do anything but increase the disparity between the desperately poor population and a few very wealthy individuals on the continent – and off it, too, of course.

It would be a refreshing change if such promises were taken out of the realm of white-washing and lip service, breaking the precedents set to date on the continent in Nigeria, Chad, Angola,

Cameroon, Gabon and Equatorial Guinea, where oil has been anything but a blessing to the average citizen.

The Extractive Industries Transparency Initiative does not, however, impose mandatory requirements on companies to publish details of their financial dealings in these resource-rich nations. Rather, it places the onus on the governments of developing nations to be more transparent. But it takes two to tango, and as many Africans have suggested to me over the years, it is just as important to expose and crack down on at the corrupters as it is to expose and crack down on the *corrupted*. In the past, discussions about corruption and good governance have tended to focus on governments and elites of developing countries, as if they alone were at fault and responsible for the corruption, ignoring those who would – and do – corrupt them. Raymond Baker of the Brookings Institute, who has spent 45 years looking at corruption, estimates that at least one trillion US dollars of dirty money crosses borders each year. But he notes that the bulk of the effort to stop corruption "has been focused on those corrupt countries without much work being devoted to the facilitative role played by western countries."[150]

Nicholas Shaxson points out that "it is not unlawful for a United States bank to receive funds derived from alien smuggling, fraud, racketeering, handling stolen property, contraband, environmental crimes, trafficking in women, transport for illegal sexual activity, slave trading – and many other evils," so long as the crimes are committed abroad and not in the US itself.[151]

Some first-time visitors to Sierra Leone, swayed by all the negative publicity given to corrupt African leaders and governments, might be surprised by the large billboard at the international airport in Lungi: "Welcome to Sierra Leone," it reads, almost plaintively. "If you cannot help us please do not corrupt us."

Enter another encouraging, broad-based coalition that could just pressure the corporations themselves to lift the veil on their financial dealings in the resource-rich, poor countries. In 1999, Global Witness had started the ball rolling with a report detailing the extent of the complicity of oil companies and banks in the plundering of Angola's oil during four decades of civil war.[152] In 2002, George Soros, Chair of the Open Society Institute, linked with Global Witness to set up the Publish What You Pay coalition. Today, 300 NGOs from around the world make up this coalition, which calls for the mandatory disclosure of the payments made by oil, gas and mining companies to all governments for the extraction of natural resources, and likewise, calls on governments of resource-rich developing countries to publish full details on revenues[153] Publish What You Pay aims to help citizens of resource-rich developing countries hold their governments accountable for the management of revenues from the oil, gas and mining industries, so that natural resource revenues in developing countries will serve as a basis for poverty reduction, economic growth and development rather than exacerbating corruption, conflict and social divisiveness.

In June 2004, an Australian company said it was taking out oil concessions in Mali's north. President Amadou Toumani Touré was ecstatic; he said he had dreamed of this.

Many Malians I know – students and activists and members of civil society groups all of whom pay close attention to current events on their continent – are terrified by the interest in oil that may lie under the desert sands in its north. They have seen what happens in other oil-rich nations and said they do not want to suffer the consequences of black gold under the sands of the Sahara.[154]

Unlike many free-market economists who see the world in shades of dollar-green, they told me they would prefer to remain poor and socially healthy than plunge into the social and political turmoil that oil, diamonds and other precious resources can bring to African countries. Malians told me they prayed that any oil they had would be too little and expensive to exploit to interest foreign companies.

8

White elephants and 800-pound gorillas

What makes me nearly apoplectic – and I very much want to say this – is that the Bank and the Fund were fully told about their mistakes even as the mistakes were being made. It's so enraging that they refused to listen. They were so smug, so all-knowing, so incredibly arrogant, so wrong.

Stephen Lewis[155]

We are no longer, at least not in theory, colonies. But our countries are submitted to draconian economic and structural reforms that we didn't ask for, and about which the majority of the population was not consulted, and which in addition, impoverish and subjugate us.

Aminata Dramane Traoré.[156]

In 2002, all 191 UN member states signed the United Nations Millennium Declaration and the eight Millennium Development Goals, known in development circles as the "MDGs." Top on the list of positive undertakings was the pledge to eradicate extreme hunger and poverty by 2015; second was to achieve universal primary education. They could only be met, said the official statement, if international agencies and lenders stopped doing "business as usual."[157]

In some ways, this declaration was an admission that more than two decades of Structural Adjustment Programs developed and implemented by the World Bank and International Monetary Fund had not succeeded in Africa and that extreme poverty had risen.

Economist Jeffrey Sachs likens the prevailing development economics of those programs to 18th century medicine, "when doctors used leeches to draw blood from their patients, often killing them in the process." Although once a proponent of such free market economic reforms in Bolivia and Russia, Sachs seems to have changed his views. He describes Africa's plight this way: "In the past quarter century, when impoverished countries have pleaded with the rich world for help, they have been sent to the world's money doctor, the IMF. The main IMF prescription has been budgetary belt tightening for patients much too poor to own belts."[158]

Sachs is not the only outspoken critic of the economic policies that have cut African budgets and government spending to – and then into – the bone. "Despite the dogmas of the 'market fundamentalists,' … the private sector of Africa cannot lead the drive for development,' writes Gerald Caplan. "Only governments can provide essential services to all, whether schooling at all levels, proper health care, or justice and equality for women."[159]

There is widespread agreement among African economic researchers that Structural Adjustment Programs have caused social unrest, a collapse of health and education in many countries and political instability.[160]

For a long time, the World Bank and the IMF ignored this reality. In 1994, despite all the evidence to the contrary, the World Bank stated that "adjustment is working." Then there were some quiet admissions that "nobody has all the answers" and "development everywhere is a complex phenomenon" and that there were "rapidly changing realities." Eventually the Bretton Woods institutions began to speak of "policy dialogues" with Africa.[161]

In 2001, James Wolfensohn,[162] president of the World Bank, travelled to Africa with Horst Köhler,[163] head of the IMF, to meet with selected heads of state. Maybe the "policy dialogue" was starting? Their auspicious trip began in Bamako.

It was February and that meant that the annual dry season – nine months of blowing dust in cloudless skies – had arrived in all its overheated glory. At Senou International Airport in the Malian capital, hot winds blasted across the vast open expanse of runway and fields of grass faded yellow and brown by the Sahelian sun.

A warm and noisy traditional Malian welcome had been rolled out to welcome the two very, very important men, So had the red carpet, which was laid from the door of the VVIP lounge, normally reserved for visiting heads of state, all the way across the hot tarmac to the spot where the incoming Air France Airbus would eventually park to cool its jets after a long haul from Paris.

Fabulous traditional dancers from Dogon Land in the east of the country had been bussed in and were lurching about on very tall stilts; whooping and swooping all over the place with masterful choreography.[164] Drums were pounding, the national orchestra was belting out its own classic Malian melodies, and nobody seemed to mind that the five separate musical groups were all playing different tunes at full volume. Hundreds of toddlers had been pulled from their *maternelles* – kindergartens – in Bamako, dressed up in smart little pinafores and uniforms and lined up either side of the red carpet, where they had been standing like quiet little lambs, bewildered and doggedly obedient for several hours in the blazing sun.

Now, as the aircraft touched down and the dignitaries emerged and were quickly surrounded by security men and their Malian ministerial hosts, bossy matrons started pushing and shoving the children into action. They handed them miniature flags bearing the World Bank logo, and instructed them to sing and wave the flags to welcome the VVIPs. The children, of course, had no idea who these visitors were. But the local press did; they had turned out en masse for the arrival in their impoverished country of two of the most powerful men on the planet.

This was before the 9/11 attacks in the US would put a damper on what had been a growing anti-globalization movement and protests wherever and whenever world leaders gathered to talk global policy. The austerity programs imposed on Africa and the developing world had caused rioting there for years, but, as Nobel Prize-winning economist Joseph Stiglitz notes, "their protests were largely unheard in the West."[165] Then the protests spead to the developed world, at meetings of the World Bank and the IMF, of the World

Trade Organization, and of the elite annual get-together of the global oligarchy at the World Economic Forum in Davos, Switzerland.

This was still six months to go before the World Trade Centre would crumble in New York and radically change the world mood and the amount of freedom available to any dissenters on Western foreign policies. Some at the helm of major global institutions were showing some concern about their increasingly negative public image and were taking measures to improve it. This trip to Africa by the heads of the World Bank and IMF certainly seemed to suggest that they wanted to try to mend a few fences.

Horst Köhler was still fairly new as Managing Director of the IMF and this was his very first trip to Africa in that capacity. James Wolfensohn, on the other hand, knew his way very well around Africa – at least the parts of it one finds in the air-conditioned five-star hotel suites and conference halls that a World Bank president is likely to experience during an official trip on the continent.

In a short statement to the press in the marbled and cool interior of the VVIP lounge at the airport, Mr. Köhler said, "I've come here to Mali together with my colleague and friend, president of the World Bank James Wolfensohn, to demonstrate the commitment of the International Monetary Fund and the World Bank to support Africa's efforts to fight poverty and to demonstrate in Mali that we are committed to support efforts to regional integration that we feel are important to combating poverty."

This sounded quite promising.

I had been looking forward enormously to the arrival of these two men, hoping that the press would be given the time and opportunity to ask them some questions to which I had been looking for answers for years. About how Africa's debt was incurred, about privatization that didn't seem to have greatly benefited anyone except the foreign investors who had grabbed up profitable African utilities and mines and about economic austerity policies that curtailed public spending on education and health, which would have led to a coup d'état or at least a very rapid change of government in any Western country that tried to impose similar policies at home.

A couple of public relations officers of the Bank and IMF had flown in a few days earlier, not to answer any of these questions but to offer a vague overview of their bosses' itinerary and the purpose of the trip. They said the two men with their delegations of Bank and IMF Vice Presidents and high-level technocrats would make four stops on the continent – Mali, Nigeria, Tanzania and Kenya, where they would be meeting with specially selected African heads of state, ostensibly to "listen" to them. They would be discussing new blueprints for private and foreign investment that would hinge on good governance and democratic reform in Africa.

One of the master plans intended to foster development and ease poverty on the continent was known as the New Partnership for African Development, or NEPAD for short. A few wry West African journalists chuckled sardonically about this new "knee-pad thing" that had been developed by the presidents of South Africa, Nigeria, Senegal and Algeria. The journalists wondered aloud if this "knee-pad thing" was for African presidents so they wouldn't hurt their knees when they were begging and grovelling before their political and economic masters in the West.

But such irreverence was usually kept fairly quiet, in deference to the World Bank and IMF information officers, Nigerian and Cameroonian respectively, who had jetted in to prime the press. They briefed us about the importance of this African tour by the two men who, they said, were putting "Africa at the centre."

The press officers admitted that the two men would have no time to move outside Bamako or visit any communities to see first-hand what extreme monetary poverty looked like. But, they told us, Mrs Wolfensohn and Mrs Köhler would be visiting some local charities in the Malian capital, while their husbands met with Mali's civil society at the Congress Palace in Bamako.

When, on day two of their visit, we (the press) arrived at the Congress Palace for that meeting with civil society, we were surprised to find chains and padlocks on the doors, and bullet-proof-vested security men, wired from their wrists to their ears, talking into the cuffs of their suits, manning the closed entrance. They were checking special passes that had been issued to only a few journalists – three of us from the BBC had been accorded only two – and to a select group of Malians invited to attend this meeting with the World Bank and IMF bosses.

And as for the civil society represented inside, in Bamako, at least for the visit of Wolfensohn and Köhler, the term *civil society* took on a peculiar new meaning. Although civil society is a term with many definitions, it generally refers to all of the voluntary civic and social organizations and institutions that form a functioning society, as opposed to commercial institutions and the structures of the state that are backed by force. It generally encompasses all manner of organizations and associations; registered charities, development NGOs, community groups, farmers, women's organizations, faith-based organizations, professional associations, trade unions, social movements, self-help groups, business associations, coalitions, activists and advocacy groups. A major body of scholarly works examines the complexities of the role and the diverse, inclusive composition of civil society. But on this occasion in Mali, civil society was exclusive. It included guests specially invited by the World Bank and IMF offices in Mali because they worked directly for or benefited directly from the World Bank's micro-projects in Mali, projects involving small grinding mills for grains or a well here and there.

Non-civil society – a truckload of gendarmes in full riot gear – ensured security outside the palace and kept a close eye on the handful of protestors from Jubilee 2000, the international coalition that for years had been campaigning for the cancellation of Africa's debt. The protestors waved banners comparing Africa's debt to "economic circumcision" and told us (BBC and Radio France journalists) they had learned of the IMF and World Bank visit to their country only two days earlier, from the international media, BBC and Radio France International. They were complaining bitterly that they had not been invited to attend the much-touted meeting between the World Bank and IMF bosses and representatives of Mali's civil society – given that they represented civil society better than did the invited guests inside.

When Wolfensohn and Köhler and their entourage pulled up, their security men tried to steer them past the protestors and bullied journalists out of the way with their elbows. Much to their credit, the two men ignored their hired thugs and approached the small group of protestors, who were chanting *"Annulez la dette,"* cancel the debt.

"What do you want me to do?" James Wolfensohn asked the group, superfluously I thought, given that they were busy chanting three words that answered his question.

Then Horst Köhler tried to engage the group from Jubilee 2000 in a discussion on the merits of money-lending, from his European-trained, macro-economist point of view. "People must borrow money to make money," he said to them, while an aide translated his German-accented English words into French. "You need credit for development."

The reaction was raucous, with protestors shouting that most of the debt had been incurred by unelected presidents and no one except those presidents and the lenders had benefited. "We don't want our countries to borrow your money. It doesn't help us at all," said one Malian woman.

The protestors crowded in, eager to communicate their African perspective on credit, debt and development to Wolfensohn and Köhler. A grey-suited bodyguard began pushing people back, muttering, "This is not a press conference."

For a few minutes, once again to their credit, Wolfensohn and Köhler ignored the thugs in suits there to guard them, and continued to counter the protestors' complaints about bad credit and big debt with their textbook economic logic that credit would beget wealth. But eventually the bodyguards got the upper hand and led their wards away from the protestors and into the Congress Palace for a far more pleasant encounter with about a hundred carefully chosen Malians who had nothing but praise for the World Bank, the IMF and all their good works in the country.

In fact, things were so calm and polite inside the heavily fortified confines of the *Salle des Banquiers* in the Congress Palace that some Malian journalists described the meeting as a "charade" and "a joke." The Malian government under President Alpha Oumar Konaré had orchestrated the event very carefully indeed, making sure the visit had no advance publicity. That ensured that groups opposed to World Bank and IMF policies had little chance to mobilize for demonstrations.

Outside, I found several people from non-governmental development organizations pacing the pavement, furious to be locked out of a meeting where they could have given voice to their concerns about what was ailing Africa. Kevin Ray from the British NGO, International Service, was one of those left standing outside in the heat. He said he had just heard about the meeting on BBC radio, and knew that it would be too late to rally any of his Malian development partners in local NGOs, so he decided to rush down himself to attend the meeting with civil society, "to see what it's all about." Unfortunately, as he found out, the doors were locked. "We couldn't get in, so we're talking to you instead," he said, laughing. Ray had grown up in Africa, and had adopted the African saving grace of laughing instead of crying over frustrating realities that were *faits accomplis*.

That evening, my colleagues from the BBC and I asked the information officers to arrange interviews with a couple of IMF technocrats and Vice Presidents of the World Bank – there are a lot of those who had accompanied their bosses to Africa.

My main aim was to put to them a list of questions that BBC listeners in Africa had sent to producers in London for a program called *Postmark Africa*. These started with why the Bretton Woods institutions refused to cancel the debt, then asked where all the money had gone from all those loans and why it had been loaned in the first place, and to whom exactly.

My colleague, Saïd Penda, from the BBC French service, wanted answers to the same questions, which he fired off like bullets, cutting off his interviewee each time he resorted to technocratic mumbo-jumbo rather than offer a lucid reply that would fit into a short radio report. We had each completed one interview when the Cameroonian woman who had flown out from Washington in her official capacity as an IMF information officer put an abrupt end to the interviews.

"You can't ask questions like that," she said, pulling us aside. "Look, you'll never get anywhere as journalists if you ask questions like that."

Saïd, himself Cameroonian, studied her for a moment – moving his eyes from her impeccably made-up face, down the length of her very expensive red skirt and jacket suit to her stockinged legs and shining black stilettos. "If by 'getting anywhere,'" he said, "you mean getting myself into a traitorous position like yours, then you're right, I'll never get anywhere."

After that, we were cut off. No more one-on-one interviews with World Bank VPs or IMF VIPs. It wasn't until the end of the two-day visit, during a press conference with Wolfensohn, Köhler and the participating presidents – Omar Bongo of Gabon, Abdoulaye Wade of Senegal and Olusegun Obasanjo of Nigeria – that I was finally able to pose some of the questions from BBC listeners in Africa.

One of these, how Africa's massive debt had been incurred, was passed on to President Wade of Senegal, who had just been elected in his country. He said that on assuming office he was shown the figures for what his country actually owed to the Western donor countries and the Bretton Woods institutions, in the billions of dollars, all loaned presumably to foster development in Senegal. He said he then made a tour of his own country, looking at the villages without running water, the ailing railroad, the terrible roads, the squalor and poverty of the market area of his capital, Dakar, and asked himself where all the money had gone, what his country had to show for all that debt.

James Wolfensohn made it clear that they had come to Africa to try to change the negative image of the Bretton Woods institutions and described the summit with African presidents in glowing terms as "a break from the past." But he and his entourage studiously avoided any talk of cancelling debt, saying only that debt relief had already reduced it by 65 percent.

Horst Köhler said, "Debt had built up because there was not made good use of the money and this had two sides, not good policy at the receiver side and not good policy at the creditor side." He promised that, "Credit will remain an important instrument to finance development, to get out of poverty." He sidestepped the question of debt cancellation.

Gabonese President Omar Bongo countered, saying that full debt cancellation was the only solution for poverty in Africa. It's a shame that this came from President Bongo. His own wealth is legendary. At this time, he was married to the daughter of another wealthy African president, Denis Sassou-Nguesso of the Republic of Congo. I had watched Madam Bongo parade about in this same Congress Palace, draped with the worth of a health-care centre dangling in jewels from her neck and ears, while attending an African First Ladies' conference on the staggering death rates of African women giving birth. A friend who worked with the United Nations in Mali told me that Madam Bongo's daytime jewels were nothing compared with those she donned for the dinners in the evening. She had sat across the table from the First Lady of Gabon one evening, wishing she had sunglasses to protect her eyes from the slivers of light cast by Madam Bongo's cascading neck-to-navel sheath of diamonds.

President Bongo had lived *very* well from the oil revenue in his country and been one of France's main men on the continent. So he wasn't well-placed to complain about economic injustice or inequities exacerbated by World Bank and IMF policies; he was himself one of those leaders that had enriched himself greatly at the trough of foreign capital – especially oil money – moving through his country. But he still evoked gales of laughter when he said that for the wealthy Bretton Woods institutions, debt cancellation in Africa could be written off as "a small loss of profits."

As the press conference wrapped up, Horst Köhler made his way down the aisle of the conference room in the Congress Palace, where I was packing up my camera and recording equipment. He reached for my hand, pumped it heartily up and down and said to me, "Don't worry, we are changing, we are changing!" He looked as if he meant it.

The people on the streets, however, were not impressed. Those I interviewed said they hadn't bothered to pay any attention to the coverage on state radio and television because it was "more lies." "It's a waste of time and money," said one roadside trader.

A group of money-changers sitting in front of the main bank in downtown Bamako responded to my questions about the World Bank and IMF visit by saying they would be happiest if all the money flowing into the country in the form of loans was stopped, because "it just comes in through the door and goes out again through the window, making our politicians rich and making us poorer."

In another part of the city, the African Initiative for Ethics and Culture, a coalition opposed to the Bretton Woods policies, summoned the press and delivered a post-mortem on the summit, which they described as "humiliating" and "dishonest." They contended that the World Bank and IMF caused the very poverty they were pretending to cure, and said the two institutions were in no position to speak about democracy and good governance when they themselves were anything but democratic.

One member of the coalition was Aminata Dramane Traoré, a leading light of Mali's civil society. Although I had heard one German development expert working in Mali describe her as a "crazy woman," many Malians respected for her outspoken and articulate critiques of the Bretton Woods operations in Africa, which included two books on the subject. I asked her if it wasn't a good thing that the leaders of the World Bank and IMF had come to Africa to meet with Africans heads of state and, as they said, "to listen." She could barely contain her indignation.

"By coming here, they are just hurting us," she retorted. "They are hurting us. It's not fair. They are not listening. They don't listen. Actually they know what we want; they know what they should do. The *raison d'être* of these institutions is just to make profit. You cannot tell the poorest that you want to alleviate poverty when your *raison d'être* is profit. This meeting was prepared secretly a few days ago; we didn't know about it till a few days ago, [didn't know] who will be the heads of state coming here. Myself, I was not invited as a civil society person to tell these people what I think. They avoid people who tell them the truth."

"But if you read their statistics, if you read their economic indicators," I countered, "they put Mali forward as a great success story."

"Just go in the street," she replied. "Ask the ordinary Malian person the way they are living. It's just pitiful that these people give themselves the right to assess our leaders. They don't have the right to tell African people who is good and who is not. The main issue now is that nowhere in the world you can achieve local democracy while people from outside are dictating to the elected decision-makers what they are supposed to do."

Why, I asked her, didn't Africa's elected decision-makers and leaders just say no to the economic policies of the Bretton Woods institutions?

"Because they need financial means. You know all these Machiavellian strategies for decades to give loans to bad leaders, you know all the story of debt, external debt in Africa, now we are like people in a jail because some people outside suppose that you owe them something. But we don't owe them anything. They took everything from us: mineral, agricultural and now financial resources. It's a shame. Our leaders are supposed to report to us. They [Wolfensohn and Kohler] don't have the right to come [to Africa] and say they are listening; they are not listening. And suddenly you are informed that they are here with 12 heads of state. This can demonstrate how strong they are. We elected 12 heads of state [in Africa] and they are coming today to sit and report to them [Wolfensohn and Kohler]. I want our presidents to report to *us* first!"

Because of the power of the World Bank, some people described it as an "800-pound gorilla." This is not my term for the Bank; I learned it from the woman who was Country Director of the World Bank in Mali in 2000. I had tried repeatedly to obtain an interview with her, or simply meet up for a casual chat that I hoped would touch on corruption in Mali, which Malians said was at an all-time high under their President Alpha Oumar Konaré.

The US and other Western countries continued to praise Mali under President Konaré as a "model democracy" on the African continent, despite the fact that he had come to power for a second five-year term in a seriously flawed election that had been boycotted by the opposition. So I was curious about why all the Western diplomats couldn't say enough good about the Malian president, at the same time that rumours were rampant that the World Bank office had allegedly compiled a list of a hundred well-connected people within and around the government who had gone from rags to riches in the past ten years. They were known as "Mali's Millionaires of Democracy."

I also wanted to know why the World Bank had just postponed Mali's membership in the exclusive new club for pauper nations that had been created for Highly Indebted Poor Countries, commonly referred to as HIPC, for short. HIPC was the Bank's response in 1996 to growing worldwide pressure from civil society, social justice and church groups, and non-governmental organizations and that had long been lobbying for a cancellation of Africa's debt, which they had calculated would be about 350 billion US dollars at the turn of the millennium. The Bretton Woods institutions came up with the HIPC scheme to reduce debts, but only for countries that qualified. To qualify, a country had to conform to a rigid list of economic rules, behave like an obedient pupil in the Bretton Woods school of draconian economic reform.

Mali *seemed* to qualify. Two US secretaries of state, first Madeleine Albright and then her successor, Colin Powell, had flown all the way to Bamako for quick stops, long enough to extol the virtues of Mali's excellent president. Why then, I wanted to know, had the World Bank just postponed Mali's debt relief? What had gone wrong in the model democracy?

This was the question I wanted to put to the World Bank representative. She finally found time to fit me in, not for an interview but for a meal at the city's Thai restaurant, an exclusive little place in Bamako's old downtown, where the cost of a dinner for four was about the same as the average annual per capita income in Mali.

It was clear even before she ordered our Thai delicacies that she had no intention of telling me much of anything about HIPC or why Mali's qualification was being postponed. I suspected it had to do with the new private cell phone company that a few of the president's men had set up, in a very dubious way using state funds and connections.[166] At this point, the revolution in wireless communications was just beginning in Mali, and the president's inner circle was allegedly behind the new and highly lucrative cell phone company.

I asked the World Bank country director if this was what had prompted the delay in Mali's HIPC approval. She shushed me, fingers to her lips, and glanced about the small restaurant, warning me not to mention the name of that company; there were "spies" all over the place.

So I moved to another question many Malians had been asking themselves. Why was the World Bank pressing the Malian government to cut back on bursaries for deserving and needy students in secondary schools in the country, a measure that would preclude anything but primary school education for most Malian youngsters. One of these bursaries was really a tiny amount, about 50 US dollars for *an entire year* to pay lodging, meals, transport for lycée students who often had to move to a city to find a school to attend. She replied tersely that Mali was a poor country that could not afford stipends for its high school students. She did not seem interested in discussing Bank policy.

The meal turned out to be a long and very awkward. I struggled in vain to make polite small-talk as she expounded on her successful career and on offers she had from the World Bank to move on to reform and "save" bigger and richer countries in Africa, Nigeria being one of those. She told me she felt very much like a "missionary."

I asked her if she found it difficult as a young and single woman to hold such a powerful position in a very traditional, male-dominated country like Mali. She said it had been at first, but people had got to know her now, although she admitted she could still silence a room with her entry, as "the 800-pound gorilla."

It was an unfortunate choice of words. In one of those horrendous moments that mortify long after they have cemented themselves like rigor mortis in the memory bank, I suggested that she shouldn't be so hard on herself because round and shapely women were greatly appreciated in Mali and surely she didn't weigh *eight* hundred pounds. After swallowing a couple of times, she corrected me through a grimace intended to be a smile, saying no, she had not been talking about *herself*. "That's what people here call the World Bank," she emphasized. "The 800-pound gorilla."

A few weeks after the disastrous lunch, the Bank held a press conference at its headquarters in Bamako. The press were invited to listen to and ask questions of a blue-eyed gentleman man who had just been named Executive Vice President of the International Finance Corporation (IFC), part of the World Bank Group.[167] He was a soft-spoken German who explained to the Malian press corps how the IFC would be making loans to local entrepreneurs to promote economic growth in Mali.

Throughout his talk, brimming with optimism and rhetoric about fighting poverty with credit and building the private sector, one phrase kept popping up to justify all the reforms that the World Bank and its most powerful members in the West were spreading around the globe.

There is no more room for ideology in government, he said, and privatization was key, be it in energy, communications, water, railways, mines, anything and everything. When Malian journalists asked whether the World Bank was going to force the government to privatize Mali's cotton company, CMDT, he replied obliquely, saying only that governments should limit their role strictly to social services.

A year earlier, the World Bank in Mali had praised the CMDT as a shining example of how a parastatal and partially foreign-owned company could work in Africa, and work well. This was before world prices for cotton hit all-time lows, and the CMDT was still making record amounts of money, which were shared by its French co-owners and the Malian government, with plenty put into local infrastructure in cotton-growing areas because its owners and managers had a vested interest in seeing that their communities benefited from the profits.

Now the World Bank was hinting about the need for the government to break up the CMDT into smaller pieces and sell them off to investors. Privatization was a condition for more loans – and for debt relief. Mali had already sold off the energy company to a French firm (state-owned), the communications company was on the auction block and being 'invested' in by French firms, and Air Afrique – the airline owned jointly by 11 francophone African countries and France – had just been grounded; many of its routes taken over mostly by Air France (which was at that point, still state-owned).[168]

Many Malians were wondering what exactly the World Bank meant by successful privatization of Mali's public sector firms, which had been bought by French state-owned ones. They were deeply concerned about the fate of the CMDT and its employees if it were sold to foreign interests, as other state companies had been. It was true that CMDT suffered from corruption because of the lack of checks and balances on its management, but it was also true that the company and its managers were very much part of the Malian social fabric and deeply rooted in the rural cotton-growing areas where CMDT provided many community development services, including roads and schools, for cotton farmers. Next to the inefficiency and corruption that has been documented in Iraq among the enormous American corporations with close ties to the Bush administration – the supposedly efficient and accountable private sector – the corruption and inefficiency of the parastatal CMDT are truly negligible.[169]

After the press conference, I was able to ask the IFC Vice President some of the questions that preoccupied people in Mali about privatization of the cotton company. I began with the simple question: Did the World Bank intend to force the Malian government to privatize the parastatal cotton company?

He said that governments should stick to social services, health and education. Government should not run business. Government had no place in business.

I asked if that was a yes or a no, if the World Bank intended to force Mali to sell off its cotton company.

He replied that there was no more room for ideology in government.

I said he didn't answer my question, and repeated it.

He repeated that there was no room for ideology in government. That time had passed.

The World Bank country director interrupted me, saying that my time had run out. I tried one more time, asking him for a yes or a no to my question.

He reiterated his point that governments had no business in business, that there was no room for ideology there.

"That sounds like an ideology to me," I said, as I was gently pulled away and firmly told the interview was over.

Frustrated by futile attempts to get direct answers from various World Bank and IMF officials about privatization, debt relief – and also details of how the debts had been incurred – in December 2001, I set out to examine one of the mega-projects in Mali, which at that point accounted for about a third of Mali's 3.3 billion-dollar debt.

The Manantali hydro dam, one of the largest in Africa, was constructed in the 1980s, creating a lake 80 kilometres long and 40 wide. The lake flooded parts of one of Mali's most bio-diverse wildlife reserves, the only one that harboured chimpanzees, an endangered species. After the concrete was poured and the lake filled up, the unfinished dam sat there for a decade.

The foreign experts who conceived it, ostensibly to bring hydro power to Mali, Senegal and Mauritania, and the foreign companies – French, Canadian and German (among others) – that benefited from the contracts to create the massive concrete structure, had long since packed up and gone home.

In 1994, France devalued the West African currency, the CFA franc, by half. The CFA franc was used in former French colonies in Central and West Africa, and remained pegged to the French franc. Overnight, debts in these countries – calculated in US dollars – doubled as the worth of the CFA halved. Instead of owing a quarter of a billion dollars for the construction of the dam, Mali and its neighbours suddenly owed twice that amount.

In 1998, the World Bank, the African Development Bank and also the Canadian International Development Agency (CIDA) agreed to finance a new phase of the Manantali dam, despite numerous studies that had already shown it had caused innumerable health, economic and environmental problems downstream. The Canadian government ignored these, perhaps because a number of Quebec companies stood to benefit from the Canadian financing. The energy watchdog group, Probe International, used Canada's Access to Information Act to learn that CIDA paid almost 20 million dollars (Cdn) for turbines and alternators provided by Sulzer Canada of Quebec, another seven million to a Montreal consulting company for installation supervision and still more for a fishery study done by Roche International of Sainte-Foy, Quebec.[170]

When I visited Manantali in 2001, foreign contractors were back, putting in turbines and a power station to make the dam operational. By the time it would start to produce electricity in 2002, it would have cost about a billion US dollars. This was money loaned to Mali by international financial institutions and paid out to the foreign contractors, money that showed up on Mali's ledgers as debt.

Since only about one percent of Mali's estimated 11 million people had electric power in their homes, approximately 100 thousand people would enjoy Manantali electricity in their homes though all Malians would feel the effects of that debt. Most of Manantali's electric production would go to relatively wealthy city-dwellers in Mali and her neighbours.

By the time the dam was producing power in 2002, the national electricity company, *Energie du Mali*, had been privatized because privatization was a prerequisite for debt relief under HIPC. *Energie du Mali* was sold off to *Energie de France,* and a private operator, SOGEM, had been set up to handle the sale of Manantali power in the three countries. Any profits Mali might have accrued by producing and selling its own hydro power headed out of the country. The new French director of the no-longer-Malian energy company then announced that electricity prices would not drop when Manantali hydro came on-stream, even though it was five times cheaper to produce than the electric power being produced by diesel and gas-turbines in the country.

In the end, even if the dam did produce profits, it would not be the Malian people who would reap them. But some Malians paid an even higher price. When Manantali was constructed, 20 thousand Malians were pushed off their lands to make way for the lake and were promised that they would be resettled with good homes and good lands downstream from the dam.

Fifteen years after their expropriation, I dropped in to the resettlement village of Bamafélé, looking for those good lands and good homes. They were nowhere to be seen. To find them, you had to drive a couple of kilometres upstream towards the dam, to the gated, well-lit compound where foreign contractors stayed. Their compound included a private health centre, a swimming pool and tennis courts.

Damba Dembélé, the school director in Bamafélé, spoke emotionally about the suffering the dam had caused. "Truly, when they told us we would have to leave the land of our ancestors, our farms, our villages, the spirits of our grandparents who still dwell there, it seemed surreal, like a bad dream. We were happy there, we had fertile land. When we were moved to here, we had so many problems – poor land, no pastureland for our animals, and all those problems remain."

Soft-spoken Doubafing Suco told me that at the time of the resettlement she was a teenage student in Dembélé's class. She said the displaced people were cut off not just from their land, but also their past. "For the elderly people, it was a catastrophe," she said. "No one wanted to leave their villages. They wept and wept and wept; no one was happy, but what could we do? When we arrived in the new sites we noticed that lots of people were dying, almost all the old people died shortly after we were resettled."

Dembélé looked up at the high tension wires carrying power from the dam to distant cities, and then made a sweeping gesture that took in the entire village of Bamafélé, drawing my attention to all that the displaced villagers did not have – no health centre, no fertile land, no running water … and no electricity. He said he was tired of promises and projects that never bear fruit.

"I believe that the people who should have benefited first from that electricity were the population along the Bafing River because we suffered most by leaving behind our villages. Really, we were not involved in the conception of this project; billions [of CFA francs] have been invested here. The first to benefit should have been us. Instead we're the very last – that's if there are any benefits for us."

As we sat together in Bamafélé, watching barefooted children chase guinea fowl and pound millet in a tall mortar, a plane circled overhead, bringing in a World Bank delegation to monitor progress of the Manantali power station. The project was financed with an additional half a billion dollars worth of credit – of debt. Dembélé watched the plane until it descended out of sight, landing at the Manantali airstrip. He turned to me. "Every time delegations come here we tell them, we repeat the same things, how we were forced to move here, how we live here, but it always falls on deaf ears, they don't listen."

Back in Bamako, I again called up the World Bank office. I wanted to know how, exactly, the World Bank was easing the burden of debt, for which Mali (and Africa) clearly had very little to show. Fortunately for me, there had been a change at the helm at the World Bank Mali office and I was able to secure an interview with the new country director.

During his visit to Bamako, James Wolfensohn had said that it was clear that debt relief could free up money for social purposes, and that "the impact of no debt relief in the past has been that too much money has been used for debt repayment and too little for social purposes and so the very simple rationale behind the HIPC is to make the balance more equal."

But what did a country need to do to make the balance more equal and qualify for HIPC debt relief? That is what I hoped Judith Presse, the new World Bank Resident Representative in Mali, would explain.

"Mali or any other country involved in the initiative," she said, "needs to show that they are managing their macroeconomic framework in a sensible way and that they are managing their policy in a sensible way, using funds responsibly. Also it may involve continuing programs of privatization where that is appropriate. The other area is that they actually undertake and prepare a poverty reduction strategy, participatory, with the public at large, the civil society, NGOs; all give their input on how best to focus the debt relief that the country will be benefiting from. That strategy needs to be prepared and reviewed by the international community."

"But how, exactly, does it work?" I persisted. "What does it actually mean for, say, Mali?" She turned my questions over to Youssouff Tchiam, Senior Economist at the World Bank office in Mali, who laid it out this way.

"Debt will be reduced by 817 million [US] dollars over [a] 30-year-period," he said, "with about 42 million [US dollars] for the first ten years, and 22 million for the remaining 20 years. Instead of paying back [this money to creditors], they will spend it to fight against poverty. In year 2002, if for example Mali has to pay 100 million [US dollars] to the World Bank, they repay only 62 million, and 38 million will be used for health, water supply and to fight against poverty."

Tchiam admitted that the debt relief applied only to the debt as it stood at the end of 1999, at 3.3 billion US dollars. He said that any new loans, any debt incurred after that deadline, including all those being dispersed in the official 'fight against poverty' that involved expensive foreign expertise, were not covered by the program.

Another Malian economist in the employ of the World Bank spoke with me later about debt relief, in a casual conversation that was off the record and thus much more candid about the HIPC initiative. He suggested it was a smokescreen that would do little to solve the debt problem, but would make it look like as if something were being done.

He explained it this way. In the late 1990s, Africa's debt had reached crisis proportions. It had been building for three decades, while international lending agencies and the donor community had been handing out big loans to the continent. The money, he said, had mostly gone into mega-projects or studies that employed the services of Western companies and experts, or into invisible numbered bank accounts and other offshore holdings of an African oligarchy created and supported by the West. The people of Africa were left with countless white elephants, a super-rich class of overlords versed in the fine arts of international corruption and offshore accounting, and with a debt that precluded much spending by their fledging democracies on health or education – human investments that would let Africa develop itself in its own way.

By the late 1990s, international pressure was mounting for debt cancellation. African governments were spending more to service their debts than they were on health and education combined. The Bretton Woods institutions and their major shareholders in the West recognized the problem, and also realized that if something were not done, some of the poorest countries would soon not be able to keep up the payments and might start to default on debt payments. Hence, the need for the HIPC program. At least that was the cynical view of the Malian economist working for the Bank in Mali.

HIPC would be limited to only the world's poorest countries. To qualify, the countries would have to meet free market conditionalities and spend the money that would have gone to service their debts on health and education programs. But in the view of the Malian economist, that money was just theoretical. He said the World Bank knew that the countries involved had no money with which to service their debts, and thus would have no money to put into social programs. But that didn't stop the World Bank from boasting that it was helping African governments pay for health and education, and relieving debt at the same time. He called it a "charade."

Aminata Dramane Traoré was less charitable in her assessment of HIPC.

"I think the HIPCs are against the poorest, mainly youth and women. I don't want to think in terms of debt relief, [this debt] relief means a lot of mechanisms will be working in order to tell decision-makers to do this and that. And what they want us to do is to keep the door open for what they call foreign investors … we are still waiting for them, they are not coming at all, except in water and electricity, to sell services to the poorest. It's also an argument for the IMF and World Bank to interfere not only in macroeconomic decisions, but even in the political area. We are supposed to be a democracy, but they have the tools to dictate to elected decision-makers what they are supposed to do."

"But they say there that their priority is fighting poverty," I said. "In fact they're even dispensing money to …"

She cut me short. "They are producing poverty!" she cried. "They are producing poverty … even to be eligible for the HIPC, your debt is supposed to be 250 percent of your exports, which means you are supposed to be in debt up to a certain level. They push for more indebtedness … and it's in their own interest, because they are selling money."

I tried again. "But the World Bank here says that the HIPC by eliminating 38 percent of debt by reducing repayment by that much, money can go into education."

"Why do they refuse to cancel? Why do they avoid this central question? Do you want to help? Or do you want to play? It's like a game. You play with the life of people, the poorest."

I asked Judith Presse at the World Bank if it wouldn't be fairer to eliminate the debt than to reduce it minimally over 30 years with a complex debt relief scheme that locked HIPC countries into a fixed set of public economic and social policies.

"I think a 40 percent cut in the debt is more than minimal," she replied. "… as for totally cutting the debt, that's really an issue for the member countries of the World Bank who constitute the Board of Directors and they would have to take a decision on that. That is not the management of the Bank who could take a decision like that; it's the shareholders, the owners, who have to do that."

The major shareholders of the World Bank are the wealthy developed countries, with the US heading the list. The president of the World Bank has always been an American, chosen by the United States. The head of the IMF is traditionally chosen by Europe and is, by convention, European. The Paris Club is an informal group of financial officials from 19 of the world's wealthiest nations.[171] It generally takes recommendations on debtor nations from the IMF and offers HIPC debtors more leeway than it does other countries, which is another carrot or stick that can be used to persuade African governments to swallow the free-market economic policies.

Today, the Bretton Woods institutions have stopped calling the economic reform "structural adjustment," which African economists agree failed rather spectacularly across Africa, causing untold hardship and political instability. The favoured recipe for Africa has become the Poverty Reduction Strategy Paper (PRSP), drawn up by and for each country to tackle poverty from all sides, with a good deal of influence from the Bretton Woods institutions that still seem to believe that one size fits all.

The consensus of African economic researchers who gathered in Dakar, Senegal, in 2005 for a conference on how they might make their voices heard in African policy-making is that the Poverty Reduction Papers are just Structural Adjustment Programs in a new disguise.[172] Economist William Easterly calls these Papers another of those Big Plans of "Planners" who are far removed from the problem and are unaccountable when their plans fail.[173]

Widespread criticism and campaigns led by civil societies and NGOs have, however, not been in vain. In 2005, 139 donor governments, multilateral agencies and governments from developing countries agreed to sign up to the Paris Declaration of Aid Effectiveness. Donors committed themselves to giving more ownership to governments in developing countries. They committed to more harmonization of their cumbersome procedures and to aligning their efforts more with those of the governments of developing nations. They also agreed to ensure aid really was channelled towards poverty reduction. Such measures, according to the European Network on Debt and

Development (EURODAD), a coalition of 48 NGOs from 15 European nations, could make aid more effective in achieving the Millennium Development Goals.

In a study of aid in Sierra Leone, EURODAD recommends that donors stop tying their own aid disbursements to the harsh and rigid economic conditions set by the IMF.[174] It also points out that ownership of development is still in the hands of donors and lending agencies. These tend to meet behind closed doors with governments in developing countries, so that the public and civil societies do not know how much money is coming into their countries or how it is being spent. This undermines democracy and reduces the power the public should have to demand accountability from their own government. In addition, donors tend to assess how much ownership is handed over to a national government by looking at the alignment of its policies with those in its Poverty Reduction Strategy Papers, which are developed mostly by the World Bank as a condition for the HIPC. EURODAD calls this "circular donor-driven logic."

And according to ActionAid, the IMF continues to impose strict conditions on aid that actually impair efforts to achieve the Millennium Development Goals. One of these, extremely low wage caps on the civil service, makes it impossible for governments to pay teachers anything more than a pittance, or to hire enough teachers to reach the Millennium Goal of universal primary education.[175]

In July 2005, the G8 leaders meeting in Scotland agreed to forgive the debts of Africa's least developed countries, provided that they adhered to the same conditions the HIPC imposed on them.[176] The IMF protested, saying this would reduce their financial capacity of dispersing loans for development and investment on the continent. In January 2006, debts owed by 19 of the world's poorest countries to the IMF were written off. But in March that year, Oxfam noted that key promises made by then British Prime Minister Tony Blair's African Commission to ensure fairer trade and to control arms dealing had not been kept.

On April 1, 2005, US Deputy Defence Secretary, Paul Wolfowitz, founding member of the neo-conservative and hawkish think tank, Project for a New American Century, a believer in pre-emptive strikes and of "deterring potential competitors from even aspiring to a larger regional or global role," was named the new president of the World Bank.[177]

He said poverty reduction would be the "primary mission" of the Bank under his leadership, "especially in Africa, the continent which most desperately needs it."[178] He also said he would focus on the scourge of corruption, refusing loans to corrupt leaders.

Two years later, Wolfowitz himself was accused of nepotism in a scandal after offering his partner, Shaha Riza, who also worked at the Bank, a new position with a salary close to 200 thousand US dollars. After fighting to remain on as head of the World Bank and even apologizing for his handling of the matter, he was eventually forced to step down in June 2007. President George Bush then pushed for an American successor, and didn't have to look far to find one.

In June 2007, Robert Zoellick, former US Deputy Secretary of State under Condoleezza Rice and a campaigner for George Bush in the 2000 elections, was named president of the World Bank. After his appointment, the Global AIDS Alliance described him as "a close friend to the brand-name pharmaceutical industry" that has so often blocked generic medication for people affected by HIV/AIDS.[179] Greenpeace drew attention to his role in mounting a legal challenge against the European Union on its refusal to adopt bio-tech (genetically modified) crops and food, which are now being pushed on Africa as well.

Zoellick is also a former Chief Executive Designate at the Center for Strategic and International Studies (CSIS), and is a former Executive at Goldman-Sachs a "leading global investment banking, securities and investment management firm." Like Paul Wolfowitz before him, he is also a signatory on the extremely hawkish letter from the Project for the American Century sent to Bill Clinton, calling already in 1998 for the overthrow of Saddam Hussein in Iraq.[180] He is hardly a neutral figure or someone with any obvious understanding of, or interest in, the needs or realities of the people of Africa.

I keep recalling that moment back in 2001, when an enthusiastic and apparently sincere Horst Köhler gripped my hand and assured me that "We [the World Bank and IMF] are changing." I wonder what kind of change he was talking about.

The World Bank continues to strive, it claims, for poverty reduction and to reform Africa's economy with privatization schemes, subsidized investment opportunities for large multinationals and with attempts to develop and impose taxation schemes on the African people, right down to the pre-teenage girls trying to sell a few roasted peanuts from a tray they carry about on their heads. Yet World Bank employees are themselves, mostly tax-exempt.

After the scandal with Wolfowitz and the high-salaried position he was offering to his partner in the Bank, the *Wall Street Journal*, which defended Wolfowitz and blamed Europeans and World Bank staff for his resignation, nevertheless had this to say about the World Bank and its 10 thousand employees, "… no fewer than 1,396 have salaries higher than the U.S. Secretary of State; clearly 'fighting poverty' does not mean taking a vow of poverty at 'multilateral' institutions … Even sweeter, all of this is tax-free to non-Americans. U.S. employees have to pay U.S. tax but have their income taxes reimbursed by the bank."[181]

Salaries of UN diplomats are also free of tax; and anyone who heads a UN mission in a country – the United Nations Development Program, UNICEF, World Food Program, and so on – is granted diplomatic status, with all that entails, including luxurious housing, a vehicle with driver, moving allowances, the whole kit and diplomatic caboodle. The right-wing CATO Institute refuses to acknowledge the immense value and accomplishments of the UN in development, peacekeeping and peace-making missions, and also in helping from time to time and to a small extent to act as a counter-weight to multinational corporations in Africa. CATO's outright condemnation of the only world body that exists to struggle for noble human goals of sharing and equity on this planet is unfortunate at best, downright irresponsible at worst. But the Institute does make some discussion-worthy points about the privilege that the UN allows itself: "Salaries of administrative staff include an 'assessment' used to offset tax liability in most cases, so many of the staff salaries are tax-free as well. In addition, UN employees receive monthly rent subsidies of up to $3,800 and annual education grants of up to $12,675 per child."[182]

Fighting poverty around the world appears to be quite a profitable business for some.

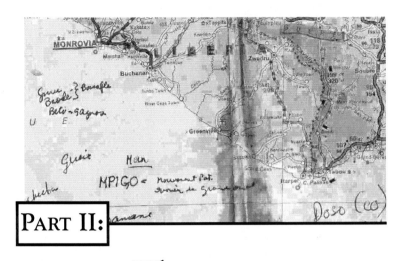

PART II

The inevitable curse

9

Coffin of gold

The happy conviction of European conquerors that they were bringing civilisation to Africans against whom the Gates of Eden had barely closed may still have its adherents, yet not among those who have looked at the evidence.

Basil Davidson[183]

I've spent many years trying to understand the hubris of those in financial institutions who make decisions that affect millions of lives in Africa. I've spent many years trying to understand why so much of the world continues dismiss a continent of more than 50 different countries and regard it as if it were one monolithic never-ending disaster zone unworthy of respect or of the right to be listened to. In the end, I learned most by recalling my own ignorance, my own complete lack of knowledge of the continent before I had the good fortune to live there.

After 12 years of basic schooling, with its countless history classes and hours of reading social studies, history and geography textbooks; after memorizing dates and names of civilizations, kings and queens and emperors and the wars they fought, the lands they conquered, their great intellectual feats; and then after several more years of university, I don't recall reading about or hearing a single reference to a great African leader, thinker or civilization.

Rome was covered. Greece was covered. Mesopotamia and so-called classic civilizations: also covered. But sub-Sahara Africa's place in our entire school curriculum in eastern Canada was to be found on a very few pages in a grade four social studies text, where we read about a boy called Bunga who lived in a mud hut surrounded by banana plants. He had no discernible or remarkable human culture or civilization. When we children got together in the playground at recess after learning about Bunga, we invented a language for him and called "ooga booga" to each other. I would like to think we were not being disparaging. But of course we were. Our curriculum was disparaging.[184]

We learned about the 'great' white explorers who had 'discovered' continents such as Africa and the Americas, as if they were empty lands awaiting the arrival of these Europeans. As far as I knew from my schooling in Canada, Africa had no civilization at all. At best, it was treated as a great black hole. At worst, it was portrayed – as it often is even today in our media – as a poor, squalid, pitiful, perpetually hot and hopeless continent.

There was certainly nothing about great and learned scholars, immense wealth and knowledge of the principles of democracy, equality, tolerance and social justice. All of these seemed to be exclusive to the West, and its civilization, according to our curriculum. The same can be said of many curricula in Africa itself, which have tended to use European books and sources and their points of view. Malian historian, philosopher and Africanist, the late Amadou Hampate Bâ, captured the problem this way: "Until the lion tells the story, the story of the hunt will always glorify the hunter."

One begins to wonder how Africans have managed to survive and thrive over the 250 (or more) thousand years since *Homo sapiens* evolved in Africa, without Western development aid. Surely Africans should all have died out long ago if they are as unable to feed themselves and anxious to kill each other as media stereotypes would have us believe?

I do recall spending time in school learning about the great pyramids of ancient Egypt. Like many before me, I fell under the spell of the secrets of the pharoahs' tombs, developing a great fascination for the golden masks and ancient treasures looted from Africa. But somehow, it didn't register that Egypt was on the African continent and certainly the ancient Egyptians were never referred to as Africans.

As a teenager I remember reading Erich von Däniken's book, *Chariots of the Gods,* which was later turned into a blockbuster movie.[185] In these masterpieces of not-very-subtle prejudices, von Däniken looked at great architectural feats of ancient peoples not considered to be part of the cradle of European civilization – the Egyptian pyramids, for example, and the Inca desert drawings in Peru and Mayan burial tablets in Palenque, Mexico. He concluded that these great works had been inspired by or else actually were the work of extraterrestrials, the implication being that surely all those little brown people so far from Europe could not have accomplished such things all on their own.[186]

In *Chariots of the Gods*, von Däniken credited aliens for the great non-European endeavours, and he missed mentioning the remarkable feats of people in sub-Sahara Africa – as if there simply weren't any worth mentioning. For a long time, I didn't see the flaw in this Eurocentric reasoning. I wasn't alone. Von Däniken's first book sold 60 million copies. After 26 books and an extraterrestrial theme-park in Switzerland, he claims to be the most successful non-fiction writer of all time.[187]

Eurocentric views do sell well, and not just among Europeans; people all over the world have succumbed to them.

In a less extreme way, it seems the great civilizations that were recognized as such in much of our literature and in school texts tended to be those that emerged in what we tautologically called the cradle of civilization. That is, civilizations that laid the foundation for ours today.

In 1955, in his introductory book to West African history, British professor, J.D. Fage, succinctly depicted the circular reasoning that has inflated Europe's opinion of itself and shaped the way it has regarded and treated Africa for centuries: "In the case of Africa in general and West Africa in particular, a number of factors tended to strengthen these Europeans' sense of superiority. They were woefully ignorant of the achievements of Africans in the past. They then knew nothing, for example, of the great life of Ife and Benin. When this did begin to be revealed to them, they at once assumed that it could not be purely African achievement: it must stem from some forgotten influence from the classical Mediterranean civilization that lay behind their own culture. They knew very little of the great African empires of the past, Ghana, Mali, Songhay and the like."[188] These covered huge territories that covered vast swaths of the continent, and to it can be added many more all over Africa, in what are today Zimbabwe, Ethiopia, Nigeria and others.

A great many people in Africa kept much to themselves in relatively quiet villages, governed by low-key traditional chiefs accountable to elders, who ruled by consensus. They kept the peace without any centralized hierarchy and without military force or imperial ambitions. Unfortunately, there has been a tendency for some Western people to dismiss these and similar cultures around the world, including native ones in North America, as primitive or uncivilized. Because their greatest constructs are not physical – such as intricate social systems designed to keep harmony among themselves and with the natural resources on which they depend for survival – these peoples are overlooked by those seeking the great monuments, pyramids and walls that, to them, attest to advanced civilizations. Alas, these seem to be the criteria that many in the West use to decide which peoples or cultures are advanced and which are evolutionary backwaters, worth annihilation and perhaps the centrefold of an adventure travel magazine just before they vanish.

African civilizations and achievements were and are pretty much off the Western map. They didn't make it into any curriculum I followed, nor into the anthropology texts I studied, which focused more on Africans living in tribes with low-level chieftaincies that governed by consensus. Early anthropologists often reinforced and perpetuated the myth that cultural evolution followed a straight line towards progress, toward the European ideal.

Polish anthropologist Bronislaw Malinowski founded the school of functional anthropology that took a holistic approach to the study of all the interacting components of a culture. He also taught at some of the most prestigious universities in the Western world and conducted field work with tribal cultures all over the world. Nevertheless, this illustrious European intellectual concluded: "Looking from far and *above, from our high places of safety in the developed civilization,* it is easy to see all the crudity and irrelevance of magic. But without its power and guidance early man could not have mastered his practical difficulties as he has done, nor could man have advanced to *the higher stages of civilization.*"[189] (emphasis added)

Many of the ideas about Africa and Africans that were formed and spread by early colonists and explorers reek of ignorance, hubris and racism. Yet they are still circulating, sometimes at a subconscious level, in some sections of European society a century after they were spread.

Here is a journal entry from 1863 about the Latooka people of Sudan by the British explorer, Sam Baker, whose forays along the Nile were supposed to be humanitarian: "I wish the black philanthropists of England could see Africa's heart and entrails as I do; much of the sympathy would subside. Human nature viewed in its crude state as pictured among African savages is quite on a level with brute nature, and not to be compared with the noble simplicity of the 'dog.' There is no gratitude; no pity; no love; no self denial; no idea of duty; no religion; but greediness, covetousness, ingratitude, selfishness, cruelty. All are thieves; all are idle; all are envious, and ready to plunder their neighbors."[190]

More than a century later, I have heard similar rhetoric and loathing coming from the mouths of a few Westerners in Africa; some were in the oil or mining business and some were development experts and some worked in grassroots NGOs claiming to be charitable.

Worse still is that I have occasionally heard the same kind of comments coming from the mouths of Africans themselves, sometimes about other ethnic groups, sometimes about whole nations, and sometimes about the whole continent. Self-loathing is a tragic and enduring legacy of colonialism and it's a by-product of neo-colonial interference in Africa, which continues to dismiss and denigrate African traditions, knowledge and faiths.

During his visit to Africa in 1998, the very first significant trip to the continent by an American president, Bill Clinton made a remarkable admission even if it was an audacious understatement: "I think it is worth pointing out that the United States has not always done the right thing by Africa. But perhaps the worst sin America ever committed about Africa was the sin of neglect and ignorance."[191] Leaving aside for a moment other significant sins – including slavery, America's covert operations, or just the furthering of American interests on the continent to the detriment of African interests – Clinton's point about the sin of ignorance was a valid and important one.

I now know – but only because I had the privilege of living in Africa for so many years – that sub-Sahara Africa did indeed see the rise and fall of many centralized empires that were rich enough, stratified enough and belligerent enough to conform to Western notions of what constitutes a civilization. One of those was the Mali Empire. When I landed in that country in 1997 to live and work, I had a lot of history to catch up on and lots to learn about Mali and its ancient empire.

It is a truly humbling and humiliating experience for an adult to start at the beginning like a child. It means learning from scratch everything about an entire nation, its many groups of people and their histories.

Fortunately, there was no shortage of history teachers in Mali. Just about every man, woman and child in the country was immersed in, incredibly well-versed in and inseparable from their own past, of which they were also inordinately proud. They were more than eager to fill in hopelessly ignorant newcomers on the Mali Empire and its great leaders, starting with its founder, Sundiata Keita. Seemingly without exception, Malians – from our elderly landlord, to the welder who came to work on window frames in the house, to politicians and journalists, or just men and women on the street – could and would tell me about Keita, their great ancient leader. Eight hundred years earlier, Keita almost succeeded in putting an end to the hegemony of quarrelling city states in West Africa, bringing many of them in under the fold of the Mali Empire. At one point Keita gathered leaders of these smaller nation states together in what is today the village of Siby,[192] nestled in the red cliffs of the Mandingo Mountains about 60 kilometres west of Bamako for a conference that would produce a prototype for a democratic constitution.

Keita was not only a remarkably astute military leader and emperor, he was also relatively progressive on the issues of human rights and equality, working with some success to have slavery phased out and to have slave-owners incorporate their slaves into their own families. Keita governed an empire that would become at its zenith, one of the richest civilizations on earth, even by Western definition. At one point, it stretched from what is now northern Nigeria right across to the West African coast.

One of the reasons for the growth of the empire was gold, which was mined in what are today the countries of Mali and Guinea, and was transported along the trade routes that crisscrossed the empire. These trade routes linked northern Africa, the Middle East and southern Europe with peoples south of the Sahara Desert in Africa's forested coastlands.

Malians know all about their golden history and the great feats of Sundiata Keita, who remains an icon in much of West Africa today. They also know that gold helped create that flourishing and wealthy civilization.

They delight in reciting to visitors the saga of another great emperor, Kanku (King of all Kings) Musa. He made the *hajj* pilgrimage to Mecca in 1324 AD, travelling with an entourage of 60 thousand porters and 500 slaves, each carrying a golden staff weighing about two kilograms, in a caravan of 100 camels. Each camel carried 130 kilograms of gold.

As Kanku Musa moved east across Africa, he had a mosque constructed in every village through which he passed, including the Djingereber Mosque in Timbuktu, in which the people of Timbuktu still pray today.

When the emperor reached Cairo and began handing out lavish gifts of gold, the sudden glut of the precious metal on the market made the world price plummet by half, and the name "Mali" became synonymous with incredible wealth and with gold.

This was at a time that Western Europe was just emerging from the Middle Ages, and the Renaissance was just a glimmer on the Medieval horizon. During the Dark Ages in Europe from 600 to 1000 AD, the Andalusian civilization that encompassed North Africa and southern Europe, Africa's Moors provided Europe with its scientific foundations and scholarship that would eventually lead to the European Renaissance.[193]

Futile or not, I like to amuse myself by musing about what would have happened had Kanku Musa made his way not east towards Mecca but north instead, from sunny Africa into cold and dreary Europe in the winter of 1324 AD. The black emperor from Africa might have looked around at Medieval Europe, and decided that its filth, gloom, disease and misery earned it the name of the Dark Continent.

European culture is by no means the only one that makes unfair judgements about other continents, peoples and perspectives; this has been an unfortunate pattern throughout human history and remains so today. But because Western culture has been so powerful over the past few centuries, unfair Western judgements have been translated into policies that have helped to diminish – and sometimes destroy – other cultures and peoples.

Given the tiresome belief that prevailed and still prevails among some northern people with supremacist views, that the West has a monopoly on civilization, holiness and scholarship, I suppose it's no surprise that our history books have ignored the Mali Empire. And that they've neglected to mention any of the other great civilizations, or the small ones with no great leaders or buildings or military forces, which flourished in Africa long before there were any pedantic colonists or fervent missionaries trying to march Africans towards Western-style progress and doctrines of development.

Fortunately, Malians don't need foreign historians or even history books to tell them about their own past. They recall Mali's Age of Gold as if it were yesterday. Or as if it were connected directly to their today, which it is, really, thanks to their griots: the oral historians who remind them constantly of their own heritage and ancestry.

Unfortunately, Malians don't seem to have the same wealth of knowledge when it comes to the gold coming out of their soils today. Perhaps that's because the gold doesn't seem to be doing them a whole lot of good. Each year the United Nations ranks Mali near the very bottom of the list of the world's least developed countries, with sorry statistics on life expectancy, early childhood and mother morbidity, access to safe drinking water, formal education and health care. None of these conveys much of the human drama and courage of Malians in their struggle to make it from one day to the next.

I haven't tried to survive on less than a dollar a day, so the only way I can try to grasp how little that really is, is by considering my own spending habits. What cash most Malians, indeed most Africans, see in a year I might spend on cat food – or on deodorized, clumping kitty litter.

Since the dismal statistics in Mali aren't quickly changing for the better, even as Mali's gold production rises each year and gold prices rise, we again have the question of who exactly is profiting.

When I put this question one day to some Malian friends, they replied with indignation. However, their anger was not directed at those taking the gold out of the country. "If Canadians were so stupid that they allowed Malians to come and take all their gold for big profits, then we would do it. If Malians are so stupid they allow foreigners to take all our gold for big profits, then the fault is our own," said Amadou, a classical pianist who earned a few dollars each night playing Las Vegas style lounge music in a Bamako hotel, frequented by foreign business people and mining executives.

The average citizen of a G8 country may not know immediately where to find Burkina Faso, Mali, Niger or Sierra Leone on the world map – four countries which along with Guinea Bissau constitute the five least developed countries on the planet.[194] But the Executive Boards of mining giants such as AngloGold and Barrick Gold do. Important people sit in those boardrooms with their eyes, and hands, on precious resources the world over. Canadian-based Barrick Gold has worked extensively in war-torn areas of the Democratic Republic of Congo. Barrick's Board has included Canada's former prime minister, Brian Mulroney and former US President George H.W. Bush as "Honorary Senior Advisor to Barrick Gold Corporation."[195]

Investors are constantly on the look-out for Africa's gold, diamonds, titanium, base metals, uranium and other natural resources. And they know very well where these countries are and whether the presidents and governments there are malleable – as African presidents beholden to lending agencies tend to be.

It is often easier to find out from the business pages of our newspapers what lies under the soils of African countries than it is to find out from the features and news pages anything about the people who live on their surface.

Sometimes, it's even easier to find out about mineral deposits or mining operations in Africa from the business pages of major Western newspapers than it is to find out about them even in Africa itself. Despite numerous attempts during my first three years in Mali, I was not able to gain access to any of the gold mines in the country. All I could glean were scattered hints that all was not well in Gold Country to the west, near the regional capital Kayes, home of the giant Sadiola mine.

There was no paved road to Kayes. Forty years after Mali's independence from France there was no paved road leading anywhere west of Bamako. To cover the 450 kilometres of rough mud road and track between the capital city and Kayes could take days in an ordinary car, or be a one-day marathon in a four-wheel drive vehicle, and that only during the dry season. During the rains, it might be impossible to get there by road. There was a railway dating back to colonial times, with a train of aging Canadian cars. They ran on a tired track that led from Bamako to Dakar in neighbouring Senegal, passing through Kayes. The train derailed frequently and bridges sometimes washed away in heavy rains.

The gold mining companies avoided ground routes and used small planes to move between Bamako and their mines around Kayes. Teachers from the American International School of Bamako regularly visited their branch school near Sadiola, using a plane offered them by the gold mining companies. One teacher described the situation around Sadiola as a kind of "apartheid," with a walled city where the mostly white South African (as well as Canadian, American and other) mining executives lived in astounding luxury. Isolated on grounds that had been expropriated from ordinary Malians, who were no longer welcome there – except as servants.

Malian reporters in Kayes wrote of numerous trucks loaded with cyanide overturning on treacherous roads in the area and spilling the toxin all over the place with no clean-up operations at all. In 1998,

82 local community groups had banded together to form an organization called Living Forces. Its members regularly begged the government to do something to ensure the safe handling of all the toxic substances that are used in or produced by the region's gold mines, specifically citing cyanide and hydrochloric acid. The government ignored
their complaints and did nothing to rectify the glaring omissions in
Mali's contractual agreements with the multinational mining conglomerates operating in the area, which failed to require those companies to contribute to the construction of safe roads or infrastructure. The Living Forces Community Group called the foreign mining
conglomerate a "state within a state."

With these stories in hand, I went to see the then minister of
mines and water, a left-leaning, outspoken university professor not
long for his post. He complained bitterly about how the giants in the
gold business, AngloGold and Randgold, played impoverished countries in the region off each other, pushing down the percentage of
gold revenue that the governments of the various countries asked for.
He said they threatened that if Mali wouldn't come down to a percentage lower than, say, Ghana, or Burkina Faso, the company would
not work there. The corporations and those who invested in them
probably called this good business. The Malian minister called it
"blackmail."

At the same time, he said, Mali did not dare to demand too
much, lest it upset the World Bank and IMF, both of which were
pushing the African governments to open doors to foreign investors
to help develop their countries – and help them service their debts.
Donor countries that are also creditors may not care all that much if
foreign investors are plunderers or not. In fact, until very recently
when China and other Asian countries entered the fray, the plunderers of Africa's resources came almost exclusively from the Western
countries that are often collectively called the donor community.
With some exceptions, Western diplomats seem to be in place primarily to take care of such business and to encourage, in the most diplomatic terms, the local politicians to keep the doors open to investors,
if they know what's good for them. It often is good for the local Africa
elite to stay open for business; hefty bribes from foreign investors
often help cement local support for a mining or oil concession or any

large construction contract. Whether it's good for the local people isn't necessarily an issue.

The minister of mines went on to speak about Mali's on-going court case against Sabena, at that time still Belgium's national airline. He said that back in the late 1980s, customs men in the capital Bamako had grown suspicious that Sabena was flying undeclared gold out of the country, and the Malian authorities had boarded a plane one day to find that this was indeed the case.

Mali's hopes of a guilty verdict, with compensation, in this case were dashed when Sabena went under in 2001. But when I spoke to the minister early in 2000, he said that the gold mining companies continued to ask for the right to export their gold directly by air from their mines and airstrips in western Mali, without passing through the capital. And he continued to say no. Clearly, he didn't trust them.

He wasn't the only one. It took a heavy coffin that wound up in a morgue in Bamako to reveal the full extent of the country's mistrust. Even if Malians didn't talk much about their gold – at least not in the present tense – that didn't mean they were unaware that foreigners were digging into their gold mines, or mean they believed that foreign mining giants had Mali's best interests at heart.

I got wind of the trouble the day after the heavy coffin landed at a morgue in the Gabriel Touré Hospital in downtown Bamako.

According to the Malian government officials, the coffin contained the body of a deceased South African. He had been working for a subcontracting company called MAED Offshore, which was developing a major new mine in western Mali for South Africa's AngloGold. The same government official said that the man's body had been found in his hotel room in the town of Kayes. The police had been called and after examining the body, had pronounced the death natural.

Although Kayes is in the heartland of Mali's rich goldfields, which were then producing about 20 tonnes of gold a year for export, the town was not nearly as well-endowed as the mine's walled towns. The regional hospital in Kayes had no refrigeration unit. The coffin had been sent by plane to the capital city, where it was shuttled about from one hospital to another until it finally landed at Gabriel Touré, the only hospital in the city with a morgue in which the refrigeration worked. It was to be stored there until it could be loaded onto an Air Afrique plane bound for Abidjan in neighbouring Côte d'Ivoire, from where it could continue to South Africa.

That is when things began to go off the rails. First, Mali's largely Muslim majority was unfamiliar with coffins and all they entailed. Malians following Muslim tradition keep funerals and burials simple and inexpensive by wrapping bodies in blankets or mats and by burying them within 24 hours after the death. So the big coffin in itself was already a curiosity when it arrived at Gabriel Touré Hospital after its voyage from Kayes. That meant many people had laid eyes on it and that interest was growing, along with suspicion that the South African mining companies were up to something.

Malians had not forgotten the scandalous Sabena plane allegedly full of undeclared gold. And this time word went round very quickly – as it is wont to do in Mali where, as Malians put it, "we all know each other" – that the coffin weighed 300 kilograms, too heavy to contain a body. *Radio Trottoir,* as the rumour mills on the street are called, claimed that the coffin did not contain a body; it was really full of gold.

The Gabriel Touré hospital is in the city's heart, which is a massive, chaotic and dizzying market. Markets are full of people who are easy to excite and galvanize into mass action. Thousands of angry Malians thronged the hospital, blocking the exit and demanding that the coffin be opened.

The police moved in, dispersing the angry crowd with tear gas, and the coffin was whisked off to the airport in the back of a green *Sotrama.* In the VIP lounge at the airport, the coffin was X-rayed. Government officials told me that inside the heavy zinc and wood coffin there was indeed a human body and nothing else. But the mobs of furious people were unable to see the evidence themselves, and didn't much trust their government not to be colluding with the mining companies. The X-ray didn't kill, or even diminish, the rumours about a coffin full of gold, rumours that were duly repeated by the country's lively private newspapers and radio stations.

The director of mines summoned the press and lambasted the journalists for seriously threatening Mali's normally good relations with South Africa, damaging its international reputation and threatening foreign investment.

The local press were not convinced and not to be silenced. For weeks afterwards, the private papers continued to question the official version of the infamous coffin story, saying that "to doubt" had become "a patriotic act in Mali."

This was not the first time in Africa that I had seen stark evidence that despite the good manners, the hospitality, the ceremonial dancing and drumming and the kowtowing to foreign visitors, there is a deep and underlying distrust of foreigners – or rather the motives of foreign investment and often even development assistance on the continent. This profound mistrust and growing resentment extends to their own governments that dance to the tunes of foreign investors and Western donors.

The coffin incident recalled for me equally telling rumours I heard back in 1985 in Cameroon about the Chinese-built Congress Palace on a mountaintop in the capital, Yaoundé. Popular wisdom had it that the Chinese had chosen the location because it was a veritable diamond mine, and that the many unexplained deaths of Chinese workers (and thus coffins leaving the country almost once a week during the construction) were indeed explicable. Common belief was that the coffins had contained diamonds on their way to China.

There was also the view that I heard expressed by people in many walks of life and in many African countries over the years: that family planning programs in Africa were a Western plot to reduce the world's black population. In Sierra Leone, students told me that AIDS stood for "Americans Intent to Discourage Sex" or "American Ideology to Destroy Sex." Some Africans maintained that HIV had been invented by the CIA to decrease the black population.[196]

In 2007, the Catholic Archbishop of Mozambique, Francisco Chimoio of Maputo, told the BBC, "Condoms are not sure because I know that there are two countries in Europe – they are making condoms with the virus on purpose. They want to finish with the African people."[197]

What interested me more than the actual details of these conspiracy theories – as wild as they seemed to me – was the simple fact that they existed and were so widely believed. The deep suspicions seemed like a warning; suggesting that Africans knew that they were victims of geopolitical games and knew that much of the rhetoric about fighting poverty and other ills was largely empty. They knew the odds were still stacking up against them, knew that some of those claiming to want to aid Africa had selfish or blinkered agendas – and also knew that there was precious little they could do about it.

Malians understood that their gold was being blasted out of the earth by foreign-owned gold mining companies. They realized better than anyone that they remained as monetarily poor as ever, poorer every year in fact. In some years, their country might be experiencing economic growth that showed up as single-digit figures on World Bank ledgers, but there was little mention in the reports of how equitably that new wealth was being distributed.

Malians also knew there was nothing they could do to stop the mining or ensure that some of the wealth trickled down to them. A mob of empty-handed people couldn't do much against a high-security fence and guards, who would call in the police and military should they face a popular uprising around a massive gold mine. A bigger uprising that surpassed the capacity of the security forces might justify government requests for foreign troops or military support to prop up an unpopular regime failing to defend national interests.

But a coffin loaded with gold? That was another matter. A coffin was something small and tangible, something they could target. For average citizens, it symbolized something much, much bigger – their lack of faith in their own authorities to protect them from foreign exploitation.

In short, many people on the continent were very sceptical. And even if they didn't always have the facts right, I was to learn that they did have good reasons not to have much faith that foreigners working on their soil, especially multinational mining giants, had anything but interest in their own profits at heart.

Weeks after the coffin story finally faded from the pages of Mali's private press, I was invited to a dinner party in an exclusive part of town. Most of the residents there were well-heeled executives representing multinationals, or diplomats from the European Union or Arab countries.

It turned out to be one of those soirées that tropical dreams are made of – with just the right china; lots of weighty, superfluous cutlery; little bits of expensive imported food arranged beautifully on large plates, served up with utmost good (French) taste; oodles of wine (French) served in gleaming goblets; not a speck of dust in sight and plenty of small talk skirting around any big or even real issues. Discreet and well-trained house-staff move about with smiles and not a sound. I was reminded of an essay by V.S. Naipaul on the French society he encountered in Abidjan, the capital of Côte d'Ivoire, back in the good old days when President Félix Houphouët-Boigny was still alive and running his country like a model French colony.[198] Naipaul met a woman from Martinique who detested the French rigidity on manners and their fussiness about having the "correct glasses, the correct cutlery, the right wines." He went on to say, "For the *petits français* – and especially in a place like Abidjan – these things were like moral issues."

At the dinner party in Bamako, it was much the same. The French women present looked to have stepped out of the same beauty salon just moments before their gushing, breathless arrivals. They were classic colonial beauties with blonde hair looking stiff and dangerous to the touch, with plenty of gold dangling around thin necks or around deeply tanned wrists and fingers, even ankles.

A delightful young woman cut from a different mould altogether sat next to me; she was fresh-faced and chit-chatting without reserve. She told me she was a native of Hong Kong, but that she had immigrated with her French husband to Australia, where they were now citizens. Then she introduced her husband to me, saying he worked at the Sadiola gold mine.

I smiled and did my very best to look pleasant and not overly curious.

"That must be interesting," I said.

"Oh, it is, it is," he said with a bold smirk. "I do personnel, human resources. Malian staff and security."

I bit back the questions that were falling all over themselves on the back of my tongue, ready to tumble out onto the beautiful white tablecloth and ruin a perfectly lovely dinner and certainly seal the lips of this swarthy, weathered French man who looked muscular and rough and ready for anything *but* human resources.

After many years of trying, I have still not come even close to mastering the fine art of diplomatic small-talk, which involves more smiling (or at least tooth exposure) than real talking, more polite murmurs than words and more words than real thoughts, and probably more dishonesty than any other form of human communication. But duplicitous discourse can also be a very useful tool for prying loose nuggets of information.

"That must be *very* interesting," I ventured.

He grinned and nodded. He said it wasn't as interesting as some other jobs he had had over the years, as a member of the French Foreign Legion. These had taken him to Cambodia, Angola, and a long list of other countries that had been torn asunder by war, rebellions and covert operations led by mercenaries over the decades.[199]

"Of course, this is the same kind of work," he continued. "Human resources in Mali means keeping them where they belong. When the Malian mining staff threatened to go on strike recently, I solved that very easily."

"Really? How?"

He laughed. "These people are not sophisticated. I called a meeting, all the Malian workers, for negotiations, you know? Then I went to negotiate." He laughed again. "I went to negotiate with my AK-47. I pointed it at them and asked if they wanted to keep their jobs, or if they wanted to leave right this minute, and never set their foot near the mine again. They all chose to keep their jobs. And they've been quiet ever since."

"A while ago," I said slowly. "I can't remember when, exactly, but not long ago I seem to recall there was a terrible commotion about a coffin of gold?"

"Oh my God, that was awful," said his wife. "The people here are just impossible. As if Anglo would smuggle gold out in a coffin. It's ridiculous. Ask my husband, he'll tell you."

I didn't have to ask; he was delighted to amuse a fellow non-African with his heroic role in repatriating the coffin with body to South Africa. This involved summoning the police to disperse the crowds at the hospital, then leading a high-speed race to the airport, with the coffin-bearing van squeezed between police cars with their sirens blaring.

At the airport, he said, he found that airport staff had already heard the rumours and were in an uproar. He ran the coffin through the X-ray, and then had it taken outside onto the tarmac for loading onto a southbound Air Afrique plane, but encountered resistance from the crew and airport staff, who didn't want to have anything to do with the heavy box – no matter what it contained.

No South African diplomatic mission had yet been established in Mali, despite the South African interest in Mali's gold and in the valuable ancient manuscripts in Timbuktu.[200] So the British Consul was summoned, a wonderful woman who had lived 30 years in Mali and knew the ropes and just about everyone who held them. Even she was unable to do very much to defuse the situation. Diplomatic niceties don't work very well with angry mobs, which by then had made their way to the airport.

The French mercenary took up his tale. "I had decided that the coffin was going on that flight. So I had it loaded into the *Sotrama* again, and I drove that van out onto the runway. The Air Afrique plane was already taxiing away from the terminal for take-off, so I sped up and stopped the *Sotrama* in front of the plane and got out with my gun. The pilot had no choice but to stop, and security personnel from the airport came out and loaded the coffin into the plane."

"So it really did contain a human body?" I asked. "People said it weighed 300 kilograms, too much for a body."

"The guy was big, you know? Heavy guy, over 100 kilograms, and the coffin was solid wood, another 200. I mean it is ridiculous in any case. Do you really think that Anglo would bother trying to smuggle a quantity of gold that small out of the country?"

He had a good point. Small-time theft is beneath the big-time operators digging Africa's riches out of the earth.

10

All that glitters is ... taken away

... the very term investment badly distorts what's really going on.
Plundering, looting and exploiting the non-renewable resources
of Africa is a far more accurate description.

Gerald Caplan[201]

In my fifth year in the Mali, in late 2002, I finally obtained an invitation to accompany the country's new minister of mines and a team of Malian journalists on a day-trip to Morila, the country's newest gold mine.

On the short flight to the mine, I found myself seated beside a South African employee of the South African mining giant, who told me he and his wife had recently applied for Canadian citizenship and that he now lived in Toronto – when he wasn't in Mali. He said things were deteriorating in South Africa, "if you know what I mean," and that he and his wife, as white South Africans, felt their futures were in Canada.

He went on to tell me about the wonders I was about to experience at Morila, especially the man-made lake that was filled with water pumped 40 kilometres from a small river, a tributary to the Niger. And as for the clubhouse, that was something to behold; he was very proud of it because he helped to design it. He called it the "Sahelian Club Med." There were pleasure craft and a wharf on the man-made lake, he said, and lovely watered gardens, a fine bar and restaurant, with food, wine and other drinks flown in from South

Africa. He said he often drove down from Bamako in his Land Cruiser to spend weekends there.

"You will be very impressed with our Club Med," he said. "It takes a white man to create something like this in Africa. Africans just don't know how to make the most of their environment."

We were starting our descent in the little prop plane, coming to the end of the flight from Bamako. By looking over my neighbour's shoulder and through the large oval window of the plane, I caught my first glimpse of the Morila mine and the vast mine crater: a gaping brown wound in the pale green tapestry of the landscape below.

The more typical green mosaic of small farm fields dotted with trees is known as the "parklands," the name given to the traditional farming system in Africa's Sahel. I have always thought the Sahelian landscape subtly and hauntingly beautiful. Over many centuries, it has been sculpted by Sahelian farmers with their digging sticks and by their ploughs pulled by oxen across fields, to create farms where trees and annual crops complement each other. Sahelian farmers nurture and protect a range of trees valuable to them for food (fruit, leaves, spices), medicinal and wood products on their land. Interspersed with the trees and neat patterns of crop fields are intricate arrangements of mud dwellings with thatch roofs.

Next to the picturesque and gentle landscape that the African villagers had made, the Morila mine crater below us looked cataclysmic, like something a nuclear bomb or a falling asteroid might have left in its wake.

We landed on the dusty airstrip and were met by public relations people there to welcome arriving passengers in the two small planes: one carrying the minister and government officials and the other mainly for journalists. We were given Morila Mine baseball caps and led to the clubhouse next to the man-made lake for refreshments and a pep talk from our hosts, before heading out in buses to be shown the mine – or at least the parts of the mine that the executives of the South African companies wished us to see.

First, we made a quick stop at the edge of the immense crater; about one and a half kilometres long, nearly a kilometre wide and over 100 metres deep. Trucks that looked like playthings so far below us, I was told, were mighty giants carrying 80 tonnes of rock and moving about on tires that would dwarf a very tall man.

Our South African guides, including the mining director, gave us a quick rundown of the mine's vital statistics. It had been in operation almost two years, and over the next ten they planned to extract 195 tonnes of gold, worth more than 1.5 billion US dollars, for a projected profit of close to a billion (much more, as gold prices rise). To do so, they would be blasting 30 million tonnes of rock out of the earth in explosions that would be felt many kilometres away.

Next stop was the explosives centre, where experts combined commercial fertilizer with diesel to produce the materials they needed to blast their way into the bowels of the earth. They used one kilogram of explosive per square metre of rock, 300 tonnes of explosives each month, at a cost of 300 million US dollars over the lifetime of the mine.

Gold mining, it appeared, is about as gentle and environmentally compassionate an operation as the international financial system that has at its base the precious metal and market forces. It's also very dirty: the production of one gold ring can generate 20 tonnes of mine waste.[202]

Still, it was "safe, very safe," according to the congenial and candid South African technical expert at the end of my microphone. He laughed off my suggestions that the explosives centre could be a prime target for disenchanted persons looking for the ammunition to bomb their cause into headlines.

"The dangerous things are accessories, your detonators and your boosters, your cortex," he said. "And that we guard 24 hours a day."

And did the daily blasts bother the villagers in outlying hamlets?

"No, no," he said. "They're about three kilometres away, so they will just hear the rumbling effect in the background. We actually went and did tests to show them there's no problem; we had a lot of spectators, so they wouldn't be scared of the whole system. So they have no problems with that."

I asked him if open pit mines that tear into the earth's surface were really preferable to the underground mines that his company operated in South Africa.

"Preferable for the miners themselves," he said, with a laugh. "But not for the landscape."

Surface mines like the one in Morila, he explained, were cheaper.

After that it was back to the clubhouse for an executive lunch in an executive dining room. I had seen the likes of this facility before in Mali, but only in the five-star Hotel Salam, where World Bank and IMF personnel, diplomats, business people and conference-going development experts generally stayed while in Bamako. Apart from some beautifully tooled leather on its walls and intricate African motifs in the gleaming tiles on its floors, the Salam and hotels like it are designed to allow their mostly foreign guests to forget which continent they are on. The Salam dresses up its Malian waiters and doormen in burgundy livery, making them look like purple penguins, and it hermetically shuts out heat, dust and ordinary Malians.

Morila's clubhouse was much the same. From inside, the impression I had was that everything glittered at the Morila gold mine. The man-made lake glinted in the sun, offering vague dreams of a seaside resort rather than dry Sahelian poverty. The official Morila PowerPoint presentation painted a wonderful picture of this lucrative gem of a mine in Mali's hinterland. With recent production being what it had been, we learned it had become one of the most profitable gold mines on the planet.

Johan Botha, director of the mine, told me that in the third quarter of 2002, they had extracted 15 tonnes of gold from the mine, triple expected amounts. A typical grade of gold in rock, he told me, was just under six grams per tonne. The seam they struck in Morila was ten times that, he said: between 50 and 60 grams of gold per tonne of rock. He figured Morila to be "one of the world's top ten operations." In his 30-year career in gold mining, he had "never seen anything like it."

Apart from the rich seams of gold in the earth, I wanted to know whether there were other particular advantages to working in Mali – low labour prices, flexible environmental rules, tax breaks and other incentives, which made gold mining here particularly profitable?

"I can say that the current convention texts in Mali are extremely favourable," Botha replied. "They must be among the most favourable in the world and I think this is what's bringing some of the big gold mining companies into Mali at the moment; it's very favourable."

I asked if there were any downsides – environmental damage, that sort of thing.

For an answer, Botha directed me outside, where he said I would find the company's on-site environmental director, flown in from the North American division. Indeed, there he was, relaxing lakeside in a deck chair in the shaded garden bar, staring off into the distance. Something in the map of broken veins in his florid, sun-burned face suggested that this might be a place he spent a lot of his time in Morila, monitoring environmental impact.

I asked him if he had any concerns at all about blasting a hole that size into the fragile Sahelian landscape, where vegetation and arable land, not to mention water, were already in such short and precarious supply.

He dismissed the suggestion that the Sahelian environment was more fragile than others, ignoring the rapid rate at which it had been turning to desert or the spectre of famine that was always just one failed crop away. He observed that during the rainy season vegetation grew quite quickly.

"And the lake?" I said. "Has anyone looked at what has happened to the Bagoé River from which all this water is pumped?" The Bagoé is a tributary of the River Niger. The Niger was silting up because of sluggish flow and it was running lower each year, no longer irrigating vast stretches of crucial rice fields in Mali's north, causing food shortages there. I wondered if he was concerned about siphoning off precious river water for the lake at Morila.

He replied that he hadn't yet got to that issue because he'd been there only two months. But he thought the lake itself was an important reservoir, holding enough water to keep the mining operation going for four months, so that when the river was low, no water needed to be pumped from it.

I glanced at the small wharf, recalling that the man on the plane spoke of pleasure-craft and weekends he spent in them, fishing in the man-made lake. There wasn't a boat in sight. It looked as if the mining company had decided to remove them for the occasion of the visit of the Malian minister and journalists.

"So it's not just a recreational lake for fishing and boating?"

"The recreational pursuits come afterwards," he replied quickly.

Our tour carefully sidestepped the area where waste was stored behind a large dam, so I asked him about it, requesting details on what substances the mine did discharge. He said there were some "water surface discharges" in the wet season but that the mine complied with "World Bank guidelines" and national standards for any releases, and that they monitored the groundwater carefully.

I pressed for details on the substances they were monitoring.

Here is his exact reply, word-for-baffling-and-waffling-word: "Cyanide is one of the parameters that we carefully monitor. We are blessed to a certain degree that cyanide is an artificial compound composed of carbon and nitrogen. When properly treated it decomposes back into carbon dioxide and nitrogen oxide and therefore as long as we watch it while we have control over it and decrease that concentration, we're not typically going to run into problems with it. We're going to, again, meet World Bank standards which have, for all species, cyanide standards and we would not release if we didn't meet those. It's basically very, very difficult to detect with even the best of methods and not toxic to drinking water purposes or for the most sensitive species, which are usually aquatic life species. The underlying concern we have is when you dig up rock you make that rock more susceptible to dissolving certain minerals into basically the groundwater system. We have a slight potential here, as does any mine, for the generation of a small amount of acid from the sulphide minerals that accompany the ore. In the process we could dissolve a few metals and therefore many of the metals, iron, copper or manganese or conceivably a little bit of arsenic, we will monitor for those on surface water and groundwater to ensure that we're meeting the World Bank standards and the World Health Organization standards for potable water supplies."

I have no idea what exactly he was trying to say – or not to say – and I still wonder if he did either. Or perhaps he had decided that jumbled jargon was the best defence against anyone seeking clear answers to straightforward questions.

So I moved on to my next question, wondering aloud what would happen when the mine was closed down – what the mining companies intended to do with the mountains of rubble, the crater in the earth, how they would heal the wound. He said they had a "closure plan" that was "refined on a daily basis."

For the record, for the day that Morila mine closes and Malians wish to know what the environmental director said the South African mining companies pledge to do, here it is: "reclaim that land with vegetation for wildlife, using adapted species of grasses and trees;" and "the hole itself can become a lake, which local communities will maintain."

So, all was well at Morila. We had had a splendid gourmet lunch and been on a tour that showed us the impressive parts of the mine that the foreign personnel inhabited and ran. There were spotless and cool offices, the clubhouse and restaurant. It was a very profitable and lavish operation. There had been start-up loans from a consortium of banks, dealt out by the World Bank: 150 million US dollars to get the mine into the ground. The mining companies had given back to neighbouring communities about 100 *thousand* US dollars worth of school rooms and roads.

After lunch, it was the turn of some Malian mine workers to speak their minds to their government minister, without the mining executives on hand to eavesdrop. The workers had not had the benefit of the sumptuous lunch to which the visiting politicians and journalists had been treated. They weren't feeling magnanimous towards the mining companies.

Fousseini Touré, secretary general of Mali's mining union, said there was a serious problem of racism. "It's like Apartheid," he told me. "That is why we were on strike in October." In one of the three mines in operation in the country, all three run by the same South African mining companies, he said, some of the South Africans spat in the faces of Malian workers and tore up official documents, and then refused summons from Malian gendarmes. The Malian miners went on strike; the South Africans in question were expelled. Touré said that was not enough.

"We are the third biggest producer of gold in Africa, but it's pathetic that we don't profit at all from what we produce," said a Malian mining technician. "We read on the Internet that AngloGold has pronounced Morila the most profitable gold mine in the world, and yet most workers here get no lodging or training, or even health care. In South Africa, AngloGold is paying for anti-retrovirals for its staff that are HIV-positive, and here they take all our medical costs off our salaries."

Furthermore, the mining company provided housing for only its professional Malian workers – 90 of the 440 men employed there. The rest had to seek a tin or thatch roof over their heads in the neighbouring village of Sanso.

That was where we headed next, leaving behind the luxury of air conditioning in the mine headquarters to travel 13 rough and dusty kilometres to the village of Sanso.

We might as well have travelled 13 thousand kilometres.

Sanso was, to put it mildly, a sorry place: a collection of crumbling mud huts along a rural path in Mali's hinterland. It looked like thousands of other villages in the country, except that its social equilibrium and cohesion had been decimated. Sanso had been invaded by hundreds of male workers seeking rooms, water and female consorts. It was now beset by new ills, ones it had never known and had no means to cure. The only sign that we were anywhere near Morila gold were hand-painted signs indicating transport pick-up points for Malian mine workers.

First to speak to me there was Sounkalo Togola, mayor of the rural *commune* – municipal division – of Sanso in which Morila was found on Mali's newly decentralized political landscape, as it had been mapped out by foreign development experts.[203] Togola didn't give me a chance to ask him a question before he started his lament.

"Of all the 702 mayors in Mali, I am the one with the most problems," he began in his halting French. "And all of those problems are because of that gold mine. We now have all kinds of people coming to Sanso so we have all kinds of problems we didn't know before. We have prostitution, hundreds of Ghanaian and Nigerian girls have come here. Local girls are leaving their husbands who might have only 500 CFA francs [about one US dollar at that time] in a week, to go with the mine workers who might have 10 thousand CFA [about 20 dollars] on hand. Sanso has become a republic apart. The mine imports all its food from outside. Very little trickles down to us in the community."

Where the mine now sat, he said, people once farmed. When their land was expropriated, the compensation was not enough for all they lost, according to the mayor. He also complained bitterly about the daily explosions that shook homes and rattled lives. He said very few local people were hired to work in the mine because they were told they were "not qualified" and the mining company didn't want to spend any money to train them.

"And what will happen when this mine is gone?" he continued. "We are afraid of what will become of it. The landscape is ruined. What will become of us?"

The mining minister had arranged a meeting in Sanso, to be held in front of the mayor's office, a ramshackle old structure dating back to colonial times. At the meeting, villagers, traditional chiefs and local officials were to talk openly about the effects of the mine on their communities and lives. The minister, the mine director and a few of his officials had all made their way to Sanso for this 'roundtable' meeting. The meeting took place not around a table but around a tree outside the mayor's office. The tree offered a bit of shade and some respite from the ferocious sun. It did nothing to cool the tempers of the villagers who came to speak their minds.

I had the impression, confirmed by the villagers I asked, that the mining executives seldom ventured beyond the fence that separates their mining enclave from, well, Mali. So this was the first time the people of Sanso and most of the mine workers had the chance to confront, face to face, the executives of the mine that the mayor said had made their lives in Sanso a living hell.

It was an unusual display of hostility in polite Mali, but I was not sure that any of the mining officials quite grasped the extent of it. They sat in their white plastic garden chairs looking uncomfortable or even bored while one after the other, local people shouted angrily. Only one of the mining executives present for the meeting, a Canadian originally from Québec, spoke Mali's official language, French. None of them could understand the heated accusations being hurled at them in Bamanankan that afternoon.

Most animated in his condemnation of the mine and the foreigners who ran it was the elderly chief of Sanso, Tsi Mariko. He cut a dramatic figure of authority in his blue woollen toque, his magnificent turquoise *boubou* robe heavy with intricate embroidery, and plastic flip-flops on his weathered feet. The chief clutched a long spear pointed skyward, which he pounded into the ground to punctuate a shouted list of wrongs he felt the mine had caused in his community. He said the prices of the most basic foodstuffs and even water from a few ailing local wells had been driven up by shortages caused by the influx of workers. His village had no decent road, no good water supply, no electric power. All it had was the fallout of the gold mine – dust, noise and social upheaval.

Even if mine director Botha looked blithely unaware of, or unconcerned by the litany of complaints, Mali's minister of mines, Hamed Diane Semega, was absorbing every damning word.

He was caught in the middle. Minister Semega was painfully aware of the need for such mines if Mali were to conform to the demands of the international donor/creditor community and the World Bank and IMF, and attract foreign investment to increase its economic output. So, on one hand, he had to appease the foreign investors wishing to get at Mali's gold and take it out of the ground, because this is the reality of governing in a young, independent African country for which economic independence remains elusive.

On the other hand, as a Malian and a government minister, he knew he was supposed to be defending the rights of his own people. And they were telling him in no uncertain terms that afternoon that they were fed up with the gold mine that was bringing them grief.

A high-ranking official from the minister's office hinted to me, when we were out of earshot of the crowds, that one of the reasons the minister had made the trip to Morila was because there was deep suspicion – not just among the public but also in the minister's office – about the way gold mining companies worked in the country. He pointed out that elections in May 2002 had brought a new president, Amadou Toumani Touré, to power in Mali. Touré had just formed his new government, and there was no way of knowing what gentlemen's agreements may have existed between foreign investors and the former government. In whispers, the official told me that the mining companies had begun to report the remarkable production at the Morila mine in June 2002. He said this coincided with the inauguration of the new president and government, and the naming of the new mining minister. He alleged that the mine could have been producing record amounts of gold all along under the noses of former ministers, with or without their complicity.

The mining technocrat said that unlike previous ministers, Minister Semega had worked extensively with Canadian gold exploration companies in Mali – numbering in the dozens – and thus he knew how the mining sector worked. He alleged that perhaps it was the arrival of a new and savvy minister that had spurred the mining companies to begin announcing high production levels, out of fear that the new minister would catch on. Another possibility, he suggested, was that the mining companies were pushing to get as much gold out of the ground as they possibly could in the first five years of the mine's operations, before their generous tax exemption expired and they had to start paying a corporate tax of 35 percent to the Malian government.

It was impossible to tell how much substance there was to these allegations without a full-blown investigation by professional and independent auditors. The director of the mine denied them categorically when I put them to him. He said that every single bar of gold that left the mine was accounted for by the consortium of banks that financed the mine in the first place.

But at the end of the tour, when I had a chance to speak to the minister and to voice the suspicions that came from his own staff, he told me this kind of conspiracy theory and suspicion underlying gold mining in his country was the reason he had arranged for the tour of the mine in the presence of Mali's press corps.

"Gold mining is not an exact science," he said. "We have to be transparent. I need the co-operation of the gold mining companies. I tell them to help me make them visible and transparent. When I came to the office and had a chance to talk to the mining companies, I told them to 'help me help you guys, because visibility is the key. You're dealing with gold in a poor country, you know what that means: it's a sensitive issue. So you have to open up, make yourself available to people and let people know what kind of business you're engaged in because it's a complex business.' Gold mining in an industrial way is difficult, complex, and it requires a lot of expertise and money."

Semega said Mali needed the huge foreign companies to develop its mines, to develop its economy. The gold mined by large conglomerates was exported from the country as gold bars. Local goldsmiths in Mali had told me they had to get the small amounts of gold they need to fashion jewellery from artisanal mines in the country, local men working with shovels and buckets and digging by hand into the earth. Artisanal mines can also be very hard on soils and the landscape, destroying valuable farming land, and they tend to operate beyond the reach of any regulatory body or revenue agency. But they *are* local.

The minister of mines defended the attractive tax breaks and terms Mali offered the mining giants, saying it took an enormous amount of investment for gold exploration and exploitation. Investors, he said, "have to know that their investments will bring profits."

"Mali is a rich country but without money," he said without a smile, while noting the one that I was unable to suppress. "That might make you laugh. You have gold everywhere, and gold is a sign of wealth, but you have to go down deep to get that gold out and that requires a lot of money. We don't have that kind of money in Africa, let alone Mali. So we appeal to foreign companies to come and develop the mines, and we benefit from that." He said the Malian government had a 20 percent share of Morila, while the two South African companies owned the other 80 percent, and the mine would generate for Mali about 70 million US dollars over its ten years of operation.

What about the five-year tax exemption, I wanted to know, which meant that all the windfall tonnes of gold and enormous profits being mined in the first years were not taxed? Was it fair that the mining companies should be given such generous tax breaks in such a desperately poor country?

"You have to be attractive if you don't have the money to do the mining yourself," he replied. "So in order for others to come and put there money in here, and not in neighbouring countries where there is also potential, you have to open up. It's the dilemma of a monetarily poor country: we're not a poor country when it comes to resources, but poor when it comes to access to financial markets, and that puts limitations."

I countered that the South African mining giants had actually invested 150 million dollars loaned to them by a consortium including the World Bank, wondering aloud why such loans could not be made available to African investors or consortia.

"I'm a Malian," replied the minister. "I'm dedicated to my country and if I could generate the finances to mine our gold and make it stay here in Mali that would be nice. But unfortunately, to be realistic, that is not possible here."

"I can see," he said despondently, "that not everything glitters in Morila."[204]

As we journalists lined up to clamber back into the small plane for our return trip to Bamako, mining officials offered each of us each a bag of Morila goodies, which, when we opened them on board the plane, turned out to contain gold pens engraved with the mine's name, perhaps to sweeten any articles the press intended to write. I should have made a show of refusing the gift, loudly condemned such not-very-subtle bribes, but I didn't. Such is the power of gold. For a few weeks, I put the pen away, intending to give it to someone who truly needed the money it might fetch if sold, of whom there were millions in Mali. I eventually slid it onto a pocket of my reporter's bag, with that noble intention nagging away at me. I sincerely hope that I would eventually have given it away. As it turned out, I didn't need to. Someone nicked it during a press conference. Lesson learned, justice done.

Since then, and partly because of the minister's trip and the publicity about the disparities at the Morila gold mine, there has been growing scrutiny of the economic and social effects of gold mining in Mali. One study showed that there is a need for the mining companies to spend more in the areas around the mines on community development, to offer more in the way of compensation to those who lose their land to the mines, and that there needs to be some mechanism to ensure that government revenues from the gold mining are better distributed so that the Malian people benefit from their gold.[205] Remittances from Malians living abroad to their families back home still exceed the revenues generated in the country from its gold. Such studies are extremely valuable, and would be even more so if would-be investors in gold exploration and mining companies in Africa were made aware of them, if corporations were not bound by law to try to increase profits for their shareholders no matter what the environmental or human costs,[206] and if consumers could also know where the gold they buying comes from, how it is mined and by whom.

11

Washing the blood from the diamonds

> *To tear treasure out of the bowels of the land was their desire,*
> *with no more moral purpose at the back of it than there is in*
> *burglars breaking into a safe.*

> Joseph Conrad[207]

Controversial and sensitive as it may be, gold mining in Mali has so far remained a *relatively* benign business when compared with some other extractive businesses on the continent. Foreign exploration companies (the majority of which are Canadian, or at least listed on Canadian stock exchanges) take out concessions and seek out the rich gold deposits. Foreign conglomerates then fence in the sites and mine the gold, employing a few hundred Malian labourers so that at least a small amount of the revenue generated trickles down, along with some nasty toxic wastes. Social, environmental and economic upheaval is localized, and the government receives both taxes and a share of revenue from the profits of the country's gold. Poverty around the mines may persist and the environment suffers, but at least peace prevails.

There is a much more tragic story to be told about the fate of African nations rich in precious resources. It goes back more than a century to the blood-soaked colonial period of European plunder on the continent, and back even further if one includes the trans-Atlantic slave trade as a type of resource extraction. Whether the business was the trade in human beings, or ivory and rubber as it was in Belgian King Leopold's Congo, or in diamonds and oil that later drew the foreign business interests, the extraction of riches from Africa has spawned conflict. The term "crimes against humanity," was coined in the late 1800s by George Washington Williams, an African-American who visited King Leopold's Congo, to describe the atrocities of cutting off hands of labourers who didn't work hard enough, kidnapping wives and shooting people for sport.

This is not to say that African people, politicians and business interests can be absolved of all the blame for conflicts on their continent. There are politicians in Africa who inflame ethnic rivalries to gain political leverage and there are people in Africa who continue to allow themselves to be divided along ethnic lines. African Unity remains as elusive a dream as it was in the days when Panafricanists such as Ghana's first president, Kwame Nkrumah, waxed eloquent about the great things a unified Africa could achieve. The continent is divided along ancient ethnic and cultural lines that have been exacerbated and in some cases perverted or soured by the lines that have been drawn more recently to separate people along lines that are religious, political, linguistic and nationalistic.

The conflicts in Rwanda, northern Ghana, the Casamance region of Senegal and more recently in Kenya are examples of turmoil sparked by politics played along ethnic lines. But each of these also has an important historical context involving colonial policies of poorly drawn borders, ethnic favouritism and land distribution or ownership that sowed deep ethnic divisions and helped lay the foundation for ethnic rivalries, resentment and conflict. To reduce such conflicts to "tribalism" is to deny history.

Other conflicts have nothing to do with tribalism. There is a deeply troubling correlaton between the location of resources being sought by the world's industrialized nations and their corporations, and the incidence of conflicts in Africa.[208] It's a relationship that is not difficult to see once you start looking. First, you take a look at the African map and list the countries with the most lucrative natural resources. Then, beside it, make a list of countries that have recently been or are still plagued by conflict – often with proliferating or splintering groups of shady, heavily armed rebel groups or militias. Yet the underlying relationship between key resources and conflict in Africa rarely receives media coverage. "The amorphous news spin is America has to protect its strategic interests and national security," writes Rod Chavis of the Africa Studies Center at the University of Pennsylvania. "Without access to certain raw materials from Africa, Western industrial capacity would wither much like a raisin in the sun."[209]

Although by no means exhaustive, here a list of African nations that have suffered from turmoil and conflict, paired up with the natural resources they have in abundance: Sudan (oil, gum arabica[210]); Liberia (timber, rubber, diamonds, gold, iron); Sierra Leone (diamonds, gold, iron, the black sand called rutile that contains titanium dioxide); Nigeria (oil); Niger (uranium); Angola (oil and diamonds); the Republic of Congo with its capital Brazzaville (oil and timber); Algeria (oil); Chad (oil); Central African Republic (diamonds, uranium and timber); Guinea (bauxite, diamonds, gold).

Then there's the Democratic Republic of Congo (DRC), capital Kinshasa, which has the fortune – or misfortune – to have all of the above in addition to a whole lot of other increasingly valuable minerals and export commodities: cadmium, cassiterite, cobalt, copper, manganese, tin, zinc, many of which are of strategic value in aerospace technology, as well as having coffee, timber and palm oil, used increasingly for biofuels. The Pole Institute asks how the country can have so many valuable exports and still have such poverty that life expectancy is "renewable every twenty-four hours?"[211]

The Democratic Republic of Congo also has half the world's supply of coltan, a mineral that can withstand high temperatures and stress. It is used in capacitors in computer-based technologies. The US Pentagon classifies the coltan derivative, tantalite, as a "strategic mineral." Tantalum is found in cell phones, stereos, computer chips – you name it. And most of us use it without a clue as to what it actually does – let alone where it comes from and what havoc has been caused by its soaring value as a commodity.

According to the human rights groups and NGOs that struggled to end the bloodshed in the Democratic Republic of Congo, one of the things coltan can do (apart from acting as insulation in cell phones and electronics) is cause a lot of death. Its exploitation and export from Congo (often via Uganda and Rwanda) fuelled conflict in the country. Rebel groups sold it to bring in millions to purchase more arms and fight for territorial rights that gave them access to still more mines.

The country's coltan belt is home to many ethnic groups, which have been at odds since King Leopold's policies of divide, rule and plunder in the Belgian Congo deliberately turned ethnic groups into rivals.[212]

In 2001, a UN Panel of Experts was put together to examine the illegal exploitation of resources in the Democratic Republic of Congo. The panel submitted its report to the Security Council in 2002.[213] It pointed to the direct involvement of six other African countries in the conflicts in Congo – Rwanda, Uganda, Burundi, Zimbabwe, Angola and Namibia. The UN reacted to the report by demanding the withdrawal of those foreign armies from the Democratic Republic of Congo. Under increasing international pressure, they complied, more or less.

Yet independent non-governmental organizations have blamed multinationals for much of the fighting in Congo.[214] They said that the corporations had developed what they called "elite networks" of "key political, military and business elites to plunder Congo's natural resources that in just five years of conflict caused the deaths of more than three million civilians."[215] The Western corporations cited for their involvement with local rebels and militias are, as Gerald Caplan notes, "chock-a-block with the world's political elites and retired politicians who are household names … It is as pure an example of the Great Conspiracy as can be imagined."[216]

In 2004, an NGO letter to the UN stated that: "Recent devastating conflicts have been triggered, funded and exacerbated by the exploitation of natural resources including timber, diamonds, oil, water, ivory, coltan, cobalt and gold."[217]

And despite the ceasefire agreements, the UN monitors and peacekeepers, and the countless high-level meetings intended to restore order, militias continued to kill and maim in the Congo in the lead-up to the presidential elections of 2006, and then afterwards as well. The Western media hardly covered the conflict, and have been "singularly uninterested" in mentioning the names of the corporations involved or investigating accusations about their involvement in Congo's resource wars.[218]

In January 2008, on the eve of a peace deal signed by rebels in North Kivu, the International Rescue Committee (IRC) announced that the conflicts and their aftermath in the Democratic Republic of Congo had resulted in 5.4 million deaths since 1998, more than in any other conflict since World War II, with 45 thousand dying each month.[219] It's too easy to write those numbers down and too hard to conceive from afar what they actually *mean*. And as of this writing, news is emerging that both government and rebel groups in Congo are rearming, gearing back up for conflict.

A long and sinister supply chain stretches from the blood-soaked soils of the Democratic Republic of Congo to the cell phone I own. Around the world consumers continue to buy and enjoy consumer items without any idea of their origins – or where they will go when they discard them for some gadget that is newer, trendier or more convenient.

As I write this, my fingers move over the keys of a laptop that may well contain tantalum made from Congolese coltan, tainted with the blood of some of those innocent Congolese civilians on the battlefield cum mining region in a distant country. It makes my stomach uneasy, but it doesn't stop me from using the computer. We are all woven into the bloody fabric of conflict in Africa.[220]

These conflicts are often unspeakably brutal, with horrific atrocities and civilian suffering that the outside world and the mainstream media may simplistically label "ethnic conflict" or "civil strife," paying no attention to the root causes of the fighting. Even if the mainstream media in the wealthy world avoid dwelling on the correlation between resources and conflict, other groups are documenting the tragedy of resources as a curse rather than blessing, and are working hard to end the curse.[221]

Competition between France and the US for resources was a factor in the civil strife in the oil-rich Republic of Congo (with its capital Brazzaville). The competition today between the US and China for oil in Chad, Angola and Sudan has had enormous implications for the people of the region. It is also a major factor in the on-going human catastrophe of Darfur in Sudan. China relies heavily on Sudanese oil. This makes China unlikely to make any public noise, or to agree to UN Security Council sanctions that punish the China-friendly Khartoum regime for supporting the Janjaweed militias that commit atrocities in Darfur.[222] Who is supporting the rebel groups fighting against the Janjaweed? That is a question that begs for an answer, but the answer isn't likely to be found while it's impossible for citizens to track the clandestine sale of arms to such groups and the work of secret services.

In the view of Nicholas Shaxson there is no way to tackle the problem by pointing fingers at corrupt African rulers or at the oil companies "from whose oily teats the rulers suckle." Rather, he concludes, "My revulsion is now directed less towards these actors and more in two other directions: first, toward oil itself – the dirty, corrosive substance – and, second, toward the *system* – the global financial architecture."[223]

The same might be said of the effects another corrosive substance can have; this one not dark and dirty but glittering and beautiful. A substance turned successfully by De Beers into a must-have symbol of love and fidelity – diamonds. Half of the world's diamonds come from Africa.

In Angola, decades of war have been financed not just by oil, but also by diamonds.[224] It was in this conflict that the controversial mercenary firm, Executive Outcomes, successfully recaptured an oil installation for Canadian company, Ranger Oil, from the UNITA rebels.[225] Executive Outcomes' soldiers of fortune came mostly from the ranks of Apartheid-era security forces in South Africa. In Angola, many of them had once fought against the MPLA on behalf of the South African government in the Apartheid and Cold War years. In the 1990s they now found themselves hired by the MPLA to train its soldiers and to fight *against* UNITA, often for protection or control of oil and diamond installations.

Executive Outcomes was founded in 1989, and was linked from the start to a murky corporate maze that involved men whose names have become synonymous with trouble spots in Africa. One was Lieutenant Luther Eeben Barlow of Apartheid-era South African

Defence Force and the elite special forces 32 Battalion. Another was Simon Mann, who later found himself in prison in Equatorial Guinea for the failed coup he had co-plotted in that country. Another was Tony Buckingham, a wealthy Briton with his hands all over Africa's resources. The names Mann, Barlow and Buckingham, along with those of Michael Grunberg, Nic van der Berg and ex-Scots Guard member Tim Spicer do seem to come up again and again where resources and conflict coincide in Africa.[226]

The layers of companies and shadow companies with which Buckingham has been associated were unravelled somewhat in a 1998 article in *The Independent* (London) newspaper.[227] It stated that the Canadian company, Ranger Oil, which first hired Executive Outcomes in Angola, reportedly had links to Heritage Oil and Gas, which was controlled by Tony Buckingham and which "made him a multi-millionaire." Furthermore, Heritage Oil and Gas (headquartered in Calgary with a Canadian registration),[228] along with Buckingham's other companies, DiamondWorks and Branch Energy (the latter a subsidiary of the former), shared offices with the security company Sandline International, at 535 King's Road, in Chelsea. The UK charity, Campaign Against Arms Trade (CAAT), sees these military companies as a front for the real business of mineral extraction. The issue here is that Buckingham's companies managed, in the heat of civil wars, to obtain mining concessions in two countries in which Executive Outcomes helped regain control of mines for corporations and government – Angola and Sierra Leone. Against all this evidence, officials from these security and mining companies periodically deny there is any link at all.

Much has been written about the civil war in Sierra Leone, which began in 1991 when Revolutionary United Front or RUF rebels marched into the country from neighbouring Liberia. The conflict continued for 11 years, almost twice as long as World War II. Atrocities were committed by the RUF rebels, who forcefully recruited many children. But equally horrific crimes were committed by all sides during the conflict – government soldiers, traditional hunters known as Kamajors fighting with the Civil Defence Force, the Nigerian-led ECOMOG peacekeepers, and also by the hybrid group of renegades that emerged during the war known as "sobels" who were said to fight as soldiers by day and rebels by night. The conflict took as many as 100 thousand lives, resulted in thousands of amputees and displaced half the country's population. All that suffering was fuelled by diamonds.

Much has been also been written about Sierra Leonean diamonds; way back in 1957 Ian Fleming, best known for his 007 thrillers about the fictitious James Bond, wrote a non-fiction book called *The Diamond Smugglers* about the negative economic effects of the glittering stones on the economy of Sierra Leone, then still a British colony. More recently, there have been numerous books, studies and documentary films dispelling the myths that diamonds are a girl's best friend. Hollywood has also contributed to the growing consciousness about the dark side of these sparkling stones with Edward Zwick's blockbuster, *Blood Diamond*. So did American rapper, Kanye West, with his song "Diamonds from Sierra Leone."

These exposés have done a great deal to reveal that no diamond, no matter how polished and beautiful, can be taken at face value as a natural symbol of love, as De Beers would have the world believe. Throughout the war, rebels – and others involved in the conflict on all sides – sold diamonds to a wide range of foreigners to purchase both the armaments and the drugs needed to fuel the insanity and the willingness of the young rebel or other recruits to follow orders and keep up the slaughter. Diamond wealth paid for the drugs and the weapons and prolonged the nightmare, the atrocities that caused suffering on a scale that is inconceivable for any of us who have not experienced it. The forced recruitment and drugging of children who were sometimes made to watch their own family members being killed; the rapes; the amputations of arms, legs, ears and noses of innocent civilians, including children.[230]

The work of Partnership Africa Canada, Global Witness, a UN Panel of Experts and many others who helped document and publicize the link between the conflict and diamonds eventually led to the international certification system for diamonds, known as the Kimberley Process.[231] This was intended to separate blood diamonds coming from conflict zones from those mined in areas enjoying peace, and it has made great progress. About 60 billion dollars worth of diamond jewellery are traded every year and the monitoring mechanism of the Kimberley Process makes it possible to assess how many smuggled diamonds land on the international market, which should also reduce the illicit trade of the gems.

However the chain linking the miners with the eventual purchaser of a piece of diamond jewellery is extremely long, circuitous, opaque and subject to abuse. Peace has been restored to Sierra Leone, as it has to Liberia, so diamonds from these countries are no longer considered conflict diamonds under the Kimberley Process. But does that mean they are *peace* diamonds? Ethically produced?

It's one thing to read about the way diamonds fuelled the war in Sierra Leone and to hope that with the publicity engendered by these many detailed books, reports and studies – not to mention the Hollywood film – everything has changed and that in future all the diamonds dug out of the earth will be mined and sold fairly.

It's quite another thing to visit Koidu, the capital of the diamond-rich Kono District of Sierra Leone, to see the reality. This region has produced billions of dollars of worth of diamonds in the past three decades. But on my visit I saw squalor up close and painfully. By day, I walked the roads studying the burned out wrecks of buildings and vehicles. By night, by the light of candles and small kerosene lamps made from old tin cans, I walked the same roadsides to find a meal of rice or a simple omelette. The town has no electricity, no running water. I absorbed the contradictions and tried to reconcile the local realities with those missing billions.

In February 2008, I made my third trip in just one year to Kono District. I had been there previously to get images – photographs and footage – of the desolate, dusty, impoverished diamond town. I took photos of the destroyed, burned out and looted buildings still riddled with bullet holes, and of the gaping holes with mountains of brown sand and silt beside them that constitute the artisanal mines and which stretch as far as one can see from atop the central hilltop. There I took the photo of the woman on the cover of this book, as she strode the dusty road underneath a rusted and broken sign for a long-gone "Hollywood Cinema." Baby on her back, she smiled and nodded in shy delight when I asked if I might take her photograph.

The entire town of Koidu and the countryside for miles around it have been turned upside down, inside out, in the mad search for the gems. What could have been valuable farmland bordering streams now resembles moonscape, with man-made mountains of light brown soil and sand everywhere. The extent of the environmental devastation has never been assessed. The amount of human energy squandered to dig up invaluable farming lands in the mostly vain hope of striking it rich is incalculable.

Main streets in the towns of Koidu, Kenema and Bo are flanked by shops belonging to local diamond dealers. The signs are mostly hand-painted illustrations of bluish cut diamonds. One announces, "We sell rice. We buy diamonds." The diamond dealers sell electronics or mining materials or imported foodstuffs – Heinz beans, canned milk, rice. It would be almost impossible to monitor how many diamonds change hands in these dank little shops every day. And the borders with Liberia and Guinea are not far away; they are porous and easy to cross with, say, tubes of toothpaste filled with tiny stones. There are countless ways of smuggling tiny stones. When I was filming there, one diamond trader showed me how he could slip a diamond into his mouth, eat a bowl of rice, and then, with a smile, he reached in and extracted the tiny stone from its hiding place between his teeth. He said he could have kept it there for days, undetected.

The pictures I collected on the earlier trips are disturbing. In the pits young men who look far older than their years – many of them are still teenagers – are bent over shovels and sieves, day after scorching day working in the muck, searching for diamonds. Drenched in sweat, their hands blistered and sometimes bleeding and their legs full of open sores and insect bites, they dig, wash the dirt, dig some more, wash some more dirt. All the while they keep hoping that the next shovelful of dirt will contain a diamond. Filthy ponds of water collect where they spend their days digging – part cess pools, part ruined streams.

I had more than enough images, not just on my hard drive but also burned into my brain. However, I had yet to spend time talking to the young men doing that back-breaking work or hearing their stories and learning how the complex and opaque system of artisanal diamond mining works.

My lessons began in the "Youth Plot," better known as the "hustling area" not far from the centre of the town. There I met dozens of angry young men who swarmed the notebook- and camera-carrying strangers in their midst. Many were ex-combatants, young men who had been drugged, beaten, tortured and forced into the ranks of the RUF rebels that occupied the diamond mines for a good part of the war, working with smugglers who found willing buyers all over the world to finance their continued assault on the Sierra Leonean population. Years later, the young men were still there, trapped in the diamond pits. They said that without education, without other options, and with relations still strained with the elders in their native villages because of the conflict, they had no choice but to work as artisanal diamond miners.

There are estimates that up to a quarter of a million young men work in the artisanal mines in Kono and Kenema Districts of Sierra Leone. But the system of who employs them, where the diamonds are going and who profits, is as clear as the filthy brown water that churns around the legs of the miners in the pits. How, I wanted to know, did it work?

As their tempers cooled, and we (myself, a German journalist and a team of Sierra Leonean development workers) explained to them that we had come to hear their stories about work in the mines – they finally opened up. They said they worked for men who have the means, the political connections and money, to obtain mining licenses. The men of means who had the mining license (or claimed they did) – be they local chiefs, Lebanese, Gambian and Malian merchants, Sierra Leonean politicians – might agree to host the miner and his family (if he had one) in their compound, give them a place to sleep while they work. Or, they might agree to pay miners in their employ 1,000 or 2,000 Leones a day (about 30 and 60 cents, respectively) for a day in the pits that lasted from dawn to dusk. Or, the owners might agree to feed them, give them a meagre plate of rice each day.

So when – if – the miners did find a diamond, they had no choice but to take it to their employer who decided on his own what it was worth and dictated the price. The employer would point out that the miners were in his debt as he had provided them survival rations.

Those who toiled in the pits had no more rights, or rights to profit from any diamonds they might unearth, than indentured workers or slaves.

"He says that he has spent his money on us and so he gives us any amount he want to for a diamond, and then he takes away millions [Leones]," said Mohamed Barry. "Diamond is a waste. It's a curse because those who come from away are taking away the diamonds and making profit. The diamond miner does not profit. Human rights people should look at this problem. It will bring us to fight among ourselves if it continues. We the youth cannot develop, we have no means to support ourselves."

Miners could work for years without finding anything of value at all. Twenty-one year old Tamba Silamie told me he had been working in the mines for the past three years, seven days a week. He had never found a diamond. Of the dozens of young men who spoke to me over the two days that I roamed the town and the mining pits, I found no one who had ever found a diamond that had fetched more than 80 thousand Leones (the equivalent of about 25 dollars).

"We do straining, straining, suffering," said Abdullaye Freeman, better known as Uroy, whose face was awash in sweat under a Toronto Maple Leafs woollen cap worn as insulation against the raging sun. He began mining in 1985, had one wife of 22 years and five children. During the war he took refuge in Guinea. Then he came back, and for the past five years, had been putting in 12-hour days. "We do this because we are not idlers, we don't want to be thieves. I didn't go to school, I have no work and I am hungry. I have to work diamonds to support my family."

Did he have any money? Was he able to feed and school his children?

"Not today. This morning I beg my neighbours for food," he said. "We find no diamond here now." I watched him as he piled a shovelful of dirt into the sieve, held by one of the group who stood in the fetid stream of water and waste. Tiny blackflies that swarmed the water-filled pits had turned my exposed shins and ankles into a mass of itchy red welts. The man working the sieve did so with incredible dexterity, using his bare fingers to scrape out gravel then swirl the sieve to make any diamonds or diamond chips move to the centre. It takes enormous strength and skill, the eyesight of an eagle, and endurance beyond anything I can imagine to do this work.

I asked the group of men if I might take a turn on the sieve, just for a minute, to see how it felt and to learn how it was done. They roared with laughter, shared the unintended joke with the women and girls gathered behind us on high dry ground, preparing rice for meals.

"You will die after five minutes in that water," said Uroy. "This no work for white man."

Not one of the dozens and dozens of miners who spoke to me in Koidu could tell me what diamonds are used for, what they look like when they are polished and cut. They had never seen one. "All we know," said Uroy, "is that white man pay plenty for them so they have value."

Uroy said he wanted to return to his village of origin and go back to farming to feed and sustain his own children the way his father had done and his grandfather before that.

The east of Sierra Leone was once considered the bread basket of the country, or more specifically the rice, cocoa, coffee, palm oil, fruit basket. But not only diamond mining and the conflict have killed farming here. The closing of the dilapidated railway link in 1974 on the recommendations of the World Bank, the lack of a passable road network in the region that would permit farmers to get their produce to market, as well as the dumping of cheap, subsidized food from other continents for many years – all had rendered the country's farming sector moribund. Swamps that once produced enough 'country rice,' as the delicious local variety is called, that once fed the nation have been abandoned. This was in early 2008, just before global food prices sky-rocketed, driven upwards largely because of the mad rush towards biofuels and commodity speculation, which would put an end to cheap imported foodstuffs from subsidized over-production in Europe, Asia and North America.[232]

In early 2008, imported – dumped – white rice from Asia still filled the markets of Sierra Leone. Cheap palm oil from Malaysia was ubiquitous. Local farmers could not compete. Once-thriving cocoa, oil palm and coffee farms had become overgrown tangles that can be rejuvenated only through heavy labour. Labour that only strong young men can provide. In a country that can no longer assure its own food security, or offer any kind of decent employment to its sons and daughters, there is a great need for the youth to move back to the rural areas to work farms and produce food. Many feel betrayed by their own leaders and by the outside world.

Sierra Leone's Special Court continues to try those accused of crimes during the war, at a cost of more than three million dollars a month in 2007.[233] Donor countries cover these costs. It is expensive to develop and hire the First World facilities it occupies in Freetown and The Hague, pay the salaries and travel expenses of hundreds of European and North American police investigators, lawyers, and staff who work at the Court and the Mongolian forces who secure it. UN and NGO four-wheel drive vehicles constitute much of the vehicular traffic in the country, suggesting that there is aid and development money around.[234] But countless young people who were dragged into the fighting, whose lives and educations were completely disrupted by the war or whose limbs were hacked off, remain at a loss, unable to find work or income to cover even basic daily needs.

It is small wonder that so many wind up in the diamond fields at the mercy of the lease-holders and the international diamond market. A few development organizations are working directly with the destitute youth to help them escape the mining trap by returning to their villages. They provide the miners with basic farming tools, seeds for planting, sacks of rice, jugs of cooking oil, and transport for themselves and their young families to their original rural communities. They also lay the groundwork by negotiating with elders in those villages to heal the rift that was both a cause of and exacerbated by the war.

I tagged along on one of these resettlement missions. Six weeks earlier, 50 young men had been given the provisions and transport they needed to go back to their village about 30 kilometres (a three-hour ride in a vehicle) from Koidu. This time, it was the turn of their wives and young children to join the men in the village. Shortly after dawn, they gathered in Koidu at the loading point with the small bundles that constituted all their worldly possessions. They laughed, talked, milled about and waited – eternally patient – for the eight hired vehicles that would ferry them to the village. When they did, I wondered how many of the eight would make it over the mud and stone path that was a typical road in Kono District. The vehicles were held together by tape, rope and one had branches serving as suspension on the dubious undercarriage. I'd seen far better vehicles abandoned on farms or sitting in junk yards in eastern Canada.

The children looked dazed, but none was crying or complaining. I watched as they crammed themselves into the vehicles. One by one, the vehicles pulled away. By the time we reached the edge of town, two vehicles had broken down and the police had asked the Sierra Leonean organizers of the resettlement for a bribe to let the remaining six vehicles pass their checkpoint. As they negotiated with the police – politely but firmly avoiding paying the bribe – the women and their daughters in a maroon *Pajero* emblazoned with large faded stickers of Madonna blowing the world a kiss, started to sing.

"We tank He for what He do for We," was the refrain. It was another of those powerfully humbling moments in Africa. Squeezed into a dilapidated vehicle, under the relentless and vicious sun of late morning, with nothing to eat or drink since dawn, their bundles of worldly belongings smaller than the bag of garbage I might throw out each week in Canada, heading off to a completely new life in a village they might not remember or even know, these women and girls were thanking God for all that He'd done for them.

Two more vehicles broke down along the way, but by then, the other two had been repaired. These continued on their way thanks to that incredible ingenuity for keeping outdated, tired and apparently irreparable machines and vehicles working against all odds, which is one of Africa's trademarks.

As the vehicles pulled to a stop on the long straight stretch of mud road that ran through the village, the men rushed to embrace their wives and children and the villagers threw themselves into the arms of the newly arrived. There was dancing, singing – jubilation. Many of them were long-lost brothers, sisters, sons and daughters. Many were strangers they had never met. It made no difference. They were all welcomed with rejoicing. Watching them, I felt something akin to envy for their resilience, solidarity and ability to find joy where I would surely miss the opportunity.

There is an urgent need for more resettlement programs to get the country's youth back into productive paying work in rural areas and out of the shanty towns of Freetown and out of the mines. The former government under President Tejan Kabbah offered no support at all for the tens of thousands of young people trapped in the diamond pits of Kono District, and in the related service industries in town – making shovels, sieves and buckets. Nor did the political elite seem too concerned during the crucial post-war years about the burgeoning slums cobbled together from rubbish and filled with despairing youth in the once-beautiful capital, Freetown, as they cruised the miserable roads and the magnificent Lumley Beach strand in their new luxury vehicles.

As Sierra Leonean journalist and academic, Lansana Gberie, says, the "effete and crass political elite in Freetown" in the form of the government in power after the end of the war, "appeared, like the Bourbons, to have learned nothing and forgotten nothing."[235]

On the roadside in Koidu town, in the searing afternoon heat, I stopped in front of one of the tiny workshops where scrap metal is recycled into buckets for the mining. Inside, an elderly man turned a bellows wheel to fan a flame where he was smelting the metal and shaping it to form panels for the buckets. He flashed me a huge grin for a photograph. A boy – maybe ten years of age – struggled with a rusted piece of corrugated metal, tracing and then cutting out bits to be fashioned into buckets.[236] It was dangerous work. The metal was sharp. He wore no protective gloves or goggles, and it looked as if he might eat once a day, at most. The red t-shirt he was wearing said, "Canada kicks ass."

I recalled the man I met in a popular Lebanese haunt in Kenema, another diamond town in Sierra Leone. I had noticed him sitting there, looking rough and ready with his tanned and weathered face, his yellow-grey hair long like an aging rock star's, sipping on his can of *Carlsberg* beer imported from Denmark.[237] I had seen so many men like this colourful character over the years in out-of-the-way places in Africa where weapons and precious resources are abundant that I didn't give him a second thought.

I was there with a team of Sierra Leonean development workers and I'd ordered a can of pineapple juice. Naïvely – or rather with false hope – I had hoped for fresh juice given the abundance of pineapples growing near the town of Kenema, or at least a can of pure pineapple juice from Côte d'Ivoire. Instead, the waitress had brought me a tiny can suitable for a very small thirst, of *Disco Pineapple Juice,* that claimed to be "100 % fresh drink" all the way from Arizona, USA. I complained to my Sierra Leonean companions, saying it was time they began producing and consuming their own pineapple juice. They told me they didn't know how. I argued that they had not known how to use cell phones a decade ago, and could now manipulate cell phones better than any Canadian I knew, at least any Canadian my age. I said they could learn. They argued that they had no financial means to set up a processing plant. My lecture fizzled out.

I moved to the back of the bar to pay for the drinks. As I passed him, the man called me over. "You Canadian too?" he asked.

I said I was. He said he could tell from the accent. Then he wanted to know what I was doing there. Seeing the mines, I replied. He told me his name was Paul and asked if I was doing "some mining." I said I wasn't. He said I should; there was lots of fun and money in diamond mining. He himself had been in "the area" since 1992, doing "business." He smiled, but refrained from elaborating when I asked him what business exactly and what it entailed. The look on his face told me that my question was stupid. There was only one business in Koidu and Kenema, and that business was diamonds – dealing them and mostly smuggling them.[238]

Far better for the morale to focus instead on Canadians such as those at Partnership Africa Canada who have worked with Africans to bring the issue of conflict diamonds and the plight of the artisanal miners to the world's attention. After pushing so hard to have the Kimberley Process set up to end the trade in conflict diamonds, Partnership Africa Canada went on to launch the Diamond Development Initiative. The initiative is specifically for the million or more young men – some of the poorest of the poor on the planet – who toil in Africa's alluvial diamond mines. It is working to encourage better work environments and better prices for diggers and aims to accomplish this with education for miners, access to credit and artisanal mining equipment, training in diamond valuation, and working with governments to streamline marketing and improve labour laws.

It will need a lot of political support, and a lot of donations. In my dreams I see donations to this initiative becoming the most sought-after, must-have engagement gift, along with the diamond engagement ring, in North America and around the world.[239]

Giving some rights and support to artisanal miners, some hope that their hard work may pay off in small profits for the diamonds they toil to find, might also put a bit of a squeeze on some of the big, foreign investors that pop up all over where resources are rich and people are poor. Investor does seem an awfully kind word to describe mining magnates who extract and exploit.

The proliferation of mining investors in Sierra Leone is nothing short of mind-boggling. Equally challenging is the task of tracking down the owners, directors, their actual addresses, and their alleged licenses to explore for and exploit diamonds. The major shareholders of the companies tend to change as often as their names and addresses.

Partnership Africa Canada, Global Witness, Sierra Leone's Network Movement for Justice and Development (NMJD) along with the broader-based civil society group, Campaign for Just Mining, have tried very hard to get to the very heart of this troubling diamond matter, especially the corporations involved in the diamond sector. It is not an easy task. NMJD reports that, "For some companies, even basic information like telephone number, number of people employed, environmental management plan, to name but a few, were not provided. Mining companies operating in the district are unwilling to divulge information on their status and mining in Sierra Leone is perceived by many as a money laundering arrangement and to all intents and purposes is shrouded in secrecy."[240]

It is extremely difficult to keep track of just who is exploring for or exploiting what in Sierra Leone and it's especially difficult to monitor concessions. African Minerals, formerly the Sierra Leone Diamond Company (SLDC), says that it was established in Sierra Leone in 1996, which means during the war, when rebels, soldiers, ECOMOG and others were all vying for control of the country's diamond mines. This is a period Sierra Leoneans call "Operation Pay Yourself." Executive Chairman of African Minerals – as of this writing – is the Romanian refugee Vasile Frank Timis, reportedly the 607th richest man in the UK, who was convicted three times for drug issues in Australia, where he had obtained refugee status.[241] Timis owns three London firms that focus on African oil, diamonds and gold. In Sierra Leone, where he is a frequent visitor with remarkable access to the authorities and to the newspapers he pays to fill pages with his photo and praises, he has also been turning his attention to iron ore.

Patrick Tongu, who heads the Kono District office of the Network Movement for Justice and Development of Sierra Leone, told me that people in Kono allege that Timis' company, African Minerals, has been grabbing land, claiming "concessions" about which they know nothing. African Minerals boasts on its website that it "has assembled the largest portfolio of mineral rights in Sierra Leone, covering approximately 41,236 ^{km2}."[242] That's more than half of Sierra Leone.

Then there is Koidu Holdings, which runs the largest industrial diamond mines in the country. To know how this conglomerate got hold of the two concessions it has today, you have to go back again to 1995 and the mercenaries from Executive Outcomes. This was four years after the first RUF rebels marched into Sierra Leone from neighbouring Liberia. At the time, the country was still being ruled by a military junta led by Captain Valentine Strasser, and the RUF had occupied many of the mining areas and were encroaching on Freetown. Strasser hired Executive Outcomes to come in and help the beleaguered army of Sierra Leone defend Freetown from advancing rebels and to help retake control of diamond-mining areas in Kono District. The mercenaries were successful on both counts, at a cost of a million dollars a day.[243]

After the intervention by Executive Outcomes, Branch Energy, one of those companies that shared some directors and offices with the mercenary firm, was granted diamond concessions in Sierra Leone. In 1999, the hired soldiers were back, this time under the name of Sandline, to help the Sierra Leone government with weapons (during a UN embargo), training and men.[244]

After peace had been restored to the country, Koidu Holdings began to exploit the mining concessions acquired earlier by Executive Outcomes/Branch Energy, then DiamondWorks, one of

Tony Buckingham's companies registered in Canada. It's a tangled web that makes one's head ache and spin.

Buckingham, like many mining executives, has a fondness for Canadian registration for his companies so they show up on the Toronto Stock Exchange. Canadian registration is like a flag of convenience, as journalist and author Madelaine Drohan notes; companies with Canadian registration may keep their head offices in convenient tax havens to avoid paying Canadian taxes. "It's clear what the resource companies get out of the deal," she writes. "… the ability to call themselves Canadian with all that entails: a positive national image, a solid reputation for mining expertise, and access to government resources through our embassies abroad."[245] Ironically, it is just this laxity in Canadian securities regulations and the lack of transparency in the overseas operations of mining companies that is damaging Canada's reputation internationally.[246]

One of these companies was DiamondWorks, of that confusing nexus involving Tony Buckingham and his mercenaries. The genesis of Koidu Holdings goes something like this: In the beginning and during the war, three Canadian – at least registered in Canada – junior companies obtained diamond exploration concessions in Kono District. After retaking those holdings from rebels, the mercenary outfit Executive Outcomes obtained diamond concessions in Koidu and Tongo Fields and begat Branch Energy. Branch Energy was swallowed up by DiamondWorks, which then became Energem on the Toronto Stock Exchange, before selling Koidu Holdings to the Israeli-American Beny Steinmetz Group.[247]

One of Koidu Holdings' concessions is right in the town of Koidu, where diamond mining is officially prohibited but where mining is rampant. Koidu Holdings is now fenced in and protected by guards belonging to G4S Security. Police reforms quietly pushed through in Sierra Leone under the previous government of President Tejan Kabbah allowed the nation's police to be seconded to private security companies such as G4S (which claims to be the world's largest), and to be paid and armed by them. So in addition to the G4S guards at the heavily fortified gates of Koidu Holdings, Sierra Leonean police officers – armed – also keep away the masses. In some cases, they even keep away Sierra Leonean parliamentarians and government officials seeking to enter the concession, as happened in 2007 when the Network Movement for Justice and Development organized a fact-finding trip to Koidu.

Since it began exploiting the concessions, Koidu Holdings has been blasting away the remnants of homes in Koidu and blasting giant holes in the earth as it goes about unearthing kimberlite – and the diamonds it holds. Patrick Tongu of NMJD said that while the blasting is going on, people have to leave their homes and children abandon their schools in the area to avoid the flying rocks and debris. People who had lived in the area for 60 years – many of whom spent the war as refugees in neighbouring Guinea and returned to Koidu after the war to find Koidu Holdings fencing in the area – have now lost their homes. An environmental impact assessment stated that Koidu Holdings had to relocate – build new houses for – 384 households displaced by its operations. By the end of 2007, only 70 had been built and even these were said to be below standard. Letters of protest from the affected communities to Koidu Holdings to end the blasting, to compensate for the loss of homes and land, and to compensate too for damage done to four schools by the blasting, had been ignored.

On December 13, 2007, the community staged a protest, saying they would disperse if Koidu Holdings cancelled the blasting planned for the day. It began peacefully. The demonstrators, including women and children, were rebuffed first by teargas by their own police, now in the employ not of the people of Sierra Leone but in the employ of the security company guarding the mine. When the police ran out of teargas, they opened fire with live bullets and killed two protesters, injuring many more.

The new government under President Ernest Bai Koroma acted quickly, closing down Koidu Holdings operations in Koidu and at Tongo Fields some 50 kilometres to the south, and set up the Jenkins-Johnston Commission to investigate the deaths. It looked promising. At first.

Koidu Holdings denied access to information on the activities of the company at all levels. According to a 2007 study by NMJD, its Chief Executive, Jan Joubert, allegedly a former mercenary with

Executive Outcomes, made his home in Geneva, Switzerland.[248] It also said that the company had undertaken no community development projects – wells, clinics, schools, sanitation facilities, bridges or roads. Statements from Koidu Holdings argued that it was the largest tax-payer in Sierra Leone and that it employed 500 local people and indirectly supported about 5,000. It was only when Joubert was forced to appear before the Jenkins-Johnston Commission that the Sierra Leonean public learned, to their shocked amazement, that Koidu Holdings was paying the government of Sierra Leone a trifling 200 thousand US dollars a year as mining lease fees. At the hearings, Joubert complained of the "interference" of civil society groups that he claimed were delaying the construction of homes for the displaced population.

The Jenkins-Johnston Commission recommended that Koidu Holdings pay compensation to all those injured on December 13, to the families of those killed, the police officers involved be prosecuted, and that there should be no more blasting until resettlement was complete, and no more blasting at all in some areas. About a month after this report was released, the company's owner Beny Steinmetz himself, jetted in to Freetown and met behind closed doors with the president of the country. The next day, and without explanation, the government lifted the suspension on the operations of the mining company, ignoring the Commission's recommendations. The civil society groups were furious and filled the newspapers with pleas for justice and explanations. All to no avail. It was business as usual.

In February 2008 when I asked the guards at the Koidu Holdings security gate in Koidu if I might take a photograph of the large and attractive signboard mounted prominently outside the fence, just beside mountains of gravel and dirt blasted from the earth, the answer from their "boss" came back as "negative." I think it worth repeating what is written on that large billboard: "Investment, development and growth in Sierra Leone's mineral resources for a better future."

"It's not development," said Patrick Tongu. "It's only destruction. Really, I wish all the diamonds in Kono District would just disappear."

"It's a grave conflict," he said of the tension between Koidu Holdings and the local people." It's a very grave situation."

Many people in Kono District spoke to me of collusion with some traditional leaders and custodians of the land – paramount chiefs – who are paid handsomely to support the mining companies and endorse their holdings, and of the involvement in diamonds (and diamond smuggling) by prominent Sierra Leoneans and politicians.

Suna Bundu who heads NMJD's program for mining and extractives said that the diamonds being produced in Sierra Leone are still conflict, or "blood diamonds." They may pass the Kimberley Process because they are not coming from a nation with an on-going war, but she said they are still causing pain, suffering, conflict and, as happened in Koidu in December, death.

Ian Smillie of Partnership Africa Canada told me the work of the Diamond Development Initiative will be to develop "ethical diamonds" and find a solution that will not label diamonds as an "unfair" product. He hoped it can apply principles already laid down by the International Labour Organization and others, which would work in the real world and could be applied to diamonds, including "third party verification that dealers, mining companies, individual licence holders and others are actually applying them." He thought this would be possible before 2013, or even earlier.

He said the biggest problem in the meantime was not to get an ill-informed consumer movement going that would further punish Sierra Leone after all it has been through. "We want to help diggers, not make life worse because people want instant ethical diamonds – and of course there are none at all right now in Sierra Leone."

If measures are not taken soon, said Suna Bundu of NMJD, the diamonds of Sierra Leone will continue to be a terrible curse on the country and continue to cause conflict. "I see Sierra Leone as a time bomb that could explode at any time," she said. "The things that caused the war – corruption, injustice, mismanagement of diamonds and other resources – are all still there. If these are not solved, I envisage another war like the one that already devastated our country."

I asked Bundu if she would wear a diamond. "No, I don't fancy them."

In all my time in Sierra Leone I never saw a piece of diamond jewellery being worn by any Sierra Leonean.

After Koidu, the Sierra Leonean development workers and I moved on to Koidu Holdings' second big diamond-extraction operation in the country, Tongo Fields. We stopped in front of its high-security fence and asked if we might take a photograph of a ruined building outside the fence, on which former UN peacekeepers had written "Zambia Army." The private security force protecting Koidu Holdings in Tongo Fields refused us permission to take a photo anywhere near their gates, just as their counterparts did in Koidu.

A few kilometres further on, we had to stop to change a flat tire. We stopped in a small village typical of the communities throughout Kono, Kenema and Kailahun Districts that were hit so hard by the war.[249] It was midday, very warm, and the empty shells of burned out homes surrounded the newer concrete and mud houses that had gone up in the village since the war.

Joseph, one of the Sierra Leonean development workers with whom I was travelling, headed straight for one of these houses. He entered then re-emerged carrying a wooden bench that he placed on the shaded veranda of hard-baked mud. He called me over to join him in the shade. I hesitated. I was remembering that just six years earlier, this village would have been filled with young combatants armed to the teeth. And even after so many years in Africa, I was hesitant to trespass on someone else's private property – a Western mindset that is deeply engrained. Two young men from inside the house joined Joseph on the porch, and called to me in Mende, while Michael translated their words into English. They also urged me to come and sit. The young men began offering me lessons in Mende, uttering greetings and waiting while Joseph translated and then gave me the appropriate Mende reply. My pronunciation evoked gales of laughter.

Soon some young women and children joined the impromptu party of strangers on the porch. One young woman plonked a chubby baby on my lap. She said the baby's name was Memuna, and that she was mine. We all laughed then, and for the next ten minutes I marvelled at the beautiful baby girl, gazing serenely into the face of a strange – and very odd-coloured – woman. Occasionally, when I tickled her little toes, she broke out in a smile and gurgled happily. Our hosts then challenged me to try carrying Memuna on my back. I earned back a few of the points I had lost earlier in the language lessons by showing them I knew how to place the baby on my back and wrap her up in a lappa to create an instant baby pouch and carrier. I think it is by far the most practical, inexpensive and satisfying way in the world to move about with an infant. You have both hands free to work. The baby feels secure close to its mother, and it is a cozy place for them to sleep. The baby can also watch the world go by when awake. I told the gathered crowd that I though Africans have it absolutely right about carrying babies about on their backs, and that I had done so with my own two children, so did my sister-in-law in Canada. They laughed. They seemed to think I was making a joke.

Or maybe they didn't have a clue what I was talking about. They wouldn't know the Western alternatives to the simple lappa, would never have seen any of the baby transport paraphernalia – the strollers, buggies, carriages – that have been invented in the name of moving around easily with small children, which have in fact made moving around with small children a logistical nightmare. The only baby carriages I ever saw in Freetown were old and battered, cast-offs sent out for sale in Africa, and they were being pushed by young male vendors. In the place of babies, they held coolers full of soft drinks for sale.

Then our time was up. The driver said the tire had been changed and we should be on our way. I scooped Memuna up in my arms, and smiling, turned to say goodbye, making as if I was heading off with their baby. There were great cries of mock protest, and much laughter, and I handed Memuna back to her mother (or perhaps it was her aunt, or perhaps the woman was no blood relation because all adults are parents to all children in villages). Lots of waving, wishes for a continued safe journey and off we drove.

I turned to Joseph, and asked him if he knew what would happen were I to walk into a house of strangers in North America or Europe, help myself to a chair and sit myself down on a porch without permission or introduction. He didn't.

"Well," I said. "I suppose there is a remote chance, in a rural community, that I would be welcomed. I might have to apologize for entering without knocking on the door. But in lots of places, there is a good chance that they would tell me to get off their property, or call the police because I was trespassing. And in some places, there is also a chance they might just pull out a gun and shoot."

Joseph and the rest of the Sierra Leonean team of development workers in the vehicle laughed with disbelief. All that happened in the village – handing their precious infant to a stranger to hold, allowing strangers to barge in unannounced and, uninvited, make themselves comfortable on chairs in their home – was simply "normal" in Sierra Leone, they said. Even in a part of the country laid waste by a decade of warfare and the cruel injustices of the diamond mining.

12

Strategic minerals, strategic games

It's so idiotic! The government buys its arms from the arms dealers. The rebels buy their arms from the arms dealers. Who wins? The arms dealers. My African brothers and sisters, you forget that you are just Blacks to them, and they don't care about your lives. They don't care what tribe you are when you die.

Ivorian musician, Alpha Blondy, at his New Year's Eve concert in Bamako, Mali, 31 December 2002.

Sometimes, commercial interests are piggy-backed onto strategic and military ones, in the quest for Africa's underground riches. Nowhere in Sierra Leone is that more obvious than when one starts to dig around in the south of the country to unearth the story of the mining operations of Sierra Rutile and Sierra Minerals, both subsidiaries of the Titanium Resource Group. If the area is known at all in the outside world, it is through the writing of Ishmael Beah, in his best-selling book, *A Long Way Gone – Memoirs of a Boy Soldier*, who fled his home town of Mogbwemo when the rebels invaded. And what they invaded and occupied was the rutile mine, where Beah's father had worked at the time.[250]

Rutile. Not a household word but very common in our households. It produces a white pigment found in paints, plastics, ceramics, food colourings (E171), medicines, sunscreens, toothpastes. It's used in welding rods and aircraft. It's also found in some of the playthings of the well-heeled: golf clubs and tennis racquets of titanium. But most significantly, rutile contains 95 percent titanium dioxide used to produce titanium metal, deemed a "strategic material" for stockpiling by the US Defense Department.[251] It is used in missiles and armour, and needed for military aircraft, such as the new Joint Striker Jet being developed jointly by the US and the UK.[252]

It is perhaps no coincidence that Walter Kansteiner III, who was part of the US Defense Department's committee that identified "strategic materials" and then US Assistant Secretary of State for African Affairs under President George W. Bush, is the non-executive Chair of the Titanium Resource Group (TRG) Board. Kansteiner is heavily involved in mining activities in the Democratic Republic of Congo, home to more militarily "strategic minerals," and a director of the African Wildlife Foundation that claims to be conserving gorillas in the Virunga Mountains, while some allege it is a cover for mercenary activities linked with securing precious minerals.[253] Also on the Board of TRG is Baroness Valerie Amos, who has "held a number of senior posts in the UK Government including Secretary of State for International Development and Leader of the House of Lords."[254]

Rutile deposits in southern Sierra Leone may account for 30 percent of the world's supply, making it of particular strategic military and commercial interest, which helps explain the involvement of such high-powered political figures on the TRG Board. The company has four exploration leases and one where mining has been going on for years.

The Titanium Resource Group is part of the corporate empire of jet-setting and controversial diamond magnate, Jean-Raymond Boulle, who has a fondness for extracting valuable minerals in impoverished and war-ravaged countries in Africa, such as the Democratic Republic of Congo and Sierra Leone. He has had close links with former US President Bill Clinton, his companies have worked on behalf of Barrick Gold (on whose Board figure former Canadian Prime Minister Brian Mulroney and former US President George H.W. Bush) in the Democratic Republic of Congo. He is alleged to have helped finance the march to power there of Laurent Kabila when he overthrew President Mobutu in 1997, in exchange for mineral concessions.[255] The UN Panel of Experts investigating conflict and resources in Congo also complained about his operations. Boulle is no stranger to Canada either. Together with Canadian mining promoter, Robert Friedland, in 1992 Boulle launched the company, Diamond Fields, which sought diamonds in Africa but was registered in Vancouver. Nor is he a stranger to the Canadian Revenue Agency, which failed to recover 190 million dollars in unpaid taxes from the Voisey's Bay nickel mine that Boulle sold to Inco, using tax loopholes he knows well.[256] Boulle, who lived in Monaco at the time, argued that he didn't owe anything in Canada because he made the investment through a company he incorporated in Luxembourg.[257]

In May 2008, I headed down to Sierra Rutile to see for myself the strategically important mine owned by such an illustrious man with so many friends in high places. I was travelling with Theophilus Gbenda who heads the country's Association of Journalists for Mining and Extractives. We stopped at the official police checkpoint for Moriba Town in Moyamba District, the entrance to an apparent state within a state – almost as if it were the Republic of Rutile. It was not a Sierra Leone policeman but a private security guard from G4S who lowered the rope to allow us to continue on the road into the town. The only person representing the Sierra Leonean government and people at the police checkpoint was a man in plain clothes who informed us he was a "Sugar Baker" (Special Branch, or Sierra Leone's secret service) and his job was to keep an eye out for thieves. I asked him for clarification: who was stealing from whom? He said his job was to prevent theft by local people *from* the two mining companies.

He meant Sierra Rutile and Sierra Minerals, the two TRG companies extracting rutile and bauxite from mining leases that cover 912 square kilometres. Its proponents claim this mining is important for economic development. But here's the question: *Whose* economic development? To restart the mine after the war, Sierra Rutile was offered a 25 million dollar loan guarantee from the US government's Overseas Private Investment Corporation, and a 25 million Euro loan from the European Commission, money granted by the European Commission to the Government of Sierra Leone to be loaned on to Sierra Rutile, with repayment of capital to begin in 2012. A spokesperson at the European Union office in Freetown had

235

told me that this loan was granted so that TRG "could have credibility when raising money on the London Stock Exchange."

I didn't say what I was thinking, which was that it seemed an ominous sign of the times that tax-payers in Europe, who would know nothing of such a loan or the company receiving it, were paying to create credibility for a mining company owned by the super-rich and digging up riches in Africa.

The company was granted a ten-year holiday on fuel import taxes and a rock-bottom royalty rate of just 0.5 percent for the Government of Sierra Leone when the standard rate is 3 percent. The IMF estimates that between 2004 and 2016, the Government of Sierra Leone will lose 98 million dollars of tax revenue because of tax concessions granted to Sierra Rutile investors.[258]

It was John Sisay, Executive Director of Sierra Rutile and commonly referred to as an "adopted son" of Jean-Raymond Boulle,[259] who negotiated these concessions.[260] Sisay is a Director of TRG and of Boulle's other Sierra Leone interests, Diamond Fields International and Gondwana Investments. Sisay's biography on the company website, accessed in May 2008, said he was President of Sierra Leone's Chamber of Mines and that he acted as an "*independent* advisor to the Government of Sierra Leone on mining related matters."[261] The italics are mine. Unfortunately I was not able to ask John Sisay about these apparently conflicting interests because he didn't respond to my many phone calls, text messaging or email. A month later, the website dropped that bit of his biography.

Sisay had been quoted as saying Sierra Rutile was "creating an economy in a part of the country where there is no economy."[262] Yet there was no electricity beyond the confines of the mine's installations, no running water and no sign of any thriving modern economy in the homes and hovels of either Moriba Town or Mogbwemo. In the one bar in Mogbwemo, just a stone's throw from the company's mining headquarters, teenage girls – some students at the town's high school – wore blonde wigs and skin-tight dresses and short-shorts to try to solicit the interest of beer-swilling South African men who work and live inside the mine perimeter. When Theophilus Gbenda stood up and greeted one of these men, extending his hand, the man roughly slapped it away and walked past him without a word.

As of this writing, Sierra Rutile has dislocated 13 communities, resettled 3,281 people, turned an estimated 190,000 hectares of what was once thriving agricultural land watered by freshwater streams and rivers into giant turbid lakes ("oceans" is how the local people describe these deep water bodies), produced dunes of sand tailings that would not be out of place in the Sahara Desert, and despoiled land for which the 'investor' has no clear plans to try to restore the agricultural wealth of the land.

From the frigid luxury of his air-conditioned office inside a tall chain-link fence in Mogbwemo, Hadji Dabo, Sierra Rutile's Community Affairs Manager and a graduate of the University of Alberta, assured me that despite all the complaints I had been hearing – and after 24 hours in the area I still had heard nothing positive about the company – the communities were happy and the company employed 1,350 Sierra Leoneans. He suggested that the people who had lost their farmlands should turn to "some alternative use of that land, such as fish farming."

Thomas Sabbah, chair of the Landowners' Federation for the eight mining chiefdoms where Sierra Rutile was operating, reacted hotly when he heard what Dabo had said: "That's an insult to us! If the almighty God had wanted us to be fishermen, He should have made oceans here. Is God a fool? He created oceans somewhere else and the Company came and made artificial lakes here."

Moreover, a consultant study done in 1989 stated clearly that because of the water quality of the dredge ponds, they "are not feasible for aquaculture fish or shrimp farming."[263]

Dabo also defended the TRG Foundation, set up in 2005 with the stated goal of improving socioeconomic conditions in the area. He said any complaints about how the Foundation was spending money were from "uninformed sources." Dabo defended its use of funds to bring in biodiesel consultants from the UK to set up a biodiesel plant to supplement the company's voracious need for fuel. This was something he said the company and people thought "reasonable."

Thomas Sabbah again reacted in anger. He described Hadji Dabo as a "traitor" to his own people. Sabbah showed me a confusing and incomplete print-out of the Foundation's expenditures and revenues;

there was no clear accounting of how the 155,000 US dollars contributed each year by the two companies to the Foundation had been spent, or what remained.

Yet the TRG Foundation featured large on the company's website with a heart-warming portrait of smiling schoolchildren in their neat blue uniforms. The outside and innocent observer, even potential investor in the company, might believe it to be a charitable corporation that does not plunder, destroy or dislocate. It takes just one visit to the mining area to dispel that myth. If you can't do that and you have access to the Internet, have a look on Google Earth at the giant lakes and denuding of the land in the Imperi Hills of southern Sierra Leone.

There were two dredges working day and night to scoop out the precious titanium dioxide in Sierra Rutile's mining lease in southern Sierra Leone. From there the rutile was ferried down the Sherbro River in barges and transferred to ocean-going ships taking it to Europe and America for processing. There is no independent monitoring of how much is actually being exported. Sierra Rutile is constructing a third dredge to increase and speed up rutile exploitation.

"We call it the disaster dredge," said Leslie M'boka, chair of the civil society coalition, Campaign for Just Mining, and also head of the Community Advocacy and Development Movement (CADEM) in Mogbwemo. "The story of rutile here is a story of unmitigated exploitation". He said that while everyone had heard of blood diamonds, in some ways the rutile was worse, because local people could not mine it themselves. Because of the deaths by drowning in the lakes, a killing by private security guards of a local citizen and the widespread suffering of the displaced people, M'boka said people should be speaking of "blood rutile."

When we finally made it past a hostile South African security officer into the cool interior of his office, Acting General Manager of Sierra Rutile, Sahr Wonday, countered that it was a "win-win" situation for the company and Sierra Leone, that the generous fiscal regime – the tax and royalty concessions – were necessary "to encourage investors."

But M'boka said that there already *was* investment in the area, local investment for and by the people. "Prior to mining, people here invested hugely in agriculture, oranges, coffee, cocoa and with the advent of mining the company has destroyed the entire ecology of the local communities."

Head of the Landowners' Association in the Imperi Chiefdom, Jacob Villa, who had undergone resettlement courtesy of Sierra Rutile and now found himself without a farm in a new community, couldn't contain his indignation. "When the company has left this place, the place will remain empty because there is nothing," he shouted. "They only satisfy us through our ears!"

He pointed out that the miniscule surface rent paid to landowners, whose land is now underwater or wasteland, was 10 US dollars per acre per year. The company decided how many acres it would pay for, and this meagre sum was then shared among chiefs and 500 community members so that Jacob Villa did not receive enough each year to pay for even half a bag of rice. He described the displaced people as "slaves." He lamented what the people had lost – their tree crops, rice swamps, farms, society bushes for traditional ceremonies, cemeteries. They were given only one-off payments for valuable perennial crops that would have fed and provided income for their grandchildren. When the communities attempted to make their voices heard, marching on the company offices in Mogbwemo, Jacob Villa and four other community leaders were arrested and held three days in prison. He said people were afraid to speak out and show their displeasure.

Mine workers showed their fear by either avoiding us, or glancing nervously over their shoulders to ensure no one could overhear when we asked them about their salaries and working conditions. Some said they were getting about 60 US dollars a month. The highest paid local employee, a supervisor who had been working in the mine since the 1980s, said he earned about 200 US dollars a month.

The local people had much to be displeased about. Gone, for good, were the rich and diverse agricultural resources of the area, the clear streams with potable water and fish, and the social balance on land that was conquered for them in ancient times by the great Mende warrior, Solondo.

"The company has even stolen our great hero," said James Beandoma, chief of Foinda, a community that was awaiting with dread and discontent its own resettlement – and destruction. "They stole that name and put it on their second dredge that they call Solondo."

In July 2008, shortly after Chief Beandoma said that to me, the dredge called Solondo, the one that Leslie M'boka presciently called the "disaster dredge," did indeed suffer a disaster. It capsized; two workers on board were killed and dozens were injured. Executive Director of Sierra Rutile, John Sisay, said this was a "very bad situation for the business." But he said the company had "the backing and we will be fine."[264]

The Titanium Resource Group had already established a subsidiary company to work in the area – this one in agribusiness. It would partner with American agribusinesses and investors and also with Chiquita, formerly United Fruit Company that through its connections to American administrations and the CIA, caused so much political and social turmoil in Latin America for decades. The plan was to secure tenure or ownership over 1000 square kilometres of Sierra Leone's fertile coastal plain into biodiesel (palm oil) and banana plantations. This made civil society groups furious, who said the inevitable result would be that still more local people would be robbed of both their own lands and livelihoods, and forced by sheer need to work as labourers on the new plantations.[265] Africans were once stolen from their homes and shipped as slaves to the Americas to toil on giant agricultural plantations there. Now it seemed the giant agribusinesses and mining investors had decided to reverse the flow, move into Africa to turn the local people into modern-day slaves right where they lived, as ill-paid and ill-treated labourers on what was once their own family land. Land and livelihoods destroyed.

And all the while such investments supplied Western commercial, defence and aerospace industries with resources crucial for their continued defence of their own interests in Africa, feeding the military and industrial complex so it can export military hardware back to the war-torn countries that produced the raw materials, and – perpetually – fuelling the so-called war on terror.

"I have always believed that the average European is a very fair person," writes Baffour Ankomah, editor of *New African* magazine. "If they knew what their governments did, and still do, in their name abroad, they would always be in the streets, demonstrating."[266] Much of what Western governments do in Africa, however, is hardly visible, even in Africa because, as journalist Cameron Duodo puts it, it is "done through nods and winks."[267] He notes that if you see any country or leader in Africa getting "the treatment" from the British media, you can be sure that the "mindset" is at work, that is: if the British media start zeroing in on real or concocted crimes of any African leader, that leader has somehow fallen out of favour with the Western establishment. Which in turn means, he is not playing by the unwritten rules of the neo-colonial game.

But how do the Western powers come up with and enforce these unwritten rules, sealed only with winks and nods? There are many ways. There are annual elite get-togethers of power-brokers at Davos, Switzerland, and also of the G8 leaders. Baffour Ankomah points to the meetings of the Western 'secret societies' – the Bilderberg Group, Council on Foreign Relations, the Trilateral Commissions, the Bohemian Grove.[268] Journalist Cameron Duodo points to the instruments through which the West manipulates and controls finance and trade around the world – the World Bank, IMF, World Trade Organization. There are also secret services, which operate beyond the scrutiny of the public and even most of their elected representatives.

The five countries that currently hold permanent seats on the UN Security Council – China, France, Russia, the UK and the US – wield enormous power over global affairs and also have the dubious distinction of being the world's largest producers and sellers of arms. Canada has now joined their ranks; in 2007 a US Congressional Research Committee study showed that Canada's sale of military goods had tripled in just seven years, making it the world's sixth largest military supplier.[269] Canada is the nation that pushed through the Ottawa Treaty to ban landmines,[270] and for the most part, still rests under the national illusion that even as a major arms producer it still is an international boy scout, a force for peace and good on earth, in the tradition of its former prime minister, the late Lester B. Pearson.[271]

It is difficult to reconcile the loudly stated desires for peace, stability, equity, an end to poverty, and respect for human rights and democracy by the US, UK, France and Canada with their reliance on the export of military goods, unless one truly believes that arms make peace and not war. As journalist John Pilger puts it, "Noble words, like 'democracy', 'liberation', 'freedom' and 'reform' have been emptied of their true meaning and refilled by the enemies of those concepts."[272]

China tends to do far less lecturing about the need for peace, stability and democracy in Africa. This doesn't make it less to blame for exploiting resources and exporting arms to friendly politicians on the continent. But it does make China less hypocritical than the Western nations.

As a result of the discrepancy between what Western leaders and investors say they are doing in Africa, and what they are really doing, many in Africa have become suspicious about almost any Western involvement in their countries – even when it is genuinely altruistic and benevolent, done by NGOs with long and proven track records.

While covering the civil war in Côte d'Ivoire in 2002 and 2003, I was dismayed to hear rebels and ordinary citizens in the north of the country say they believed the Red Cross and the hard-working medical personnel from *Médicins sans Frontières* working there were foreign agents or gun-runners in disguise. I told them these were ridiculous allegations. But such suspicions were a damning comment on just how little some people in Africa trust the intentions of foreigners on their soil, if they believe that such reputable NGOs would allow their ranks to be infiltrated by spies and mercenaries.

Still, the question remains: would NGOs know if agents had been placed among their ranks? Some Western nations have done plenty to nurture the suspicions around the world that aid and development agencies might harbour agents. For many years the CIA has placed its operatives in strategic positions in Africa, not just in embassies but also in its own development organizations such as the Peace Corps.

The extent to which the CIA had been using journalists as agents came to light in 1973 during the Church Committee hearings on alleged CIA assassination plots. But it was not considered much of an issue until US journalist Terry Anderson, chief Middle East correspondent for The Associated Press, was taken hostage in Lebanon in 1985 and held until 1991 by Islamic militants who wrongly believed he was a CIA agent.

In May 1996, the House passed a national intelligence bill that forbade the CIA from using American journalists as spies.[273] However, there were loopholes. First, the CIA could employ non-American journalists, and secondly, the CIA could still use its own agents to pose as reporters. The debate on the CIA use of journalists caused Senator John Kerry to quip, "If they [journalists] weren't tainted before, they will be now."[274]

The US is not the only nation that uses journalists as spies, or vice versa. I know a prominent French journalist who provides intelligence to this country's secret service and writes favourable articles about French interventions in African conflicts. The British secret service, MI6, is also alleged to recruit journalists as informants.[275]

In Ghana, friends who had friends inside the Special Branch (Ghana's secret service), informed me there were thick files on me, and that I had been identified as a Canadian spy, apparently based on the logic that I seemed able to identify members of the Special Branch. I countered that the men whom I had identified as secret service agents hardly wore a disguise or made an effort to make their presence unknown. At demonstrations, press conferences and even on the roads of Tamale they were conspicuous in their grey sedans with no license plates. They wore the ubiquitous name-brand sunglasses, lurked about in corners talking into their sleeves, often brandished extra-long fingernails on their little fingers and distinctly suspicious bulky items under their jackets or in their trouser pockets. You'd have to have been born in a cabbage patch not to have recognized their ominous presence for what it was. Still, as a journalist, I immediately came under suspicion even though, at least to my knowledge, the newly formed Canadian secret service, CSIS, wasn't placing agents in places such as Ghana.

Years later in Mali, the Public Diplomacy Officer at the US embassy suggested to me that it was "awfully strange" that I always "happened to be near the US embassy when there was trouble there." She had called me to apologize for the seizing of my recording equipment and my temporary arrest while I was covering a demonstration in front of the US embassy to protest American support for Israel. I replied sharply that my job was to follow the news and if she repeated her ludicrous insinuation that I was responsible for making it, I would call a lawyer. I was in foul mood; I'd spent several hours on a metal chair in the scorching sun waiting for the police to come and take me away, question me and release me. Perhaps her suspicions that I was some kind of *agent provocateur* stemmed from her own knowledge of how common it was to plant agents as journalists.

The policy of recruiting spies from the ranks of charitable groups, or using charitable groups and media organizations as cover for the CIA and other nation's intelligence agents feeds the rumour mills and raises suspicions among Africans. Now some of them imagine that there is a spook behind every aid worker, missionary or reporter. This puts every genuine aid worker, missionary and reporter at enormous risk.

Well-informed American friends in Nairobi alleged in 1996 that the American representative to the United Nations Environment Program (UNEP) in that city was a medium-cover agent, and also, in their words, "a complete fool." From these strategic posts within development and media organizations, agents collect intelligence, which can be used to run all manner of operations, even arming and managing leaders of armed conflicts.

Since 9/11 it has become all the more elaborate, secretive and open to abuse. Because of increased public tolerance of secrets kept in the name of national security, and because of the privatization of 'security' contracts, public oversight of these areas has been reduced and so has accountability.

The more flagrant abuses of human rights by the US in Guantanamo Bay and other secret prisons to which suspected terrorists have been rendered by the CIA for interrogation and probably torture cast doubt that Washington had much moral ground left to stand on. And the US with its allies, have stepped up other efforts to "win hearts and minds," convert people all over the world to a more pro-Western – and sometimes pro-Christian – point of view. This kind of conversion can take many forms.

Africa is swarming with missionaries from groups that constitute the Christian right in North America. In 2000, for example, an American missionary couple settled themselves and their pulpit in

Mali's holiest Islamic city, Timbuktu, to spread the Assemblies of God version of the Gospel and to try to convert Muslims.[276]

The Assemblies of God have powerful political connections in the United States. Former Attorney General under President George W. Bush, John Ashcroft, is a prominent member of the church. Ashcroft doesn't feel the need to hide his anti-Islamic bias, and has been quoted as saying "Islam is a religion in which God sends your son to die for him. Christianity is a faith in which God sends his son to die for you." [277]

Then there is the larger, fundamentalist Christian Coalition, headed by the televangelist and religious multinational businessman, Pat Robertson. Robertson has been active in Africa over the years, befriending and signing business deals with dictators such as the late Mobutu Sese Seko of the former Zaire (now the Democratic Republic of Congo) to get at diamonds there in what was called "Operation Blessing."[278] He has also worked with Charles Taylor in Liberia to try to get at gold there, championing the Liberian warlord as a defender of Christianity against Islam.[279] Like Ashcroft, Robertson doesn't hide his views on Islam. "Islam is not a peaceful religion that wants to coexist," he said on his television program *The 700 Club*. "They want to coexist until they can control, dominate and if need be, destroy ..."[280]

The presence of fundamentalist Christian missionaries and US Generals who show up in places like Timbuktu makes one wonder just who it is that is trying to "control, dominate and, if need be, destroy."

There are many kinds of missionaries, of course. Many go to Africa to promote social justice, peace and quietly lend people a helping hand with development projects – health, water, education facilities – that lead to a few of the basic amenities that in the rich world are generally taken for granted as God-given. Many work for church-supported NGOs that work on the ground in important development projects.

They could not be more different from the proselytizing, evangelizing missionaries, who head to Africa expressly, in their own words, to "save souls" and "target Islam," and plant churches to convert people to their variation of Christianity.[281] Mali and other impoverished countries where the Assemblies of God work in West Africa graciously open their doors to these intruders, allow them to preach as they like, where they like and when they like.[282] Not for lack of trying, I never managed to convince any West African Imams to tell me what they thought of this concerted effort to convert Muslims in the region; they demurred because they did not want to sound "extremist" or be viewed as intolerant or "fundamentalist."

Religious campaigns are just one form of increasing Western infiltration of and influence on African societies. In 2004, Malian social activists and professors alleged to me that the American government was helping to create NGOs with what looked like banal, even apparently benevolent missions, claiming to be devoted to human rights issues and democracy. According to the Malian activists, the real missions of many of the so-called democracy-spreading agencies and organizations were to stir up trouble where the US administration deemed it suited their interests, by bankrolling hand-picked candidates and political parties in elections, think tanks, media, women's and youth organizations. Other countries may have been doing the same, but Africans did not speak of them to me.

In Mali, for example, a coalition of citizens who considered themselves representatives of Mali's civil society opposed to the push by the United States Agency for International Development (USAID) and the agrochemical giant Monsanto to introduce genetically modified cotton to West Africa, told me that the US embassy had been funding and organizing a group of Malians to back American policies in the country and that they called themselves Mali's "civil society." Desperate unemployed people are vulnerable to any offer of income, and some can be easily hired to defend any issue, cause, or nation. Since many of the radio stations in the country and also Mali's state broadcaster, ORTM, receive money from USAID, these same media often trotted out the pro-American civil society made by the US in Mali, to spout the benefits of genetically modified crops and to praise US foreign policies.

As distressing as this was to the citizens' coalition and Mali's home-grown civil society groups, it was still a non-violent example of clandestine meddling by a foreign power in Africa's internal affairs.

The US has been busy in recent years developing what it calls "US-Africa partnerships" that it views as the "key to waging war on terrorism." It has been building immense new embassies in capitals across the continent. These seem to be part of what Naomi Klein identifies as the "Green Zone phenomenon" that is not limited to Iraq where the US developed its own city state inside high security walls, but is present "everywhere that the disaster capitalism complex descends."[283] In Sierra Leone that new US green zone sits atop a mountain that is no longer either green or forested. It was carved out to build the Orwellian embassy and a walled enclave of lavish villas for embassy staff. The city of Freetown that spreads out far below is a chaotic, crowded tangle of shanty towns with huts constructed of bits of rubbish, better-heeled buildings surrounded by high walls adorned with razor wire, precious little access to running water or any basic amenities. At night, with its massive generators throbbing to produce cool air in and bright lights around it, the glow the gated US embassy complex emits on the hill high above the city – most of it in darkness below – is a cruel parody of heaven.

In 2003, the United States launched its Pan-Sahel Initiative (later supplanted by the much larger Trans-Sahara Counter Terrorism Initiative, with its military component, Operation Enduring Freedom – Trans-Sahara, or OEF-TS).[284] The descriptions of the initiatives, though riddled with military jargon and acronyms that effectively disguise their real meanings, suggest that these efforts involve eliminating suspected opponents, or alleged terrorists. This flies in the face of the basic tenet of justice that assigns innocence to alleged criminals until they are proven guilty.

Operation Enduring Freedom, for example, was to be operated out of the US European Command or EUCOM (this, until the new African Command or Africom is established in Africa itself) by SOCEUR, which translates as Special Operations Command Europe. It is intended to "develop an operational reach that enables the ability to detect, exploit, deter, seize, defeat, or destroy targets throughout the AOR [area of responsibility]," all rationalized and justified by what the US Central Command calls the GWOT, the acronym it has developed for its global war on terror. The word "destroy" tucked away in that list of things that Operation Enduring Freedom has "enabled" the US military to do to its "targets" is the verb that should set off deafening alarm bells.

From Mali I had filed reports about the Pan-Sahel Initiative. This American military venture offered Mali, Mauritania, Niger and Chad help to "protect borders, track movement of people, combat terrorism, and enhance regional cooperation and stability." Under the Initiative, Americans were to work with the governments of these countries (and place US operatives on the ground to assist them), "in detecting and responding to suspicious movement of people and goods across and within their borders through training, equipment and cooperation." Its goals were to support "two US national security interests in Africa: waging the war on terrorism and enhancing regional peace and security," at a cost of 100 million dollars a year.

In 2004, the US embassy in Sierra Leone issued a press release saying that in the previous eight months, soldiers from Mauritania, Mali, Niger and Chad had been brought to Freetown for logistics training "in support of the war on terrorism" with the assistance of the Sierra Leone Armed Forces and the private security firm, Pacific Architects and Engineers, PAE. PAE is a Lockheed Martin company with 6,000 employees under contract to the US government. The press release stated that Sierra Leone's Armed Forces had assisted PAE and the US Government in delivering 12 "desert mobility vehicles" overland from Freetown to Niamey, Niger. "The Niger Armed Forces will use these vehicles to combat terrorists roaming the Sahel region," it boasted.[285] These are the same Sierra Leone Armed Forces that are still desperately trying to develop and reform themselves after their pitiful performance in defending their own population from rebels, committing atrocities and engaging themselves in diamond smuggling throughout the decade-long war. More than 2,000 are former rebels who have been integrated into the Sierra Leone army; the majority are illiterate and more in need of basic education, decent housing and living conditions than anything else.

There were quite a few PAE military trucks and four-wheel drive vehicles on the streets of Freetown, many with darkened windows. When I saw them pass, I would ask my Sierra Leonean colleagues who the PAE men were and what they were doing in the country.

And every time the reply, generally accompanied by a knowing smile or laugh, was, "They're spies, CIA."

They're not actually; they're a private military corporation apparently accountable to no one except the US administration that hired them to engage in military affairs in an extremely vulnerable, war-torn and poor part of the world.

In November 2004, in an off-the-record conversation, a Malian cabinet minister decried the American military involvement in the northern desert of his country, saying they were busy handing out arms to the Tuareg nomads, whom the Malian government was still trying to *disarm* following a peace treaty with them in 1996 that had put an end to a six-year-long rebellion. The American government, along with the International Crisis Group, believed that al-Qaeda was a serious threat in the vast desert north of Mali, and the US military were busy trying to train local troops to tackle any latent or existing terrorism. The cabinet minister believed this kind of counter-terrorism initiative was counter-productive. So did other well-informed Malians.

University of Mali professor of law, Aboubacrim Ag Hindi, saw this as exactly the wrong approach. "Groups close to al-Qaeda, if they come to the Sahel region, could get support at the local level if they brought in resources," he said in 2004. "But the biggest danger in this region is not al-Qaeda. It is famine."[286]

This view wasn't shared by those in the US running counter-terrorism in the region. Operation Enduring Freedom continued in Sahelian nations. In Chad, it manifested itself in March 2004 in a firefight between the Chadian military and an Algerian group that figured on the US terrorism list: the Salafist Group for Preaching and Combat. The US reportedly provided Chad's army with communications, intelligence and reconnaissance support, which included a Navy P-3 aircraft and 100 American servicemen.

European development workers working in neighbouring Chad told me in November 2004 that they were furious about covert American operations in that country. "They are training and arming militias," said one man who had travelled throughout the country. "They're not training the Chadian army! The US forces are training *militias!*"

It's worth casting an eye towards and raising some questions as well about other US military programs in Africa, such as the US Combined Joint Task Force for the Horn of Africa – CJTF HOA in US military-speak.[287] It certainly looks as if the US is gearing up for a lot more than enduring peace.

In 2006, there were reports that the US had been backing warlords who had been fighting Islamic groups for control of the Somali capital, Mogadishu, for 15 years.[288] Some of those warlords that the US was now supporting had allegedly had a hand in the deaths of US troops in Somalia during the disastrous American military intervention there more than a decade earlier. A weak transitional Somali government had been cobbled together in 2004 in neighbouring Kenya, which tried for the most part to govern Somalia from the Kenyan capital, Nairobi. Members of the transitional government complained bitterly that the US should be working with them and not with warlords they described as "criminals" (others alleged that some members of the transitional government were themselves warlords). Analysts suggested that the US was backing the warlords because they were helping fight al-Qaeda and the US-led war on terror.

The American government refused to confirm or deny the reports that they were supporting the warlords in Mogadishu, and eventually the warlord factions were defeated by the Union of Islamic Courts. At that point two warlords fled and Reuters reported that they were picked up by a US naval ship just offshore. A spokesperson for the US Navy, said that he "had no information on that."[289]

The alleged covert American support for the warlords was a serious breach of the UN arms embargo on Somalia. British journalists uncovered dramatic evidence in the form of email correspondence that showed that the US was indeed up to illegal and covert mercenary activity in Somalia, using private "security" firms and hinting at covert British involvement as well.[290]

Even that which is in full public view can sometimes be denied too. Neither the Ethiopians nor the American government was willing to tolerate a Somalia governed by the Union of Islamic Courts, despite the fact that they had managed to end years of anarchy in the capital and taken pains to stress that they had no intention of setting up an Islamic state like that once run by the Taliban in Afghanistan. President Bush ignored these reassurances and continued to claim that the Islamic Courts harboured al-Qaeda terrorists and constituted a threat. Ethiopia and the US then went to work to topple the Union of Islamic Courts, denying their actions every step of the way. In mid-December 2006, when the Ethiopian army was amassing its forces along the border with Somalia and crossing into the country, the Ethiopian Minister of Information categorically denied it in an interview on CBC Radio's *As It Happens* program.

Then, in late December 2006, the Ethiopians moved past the denial stage, and moved into Somalia in a full-fledged attack. With military support from the US, Ethiopia ousted the Islamic Courts. There was no international outcry at all. Right after that, the Americans decided to finish the operation in Somalia by sending in bombers.

According to the US ambassador to Kenya, (who was at that point also responsible for Somalia), the air strikes were intended to hit three alleged al-Qaeda terrorists suspected of involvement in the bombing of US embassies in Kenya and Tanzania in 1998. The US ambassador later admitted that the three alleged terrorists had not been killed as has been reported by Ethiopian sources. When credible eye witness reports emerged of bombs killing innocent women and children, and entire herds of camels, he strongly denied those too.[291]

In 2005, the *Washington Post* reported that the Pentagon had created a new espionage arm, the Strategic Support Branch, to deploy case officers, linguists, interrogators and technical specialists along with newly empowered "special operations" forces.[292] This powerful organization, which had been kept out of the sight of the American public for more than two years, gave then Defence Secretary Donald Rumsfeld the authority to plan and run surreptitious missions, in "friendly and unfriendly states." It would work in "emerging target countries" such as Somalia, Yemen, Indonesia, Philippines and Georgia. It had already been working in secret for two years in Iraq and Afghanistan, "and other places" that military and civilian sources declined to name.

According to a former CIA operative, this new Pentagon weapon would fix a serious flaw in US capabilities, because previously it had been possible to get arms to foreign groups only through the CIA or a separate "ridiculously cumbersome" program managed by the State Department.[293] Now the Pentagon had what it needed to allow the US to engage more easily in guerrilla warfare.

The Strategic Support Branch recruited agents that could include "notorious figures" whose links to the US government would be "embarrassing if disclosed." Among its other shadowy and sinister tasks, the new super-covert unit known as the Strategic Support Branch was involved in "managing military attachés" assigned openly to US embassies around the world.

I often recall something said to me by a southern Sudanese rebel commander from the Sudan People's Liberation Army (SPLA) back in the mid-1990s, before peace had been brokered in a deal between southern Sudanese groups and the government in Khartoum. I was in a CIA house in Nairobi, invited there by an American man whose official position in Kenya was with USAID. But he had admitted to me that he was the "link" between the southern Sudanese rebel leader, Dr. John Garang, and the White House. He had originally approached me to write a book about John Garang (an offer he later withdrew when I said I would require editorial control and could not ignore reports of Garang's brutality), and he wanted to introduce me to Garang's men, his shadow cabinet, in Nairobi. I met them in the villa he described as CIA property – we had to park several hundred metres from its gate. The shadow cabinet for the SPLA comprised several tall men of Dinka ethnicity, sporting American university degrees and missing limbs from the war. One of them – the Minister of Finance (in waiting) – told me that once in power they would nationalize Sudan's oil. I asked him what his American backers thought of this. He said he didn't care what they thought; once the SPLA had won power in their country, they would do what they wanted in their own country. Then why, I asked him, would he be siding now with the Americans and be so happy to receive American covert military support in their war against the Sudanese government, when he virulently opposed their free market politics and oil concerns anxious to get at Sudan's oil?

He smiled. "The enemy of your enemy is your friend," he said. "Until your enemy is no longer your enemy, that is, then your friend may become your new enemy."

13

Cotton-pickin' hypocrisy

The critics of globalization accuse Western countries of
hypocrisy, and the critics are right.

Joseph E. Stiglitz[294]

If you happened to be just passing through, the Malian village of
Konseguila would appear as an idyllic and quaint little Sahelian community where life's rhythms have not changed all that much in the
past few centuries. There was no running water or electric power;
there were no telephone lines or mobile phone service either. Its
thatch-roofed mud homes nestled among the satin-grey trunks of
immense baobab trees, as broad and imposing as the back end of a
whole herd of elephants. Being an African village, there were plenty
of bright smiles and warm greetings for passers-through. But there
weren't all that many travellers wandering through Konseguila.

Mud walls, baked and bleached by the relentless sun, created a
maze of sandy pathways through the village, an acoustic cushion that
muted the sounds of village life: volleys of morning greetings among
villagers, the plaintive cries of goats and indignant mbaa-ing of
sheep, the cackling of chickens and the laughter of children as they
scampered about with makeshift playthings – worn tires propelled by
sticks, bits of broken clay pots, a pink bit of plastic that may once
have been a doll's arm.

There was no school but there was a tiny primary health centre,
painted a dusty pink so as not to show the real dust that inevitably

collects on the rough concrete walls in any Sahelian community. It had a simple birthing table, a few cots for the mothers and their new-borns, and solar panels that collected energy to heat a tank of water outside and to charge a large battery to illuminate a single halogen light over the birthing table for night-time labour.

The midwife, Adjiara Kone, had just helped a shy young woman called Sali Malle give birth to a baby girl. Both midwife and mother looked very tired in the sweltering heat that was building inside the health centre, but the tiny baby looked contented and healthy, asleep on the narrow cot in the recovery room. Apart from the bed, the solar-powered light and a simple metal tray with a few medical instruments, there was nothing else in the way of equipment or medical material in this centre. To call it a primary health centre seemed a bit of an overstatement; my bathroom cupboard in the capital Bamako was far better equipped with first-aid materials and basic medicines.

The nearest paved road was 16 kilometres distant. The only motor I could spy my first morning in Konseguila was the old diesel-run mill that transformed millet and sorghum into flour for the staple dish, a porridge called tuo. In a tiny kiosk off to one side of a large sandy plaza, a little battery-powered radio played static, interspersed with programs from the state broadcaster, ORTM, with its mix of Malian music and news in Bamanankan, which people in Konseguila spoke, and in the official language French, which most did not.

The kiosk was the village's only obvious concession to the modern world of consumer goods. Its dark interior was about the size of a closet in a suburban North American home. The proprietor sold a limited selection of dry goods in packages tiny enough that local consumers could scrape together the coins to pay for them: Nestlé instant coffee, green Chinese tea, sugar cubes, soap powder, biscuits, cans of sweetened condensed milk from Holland, mosquito coils from China, Nigerian-made matches and batteries made in Mali. Everything sold there had a very long shelf life. This was essential in a hot country where electricity and air-conditioning were as affordable and plausible as a honeymoon in Las Vegas.

The proprietor, Soumaila Kone, told me that people in the village had very little money to spend in his shop. This wasn't surprising. He saw then that I hadn't quite grasped his meaning and added that the people had even less money than they once did because the community was in crisis.

Konseguila is typical of villages in the heart of Mali's cotton country, and there are many thousands very much like it across the Sahel from Chad to Senegal. Scattered across the south of this vast nation, most villages are many kilometres from the nearest power lines, running water and pavement. All are peopled by small-scale farm families that produce Mali's main cash crop and export – cotton.

With cotton prices dropping steadily since the 1990s and plummeting in 2001 to the same levels they were during the Depression years of the 1930s, the cotton sector was now in crisis. Life in rural Mali – always extremely difficult – had suddenly become a whole lot more difficult.

Local women, young men and even pre-teen children spent up to 40 long days each October and November toiling under the blistering Sahelian sun to harvest the cotton. They stood all day plucking cotton out of prickly pods, sometimes until their hands bled, without a word of complaint.

Whenever I happened through a cotton area over the years and stopped to talk to the women in the fields, they would break out in welcoming smiles and laughter – inviting me to join them. A few minutes of cotton picking under those conditions and I felt ready to collapse: dizzy, desperately thirsty and suddenly full of resolutions about never donning a piece of cotton clothing again without a prayer of thanks.

In Mali, if the Muslim holy month of Ramadan coincides with the cotton-picking season in October and November, the cotton-pickers spend their days working in the fields without consuming a drop of water or a bite of food from before sun-up to sun-down.

Were I to really try and keep up with them, pick cotton for more than a few minutes, I would likely be one *dead* pampered North American, or else in urgent need of a North American hospital. Which is probably also true for those pampered white plantation owners in the southern US – way back when – had they not had African slaves to work in their cotton fields.

And as I was about to learn in Mali's cotton fields, the situation had not changed all that much; Africans were still paying dearly to keep cotton plantation owners in the US very comfortable indeed.

In Konseguila on a still and warm April morning, several men had gathered under the tin roof on the front veranda of the mayor's office. They were discussing the problems that had cropped up not in their cotton fields but in distant places where decisions are made that determine commodity prices.

In a corner of the veranda, a young man was hammering away on a manual typewriter that had a faulty return, which he manhandled to move the bar back and forth across the page. He told me he was doing the accounts for the *Association Villageoise* – the farmers' co-operative for the area. The ink on the page was black, but he said the balance was in the red. Cotton prices were at an all-time low; none of the men present could recall a time in their lifetime when they were paid so little per kilogram.

Cotton was their only cash crop, as it was for an estimated three million Malians, more than a quarter of the country's population. They didn't grow it for their own use. Only about one percent of the 600 thousand tonnes of Mali's cotton was processed and woven in the country, mostly to produce cotton cloth coloured with dyes made from river mud and tree leaves and roots to produce the beautiful textile known as *Bogolan*, literally "mud cloth."

The rest, 99 percent of it, was sold raw and exported to Europe and to Asia where value was added. Indigenous textile companies that once made beautiful prints with original patterns in Mali had been driven into the ground by cheap imports flooding in from outside, first from Europe and then from China.

The small, precious revenue that rural Malian producers get from their cotton provides them the cash they need to send their children to school, pay for basic health care, purchase tin sheets to roof mud-brick homes, buy kerosene for lamps and batteries for flashlights, obtain a bicycle or donkey cart and cover the costs of marriages and naming ceremonies for newborns. At least those were things the farmers in Konseguila *used* to buy with their cash from cotton, when it still brought them sufficient cash.

Cheika Kone, 52 years old and looking very dignified in a green *boubou*, spoke dispassionately, telling me he had been growing cotton for 30 years. He said that until 2003, he and others like him who produced a few tonnes of cotton on a few hectares of land, could make a good living that way. By "good living" he meant that they earned about three times the annual average income per capita in Mali – up to 1,000 US dollars, rather than less than 260 dollars a year.

Not any longer. Low cotton prices had created an economic catastrophe for farmers here and throughout Mali, and in other countries such as Niger, Burkina Faso, and Benin, which are among the poorest nations on earth.

In 2003, for the first time, Kone received less for his cotton than he spent for the seed, fertilizer and pesticide he needed to grow it. These inputs he paid for with credit from the co-operative, the *Association Villageoise*. He calculated his net loss that year at about 200 dollars. That is without factoring in the countless hours of work by himself and his family: ploughing, sowing, weeding and then the painstaking job of picking the cotton. Africans rarely calculate their labour as a cost.

"What will happen to you and the *Association Villageoise?*" I asked.

He shrugged. *"Je ne sais pas,"* he said eventually; he didn't know. "Our problems are enormous. There are people who will not be eating well this year. Everything is linked to cotton here. We are eating smaller rations now, and some families cannot eat three times in the day." He added, "We have no subsidies here. We will have to share and make do ourselves."

The mayor of Konseguila, Tiecoura Kone, said the cotton prices had brought "calamity." He said many families were selling their grain stocks from the previous harvest to get money to pay their debts, incurred by the inputs for the cotton crop that didn't pay off. "That means they won't have enough food to eat this year, and there will be hunger. It's very, very serious."

Tiecoura Kone told me he would like me to send a message to far richer cotton producers abroad – especially in the United States, where he believed the problems originated. I can finally pass that message on, on these pages: "Truly, the subsidies your government is giving you are playing havoc with our lives here in Mali. As long as your governments subsidize their farmers, we here will harvest poverty."

The subsidies that Kone was referring to were those lavished by the US government on its cotton producers as part of the Farm Bill that President George W. Bush signed into law on 13 May 2002.

A study on the effects of the US cotton subsidies by the international NGO, Oxfam, reported that 25 thousand US cotton producers reaped a bumper harvest of subsidies worth 3.9 billion US dollars in 2001-02.[295] That worked out to 230 dollars per acre of cotton in the US, about the same as the average per capita annual income in West African cotton-producing countries such as Mali and Burkina Faso. It was also an amount more than three times the entire budget that USAID allocated for more than half a billion people in Africa.

Oxfam noted that in 2001, Mali received 37.7 million US dollars from the United States in official aid or development funds, but lost 43 million because of the US cotton subsidies.[296] The 33 million dollars lost by Benin the same year because of the US subsidies was double the aid it received from Washington.

Oxfam's Mohamed Ould Mahmoud told me that in 2002, sub-Sahara countries lost 302 million US dollars as a direct consequence of the cotton subsidies in the US. The International Cotton Advisory Committee estimated that if the subsidies were withdrawn from US cotton, the world price would rise by about 26 percent, more than 20 cents per kilogram.

For Cheika Kone in Konseguila in Mali, that rise would have meant that rather than losing about 200 dollars for his cotton in 2002-03, he would have made 800 dollars. That would have made him – by Malian standards – a relatively wealthy farmer in the country.

African countries cannot afford to subsidize their farmers the way American and European governments do. Even if they could, the World Bank, IMF and the donor community of creditor nations would not allow them to do so. Subsidies smack of protectionism, and they run counter to the free-market economic reforms that the Bretton Woods gurus have imposed on African countries.

For many years, debt servicing gobbled up a good portion of the financial aid (loans and grants) that African countries received from the Western creditor nations. When Canada hosted the G8 summit in 2002 in the beautiful and isolated resort of Kananaskis in Alberta, then Prime Minister Jean Chrétien promised the focus would be Africa and the blueprint known as the New Partnership for African Development (NEPAD). The rhetoric leading up the summit of made it sound as if the G8 nations were prepared to launch a Marshall Plan for Africa. Unfortunately, that hasn't panned out.

Reflecting on why Western efforts to aid the rest of the world have done so much ill and so little good, William Easterly identifies those who have developed the grandiose economic schemes for poor countries as the Planners, and those who work on the ground with the tools and knowledge to find and implement effective development strategies as the Searchers. He concludes that there is no Big Plan that will result in universal economic development, and that "The right plan is to have no plan."[297]

Ironically, the biggest plans, one-size-fits-all free trade and free market economic policies that are trumpeted most loudly by Washington, DC, come from a place that is also a world capital of farm subsidies, ballooning to nine billion dollars in 2007.[298]

When he signed the Farm Bill in 2002, President Bush said, "I told the people, I said if you give me a chance to be the President, we're not going to treat our agricultural industry as a secondary citizen when it comes to opening up markets. The farm bill is important legislation … It will promote farmer independence, and preserve the farm way of life. It helps America's farmers, and therefore it helps America."[299]

In his speech that day, President Bush conjured up a golly-gee-and-shucks-ma'am picture of the kind of farmers who would benefit from the Farm Bill: downtrodden, hard-toiling men and women on tiny windswept farms who, without subsidies, might face foreclosure and hunger. "I understand how hard farmers have to work to make a living. I know they face tough challenges. I recently spent some time with some of my neighbors at the coffee shop in Crawford, Texas. I know how hard many struggle. Their livelihood depends on things they cannot control: the weather, crop disease, uncertain pricing.

They need a farm bill that provides support and help when times are tough. And that is why I'm signing this bill today."

On closer look, one sees that the US cotton belt is home to a very powerful political lobby. It is not made up of small family farmers. It is run by cotton barons managing agribusinesses that average, in Texas for example, about 2,000 acres (just over 800 hectares).[300]

The richest 10 percent of American cotton farmers received 73 percent of the total farm subsidies. In 2001, just ten US cotton farms received 21 million US dollars. The largest of those, Tyler Farms, an Arkansas-based corporation that controls a farm of 40,000 acres (16,000 hectares), received more than nine million dollars in subsidies that year.[301] Times must have been quite tough down on the Tyler Farms.

West African cotton farmers could teach the world a little about tough times. They might also be able to teach the world something about efficient production methods. About three million small-scale farmers in Mali produce the highest quality cotton in the world. And because they do so almost entirely by hand, they produce it more cheaply than any of the big producers in the world – the US, China and India.

The US Department of Agriculture estimates that the average cost of producing a kilogram of cotton in the US is 1.6 dollars; in Burkina Faso it is about 46 US *cents*.[302] The US subsidies have naturally led to increased production in the United States, despite the inefficiency and high cost. This has in turn pushed world prices down still further, and caused no end to the hardship and suffering among some of the poorest farmers on the planet.

Shortly after my visit to Konseguila, I attended a press conference in the capital, Bamako, which was being given by a visiting Vice President of the World Bank, Callisto Madavo, and Mali's Minister of Finance. The main item on the media agenda that evening was to have been the devastating effects the civil conflict in neighbouring Côte d'Ivoire was having on Mali's economy, yanking its economic growth from positive into negative percentage figures. But it was immediately obvious from the discussions that another major reason for the downturn in the fragile Malian economy had to do with cotton, and the effects of the US Farm Bill on Mali's cotton.

World Bank Vice President Callisto Madavo said, "The World Bank has advocated strongly on behalf of the farmers of West and Central Africa, that [agricultural] subsidies [in Europe and the US] should be removed. The influence of these subsidies on prices in the world market is substantial. And it is not just the impact on the Malian economy; it is that we are talking about a crop [cotton] that is being grown by some of the poorest farmers, so the impact in terms of poverty is severe."

Mali's then minister of finance, Bassary Touré, who had worked at the World Bank, had this to say: "The amount of money that those countries put into agricultural subsidies is five times what they give as development assistance. And we've always said to those rich countries, 'You're hypocrites. You tell us to play the rules of the open market at the same time as you subsidize your farmers.' How can they twist the arms of our impoverished farmers, when they're using extraordinary amounts of money to subsidize farmers in America and Europe?"

In March 2005, the WTO upheld a complaint from Brazil and backed tacitly by several African countries that the US cotton subsidies were illegal, depressing world prices and hurting other cotton producers. The US was given 15 months to comply with the WTO ruling. The American reaction, in the words Richard Mills, spokesman for the US trade representative, was that the US would consider all its options and "study the report carefully."[303]

On February 1, 2006, the US Congress finally agreed to scrap major subsidies to its cotton industry, despite protests from the US agricultural lobby. This looked like good news for cotton producers in Brazil, which had brought the case to the WTO, and for ten million small-scale producers in West Africa. But when the Doha round of WTO global trade talks broke down in July 2006, largely because of the issue of subsidies, Brazil again requested a new panel take up the question of whether the US had complied with the 2004 ruling that its subsidies were illegal. In June 2008, the WTO again upheld earlier rulings that the subsidies helped US cotton growers undercut foreign competitors.[304]

And long before that and as the wrangling went on incessantly, Washington and its corporate friends had found a new way to rule the African cotton patch.

The US plan for Africa's ailing cotton farmers went into action while Ann Veneman, who had also introduced the Farm Bill in 2002 and who in 2004 graduated to become head of UNICEF,[305] was Secretary of Agriculture during George W. Bush's first term in office.

The idea was this: if West African farmers couldn't sell their cotton at a good price, the US would help them out by making sure that at least the cotton that they couldn't sell was "technologically improved": modern, genetically modified (GM) Bt cotton seed produced by multinational agribusinesses and injected with the bacteria, *Bacillus thuringiensis*.

Throughout the 1990s, multinationals had been working on the ground in Africa and throughout the developing world, trying to get their GM seeds into every last farm. Their strategy had been to convince governments and local researchers to accept and promote genetically modified organisms (GMOs) and modernize agricultural production.

Even if European consumers were baulking at GMOs, the giant agribusinesses were intent on getting their biotechnology firmly rooted in the rest of the world. They did this with heart-touching claims that their aim was to combat world hunger and rural poverty and environmental pollution, claims that – coming from companies such as Monsanto – hold as much water as do the drifting sands of the Sahara Desert.[306]

The hard sell didn't exclude anyone, not even the world's poorest farmers in West Africa. There the sell was being made by USAID, the official aid agency of the American government.

In June 2004, the United States government organized a conference for selected West African ministers and heads of state in Ouagadougou, Burkina Faso, benignly called "Science and technology to harness agricultural production: West African perspectives."[307] A month later, US Agriculture Secretary Ann Veneman invited the ministers in charge of agriculture and trade in Benin, Mali, Burkina Faso and Chad to the United States to participate in a "US Cotton

Industry Orientation Program," which involved well-orchestrated presentations, tours and glad-handing.

On the ground in Africa, USAID kept the ball rolling by organizing seminars, targeting the perennially cash-starved agricultural research organizations in each country. They handed out new four-wheel-drive vehicles and computers to researchers who until then, had not had so much as an office telephone or a motorcycle to work with. Expensive studies on biotechnology were commissioned by USAID, using American universities and researchers but chalked up as part of American aid – "from the American people."

These studies were then published to show how science and technology – and biotechnology – would spur economic growth in Africa.[308] USAID funded an Agricultural Biotechnology Support Project, which pumped a great deal of money into elite American universities to promote biotechnology. This scheme wrapped itself up in biosafety apparel, ostensibly to help consumers worldwide make "informed" choices and help "help reduce poverty and hunger."[309]

The genuine African Centre for Biosafety was set up with no USAID funding in South Africa to monitor genetic engineering on the continent and examine the potential risks it posed. It works to keep track of "biotech investment" and of the organizations working to promote genetic engineering in West Africa, and to oppose the commercialization of GM crops and dumping of GM products in Africa.[310]

In 2004 at a meeting in Benin, African Union experts on biosafety called for a continent-wide moratorium on GMO introduction until adequate capacity had been built. Their recommendations went unheeded.

The campaign continued. After US embassies and USAID offices had softened up the government and agricultural researchers, in came the private partners – Monsanto, Syngenta and Dow AgroSciences – to set up trial plots and get seeds onto markets and get on with helping impoverished African farmers improve their production and eradicate hunger. Texas columnist, author and Bush-watcher, the late Molly Ivins, impertinently noted that Monsanto is a major contributor to the Republican Party and cozy with the Bush family.[311]

Agriculture Secretary Ann Veneman, under whom all this was happening, had links with Monsanto as well.[312]

And now Monsanto was one of the corporations getting a helping hand from the US government and USAID to spread its GM seeds all over Africa. So many coincidences. Many African friends told me over the years that "there is no such thing as a coincidence."

Without many people noticing, in 2002, two countries in the region – Burkina Faso and Senegal – had succumbed to the US campaign and had agreed to start field trials with the Bt cotton.

Why Burkina Faso seemed to be leading the pack of GMO cheerleaders and USAID yeah-sayers in the region was a little puzzling at first glance. Burkinabé president, Blaise Compaoré, had hosted the USAID-funded conference on "science and technology to harness agricultural production" in June 2004, and Bt cotton was already growing in his country. This seemed odd, given that for years the US administration had not appeared too fond of President Blaise Compaoré, despite US support for the coup that brought him to power and put an end to the rule and life of Thomas Sankara. After that, Compaoré had been a close ally to some trouble-makers in Africa that the US loved to hate. Among them was Liberia's former president, the warlord Charles Taylor, at least after he started fomenting war in Liberia and Sierra Leone. After Taylor's mysterious escape from a US prison in 1985, Compaoré offered him a temporary home in the Burkinabé capital, where he presumably prepared his rebels for a march first on Liberia and later on Sierra Leone.[313] In 1990, I found Taylor's name listed in the Ouagadougou telephone directory.

International human rights groups had alleged several times that Compaoré was involved in the arms and diamond dealing that had fuelled wars in Liberia, Sierra Leone and Angola. And mostly, Compaoré had always been very close to Libyan leader, Colonel Muammar Gaddafi, whom the US had for years viewed as Enemy Number One, a sponsor of terrorism, bomber of airplanes, sponsor of rebel groups – a one-man Axis of Evil in Africa.[314]

But, as they say so sagely in Ghana, no condition is permanent.

After 9/11 and the invasion of Iraq, Gaddafi seemed intent on finding a warm shoulder in Washington. In 2004, Gaddafi did a diplomatic about-face to become the West's favourite reformed terrorist and recruit into the Western fold, perhaps hoping not to die in another American attack on Tripoli like the one that had killed his adopted daughter in 1986. Almost immediately after his rapprochement with the West, Gaddafi's presidential tent in Tripoli became a *de rigueur* destination for several Western leaders, including then Prime Minister Tony Blair, then Canadian Prime Minister Paul Martin and French President Nicolas Sarkozy.

It helped that Gaddafi's country had the largest oil and natural gas reserves in Africa. Most were still untapped and the West definitely wanted to tap into them. In 2005, Chevron won a good large chunk of exploration land in Libya. The US Secretary of State at this time, Condoleezza Rice, had been a Board member at Chevron for ten years and had had a Chevron oil tanker named after her. There is much cross-pollination between the Board of Chevron and that of Halliburton Corporation, the world's largest oil fields services company, of which US Vice President Dick Cheney was formerly Chief Executive and Chairman.[315]

And thus – with oil and also promises to join the war on terror and drop any nuclear ambitions – Gaddafi was able to buy his way out of Washington's black book. But what of Burkina Faso's president, Blaise Compaoré? Apart from its gold deposits, Burkina Faso didn't have a lot of extremely valuable natural resources, except as another strategic friend on the continent. And what better way to show friendship than compliance with everything Washington wanted?

So Compaoré – a wily fellow who has remained in power despite all the allegations of assassination, aiding rebels, arms and diamond smuggling over the years – followed Gaddafi's lead, and showed his compliance any way he could. One simple one was opening the door to USAID and its corporate partners who wished to introduce GMOs. Being GM-ready showed that in all ways, Compaoré was with – and not against – the United States.

It was telling, for example, that another country that USAID had been wooing had managed to say no to the GMOs, or at least to say "not now thank you very much." That country was Benin, a tiny sliver of a nation squeezed between Nigeria and Togo on the West African coast.

As a former French colony without a lot of resources or a strategic link with the US, Benin had less to gain from succumbing to American bullying; until then it had not been a major player on Washington's map of Africa.

It was not completely free of influence though. Three years earlier, in March 2005, the American defence contractor, Titan Corp (now L-3 Titan Group), had pleaded guilty to charges of bribery in Benin.[316] The California-based defence and telecommunications company admitted to having paid two million US dollars straight into the coffers of President Mathieu Kérékou for his re-election campaign in 2001, a controversial election that he won with 84 percent of the vote.

Nevertheless, in 2002 President Kérékou's government in Benin put a moratorium on GMOs, to study the issue and to inform themselves of all the pros and cons. In 2006, President Kérékou abided by the constitutional age limit, and did not run in the elections that brought newcomer Yayi Boni to power. USAID-funded seminars and training sessions on GMOs continued unabated, and Benin remained one of the target countries the US listed as ripe for biotechnology. In January 2008, at the annual summit of West Africa's leaders held in Ouagadougou, Burkina Faso, the compliant presidents endorsed a five-year action plan for the development of bio-technology and bio-safety and their deployment in improving agricultural productivity. Benin's president Yayi Boni welcomed George W. Bush to his country a few weeks later, when the American president made Benin the first stop of his five-country Africa trip. It seemed Washington had found a new friend on the continent, strategically located in the New Gulf, and not likely to oppose GMOs any more.

Then there is Mali, also strategically important to the United States because it is a relatively stable democracy in West Africa, a secular country full of moderate Muslims, surrounded by countries such as Algeria and Mauritania that the US believes are breeding grounds for terrorists. As a result of its geographical location and its malleability, Washington pays a good deal of attention to Mali and what goes on there.

The US has erected a huge new embassy (right beside a new residence for Muammar Gaddafi and a new embassy for Burkina Faso) in Bamako. The US European Command was running clandestine military operations and a major listening post in the country's desert north, and Washington considered Mali one of its new political friends on the continent. With Amadou Toumani Touré's election in 2002, Mali had the second president in a row that US felt it could work with. The American ambassador not only showed up at the country's Constitutional Court in 2002 when it was announcing its verdict on the presidential elections, but he sat right up front in the section reserved for politicians as if he were one of those angling to rule the country.

President Touré had worked extensively with former US President Jimmy Carter and his Carter Foundation that promoted democracy and the Green Revolution with its modern monoculture agriculture in Africa.[317] It seemed he would be GMO friendly.

But the GMO plot was not unfolding in Mali quite the way the US had hoped. It had begun well enough. Very quietly, so quietly that no one had noticed, USAID and its new partners in aid (the agrochemical companies), had been drawing up a five-year contract to commercialize Bt cotton together with the country's national agricultural research institute, the *Institut d'Economie Rurale*.

Bogged down in more immediate concerns such as trying to get clean drinking water and schooling for children, Malians had not paid any attention to all the sudden US interest in helping the country's agricultural researchers and there had been no public debate about genetically modified organisms. Indeed, there was almost no knowledge of GMOs in Mali or in any of the countries targeted by USAID (just as there wasn't in Canada and the United States when GM crops were slipped into farmers' fields and then onto our tables in the 1980s and 90s).

Occasionally, pro-GM reports appeared in Mali's media. These were usually written by *envoyés spécials*, unknown African 'journalists,' who filed glowing reports on the trials of Bt cotton in neighbouring Burkina Faso. Some of these articles seemed carefully designed to cause elaborate confusion by extolling the virtues of the Bt cotton, to which the "special envoys" referred as *"coton bio."*[318]

In French, the official term for organic crops is *"biologique"* or *"bio"* for short. *Coton bio* – organic cotton – was something that NGOs and farmers' groups in West Africa were struggling to introduce and to develop to reduce farmers' dependence on expensive pesticides and also the serious environmental and health effects the have. They were working very hard at securing markets in Europe and North America for organic, fair trade cotton, as an alternative to the unsustainable, non-organic cotton in the region that poisoned soils and the farmers who worked them.[319] Those development workers and Malians working with organic cotton were infuriated to see the GM crop that the US was pushing – the *"coton biotechnologique"* (GM cotton) – being referred to as *"coton bio"* (organic cotton), obscuring the vast difference between the two.

During my visit to cotton villages around Bougouni, I asked random farmers what they thought about GM cotton.

"It is a way to re-colonize us," said one farmer. "If you need to go and buy the seed somewhere else, then I'm against it. This creates a kind of dependence and I don't like it," said another. "It is against our culture," said another, "it will take away our dignity." The responses were unanimously negative.

On the streets of Bamako, I quizzed random passers-by in front of the main post office on what they knew of GMOs. No one had any idea of what they were. One man suggested that GMO was the name of a new NGO. The others shook their heads, mystified, and then asked me to tell them what a genetically modified crop was. When I explained, they were aghast. The response of one young man was particularly memorable. "White people are so incredibly smart that sometimes they become incredibly stupid," he said, laughing. "They think they can do God's work. But only God can do that."

I'm not naïve – okay I'm not *completely* naïve – or under the illusion that aid always is or should be beneficial to the recipient *only*. This is certainly not the first time that bilateral or multilateral development assistance has been closely tied to commercial or political interests in the donor country, and clearly designed to benefit an industry or industries there.

The US makes sure that 80 cents of every aid dollar is returned to the home country. About 60 to 75 percent of Canadian aid is tied.[320] Some Canadian companies, such as SNC Lavalin International, do a thriving business obtaining development funds for construction projects around the world. One Canadian oil executive I met recently in West Africa told me he formerly worked for the Canadian International Development Agency (CIDA), and when I politely inquired about the project he had worked on, he said vaguely that it had to do with an oil pipeline in Pakistan. Another CIDA employee I met one evening in Bamako told me his work with CIDA had been a long-term project to map the mineral resources of Zaire, now the Democratic Republic of Congo. When we spoke, he was on a two-year sabbatical from CIDA, working with Canadian mining companies that had taken out concessions in that country. In the 1980s in Burkina Faso, I had met a team of Canadians who were flying an odd-looking plane so full of antennae and wires that it resembled a flying catfish. When I asked the crew what kind of plane it was, they told me it was for mapping the underground riches of Burkina Faso, whose gold is now being mined today by foreign – and several Canadian – companies.

These tales of 'development assistance,' or 'cooperation,' or 'aid,' that support multinationals involved in extractive industries or agribusiness rather than malnourished children are not the kinds of success stories that the ordinary tax-paying citizen is likely to find in glossy publications put out by agencies such as CIDA, Britain's DFID or USAID. As author Giles Bolton puts it, "Many of our governments in the West … are generally quite pleased to avoid telling the public too much about how their aid is spent."[321]

This is the kind of aid that the NGO ActionAid International describes as "phantom." The ActionAid study looked at official aid budgets of the G7 countries to show that almost two-thirds of all funds in these constituted "phantom aid." That is: they were not targeted for poverty reduction; they were double counted as debt relief; they were overpriced and ineffective (technical assistance); they were tied to goods and services from the donor; they were spent on immigration or they were spent on excess administration costs.[322] Nearly 90 percent of all contributions coming from the United States and France can be considered phantom aid. According to ActionAid, "What this comes down to is that the US government is spending the tax dollars of well meaning Americans on bloated, inefficient and manipulative programs that do little to help the poor." Also unbeknownst to many tax-paying Americans is that for many years, the top two recipients of their aid money (which can include military spending) have been Israel and Egypt, hardly among the world's least developed nations or home to the world's poorest people.

But this link between USAID and multinationals and the intense pressure they were applying on African governments to adopt GM seeds seemed particularly insidious and subversive. It was reminiscent of the notorious Nestlé campaign to promote infant formula in the developing world, by giving away free samples and dressing up its agents as medical personnel, which had earned the Swiss company a worldwide boycott and a damaged reputation among many conscientious consumers.

The offices of Mali's agricultural research organization, the Institute of Rural Economy, as well as the ministry of agriculture and some Malian NGOs, were flooded with glossy booklets that read like development fairy tales about how companies such as Syngenta were helping Africa's impoverished and hungry farmers leap into the technological age with biotechnology that would improve their lives. Nowhere did these publications mention the terms "genetically modified" or GMOs.

Unlike serious scientific publications – refereed journals with independent research papers, or reference books, which are so difficult for Malian agricultural researchers to get their hands on – these public relations booklets were omnipresent. I found dozens of copies of Syngenta booklets stacked on rickety tables in the dusty and rather poorly equipped offices of national agricultural researchers in the town of Ségou in Mali.

From its corporate website, I knew that Syngenta was a global corporation with Swiss origins, and run by a Board of Directors comprising eleven men and one woman, average age of 57.4 years and average annual incomes of, well, we just have to imagine what recompense they received for trying to help impoverished African farmers, with a little left over for their shareholders and CEO on the side.[323] And from the way it presented itself in the corporate propaganda being distributed to Malians, it looked as if Syngenta were the charity wing of a particularly compassionate church group interested only in the welfare of African farmers.

The brochure I studied in Ségou described a very sophisticated and highly developed network of agricultural agents in villages that was already set up in the region, almost indistinguishable from earlier and crucial government agricultural extension services that had been decimated or eliminated under Structural Adjustment Programs. The multinationals were spreading their tentacles all over the place, trying to take control of agricultural production.

Who needs weapons when you control food and cash crop production?

But, as the popular axiom goes in Africa, you can't fool all the people all of the time. In July 2004, copies of the USAID-Mali five-year-project to test and introduce GMOs to the country got into the hands of a small group of concerned citizens: farmers; teachers and university professors; the umbrella group of women's associations; non-governmental organizations and members of the country's civil society. They acted very quickly, forming the Malian Coalition against GMOs and organizing a press conference to expose – and oppose – what looked like a done deal between Mali's Institute of Rural Economy and USAID with its partners, Syngenta and Monsanto.

They addressed the country's parliament and prime minister, and wrote to Pamela White, director of USAID in Mali, protesting the way that GMOs were being introduced.[324] They copied their letter to President Amadou Toumani Touré, and representatives of the European Union, Canada and UN agencies working in Mali.

USAID's Pamela White replied: "In our opinion, the modern tools of biotechnology offer enormous potential to increase food security, assure the conservation of the environment and safe food supply as well as economic opportunities for small-scale farmers … We sincerely hope that a transparent and participative approach will permit the government and people of Mali to decide what role modern biotechnology will play in the future of the country."[325]

Hoping to learn more about the "transparent and participative" approach that USAID was intending, I rang them up – repeatedly. My many calls were not returned.

The letter from Pamela White did nothing to appease or reassure Malian genetics professor and coalition member, Dr. Asséto Samaké. In an ill-equipped lecture hall at the under-funded university, Professor Samaké trembled with indignation and fury as she spoke about the USAID push for Bt cotton in Africa, counting the ways that she said it would harm and not help Malians.

First, she said, was the tragic irony that it was the very same interest groups that were pressuring Mali to take on GMOs that had been making it impossible for Mali's cotton growers to sell their cotton at decent prices, with their subsidies that suppressed the world price for the commodity.

"Once again it's them [the US] making the choice to experiment with Bt cotton," she said. "The reason is that this is profitable for them and it isn't profitable for us. Already, with their simple digging sticks and limited means, our peasants manage to produce cotton at record levels, and they have a problem selling their cotton. So how can they [the US] come now and propose a new package of technologies to help our peasants double their production when the [cotton] production is already there and they can't even sell it?"

Her voice rose, her anger reverberating in the hot lecture room at the University of Mali. "It's absurd! It's absurd to propose such a thing. It's an absurd choice. The advantages that they are claiming for this cotton are absolutely false! They say that with transgenic cotton one can reduce the amounts of pesticides used on the cotton, but that's absolutely false."

Samaké said that the same multinationals backed by foreign donors had introduced the pesticides into the farming systems in Africa, and that no studies had ever been done on the effects those were having on the health of the farmers or the environment. "We don't mention pollution or the question of resistance. We don't talk about the effects of these poisons on the peasant farmers and their families. And I say to myself that any technology that doesn't make life better for human beings is a technology that makes no sense. And now, lo and behold, they come and say that GMOs offer an alternative to the pesticides, to reduce the quantity of pesticides needed. I say it's all false."

She said that cotton has thousands of predators, and the Bt cotton, infected with *Bacillus thuringiensis*, could be resistant to only two or three predators. When those were eliminated, opportunities were created for other predators to take over and perhaps even increase their virulence. Pesticides would still be needed to combat those predators as they filled the niche, and by then, the farmers would be locked into the Bt cotton and beholden to the companies that provided the Bt seed and the pesticides. These were, she noted, the "very same corporations."

"We don't have enough specialists to watch the effects of that cotton in the fields," she said. "And so it will be those corporations that send us the cotton who will come and study its effects. And perhaps in five or ten years, those same people who are sending us the Bt cotton will come and negotiate funds and projects for protecting the environment in various zones. More billions in aid to add to those sent to Africa to resolve problems that they created! And they will then profit by creating still more projects [...] when you look at the sums allocated to that Bt cotton project and at the sum allocated for their own so-called experts, it's all a big farce."

"Africa is the place for experimenting," she said. "When you come to Africa you can do whatever you like, all you have to do is knock on the right door ... the pressure [on African governments] is enormous, they [the foreign powers] play on our vulnerability, they sell us a situation and profit from the weakness of our states."

Kako Nubupko, a Togolese economist with the cotton program of the French Agricultural Research Centre for International Development (CIRAD), told me that there was a real problem of productivity of Malian cotton, but he said this had to do with decreasing support for the farmers from the national textile company, CMDT, and because poverty drove farmers with no experience of growing cotton to start trying to produce the crop for cash, often on infertile lands unsuited to its cultivation. "To say that GMOs, notably Bt cotton, are going to be the miracle solution for this problem I don't believe that for one second," said Nubukpo.

He said his biggest concern about the introduction of Bt cotton into Mali was the way it was being done. "We are in the context of weak states, that is to say that the control and preconditions for any research on biotechnology here will not be effective. So it could be dangerous to introduce technology of which we are not the masters into a system that is fragile, especially after 20 years of structural adjustment, which have removed from our countries any effective means for controlling what happens to them."

Nubupko said that both CIRAD and the Institute of Rural Economy in Mali had asked for independence in their research on GMOs, independence from the multinational companies, Monsanto and Syngenta, which he said were "unfortunately very much behind the introduction of Bt cotton in Mali." He noted that Mali had signed the Cartagena Protocol on Biosafety to the Convention on Biodiversity, which stipulated that everything about GMOs must be transparent to prevent genetic pollution.

"The difficulty we have with these multinationals is that they don't want to agree that we publish the results of our research without their approval," Nubupko told me. "And that, for a researcher, is unacceptable. My personal opinion is that we should not add to an already difficult situation for the producers this problem that will make the producers even more dependent on the multinationals."

Nubukpo told me that because of his scientific research and published reports, he had received a warning letter from the French ambassador to Mali, informing him that he could easily be posted out of the country.

In October 2005, I visited Mali's Ministry of Agriculture and its research affiliate, the Institute for Rural Economy, to get the views from some of those in favour of introducing GMOs to the country. Vehicles parked outside, Chrysler Jeeps, were emblazoned with USAID stickers. So was the new office equipment – desks, computers, printers – inside. Seydou Traoré, Mali's Minister of Agriculture, told me that Africa had been left behind, that it had not benefited from the Green Revolution and that biotechnology was a way to remedy and modernize Africa's agriculture.

I asked him if he was aware of the allegations of bribes being paid out to African researchers and government officials, or the admission by Monsanto that it had bribed an Indonesian official to try to prevent environmental impact studies of its Bt cotton.

"I simply do not know of any bribes in Mali that have anything to do with biotechnology and GMOs," he replied. "In any case, today Mali is a democratic country, where the concern is good governance. And there are institutions to fight against corruption that are already in place and working, such as the special court for corruption and the auditor general. And I think these institutions work fairly well, and if there are cases of corruption elsewhere around the debate on biotechnology and GMOs, in Mali at least right now, we are not aware of them."[326]

Bribery comes in many forms. Economist Mamadou Goïta, organizer of the World Social Forum in Mali in 2006, said that all the evidence pointed to some form of financial persuasion. He noted that the former director of Mali's Institute of Rural Economy had gone to work for the multinational Syngenta, as representative in the country. Goïta said he happened one day to sit beside the director of Monsanto's France office on a flight from Montreal to Paris, and engaged him in a casual discussion about the giant corporation's work in Africa. The Monsanto director told him that Africa was not of much interest economically for the company. Their interest in West Africa was purely "strategic" – it was just a place to introduce and test various GM seeds, which would in turn help the company convince other continents to accept biotechnology – notably Europe, where consumers were still trying to hold out.

"That means that these multinationals, helped by the US government, are trying first with all their financial capacity to corrupt our researchers," said Goïta. "They did it in Burkina, where they corrupted the farmers' organization that was trying to stop it [the introduction of GMOs]. And now they are trying to do it in Mali."

He said studies done in India had shown that Bt cotton had performed very poorly: it was not resistant to pests; it did not produce higher yields and did not bring higher income to farmers. According to Goïta, GMOs would take Africa's farmers down a dead-end road. He said that traditionally, and up until 1995 when the World Trade

Organization decided that seeds were property that could be copy-righted, farmers in Africa and throughout the tropics had always produced many varieties of seed on their own. They shared these freely with their neighbours and even with neighbouring villages. Mali's farmers, with annual incomes of less than 260 US dollars, were not in a position to purchase many seeds of any kind, let alone patented and jealously safeguarded GM seed from multinationals such as Monsanto. Goïta said that Mali's coalition had watched with interest – and then dismay – as Monsanto took Canadian farmer Percy Schmeiser to court and won their claim that even if he didn't know Monsanto's Roundup Ready canola was growing on his land, it was his responsibility to pay for the seed.[327]

In Africa, Goïta said, there was enormous danger that traditional seed varieties would be lost if farmers use GMOs for a season or two. He thought they would be completely trapped in the vice of the multinational agribusinesses. "For sure, they may give them [Bt cotton seeds] to the farmers today just to introduce them," he said. "But the farmers will not be able to pay for them the day they ask them to start paying. And that's what they do. In Pakistan, they started giving farmers the seeds for free, but later on they had to pay for them. And there were so many people that killed themselves, because they could not pay and by then, they had lost all their local seeds."

He said the greatest irony of all was that cotton production in America – the most expensive and least efficient per hectare in the world – was already largely GM cotton.

"If GM cotton is so effective and good for farmers," he asked rhetorically, "then why is American cotton, so much of it GM, the most expensive to produce per hectare on the planet, not viable enough to be produced without four billion dollars worth of subsidies?"

Mamadou Mana Diakité, regional director of a movement called Seeds of Hope and country director in Mali for the Canadian NGO, USC, was another who vehemently opposed the push to GM crops in Africa. He pointed out that in marginal areas in Africa, where rains are so erratic, subsistence farmers may have to plant up to three times before a crop starts to grow. If they have to buy seeds, he said, it would be "a disaster."

He maintained that Africa's farmers are the last remaining bastion of African sovereignty, producing and maintaining seed varieties they inherited from their forefathers that are well adapted to the difficult climatic conditions many face. USC projects help small farming communities set up seedbanks and live germplasm banks with their own seed and plant varieties, rather than depend on imported, purchased hybrid seed varieties. He said these measures are insurance for times when crops fail, helping to prevent famine. When I asked him if his approach wasn't a step backwards, whereas the biotechnology was being presented as a step forward for Africa's farmers, he reacted hotly and without hesitation.

"It's part of Western culture to believe that technology is the solution to development. I don't think in the area of food security that is true. The first thing is to bring farmers to control their own resources. And I think it's a better way than bringing them to seed resources they have to access by paying. Because once they introduce GMO crops into Africa, farmers will only access if they pay, which culturally does not fit. The way they do it is exchange seeds. With GMOs, this will be illegal."

And why did he think some African governments, including Mali's Minister of Agriculture, were extolling the virtues of genetically modified crops? "There is pressure coming from outside that they can't divert. It's very difficult for an African government to fight something being imposed by a super-giant like the United States and all those seed companies."

And so the campaign of stealth to convert the world's farmers to GMO seeds continues. Where there is opposition that translates into bans on GMOs as there has been in the European Union, the US – along with its ally Canada that has championed the use of extreme "terminator" form of GM seeds at global fora – try to have the World Trade Organization strike them down.[328] One of those who had spearheaded those American challenges on behalf of biotechnology companies at the WTO is Robert Zoellick, who went on to become president of the World Bank.

Against such Goliaths, it is nothing short of miraculous that all those little Davids in Mali and elsewhere in Africa – farmers, teachers, cash-starved NGOs – continue to stand their ground, and occasionally, win their valiant battles for sovereignty of their seeds and their farms.

14

Why do you bring your mistakes here?

Indigenous cultural knowledge has always been an open treasure box for the unfettered appropriation of items of value to Western civilization. While we assiduously protect rights to valuable knowledge among ourselves, indigenous people have never been accorded similar rights over their cultural knowledge.

Thomas Greaves[329]

As I write this, I am listening to a report on the BBC World Service. UN Secretary General Ban Ki-moon is calling for a "Green Revolution" to "transform farming methods" in Africa to address escalating food prices around the world.[330] By that he means industrial farming, which requires the use of fossil fuels – or biofuels. One of the causes of sky-rocketing food prices is the use of arable land and food crops to produce biofuel to feed the industrial world, which is in turn changing the world's climate and not surprisingly, reducing the amount of arable land available to produce food. Some call the use of food crops to produce biofuel a "crime against humanity."[331] Nevertheless, the UN Secretary General thinks industrial agriculture, a new Green Revolution, is the solution for Africa.

In early 2008, the same message came from the alpine resort of Davos, Switzerland, where a select few of the wealthiest and most powerful people in the world gather at the World Economic Forum each year – by invitation only – to talk about the future of the planet. Some Cameroonian farmers waxed philosophically to me one day:

if you have money then you have power, and vice versa. And those who gather in Davos are so rich and powerful that when they talk, we ordinary mortals should really listen carefully. Many of them are the individuals deciding the future for the rest of us.[332] "Those with power and wealth determine how things will be for those without," writes Gerald Caplan.[333]

In the rarefied air of the Swiss Alps in 2008, Bill Gates announced that the Melinda and Bill Gates Foundation was giving "306 million dollars to to boost the yields and incomes of small farmers in Africa and other parts of the developing world."[334] The founder of Microsoft Corp said, "If we are serious about ending extreme hunger and poverty around the world, we must be serious about transforming agriculture for small farmers – most of whom are women."

Some internationally acclaimed economists are also joining in the chorus for a new Green Revolution in Africa, claiming this will solve problems of hunger and poverty on the continent. The Rockefeller Foundation launched the Alliance for a Green Revolution, or AGRA, with 180 million US dollars from the Gates Foundation.[335] AGRA is chaired by the former Secretary-General of the United Nations, Kofi Annan. It issues press releases saying the Green Revolution will "breathe new life" into Africa's depleted soils and combat hunger and poverty. And the media repeat their claims almost verbatim, unquestioned.[336] Yet, if the entire world were to turn to industrial North American-style farming with its petroleum-based fertilizers and transportation, the world would be out of oil by 2014.[337]

African productivity and farming have been depressed and stifled by the very groups now clambering for its increase, and policy makers would do well to consider this. A trip to the local markets in West Africa can be educational. Before biofuel really took off and sent commodity speculators into a tizzy of mad profit-making from foodstuffs, driving up their prices and putting an end to cheap surplus produce for export, I spent a lot of time in markets. Every market I visited – in The Gambia, Burkina Faso, Mali, Ghana, Sierra Leone – was piled high with such dumped produce. Here is a short list of what I found: *Ladybug* onions from Holland; eggs from India; turkey necks and backs from the US; lentils and canola oil from Canada; corn from the US; palm oil from Malaysia; rice from the US, China, Thailand

and India and sugar from unidentified sources. There was no way that Africa's farmers could compete with such vast quantities of subsidized produce – much of it inferior quality and unmarketable in its country of origin – dumped on their markets.[338] At the same time, the European and North American negotiators at failed WTO talks on trade liberalization continued to baulk at opening their markets to more agricultural produce from developing countries, and stalled on ending subsidies to their own farmers. The Doha Round talks that had begun in 2001, failed repeatedly, collapsing yet again in July 2008, largely because of the increasingly strident demands from India and China and because of these inconsistencies and injustices in agricultural trade.

Undermined by the cheap imports, for decades Africa's subsistence farmers could hardly subsist on what they produced and youth flocked to the cities, abandoning the rural areas and farming. In cities, they could usually feed themselves, thanks to the abundance of cheap foods. Then, almost overnight in 2008, the era of cheap food ended and the hardest hit were the very poorest.

In Africa, city populations that had swollen and survived because of cheap imported foodstuffs suddenly found themselves unable to afford to feed themselves. In Freetown, people told me they were down to just one meal of rice a day, and some, unable to pay school fees *and* for food, were taking their children out of school. And suddenly, African governments were being convinced they needed to modernize and industrialize their farming, go for a Green Revolution to counter this problem that had been created far from their shores. The companies that were central to the first Green Revolution were proposing a new one based on a generation of crops that depend on genetic modification.[339]

Ignored or unacknowledged by the policy makers and the corporate lobby behind them were all the lessons on just how efficient, or rather inefficient, modern industrial agriculture was in North America and what it has done to our food supply, our health and the health of the planet and its beleaguered climate.[340] Also ignored were the overwhelmingly negative outcomes of the Green Revolution in India, documented by independent researchers, such as Indian physicist Vandana Shiva.[341]

The original Green Revolution involved the use of hybrid seeds, chemical pesticides and fertilizers produced by large agrochemical companies, and mechanized agriculture that was supposed to increase crop production. In 1970, Norman Borlaug received the Nobel Peace Prize for the miracle seeds he had developed that were supposed to "speed economic growth in general in the developing countries."

Some of the literature applauded the Green Revolution as wildly successful, although some also showed that persistent use of pesticides and chemical fertilizers without organic input eventually led to poorer soils and never-ending debt for impoverished farmers caught in the trap of borrowing money to purchase farm inputs and then not being able to repay the loans after harvest. Vandana Shiva said this of the effects this science-based agriculture had on the Indian Punjab, where it was supposed to have been a celebrated success: "Paradoxically, after two decades of the Green Revolution, Punjab is neither a land of prosperity, not peace ... Instead of abundance, Punjab has been left with diseased soils, pest-infested crops, water-logged deserts and indebted and discontented farmers."[342] Suicide rates among farmers soared. The UN announced that in 1995-96, more than a third of farmers in Punjab, the epicentre of Indian's high-tech Green Revolution, faced "ruin and a crisis of existence."[343]

All these works contain important warnings about how little we truly understand of nature's complexities, how dangerous is the hubris of those promoting policies and technologies that further aggravate and even create new problems for farmers.

In 1973, then president of the World Bank, Robert McNamara, noted that the Green Revolution had not benefited poor farmers around the world.[344]

Those promoting a new Green Revolution in Africa might also want to find out a little more about what happened with the first Green Revolution on the continent. In doing so, they might do well to talk to some African farmers, and better still, listen to what they have to say.

The lessons Africans have to offer – often from farmers who have never set foot inside a schoolroom – are telling and extremely enlightening. I was the involuntary recipient of one of these insightful lectures in 1992. This was in northern Ghana, and I was working on a survey on firewood consumption. It was part of a project that aimed to reduce fuelwood consumption by introducing improved clay cookstoves to replace traditional three-stone hearths typical of the region. My professor was an elderly woman with few teeth and a big mischievous grin. She lived in a tiny village near the eastern town of Bimbilla.

It was late afternoon and we were preparing to head back to a small NGO-run guesthouse in Bimbilla, where there would be running water for a welcome shower. The elderly woman was our final interviewee of the day. She dutifully finished answering all the questions, confirming what many women in the area had already suggested – that after their long daily treks for water, the search for firewood every two or three days was becoming their greatest physical burden – among many others.

I was pondering the sad fate of the remaining tree cover in northern Ghana, which was under ever-increasing pressure. At this point, Ghana had been rigidly adhering for a decade to structural adjustment as proposed by the World Bank to bring economic reform and with it, prosperity. The prosperity had yet to arrive. Much of the nation's remaining tropical forests to the south had come down, providing export earnings from timber and more land for cocoa production, ostensibly to stimulate economic growth and to service debt. In the Northern Region, poverty had grown and this, coupled with insatiable hunger for charcoal in burgeoning urban centres, forced many rural families – the farmers who chose to stay on the land in rural areas – to supplement their meagre livelihoods by making charcoal from wood they hacked off living trees or from whole trees they felled.

An estimated 60-80 percent of the wood energy was lost in the charcoal-making process. Some village chiefs in northern Ghana, recalling the wisdom of their forefathers who preached conservation of God-given tree resources, spoke out against charcoal-making. But they said that without that hard-got income, many of their people would not be able to make ends meet or pay school and health fees. All this was going through my mind as I packed away the questionnaire, preparing to bid the elderly woman goodbye. She, however, had other ideas.

Now that she had answered our questions, she wanted to have her say too. While Zara, the survey team's interpreter, translated her words from Nanumba into English, I hastily scribbled them down. This is what she had to say to us.

"You people with your education and foreign ways, we don't understand you," she said. "When I was a young girl, you came here and you told us to cut down the trees that we always left growing in our millet and sorghum fields. You told us to cut them down and to plant maize instead. Only maize. You told us not to plant it with beans or around the trees the way we always planted our millet and sorghum. You said we should grow it by itself. You told us to buy tractors and to use modern farming methods. So we did. We bought fertilizer. We cut down our trees, even the economic trees we needed for protecting our soil and for shea butter and our foods.[345] We bought your maize seed. We did everything you said. Our tractors broke down and we couldn't get fuel. You sent the tractors but we had no means to repair them. Next thing, you people came here and told us to never mind the tractors; tractors were not good. You said we should go back to using bullocks to plough our fields because it was better than tractors after all. Then we couldn't buy fertilizer any more because it became too costly.[346] So our harvests just get poorer and poorer. We don't have our own seed any more and we cannot afford to buy the seed you sell us. You come again and tell us we should use manure and trees to fertilize our fields. But we don't have any of the trees left that used to feed us and make the soil rich because you told us to cut them down. And so we can't find fuelwood. We spend our days walking, walking, walking to get some small firewood and water. Now you strangers come again and tell us we should plant plenty of trees, not cut them down."

She paused, finally, eyed us each carefully – myself and the Ghanaian team doing the survey. Then she ran her tongue over her lips and said, "Why don't you make up your minds? We are tired of this. Why do you bring your mistakes here?"

We had no answer for her. In lieu of a reply, we asked her if she would like to participate in a few days of training on making her own improved cook stove. She shook her head and said she'd rather wait and see. She said younger women could attend and if the cook stoves they learned to make were good ones, then one of the younger women could come and teach her how to make one. That way, she could decide for herself whether this was really a good idea, or just another mistake offered as help from abroad.

What that wise elderly woman described to us that afternoon was the advent of the Green Revolution – first time around in the 1960s and 70s. Apparently it hadn't worked very well in northern Ghana.

For decades, agricultural development programs in Africa have been based on models and scientific knowledge imported from temperate lands and industrialized countries, where disciplines are constantly being divided into smaller and smaller boxes. In North America, the mixed family farm that was the backbone of the economy in the first half of the early 20th century is now regarded as a quaint oddity, something for the nostalgia room of a local museum or a theme for a Normal Rockwell painting, no longer useful or relevant for our modern age. Banks have foreclosed on them at a great rate.

Apart from the struggle by small organic producers and a growing number of fair trade companies working with them to reverse the trend, monoculture, chemical fertilizers and pesticides have become the order of the day, both for crops and trees. Universities generally offer programs in specialized areas of agriculture, or forestry, or animal husbandry, because these tend to be separate entities in the temperate world. For decades, universities in Europe and North America turned out graduates – including African ones – who had been taught to view agriculture as something separate from forestry and animal husbandry, despite the fact that on African farms, these disciplines were and remain an integrated, indivisible whole. This, despite advice to the contrary way back in the early 1960s from French agronomist Réné Dumont, who advocated farmer co-operatives and schools devoted to agriculture for peasant farmers to improve their production and keep them in rural areas: "I hope that Africa does not copy our current arbitrary division of disciplines, which are already out-of-date without our realizing it."[347]

How were Western-trained scientists to apply their European and North American university degrees to African farming, unless they went with the European models that often didn't work on African ground?

The vast majority of Africa's farmers do as their forefathers did, combining crops, trees and livestock in highly complex farming systems that reduce risks and provide a wide range of essential products in addition to staple crops. The trees and shrubs in these systems are crucial sources of medicines, oils, timber, fruit, nuts, spices and fibre – as well as providing food security in times of crop failure and drought and maintaining soil fertility.

In the mid-1970s, a few thoughtful individuals – many from the tropics themselves – finally spoke out, saying that African agricultural development was on the wrong track. Development experts began to speak about "farming systems." A group of far-sighted researchers and development experts came up with the term "agroforestry," which was to be the new name for the very old game of integrating food crops with trees and animal husbandry, and they set up the International Council for Research in Agroforestry (ICRAF) in Nairobi, Kenya.[348] According to M. Sambasivan Swaminathan, its first Board Chair, agroforestry was "a grassroots science. All over the world, systems of agroforestry prevailed. It offered food security and nutrition. It grew out of observation, practise and traditional wisdom."[349]

The Green Revolution had not just missed its mark with Africa's subsistence farmers. It had also tended to miss or dismiss the importance of traditional knowledge and the inherent complexities – and advantages – of a traditional farm. This farm might include a market or home-garden near the homestead, staple grain or tuber crops interspersed with a wide range of valuable trees scattered in cropland over which the family had no fixed or legal tenure, and a few goats, chickens, sheep and cows for good measure. Nearby woodlands or forests supplemented needs, and fallow periods were carefully planned to avoid depleting or degrading land. Imported ideas of modern farming – as that elderly woman pointed out to me – had disrupted the traditional farming systems that protected soils and watersheds and recycled nutrients on the farm.[350]

Africa's subsistence farmers don't use phrases like "recycle nutrients," or publish their wisdom in peer-reviewed journals or official reports. They just grow crops and manage trees for the welfare of their own families and communities, often cultivating communal fields that serve as a food safety net for those in need. Diversity is their best protection against crop failure and famine, and it is this diversity that agroforestry both recognizes and promotes. It was also a defence against the spread of deserts – both the Sahara in West Africa and the Kalahari in southern Africa.

Climate change researchers have warned Western donors and African politicians that they should not pursue development policies that exacerbate the "shifting sands" of the massive desert dunes, turning semi-arid regions into desert. An Oxford University team specifically cited European support for livestock production in Botswana, which increased pressure on already fragile water resources in that country.[351]

Africans have not benefited from the energy-guzzling lifestyles that contribute so much to climate change, but that doesn't mean they are being spared its ravages. Rainfall is projected to drop still further in some of the continent's driest zones. Some reports suggest that Africa is being hit first and hardest by climate change; that it is losing as much precious water to climate change each year as it actually uses.[352]

New international and UN programs are springing up to help Africa adapt to climate change, while North America continues to waffle and procrastinate on tackling its own carbon emissions. International development experts across Africa often set less-than-stellar examples – running generators to power air conditioners, driving about in air-conditioned four-wheel drive vehicles that get washed every day, water scarcities be damned, importing the wasteful habit of running a vehicle engine to keep the air conditioning working, and living in immodest homes full of every appliance and amenity possible, and then reporting to donors on the 'sustainable development' they are bringing.

And now there is the new and possibly criminal push to transform food crops into biofuels to feed the hungry industrial monster – to produce more food that can in turn become biofuel. It would be a never-ending story except that Mother Nature is getting rather warm lately, and arable land to produce all this theoretical food is becoming a little scarce.

This doesn't stop the entrepeneurs who are already profiting from climate change, biofuels and food shortages. In July 2008, a group of the world's biggest agribusiness companies – Monsanto, Archer Daniels Midland, Deere and DuPont – got together and announced they would plough "several million dollars" into lobbying on Capitol Hill and national ads to build the case for biofuels, even as grain prices climbed worldwide.[353]

They set their sights overseas for more sources of land to produce them. The Titanium Resource Group, which sells much of the rutile it produces in southern Sierra Leone to one of those powerful corporations, DuPont, sought a vast swath of the country to produce oil palm, which would produce palm oil for biodiesel. Agribusinesses, working hand in hand with donors, scouted out huge tracts of land for sugar (ethanol) plantations.[354] In early 2008 I saw a proposal in Sierra Leone by a multinational investment company, "our focus is on investment and management in agribusiness, forestry and the environment," comprising several diamond magnates (some South African and British) who wanted to establish a massive oil palm plantation and industrial processing plant in the most fertile part of the country. Sierra Leone is still desperately trying to regain its own food security by rejuvenating smallholder farms, rice swamps, cocoa and oil palm plots after the devastating civil war. The multinational investors put in a few lines about how their palm oil venture was to help local producers. If they had written "cows can fly" it would have been just as believable. Their real aim was to capitalize on the escalating cost of the palm oil – formerly a poor man's food and suddenly a potential gold mine for those wishing to sell it as fuel. The observant reader would note a few words tucked into the proposal about the ready market for their palm oil turned biofuel: Sierra Leone's rutile mine.

The push towards massive plantations for cash crops and biofuels ignores entirely the proven benefits of small-scale agroforestry plots for the people who work them and for the landscape. Despite all the academic interest in agroforestry in the tropics, it still remains one of the world's best – and best kept – secrets. In the Sahel region – from Chad across to Senegal – the traditional agroforestry system known as the "parklands," in which valuable trees are allowed to grow in cropland, functioned well for centuries. In the parklands, crops are grown around indigenous trees that are carefully managed, but tend not to be planted because of taboos. Until fairly recently, fallow periods allowed natural regrowth for trees, trees that provided food security and protected against soil erosion and depletion, drought and the spread of deserts.

Most trees have many uses, perhaps none more so than the magnificent baobab. Their leaves are rich in vitamin A, and in much of West Africa are the main vegetable in sauces consumed every day. Baobab fruit is extremely high in vitamins A and C, and can be dried and made into an absolutely delicious juice with anti-oxidant characteristics and hepatoprotective activities. Its bark is used to make rope and chords. And the tree itself, a stunning display of nature's architectural genius that inspired the "Ent" characters in J.R.R. Tolkien's *Lord of the Rings* series, provides a home for beehives for local honey production. As if that were not enough, the magnificent baobab grows in a wide variety of environments across the continent. This tree of life has enormous potential, not just for Africans to capitalize on by processing and marketing its products locally for urban consumption, but also as ideal fair trade products. In 2008, the EU approved the import of baobab fruit pulp to Europe, which could provide Africa with a valuable new export.

The néré or dawa dawa tree (*Parkia biglobosa*) provides pods full of sweet yellow powder, nature's own instant cereal, and dark seeds that are fermented to produce a highly nutritious spice for sauces. Such homegrown and nutritious flavourings prevailed throughout West Africa before the advent of the Maggi cube promoted by slick television commercials. These show modern African women happily crumbling these flavour cubes into sauces boiling away in stainless steel pots in gleaming modern kitchens. This, of course, suggests that traditional spices from trees are somehow inferior, less likely to please that modern African husband in his suit and tie.

ICRAF researchers found that a single néré tree could double a family's annual income, bring in up to 270 US dollars a year. The néré tree, alas, is threatened – it grows very slowly and invasive, exotic species such as neem out-compete it.

There are also shea nut or *karité* trees (*Vitellaria paradoxa*) that produce fruit at the end of the dry season, when food stocks are low and energy is required for planting as the rains began. The seeds from these fruit produce a high-quality butter or oil with an amazing range of uses – in sauces, to light lamps, as a medicine, as a cosmetic to protect hair and skin from the ravages of dry Sahelian air. The dark residue from the butter-making process was traditionally applied to mud walls and floors, to give them a lustrous and protective finish. Consumers in North America may have noticed in recent years that many of the soaps, shampoos, skin creams they buy contain *karité*.

Another tree integral to the parklands agroforestry system – *Faidherbia albida* – is sacred to many Sahelian peoples, who believe it possesses almost mystical powers. It does what other Sahelian trees do not: loses its leaves in the rainy season and keeps them during the nine months of annual drought, offering invaluable shade during the hottest time of the year to both humans and livestock. As a result, surrounding soils are rich with animal manure and leaf litter, so the tree can actually boost yields around its base. The ancient town of Ségou in Mali is known as *la ville de balanzan*, which is the local name for the tree. There, Bamana elder and scholar Hasshim Sow told me the *balanzan* was synonymous with life itself. "It is a symbol of women, and without women there is no life. It is thus a symbol of eternity," he said. It is closely linked to his people's origin myths and history. Or it always had been, when Africans were doing their own management of the land and its resources.

Then, along came the French colonists with peanuts and maize, and instructions to Sahelian populations to plant these as monocultural cash crops and cut trees on agricultural fields. Unperturbed by the tragic irony of doing so, scientists named the tree *Faidherbia albida*, after French General Faidherbe who had governed the French Sudan in the 1800s. It was Faidherbe who introduced peanuts as a cash crop, which launched a new approach to farming in the region and led to the slow deterioration of the parklands system and its trees. Previously, traditional leaders who took care of the land and its trees imposed strict taboos on which trees could be cut down or lopped for firewood, and which could not – no live shea tree could be touched, for example.

After independence of the Sahelian countries, international experts arrived, many of whom, like colonial administrator Faidherbe before them, had little knowledge of or interest in indigenous food crops and trees. Many valuable slow-growing indigenous trees were cut down to make way for larger fields of cash crops or orchards of exotic fruit trees with which the 'experts' were familiar, such as mangoes and oranges. When desertification became a real threat, more European experts advised the planting of fast-growing exotic species such as eucalyptus trees in green belts and reserves that put them off limits to rural people in need of firewood. These thirsty trees would flourish for a few years, until they drank themselves dry and perished, poisoning the soil around them with toxins from their fallen leaves.

Neem trees, introduced from India where they are cherished for the pesticides they produce, aggressively out-compete slower-growing indigenous tree species in Africa but their leaves and fruits are often used locally to produce pesticides and even disinfectants for sores. In the Sahel, they are an indication that the intricate balance of the parklands system is being lost. Land degradation, prolonged droughts, over-grazing and population pressure continue to take their toll, but these are not problems that can be solved by monoculture and further tree-cutting. Indeed, many of the modern problems are partly the result of modern land-use policies, which ignore the crucial role played by indigenous trees and promote instead models developed in and for temperate climates, with very different land-use and land-tenure patterns.

Agroforestry researchers in the Sahel called repeatedly for a rejuvenation of the parklands. They documented the incredible value of the trees in providing food security when annual crops failed, in protecting soils and other environmental services. In an extensive survey conducted in four Sahelian countries, they compiled a people's own "top ten" list of tree species, and found that with the exception of *Faidherbia albida*, every one of them is valued precisely because it provides crucial food security. Number one on the list in three countries is baobab.

The agroforestry research teams work with basic horticultural techniques to domesticate indigenous trees, which Sahelian farmers had always managed in their fields but never planted. They use horticultural techniques – grafting, rooting of cuttings and air-layering, or marcotting – allowing researchers and farmers to reduce by about half the number of years it takes a normally slow-growing local species to mature and produce.[355] These include potentially lucrative fruit trees such as tamarind and baobab that have the potential to produce enough for local beverage industries. Were such indigenous tree products recognized and valued as they should be, they could spawn a great deal of local industry and employment, not to mention healthy drinks.

There is also enormous medical potential in the trees. A 1997 book on the medicinal plants of the Sahel documents the progress in researching the vast range of illnesses that can be effectively treated with leaves, barks, roots and flowers of locally grown trees, suggesting that herein lies the basis for basic health care. This would be a revolutionary turn-around on a continent plagued by disease and unable to afford expensive imported pharmaceuticals.[356]

Take, as just one small example, the herbal tea that is popular throughout West Africa, known as *kinkéliba*. Were it to be promoted, developed and marketed regionally and internationally by the Africans who know it and love it, it could become a new and important commodity to drive local industry and economic growth. *Kinkéliba* comes from a hearty and extremely flexible wild plant that can be a mere shrub under four metres, a small tree up to ten metres tall or even a vine-like liana that can wind its way around other taller plants to reach heights of 20 metres. It flourishes in dry areas. Its seeds are edible; its branches a good source of wood for small-scale construction, and its roots and barks have medicinal properties. The tea from its leaves is delicious, or in a different concentration, a medicine for treating an amazing array of ailments, including: wounds, fever, syphilis, sterility, bruises, sprains, jaundice, hepatitis, haematuria, anorexia, colic, blennorrhoea, colds and bronchitis. In addition, extracts from the leaf have been found to "exhibit anti-viral and anti-inflammatory properties" as well as "anti-malarial properties."[357]

When I asked if I might have some of the *kinkéliba* that I saw my colleagues drinking in The Gambia, they were astounded because, they said, they didn't think white people liked local African drinks, or were interested in local African medicines.

This is just one of countless African natural treasures that are underpromoted, under-studied and undervalued in development efforts. Not that there have not been some efforts to rectify this. Over the years, most African countries have set up modest research units to examine the effectiveness and correct doses of traditional herbal medicines, and approved several of these. Some NGOs and missionaries have also worked hard to develop these local treasures, by documenting them and trying to market them. But the impetus has not been there to turn these into viable medicinal crops to be added to smallholder farms and home-gardens and when a valuable medicinal product is 'discovered' by the outside world, this may not benefit local people.[358]

Many Africans use "chewing sticks," small branches cut from various trees, to clean their teeth, gums and mouths every morning. There is no evidence that these natural products are any less effective than the modern toothbrush, toothpaste, dental floss and other products we are advised to use for dental hygiene, which have now also taken over from the chewing stick in most of Africa. In much of West Africa, pregnant women consume small amounts of fine white clay and say it provides them with calcium. Local knowledge such as this merits study and perhaps even promotion, before it is lost in the avalanche of advertising for imported consumer goods. Unfortunately, the tide seems to be against those who would value and promote local knowledge and resources on the continent.

The World Health Organization, the UN and huge international campaigns to fight malaria – some spearheaded again philanthropist billionaires in North America – are now promoting the use of mosquito nets dipped in insecticide and of indoor DDT-spraying as key elements in the fight against malaria.[359] The much-touted "Roll Back Malaria" campaign of UNICEF, WHO and the World Bank involved rolling back controls on the use of DDT. This followed a widespread and effective campaign by corporate America, and the right-wing think tanks and front groups it funds, to convince well-intentioned citizens in Europe and North America that if they really cared about "saving the lives of African mothers and children" they would see the light and support the use of DDT, which had been banned in their own countries since the 1970s.[360] In fact, some coun-

tries in Africa had never stopped using DDT and still suffered the ravages of malaria, as mosquitoes simply developed resistance to the
chemical. Human bodies do not.

These imported solutions harness the services of well-known and
well-intentioned stars and television personalities, and well-meaning
young people who raise money because they want to help. The
machinations and motivations of the corporate lobbies, particularly
efforts such as those by ExxonMobil and Monsanto via right-wing
think tanks to reintroduce DDT, which stand to profit from these
solutions are almost invisible, unless one goes digging.

The new and internationally accepted treatment for malaria is a
combination therapy with the herbal Artemisinin derived from the
Chinese herb *Artemisia annua* as its base. Artemisinin has been used
effectively for centuries as a traditional medicine in China. It wasn't
until Western pharmaceuticals began manufacturing Artemisinin
Combination-Therapy that the World Health Organization and
other international agencies began to promote its use in their anti-
malarial campaigns in Africa. The many traditional herbal medicines
that Africans have used for generations to prevent and treat malaria
are largely ignored.

As the years flip past, the problems of disease, food insecurity and
environmental degradation grow acute in the Sahelian countries, and
still only the farmers – and a handful of agroforestry researchers and
NGOs – recognize the medicinal and food value of the indigenous
trees and shrubs or understand the effectiveness of the traditional
approach to land use. In 2008, a UN-sponsored study, which took
four years and involved 400 researchers, recommended more "natural" and "ecological" farming methods to solve the growing global
food crisis and questioned the sustainability of the model of industrial agriculture and the Green Revolution. It also noted the "consider-
able influence" of large multinationals in North America and Europe
and expressed reservations about GMOs. Australia, Canada and the
US refused to approve the executive summary of the study.[361] At the
same time, in high places, and with much more media attention than
the UN landmark study received, new 'experts' call for Green

Revolution II, perhaps unaware that the very problems they say it will solve have their roots in Green Revolution I.

I recall once waxing lyrical about the parklands system to some highly placed European development experts in Mali to work on poverty-reduction, food security and agricultural development projects. It was a social gathering, and I thought it a perfect occasion to discuss with them the lessons I had been learning from agroforestry researchers and farmers with whom I worked, about the potential of the traditional tree-based systems. Only one man lingered to hear all of what I had to say, and then, with a dismissive gesture he said, "If this were important, I would have heard of it. I *am* a development expert, you know."

Surveys designed or done by foreign experts to assess nutritional content of people's diets often ignore completely anything that is not a staple annual crop, missing the important contribution that tree products and other 'wild' vegetation make to people's food supplies and health. Sometimes journalists from big media parachute into an African country and announce that the local people are so poor and hungry that they are "eating leaves and nuts from trees." If they had asked just a few pertinent questions before they spoke, they would have known that the leaves and nuts from many indigenous trees are standard and essential fare, providing food *and* nutritional security throughout the year, rounding out diets with essential minerals, protein and vitamins.

In 1999, I listened to a four-hour speech by Mali's then Prime Minister, Ibrahim Boubacar Keita, who outlined for Parliament the country's five-year development plan, developed with the usual help of donors and the World Bank. He spoke about hydro power, gold, cotton, rice and huge irrigation projects to increase its production along the River Niger, and electricity. He spoke about just about everything *except* the importance of trees in the landscape. Yet scientists have shown that trees in the Sahel are *the* greatest defence against food insecurity, famine and land degradation.

Prime Minister Keita did take a few minutes in his long-winded speech to mention the potential of Mali's "green gold," by which he meant the precious oil from the nut of the shea or *karité* tree. Europe and North American cosmetic and pharmaceutical markets were just discovering the full value of this new commodity that comes only from Africa's drylands. *Karité* had just been approved for use as a substitute for cocoa butter in European confectionery, and for many years was an expensive ingredient in medical ointments and in creams, shampoos and soaps manufactured in Europe and North America. Rather than invest in this valuable oil from Africa, by helping to support local producers and setting up factories to process the oil themselves, however, buyers were moving into the very last villages to buy up the shea nuts wholesale for shipment to Europe. In villages throughout Mali, women told me that "a white man" had been through to talk to them, offering to buy their whole crop of shea nuts. And they agreed, even though this might bring hardship to them in the peak of the dry season, when *karité* could be processed into butter and sold at the market when other resources were scarce.

The buyers for the foreign companies were dealing with some of the poorest people on the planet – rural women in the Sahelian countries – and so were offering bargain basement prices for an African resource, to people who had no idea of its modern monetary value, and great need for small income. And many of those people in Africa who could have invested in this local resource to process the shea butter locally and establish manufacturing plants for shea products – the small but very wealthy elite – were too busy putting their money into offshore accounts.

It is by no means an unfamiliar story in Africa.

The Congo Basin rainforest that once covered a good portion of Central African's lowlands is believed to be the world's greatest repository of biodiversity outside the Amazon. By the late 20th century, that genetic treasure trove had another distinction, albeit a dubious one. It was vanishing faster than any other forest in the world, at over ten times the rate it could regenerate if it were given the chance to do so. It wasn't. And yet, the non-timber forest products offered invaluable sustenance to the populations of Central Africa, producing enormous quantities of food, spices and other essential products for ordinary people's daily needs. Hundreds of spices, all from the forest, make Cameroon's wonderful and diverse cuisine one of the world's great unsampled delights.

A specialist on the non-timber wealth of Cameroon's forests, Odelia Ngala, worked for years with the forest-dwelling populations of her country. "The forest is everything for them," she told me. "For them, the forest is life. Not because of the timber – they don't have the machinery to harvest timber – but because of the other products that they collect from the forest."

In Campo, a small town in Cameroon's southern corner near the border with Equatorial Guinea, a national reserve had been set aside, in theory to protect its 2,640 square kilometres of tropical forest from logging operations. Its protection was in the hands of two park rangers equipped with a single motorcycle and no firearms. They despaired over their impossible task.

Inside the reserve, I followed a team of Cameroonian botanists and European researchers to a one-hectare plot managed by the Global Environmental Facility where a multinational team of scientists was studying biodiversity. Occasionally the hot, wet silence of the dark forest was broken by the trumpeting of lowland elephants, the hooting of chimpanzees, and then, faint but omnipresent, the muted roar of logging machines tearing it all up. We drove past one Dutch logging camp, and the rangers told us that there were similar ones – Chinese, Italian, French, German – throughout and around the edges of the reserve. The late Steve Gartlan, a noted primatologist who for many years headed the World Wildlife Fund in Cameroon, told me that many Canadian aid contributions to that country included modern logging equipment that hastened deforestation.

In 1994, France had agreed to cancel half the debt it was owed by Cameroon in exchange for almost exclusive logging rights to its remaining forests.[362] The major beneficiary of this deal would be the French company, Rougier, operating through its subsidiaries. The broker of the deal was French President Mitterrand's son, *Papamadit* Jean-Christophe.

Foreign concerns are interested in more than logs from Africa's forests. They are also interested in the medicines that can be harvested there. Cameroonian researchers estimate that more than 80 percent of the medicines consumed in the country come from the forests. Many of these tried and true remedies that have been proven effective by scientific researchers. Yet, once that knowledge has been obtained from the local people, modern approaches are taken to harvest those valuable medicines.

One of these is found in the bark from *Prunus africana*, or the pygeum tree, which grows only in Africa's montane forests at altitudes over 1300 metres above sea level.[363] The medicinal properties of the bark for the treatment of prostate gland enlargement (Benign Prostatic Hyperplasia) were discovered – by European pharmaceuticals that is – in the 1960s. Before that, local people harvested the bark for medicinal purposes themselves, removing only narrow panels of bark so as not to kill the tree. Once the harvesting became commercial, with local people hired by large pharmaceutical interests to collect the bark, tradition was on the chopping block, just like the tree. Pygeum populations dwindled and the tree was classified in the 1990s as an endangered species by the Convention on International Trade in Endangered Species (CITES).

In Cameroon, pygeum was just one of two valuable medicines being exploited for the French Fournier Group's Fine Chemical Division by its Cameroonian subsidiary, Plantecam.[364] In the early 1970s Plantecam had set up its high-security operation behind tall walls on the Atlantic coast, near the town of Limbe. Its attractive brochure about the medicinal plants and the extracts it was harvesting was emblazoned with the words "From the heart of Africa, we care for all your needs."

The other need that Plantecam was taking care of from Cameroon was sexual potency, using nature's own Viagra, which comes from the johimbe tree, *Pausinystalia johimbe*. Researchers at the German pharmaceutical company Boerhringer-Ingelheim, which obtained its johimbe bark from Plantecam, told me that German missionaries first learned of this powerful aphrodisiac from the local people in Cameroon in the 1800s, when the territory was still a German colony.[365] The missionaries sent samples home for testing. Early studies published in European medical journals as far back as 1905 showed that the active ingredient in the bark, yohimbine, was a powerful male stimulant, dilating blood vessels and increasing blood flow to the extremities while enhancing pelvic reflexes.

In the 1970s, when Plantecam established itself in Cameroon, it began the commercial harvest of this valuable medical commodity.

The knowledge of johimbe had come from the Baka pygmy populations, for whom the entire forest had been pharmacy, pantry and hardware store, rolled into one.

Unlike many other purported aphrodisiacs, such as white rhino horn, johimbe worked – even though the effect on the African sources for the potency medicines was as devastating as it had been for the beleaguered rhinoceros. Health shops, fitness centres and pharmacies all over the world marketed johimbe in one form or another.

All of this might have been well and good for Cameroon and the Baka pygmies who harvested the bark for Plantecam, had they been compensated for their knowledge, or if they were being paid decently for their work in the forest and if the tree itself were being harvested sustainably and not being cut into extinction.

The local men who harvested the bark – many of them the Baka whose forest home had been logged out from under them and who now were forced to find their livelihoods elsewhere, *anywhere* else – told me they were paid the 200 CFA francs per kilogram of the bark, or about 50 US cents at the time. That was the price of a single capsule, containing a few milligrams of the powdered bark, on the international market. This gave the pharmaceuticals a mark-up of about 200,000 percent, profit that accrued in foreign capitals while Cameroon accrued only the loss of its forest trees.

When I visited the area several times in the late 1990s, Plantecam still had exclusive rights to both pygeum and johimbe from Cameroon's forests, which their glossy pamphlets claimed they were "protecting and nurturing." The man who headed Plantecam, a fast-talking 50-year-old Frenchman named Michel who had grown up in Guadeloupe, liked to tell me how close he was to President Paul Biya, who granted the company its monopoly on these lucrative medicines from Cameroon's forests. Michel told me that he had taken the job for the money, to pay for *"la belle vie"* that he was enjoying in Cameroon. All the props were there: the luxury Peugeot sedan with climate control, the weekend beach retreat and the nubile, young Cameroonian girlfriend – "the best lovers in the world" he told me over a ludicrously expensive dinner in the exclusive Roxy restaurant-club in Douala.

He was put out that I had brought along two Cameroonian colleagues for the dinner: one a young researcher and the other an elderly botanist who struggled against all odds to raise concern for the disappearing plant species of his country. Michel dealt with his unexpected guests by refusing to acknowledge their presence, at least not as fellow human brings. When he insisted that I try the fresh prawns, and suggested a bottle of French wine that cost about 50 US dollars a bottle, I leaned over and asked the two Cameroonians what they wanted. Loudly enough for them to hear, Michel said, "It doesn't matter what these people order. They have no taste anyway."

Neither of the Cameroonian researchers batted an eye or uttered a word.

Plantecam was aware that negative publicity was leaking out about the harvesting techniques, and also that the golden goose itself was nearly dead, at least in Cameroon's forests. It eventually opened its doors to agroforestry researchers working on horticultural experiments that would make it possible to cultivate the medicinal forest trees on farms, domesticating wild species that provided important fruits and medicines that could grow alongside cocoa and coffee, in rich and bio-diverse agroforests.[366]

Then Director of Research at ICRAF, Roger Leakey, saw this as perhaps the most promising model for African agricultural development because it would provide rural people with a whole range of tree products to market and consume, while increasing tree cover and preserving important genetic diversity. He pointed out that the value of the tree products on a hectare of land was invariably higher than the value of a staple crop such as maize or cassava. The tree products came, he said, from what he called "Cinderella trees."[367] These were trees that local people cherished for their many uses and products, which the Western research community had overlooked or missed altogether for the simple reason that they were not familiar to them. Loggers and migrant farmers did not recognize them either.

When a logging company puts in a road to go in and remove a few enormous trees of choice, they are followed almost inevitably by destitute migrants looking for land to cultivate. They often burn trees with enormous potential value either for timber or their non-timber products, clearing a couple of hectares to grow maize, for a couple of years, until the thin forest soils lose all residual fertility. Then, if they can find another plot of forest to burn, they move on and repeat the slash-and-burn process. The model Leakey and his ICRAF colleagues were promoting would provide farmers with an incentive to produce potentially lucrative non-timber forest products on their land alongside food crops. The tree products would generate income that would allow them to purchase staple food crops grown on more suitable lands – if they needed them.

It is a model that works. In 2004, I visited dozens of village nurseries throughout Cameroon. Farming groups had established nurseries where they multiplied the planting material for superior indigenous trees that came from the forest, and found they could sell the seedlings to add to their income and re-invest in their nurseries and their own farm forests.

The researchers offered farmer groups training in vegetative propagation: rooting cuttings in simple non-mist propagators with plastic stretched over a simple wooden frame that they could build themselves; marcotting and grafting.[368] They also offered them basic lessons in genetics, reminding them that plants were like people and incest was taboo, so they needed to refresh the mother plants regularly from superior trees they found in the wild.

In the tiny village of Lekie-Assi, about an hour south of the capital Yaoundé, Christophe and Delphine Missé proudly showed me around their farm, with its hectare of cocoa interspersed with a dozen species of valuable trees they had propagated in their nursery. They were using horticultural techniques they had learned at a community training session to develop planting material for indigenous fruit trees and exotics such as avocado and orange varieties.

Delphine Missé told me the huge leap for them came from knowing the quality of the fruit the tree would produce when it matured; before this they had always gone and collected wildings that grew up around mature trees, the ones "our grandparents left growing for us." The trouble was they had no idea what kind of tree or fruit the wildings would eventually produce, and the wait was long – up to 15 years before the trees would produce fruit. Delphine said that with marcots, "We start getting fruit in less than five years and we know exactly what that fruit will be like because we have cloned the marcots from good trees in the area."

"This is a huge chance for our country," said Christophe Missé, who had quit working as a teacher in a community school where he had never been paid, to work full-time in the nursery and on the farm. "These fruits are for local markets and we are producing it all ourselves."

The Missés told me that the new income had allowed them to send their 12-year-old daughter away to a neighbouring town where there was a boarding school, and to double the size of their tiny wooden home, transforming it into a two- rather than one-room hut. In front, the four smaller children were busy raking cocoa beans that were laid out to dry in the sun. They told me they now earned more selling the fruit from the trees on their farm and the marcots than they did from their cocoa.

"One day we might abandon our cocoa if the price keeps on falling," Delphine Missé told me. "We can continue with our own fruit trees and produce more of them because we can eat the fruit and sell them too."

"But that's not good for us in countries where we can't grow cocoa!" I quipped.

"Then you need to pay us more for our cocoa," she said quietly, with a smile.

I heard similar small-scale success stories in all the villages I visited in the next few days in Cameroon. The farmers had discovered that they no longer had to depend on coffee and cocoa marketing agents who had always sold them the planting material for these two key cash crops. Better still, they told me, they no longer had to depend on those cash crops – the prices for which were controlled far from their shores – to sustain their families and their communities.

Now they were able to produce and grow superior individuals of what they had always considered "forest" or wild trees, undomesticated species that produced many Central African delicacies little known outside the region, but greatly valued there. These include the delectable purple fruit *safou (Dacryodes edulis); njansang (Ricinodendron heulotii)* a nutritious nut used in sauces; Kola nut (*Cola*

303

spp), with a huge range of ceremonial and medicinal uses and bush mango, or Dika nut (*Irvingia gabonensis*) marketed throughout West and Central Africa as a thickener for sauces.

The chief of the village of Arondo-Soa and cocoa farmer, Martin Djana Nga, guided me through his 20-hectare cocoa farm, which looked far more like forest than farm to me. Interspersed with the cocoa plants laden with beautiful red pods ready for the plucking were fruit trees, both the giant ones that had been protected and managed there for years by his own father and the new 'domesticated' young trees produced in the community nursery, whose fruit quality was assured.

"This is a real treasure for me because when I go to the city I see that fruit is expensive and I look ahead at the years to come. Even if I am already dead, it will help my children and grandchildren," said the chief. "I have planted 170 fruit trees in my cocoa agroforest and I want more. In years to come I will make a lot more from this land because cocoa produces only once a year, and with all the fruit trees I have, there will be production all year round. So in January and February when I am waiting for my cocoa, I can sell fruit, and that will really help me. And not only that, my children in the future will be able to reap the benefits of this even after I am gone. I don't want them to stay poor."

He paused underneath a magnificent giant of a tree from which the small, peanut-like *njangsan* fruits had just been harvested and piled, ready for collection and cracking by his wife and younger children. He said the njangsan from just this one tree fetched the equivalent of 300 US dollars a year, and he imagined aloud the value of the fruit all the young marcotted *njangsan* trees would eventually produce.

"My wife puts *njangsan* in sauces and with fish," he said. "And if I have that, and a glass of palm wine to go with it, I am a very happy man!"

There is enormous potential in the fledgling tree revolution that agroforesters are trying to kindle in Central Africa. It offers a superb way for rural communities to reclaim marginal lands and put them into production, and to reforest areas that have already suffered from logging or slashing and burning. In Ngalli II, a tiny community nestled in remnant bits of forest in central Cameroon, a women's group that called themselves the "Rural Housewives," marched me out into the true bush – singing as they went – to show off their latest project to reclaim and reforest two hectares of deforested land.

Group member Angeline Mamoule told me that the group of ten women had managed to clear out the tangled vegetation with their machetes in just nine days, replacing it with marcots of lucrative indigenous trees that would produce both income and protect the environment. "We decided if men did the cleaning out of the area they would just cause us trouble, so we decided to do it ourselves without the men," she said. "People from the village camouflaged themselves and came to watch us from the side of the field, and we knew they were watching us. Back in the village we heard people saying, 'The way they were working we couldn't tell if they were men or they were women.'" She could hardly contain her laughter when she told this tale, and soon the women's laughter filled the new agroforest, just as their singing serenaded our trek back to the village. There they loaded our vehicle – in true African style – with enough produce to feed an entire village and bade us an emotional farewell.

But I still hadn't seen everything that tree domestication and agroforests could do for the people and landscape of Central Africa. Traditional medicine is the treatment of choice for the majority of Cameroonians, and indeed for many Africans I met over the years. Much of it comes from forests, and forests are dwindling – from the Miombo woodlands of southern Africa to the Congolese rainforests. Forests have all but disappeared completely in the lowlands of West Africa from Nigeria across through Côte d'Ivoire, to make way for cocoa, palm and coffee plantations.

The agroforesters in Central Africa have been working with traditional healers, offering them the same horticultural and nursery training they offer to farmers. This allows the healers to produce their own medicinal plants and trees, rather than trekking for days to seek them in rapidly diminishing forests. In the spectacular mountainous northwest of Cameroon where pygeum trees were once common, the tree had all but disappeared – in the wild. But pygeum was alive and

well and flourishing, or at least small marcots of it were, in the nursery of the "Good Will Farming Group," led by traditional healer
Aaron Ngong, high on the hills in the tiny community of Dichami.

Ngong said that to find cherished medicinal plants and trees he
had to trek more than 45 kilometres and sometimes for days, into the
uppermost reaches of the mountains where the last vestiges of forest
were found. Now he was propagating them himself in a nursery and a
pharmaceutical garden with 15 medicinal species growing beside his
clinic.

To show me his worth as a healer, he pulled out a photo album to
show the before-and-after pictures of some of his more spectacular
success stories – patients with cancer whom he said had been referred
to him by doctors at the regional hospital. He claimed he had cured
them with herbal remedies, which had been passed on to him from
his forefathers. He said he used the pygeum mixed with other leaves
to treat epilepsy, and also to cure "a disease we call God-fire, when
the body is burned."

This sounded a little odd to my Western ear, so I asked if his
treatments involved anything non-herbal, if he was perhaps also
invoking the supernatural and spirits.

"Nothing spiritual," he said emphatically. "My treatments are
based strictly on plants."

Some of the diseases he said he could cure were not ones even
known to Westerners, he said, including a "witchcraft that makes
your body decompose while you are alive." He said he could cure this
with combinations of medicines from trees. Noting the look of disbelief on my face, he then flipped the pages of his photo album. He
pointed to a picture of a man's face and body covered with festering
sores, which was how the patient came to him, and then free of any
blemishes, which was how Ngong said he sent him home.

Who was I to argue?

Some African friends told me they saw virtues in both modern
and traditional health care, with one complementing the other. They
said they preferred modern hospitals and doctors for diagnosis, but
then liked to take the diagnosis to their favourite herbalist or traditional practitioner for treatment.

Some people in Africa have come to believe that if they go to see a modern doctor, they have not been treated if they leave without an injection. Some doctors told me that they felt they had to treat many diseases – including various infections and malaria – with injections because then they can be sure the patient gets the necessary dose. In the pharmacies I have visited in Africa, all drugs in stock are available over the counter, and many are fakes. Pharmacists, many with no pharmaceutical training, prescribe medicines on the spot to those who come looking a cure for an ailment, bypassing doctors altogether – because people can't afford the costs, or because none are available where they live or because they don't necessarily trust them. Over the years, I've seen countless African friends fall seriously ill from the cocktails of potent and dangerous pills they pop like candies, sicker than they were when they first started on the self-prescribed medicines.

Even those patients who have consulted a physician and obtained a prescription, often go to the nearest pharmacy and purchase only as many pills as they can afford, not as many as they may need for a complete treatment. This contributes to the rapid resistance that has developed in Africa to many antibiotics. When we suffered from raging staphylococcus infections while living in northern Ghana, our doctor there warned us that the only antibiotics that were not resistant were the newest ones, the most expensive, that had just come out on the market. The others, he said, were no longer effective but they were also all that the local people could afford. This is why he often gave injections rather than prescribing pills; he could then be sure his patients had the correct dose.

Primary health workers in rural health centres are often short on materials such as syringes, or their patients cannot afford new ones. And in the structurally adjusted pay-as-you-go world of medicine in Africa today, patients are expected to pay for absolutely everything they need – from razor blades to shave hair before operations, to surgical gloves for the physicians, to the syringes the doctors and nurses use. This is a disincentive to always using new syringes, and sterilization of old ones is not always effective.

I had no grounds to doubt that Aaron Ngong, with his herbal medicines and knowledge passed down to him through generations, saved many lives and healed many bodies and souls in his village clinic.[369] The Cameroonian scientists working with him assured me he did. Now that Ngong was growing his own plants at home, rather than searching for them in vanishing forests, he looked set to keep on doing so for years to come.

Everything I've seen of agroforestry over several years and in several African countries – Uganda, Malawi, Zambia, Kenya, Burkina Faso, Niger, Mali – was convincing. But nowhere was it more so than in Cameroon. Whether they were filling their nurseries and farms with food or medicinal tree species or with both, they were guaranteeing themselves and their children a future. If prices fell for cash crops such as coffee and cocoa, the farmers always had other commodities for regional markets – fruits, nuts, medicinal barks or leaves – to fall back on. The nursery know-how gives them control of their own plant genetic resources and allows them to domesticate wild species. They bring them in from the forest and onto their farms, and replicate desirable traits of the trees and their products – quality, quantity and also the timing of peak production to take advantage of high market prices off season.

It is a sustainable development effort that, in the jargon of the day, truly is win-win. The producers stand to benefit from the income the tree products generate. Urban populations benefit from the abundance of high-quality local tree products in the markets. Agroforestry can also turn tiny urban plots into rich and diverse homegardens. The environment stands to benefit from the increased concentration of trees in the landscape to reduce erosion and soil loss. The pressure on remaining forests is reduced.

And yet, despite the impressive little tree revolution that is quietly on-going in remote rural areas all over the country of Cameroon, the agroforestry research team and the farmer groups struggled for funding. Apart from the odd modest grant, major donors – with major funding – did not appear particularly interested. Agroforestry is an approach to development that benefits Africans directly, reduces their dependence on the capricious pricing of international commodities and on imported farm inputs needed for a Green Revolution, and increases their control of their own resources. But when it comes to agroforestry initiatives that promote local industry, knowledge, crops, resources and environmental health, the big money just isn't there.

The World Bank readily loans multinationals hundreds of millions for mines and oil pipelines. Big contributions seem available mostly to those 'solutions' that require imported technology, medicines, chemicals, seeds. Aid that ties Africans to the donors' apron strings.

Solutions from afar, well-intentioned or otherwise, often turn out to be mistakes. They may hurt or hinder their supposed beneficiaries. In the case of the Green Revolution this is a dangerous gamble with very high stakes for the recipients of all this development. At risk are African seed varieties, long-term soil health, the invaluable trees and shrubs that the Green Revolution ignores and threatens or simply eliminates. Another Green Revolution could spell endless debt for the continent's farmers. It would require enormous amounts of fossil fuels that are simply too expensive and not sustainable. The loss of local varieties and seed sovereignty could spell the demise of small-scale farmers.

The words of that elderly woman in Ghana come back to haunt me: Why do you bring your mistakes here?

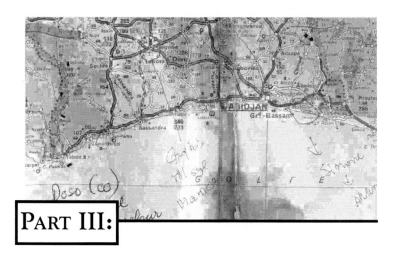

PART III:

Everyone is waving at me

15

Lots to sing about

I once asked a European colleague, who often seemed very lonely and unhappy living and working in Kenya, if her parents ever came out to visit her. She shook her head.

"No," she said. "They are very cultured people, and there is no culture here."

"No culture?" I said. "But if there's one thing Africa has no shortage of, it's culture."

"Not real culture," she said. "You know, opera, symphony, theatre. Culture!"

Africa, for some around the world, remains an amorphous blob on their mental maps, sometimes perceived from afar as a single country with a single language. A Malian friend, singer Oumou Soumaré, living in Moncton, New Brunswick, was flummoxed when one day a francophone Canadian expressed surprise that she was speaking in French, a language the New Brunswick woman thought was spoken only in Canada.

"Do you speak African?" is not an unusual question for African students attending schools and universities in North America. Others tell me they are asked how they could travel to Canada from Africa, and say they have to refrain from saying they swam or rode a bicycle across the ocean. They may be asked if they live in houses in Africa, and have to stifle sarcastic responses that spring to their tongues, such as, "No, we live in the trees." A Kenyan girl visiting us in Canada was asked how on earth she learned to speak English, which is actually the official language in her country and one of just four she spoke perfectly.

It must make Africans living in or visiting the wealthy world wonder sometimes what Westerners think they have to teach Africa, when so many seem to know so little about an entire continent. It does me. The complexities of a single country in Africa are so enormous and intricate and profound, one could spend several lifetimes trying to comprehend them. Certainly that was true in every country I lived and travelled in, and that list includes only two-thirds of the countries in sub-Sahara Africa.

What looks to the outsider like chaos – on the streets, in the markets, in the villages, popular neighbourhoods, at taxi and bush taxi stands – is not chaos at all. It is highly ordered and structured; those who live and work in these environments know who is who, what is what, and understand the complex invisible system that keeps it all together.

Each time I heard about another new social rule or group or tradition and began to ask questions about it, I usually wound up even more befuddled. Canada prides itself on being a multicultural success story. But many African nations should do the same. They comprise hundreds of different ethnic groups and languages. Cameroon, the only other nation on earth that has French and English as its two official languages, has another 24 major language *groups*, with more than 250 different variants among the more than 250 different ethnic groups. The facility with languages on the continent outshines any official efforts in Canada or even Europe to promote bi- or multilingualism. I have met many, many people without any formal education from a classroom who speak half a dozen indigenous languages fluently and who have also mastered two or three European languages as well.

In colonial times, there were strict rules against the use of indigenous languages in schools, rules enforced with "caning" – beating with a stick – of any child speaking a mother tongue. That policy I found still alive and brutally well in the early 1990s in a Catholic-run kindergarten in northern Ghana that my daughter attended.

Africa has managed to retain her languages, an estimated 3,000 of them. Some contend that if Africa is to progress and promote universal education it must dispense with the use of its own languages in the classroom, and use only official languages bequeathed to them by colonial masters – French, English, Spanish and Portuguese. Others see the retention of mother tongues on the continent as the only defence against complete acculturation and assimilation.

Because so few foreigners are able to understand what people are really saying to each other – in much of Africa everyday conversations tend to be in local languages – the people of the continent have been able to protect themselves from complete indoctrination by the multitude of "change agents," a term for development workers, who have come to live and work among them. Missionaries are aware of the importance of language in the process of changing the beliefs and mindsets of indigenous people around the world. Now known by the acronym SIL International, the faith-based organization that was once called the Summer Institute of Linguistics, has for its mission to document and investigate "lesser-known languages" – some 1800 of them around the world, to protect them from extinction and contribute to anthropology and ethno-musicology.[370] Ironically – or perhaps deliberately – this work generally leads to the translation of Christian scriptures into these languages, with an aim of converting the speakers to Christianity and the acculturation that often follows. It is only by mastering local languages that missionaries can reach the deep psyche – the soul – of the people they are trying to convert to Christianity. Missionaries are among the few expatriates – barring American Peace Corps volunteers and those who marry into Africa – who tend to speak local languages fluently.

African artists have also helped keep their languages alive by singing in their own tongues, so that their people can understand their every word. The only exception to this that I'm aware of was Kenya under its former president, Daniel arap Moi, who actually forbade Kenyan musicians to record in their own languages, actively discouraging the vibrant musical and linguistic traditions in his country.

Africa has an infinite number of things to teach the open-minded visitor. For all its troubles, for all its hardship and conflict, for all its monetary poverty and the growing disparity between rich and poor, for all the sadness on the continent, it is also full of joy. There are new trends and fashions, and fabulous artists, writers, dancers, film-makers, as well as a music industry that despite the pirating of locally produced cassettes and CDs, is thriving, driven by talent that seems to flourish among oppressed or monetarily poor people.

A whole generation of African masters laid the groundwork for the current explosion of African talent. Only a handful of African performers have ever become household names in the Western world – South Africa's Miriam Makeba and Ladysmith Black Mambazo as examples. But to gain fame in the West, it seems they had to be promoted by famous Western performers, Harry Belafonte in the case of Miriam Makeba and Paul Simon in the case of Ladysmith Black Mambazo.

When in 2005, the famous Live 8 concerts were organized around the world to coincide with the G8 summit in Gleneagles, Scotland, and to draw attention to the poverty in Africa – with grandiose slogans about making it history – top African acts were barred from the main stage in London. Bob Geldof, who organized Live 8 and who had made his name 20 years earlier as a champion of the hungry in Africa by organizing Live Aid, maintained that this startling omission of African talent on the big stage was because African acts would not attract the same crowds or television audience as would the Paul McCartneys and the Destiny's Childs of this world. The only African-born musicians who featured on the main stage were Senegal's Youssou N'Dour and South African, Dave Matthews. Other African acts were relegated to a minor stage set up in Cornwall, and they did not make it to the worldwide television broadcasts of Live 8.

Well-known British TV and radio presenter Andy Kershaw, who has done much to promote African musical talent over the years, said of Geldof and Live 8, "I am coming, reluctantly, to the conclusion that Live 8 is as much to do with Geldof showing off his ability to push around presidents and prime ministers as with pointing out the potential of Africa. Indeed, Geldof appears not to be interested in Africa's strengths, only in an Africa on its knees." He concludes: "If Geldof has genuine empathy with the continent he claims to champion, he wouldn't be telling Africa's world-beating performers that they're not worthy to share a stage with himself and his tedious friends."[371]

All of this is a sad commentary on two ills that are as closely related as the proverbial chicken and egg – Africa's apparent lack of interest in promoting its own, and the tendency in the Western world, even among some who profess to champion Africa, to ignore or under appreciate African accomplishments and talents.

Even without promotion and lucrative recording contracts, the continent is absolutely full of giant talents, as it always has been. Some of the post-independence masters who were hardly known outside their own countries, let alone around the world, were philosophers, political observers, songwriters, writers, poets and musicians all rolled into one. It would take several books to name them all and describe their musical accomplishments, but it's worth citing a few of these late, great artists and innovators who melded traditional and modern instruments to create a whole new sound. Cameroon had Eboa Lotin and Frances Bebey, who also won awards for his writing; their music gave rise to the original *makossa*. Zaire, now the Democratic Republic of Congo, had the late, great Franco. Nigeria produced the iconoclast, cult leader, Africanist and fabulous musician Fela Kuti. Ghana produced E.T. Mensah, who blended big band music with local rhythms to become known as the "father" of the musical tradition known as highlife.

They bequeathed much to the current generation of African artists, many of whom are reviving traditional instruments and combining these with modern, electrical ones to produce a mix of complex, sophisticated musical styles that often have their roots in political resistance and the struggle to conserve and build on their own heritage. The flat, silent pages of a book are not the best venue for conveying the power and beauty of the many musical forms that make Africa move. Words cannot begin to capture the fantastic gymnastics, gyrations and exuberant joy of the dances that have developed along with the amazing variety of new African music. But here are just a few of the dances and musical trends that Africa needs to share with the world.

From Congo, came *soukous* that evolved from rumba, and from soukous came a whole slew of variations, including the frenetic *kwasa*

kwasa of Kanda Bongo Man, and later the ndombolo music and dance, performed by stars like Koffi Olomide and Extra Musica. This is a remarkable and hard-to-master (for the foreigner) dance requiring gyrations of the hips, thighs and buttocks that defy the rigid skeletal structure underlying human anatomy.

Cameroon produced Manu Dibango, Ben Decca and his sister Grace, Henri Dikongue, and musicians too many to name, all of whom put their own mark on the country's trademark makossa.

Reggae, which Ghanaians assured me has its roots in their country, is popular all over the continent. One of Africa's reggae superstars is Côte d'Ivoire's Alpha Blondy who has made his name writing and performing highly courageous political songs pointing fingers at African leaders who betray and suppress their people, play with the fire of ethnic rivalries, and hinder peace and justice on the continent. Another who did the same was South Africa's Lucky Dube, until his tragic, premature death in Johannesburg in late 2007 when he was gunned down by carjackers.

The provocative and risqué mapuka dance and music in Côte d'Ivoire has its roots in traditional dances; it continued to evolve and spread in West Africa much to the chagrin of some religious figures; both Christian and Muslim leaders have called for their ban. There may be some reason for concern about the power that such a dance as the mapuka can have on a man. In one popular video in which the young mapuka dancer's buttocks begin to vibrate at an alarming rate even as she lowers herself to the floor on her stomach, a distinguished man in suit and tie seated behind a table in the audience is suddenly overcome by lust and despite the presence of his wife beside him, he leaps over the table and onto the dancer. It takes three strong-armed men to remove him.

Guinea has produced Mory Kanté and Alpha YaYa Diallo, who is now part of the group, African Guitar Summit, in his new country, Canada. Senegal has produced superstars such as Youssou N'dour, Baaba Maal, Cheich Lô, Ismaël Lô. And neighbouring Mali, as Ali Farka Touré told me, was the true home of the blues. On a visit to Mali to play with some of Mali's rising musical stars, American blues legend Bonnie Raitt mused, with a smile, on the irony of a "white-skinned, red-haired girl with Scottish ancestors" learning to play the

Mississippi blues with great African-American masters in her native America and then making her way all the way to Timbuktu in Mali, to find the origin of the blues with artists such as Ali Farka Touré.

Mali continues to pump out megastars – Salif Keita, Amadou and Mariam, Habib Koité, Oumou Sangaré, Rokia Traoré, Toumani Diabaté considered to be one of the world's greatest Cora players, and the young group of former Tuareg rebels, Tinariwen, to name just a very few. Mali also boasts a National Orchestra of singers and masters of traditional instruments that plays classical music at major events – classical *Malian* music, that is. Griots continue to produce traditional songs in praise of historical and present-day personalities.

Benin produced the firecracker dynamo Angelique Kidjo, Burundi the melodious songstress Khadja Nin, Zimbabwe the great Oliver Mtukudzi, Nigeria the phenomenal King Sunny Ade, and Congo the masterful Papa Wemba. South Africa has the Soweto String Quartet, Hugh Masekela, the Mahotella Queens, the late Brenda Fassie … and the list continues ad infinitum for that country and for the whole continent.

Today, of course, the continent is reverberating with imported music as well, and the most recent generation of its artists produce their own versions of hiphop, ragga, rap and all manner of variants thereof. Many West African musicians have lived and studied in Cuba for years, and have turned samba into a popular musical tradition and dance in the region. Lebanese music and Arabic themes are also popular, brought to the region by the very powerful and influential Lebanese community that stretches from the West African coast across to Chad, controlling much of the trade and commerce in the region – and many of the restaurants, hotels and hotspot dance clubs as well.

From Nigeria there is a huge output of wild and woolly music DVDs from artists singing the praises of Jesus and God. These are a fascinating mix of old and new – dancing that many churches might have prohibited because it looks far too much like provocative and erotic fun, with lyrics thanking God for what He has done. And what He has done, it would appear from the images, is to reward the singer's prayers with palatial homes, oodles of beautiful women, huge SUVs and Hummers, and tailored suits suitable for any tropical gangster.

Nightclubs and discos across Africa tend to play a mixture of all of the above – in The Gambia a typical evening may offer Rihanna, alongside a delightfully varied play list of currently popular African musicians performing hiphop, samba, highlife. Minds and bodies on the continent are open to an incredible range of musical traditions and beats.

All of this, despite the spread of middle-of-the-road Capital FM radio stations in some anglophone countries that mostly steer clear of indigenous African music, preferring 'hits' from the UK and the US and where presenters and announcers speak with decidedly non-African and very British accents.

Ouagadougou in Burkina Faso hosts a biennial Pan-African Film Festival – FESPACO – that brings to the screen a marvellous assortment of African films. No matter how excellent, these can never compete in Africa's video halls – and there are plenty of these in even remote areas set up to bring English and European soccer live as the new opium to the masses – with Grade D Hollywood war and horror movies, violent films from China and Bollywood love sagas from India. Nigeria's 'Nollywood' has made some inroads with its own soaps.

Across the continent, there is also a long tradition of textile making and designs, of pottery and jewellery-making. Africa's oral literature is riddled with proverbial wisdom to rival anything Aesop recounted. Africa abounds with genius, as does any continent. Only Africa does it without government interest or support, or many books to read.

Books are rare luxuries on the continent. They cost far too much for the average person to purchase, and are even a luxury for most teachers and students. The books of great new African writers such as Nigeria's Chimamanda Ngozi Adichie, Wole Soyinka, Ben Okri – and of older masters such as Chinua Achebe, Buchi Emecheta, Kenya's Ngugi wa Thiong'o, Cameroon's Mongo Beti, Ghana's Ama Ata Aidoo and Ayi Kwei Arma, Senegal's Mariama Bâ, Mali's Amadou Hampaté Bâ, to name just a few – are not easy to find in Africa except in a few major cities at First World prices. The most accessible reading material on the continent is to be found on monstrous billboards advertising caffeinated power drinks, which now complement the usual advertisements for soft drinks made by Coca-

Cola, imported beers for the elite, cell phone services, banks and cosmetics, including bleaching creams.

Another kind of reading material comes in cast-off, second-hand t-shirts from the rich world with slogans, brand names and the names or faces of pop or soccer stars on them. All of which can, to the Westerner, seem bizarre and out of context in remote villages. One that struck just such an absurd note was the white t-shirt I saw on the thin frame of a little girl trying to peddle a few bananas in the war-devastated town of Foya in Liberia; it read: "Twinkle Toes Theatre School."

For those who can afford or get their hands on them, there are also local newspapers. And sometimes interesting reading can be done from the scraps of paper – European newspapers or old UN inventory lists – that wind up on the market and are then used by roadside vendors to wrap up bread or peanuts they sell. A major source of accessible reading material is Christian literature. In the remote border posts of the war-ravaged area where Guinea, Liberia and Sierra Leone meet, where the genial officials had only school notebooks and ink pads with which to formalize our border crossing, there were stacks of glossy pamphlets from the New Apostolic Church and *Watchtower* newsletters from the Jehovah's Witnesses. Much of the Christian literature promises miracles for those who believe in Jesus Christ as their saviour, and those pastors and preachers flogging miracles – African and non-African – are enjoying something of a miracle themselves in contributions from their impoverished flocks.

What I find more of a miracle is that in many ways and in many places, people in Africa have managed to retain their traditions, culture and languages to the extent that they have. It is sad that some on the continent regard those who have retained their culture and traditions as being somehow less developed, or inferior or unsophisticated. They are anything but. And as with so many other things in Africa that at first are invisible to the outsider, once you start to learn a little of what's there, it's a never-ending lesson.

In Mali, as everywhere we found ourselves living, I had to struggle very hard to comprehend the way that society was structured in a society that could trace its lineage back to early empires in the region. I had already grappled with the notion of an inherited role in society as a noble or person of "caste" – the cobblers, blacksmiths, weavers and griots who comprised that group. This led to new lessons on the nature of each group. I was particularly curious about the griots – West Africa's singing historians, poets, historians, praise-singers – who embodied so much of the past and brought it into the present.

My lessons began with a griot of the Fula ethnic group in a small dark room that doubled as a recording studio, in which grass mats offered soundproofing, flooring and seating. Clad in a waxed damask robe of peacock green, the griot sat cross-legged on the floor, strumming away on his *ngoni,* a traditional guitar, singing historical odes detailing the histories and glories of the three successive empires that flourished in this part of West Africa between 1200 and 1800 AD – the Mali, Songhay and then the Fula Empires.

His name was Dinda Sarré and while he didn't have a penny to his name, his wealth, he told me, was his birthright of words, song and history that bring wisdom. He said he was able to sing by heart epics that could last for days and cover many centuries, so trained was he in minute details of history. Griots, he said, are veritable encyclopaedias, and, yes, they also sing praise for deserving heroes and noble feats. Like all griots, he said he was attached to a noble family, and his noble masters were obliged to listen to his counsel, and to take care of him financially.

That is how it had always been, he said.

How this worked in modern-day Mali was something about which I was very curious. As always, there was no shortage of people willing to offer their insights. The first of these was Amadou, the director of a small FM station. He was a chain-smoking journalist who could be guaranteed to turn a simple question at a press conference into a long, flowery monologue which left his quarry – usually visiting dignitaries – and also the rest of us in the press corps, scratching our heads, or just shaking them. It was difficult for me to picture Amadou as anything but a thoroughly modern man, a fellow journalist chasing after people with a microphone and mini-disk in his hands, just like me.

I was thoroughly wrong.

According to Amadou himself, who was not plagued by any false modesty, he was first and above all, a nobleman from the city of Gao in eastern Mali, once the seat of the great Songhay Empire that succeeded the Mali Empire and covered much of West Africa in the 15th and 16th centuries. Just like the young intellectual Issa, Amadou told me he was a "noble of nobles." He claimed direct descent from Emperor Askia Mohamed, revered leader of the Songhay Empire at its peak.

As proud as he was of this birthright, however, Amadou said it was not up to him as a noble to prattle on about his elevated noble status (although that didn't always stop him). Singing his praises, he said, was the exclusive birthright of a griot – Amadou's very own personal griot. Just as he, Amadou, claimed a direct line right back to Emperor Askia Mohamed, his griot was directly descended from the griot who sang the emperor's praises five centuries earlier. And if I wanted to see how this all worked, I should come and visit him at the radio station, where his griot shadowed him at all times.

The radio station was located in the heart of a hot and bustling market, nestled rather precariously on the denuded, red cliffs overlooking Bamako and the broad valley of the River Niger along which the city stretches. It was one of 16 spirited little private FM radio stations in the Malian capital, which against great odds – power failures, ancient and ailing microphones, tiny studios as hot as Hades – managed to stay on the air most of the time. The cacophony from the market – artisans hammering old car bodies into sheets of useable scrap metal, car horns, rumbling and smoking diesel motors, vendors' calls to buy – blasted up from below. Most of the windows in the station didn't benefit from glass to guarantee a lot of quiet for *Radio Liberté*. The only slightly quieter corner was the very warm little studio, a closet-sized space in which were squeezed a table with a couple of microphones, a couple of amplifiers and piles of dusty cassettes strewn about the dusty floor.

It was into this stifling radio studio that Amadou welcomed me. He was flanked by his griot, Malle Sarré, who was wearing a drab grey *boubou* robe, appropriately subdued next to Amadou's rather dashing white one. Malle, when I arrived, was chanting Amadou's name like a stylus stuck in a deep groove – for a few hundred years.

The name-chanting went on for what seemed like a very long time. Time is never a limiting factor in traditional society, or even in many modern walks of life in much of Africa, particularly when time is being telescoped – as it was that morning – by a vociferous, middle-aged griot in Bamako. When at last Sarré finished his initial recitation, Amadou told me that particular chant was about his father, grandfather, *his* father, and *his* grandfather, the family name, where they all came from, how the family lived then and lived today.

"That means we are heroes, warriors," Amadou declared. "We are proud, we are rich. We never fear fighting. We never steal, we never lie. And we always take care of our griots."

He continued, "Malle says we are descendants of Emperor Askia Mohamed, who came from Maiduguiri in what is today Nigeria, to found the Songhay Empire. And so we must behave like Askia. Sarré says to me, 'You are Big Man, you are noble, you must behave like noble, like a chief. You have your griot, your people of caste, your slave'," said Amadou, eyeing me and quickly adding, "Excuse me, that is 'slave' in brackets, not nowadays."

We were getting into sensitive territory, but he assured me that people of caste were not below noblemen on the social scale.

"No, no, no, no," he said, arms waving wildly, relishing this chance to show off his self-taught English. "Some people thinks griots are low in society. No, they are not low. They are lights, they are stars, they are moons. They are the sunlights of the society. They are the top, they are here to advise and to show; even the president of the country has to follow what the griots say. They make peace and they tell you to love even your enemy. It is only today that some people think griots are low in society. But I don't believe this."

"So if you misbehave, Amadou, what will your griot tell you?" I asked. "Will he tell you that you're not behaving well? Or will he just continue to sing your praises?"

"No, real griots never lie, never, never. This one, Mali Sarré, he never lies. Every day he tells me three things. One: never, never lie for anybody. Two: accept anyone who comes to you, from your tribe or from another tribe in Mali, or even a foreigner, White, Black, and if he needs your help you help him. Three: he tells me never believe what they say about you behind your back, never. If I lie, he will say, 'Stop, you are lying.' And I have to stop because my griot tells me."

"You make it sound as if your griot is closer to you than your own wife?"

He nodded. "About some subjects, he is closer than my wife. For instance, if it's a case of fighting with neighbours or with brothers, he's the only one who can show me the way. Because he's a man."

"And what about marriage?" I wanted to know. "If you as a noble fell in love with, and wanted to marry a girl from a griot family, what would your griot say to you?"

"His role would be to tell me first that I am foolish, I'm mad. If I fall in love with a griot girl, I have to hide it and not tell him. Because he will never agree. Never. Never." He got in a few more emphatic "nevers," then looked up with a grin. "Myself, for instance, and you, Baxter, say you are a griot and I fall down in love with you, my griot will tell me, 'Stop, this cannot be your wife. She is not your size, you do not fit her,' and he will say that I make him ashamed and if I don't stop with this girl he will kill himself. And he will find me a different woman – a noble girl."

Would he allow his own daughter to marry a man of caste? He claimed that he would give his daughter to the man she chose. But he admitted that he was against marriages between nobles and griots because they produced children that were neither noble nor griot; family knowledge of who they are and where they came from would be lost. Without such knowledge, he contended, a person was not really a person. He reiterated what Issa had told me when he said acculturated Africans who imitated *tuobabs* (the word used for white people in several West African countries) are like "bats," neither bird nor mammal.

But surely such taboos would disappear over time, I countered to Amadou. Mali wasn't in a vacuum, some kind of permanent time warp that kept it immune from cultural pollination or influence from abroad. Malians, like people from all over Africa, hold top positions in large corporations, with world bodies, and in key professions around the world. I'd just recently met Malian scientist, Cheik Modibo Diarra, who was Chief Navigator with the Pathfinder Mission to Mars, and who worked at the Jet Propulsion Laboratory in Pasadena, California. Malians were travelling all over the world to work. And at home, many were bemoaning the loss of their culture and values. There were frequent and heated discussions on state television with griots and intellectuals about which traditions Malians should be trying to preserve.

In France, there had just been a much-publicized court case involving a Malian woman of caste who was found guilty of circumcising teenage Malian girls living in France – a punishable crime in that country. In her defence, the elderly defendant said she was merely heeding tradition and her obligation as a woman of caste to look out for the dignity and status of noble families, to whom she was linked by history. One of the tasks she was obliged to perform was to circumcise girls to ensure they were initiated into womanhood and prepared for marriage. This trial, coupled with much public discussion about traditions many in Mali felt no longer fit, spawned constant debate about how African society was changing and which changes were positive, which were largely negative. In most discussions I heard, the consensus was that Africa was losing more than it was gaining by becoming more modern.

The modern world was making itself felt more every day in Bamako, I said to Amadou, so surely griots too were a tradition that was destined to disappear sooner or later?

"No, I can bet Mali will never lose our griots, no way: in Mali there can be no life without griots, you can bet it. Each family has its griots; each tribe has its griots. In Mali it would be very, very, very difficult without griots, maybe in thousands of years, but not for tomorrow, not for next year, not for two thousand years. In Mali, it's just not possible. Griots are libraries, historians, psychologists; they are history itself."

So spoke nobleman Amadou. But no matter how much he wished to paint an idyllic picture of Mali immersed happily in a utopian past in which nobles were noble and griots were griots and never the two shall mix or marry, I saw lots of evidence that this axiom no longer held.

Many of the popular singers in the country, especially the women who sang at every major public occasion, were griots. Women griots who featured large in modern urban life and on television were anything but rustic or traditional in appearance. They had a predilection for flashy gold pendants, rings studded with gemstones the size of a fist and artificial fingernails lacquered shocking shades of pink and orange. They wore shiny robes of lacy cloth in colours as powerful as their voices. They also used vast quantities of bleaching creams that turned their complexions a paler shade of pink, brown or beige. This, in turn, inspired young women of all walks of life to copy them, and eventually, even the intellectual First Lady began to pale before our eyes.

A Malian woman friend told me that because she refused to bleach her skin, she found herself being asked to stand at traditional ceremonies, marriages and baptisms, and offer her chair to the "white" guests – Malians who had bleached themselves pink to improve their social standing.

Traditions were colliding with – and collapsing under or combining with – all sorts of new influences. Keeping it all straight was hard enough for Malians. For a novice from outside, it was far more daunting and complex.

Tradition, I was told, granted only two groups of people the right to sing and make music. One of these was the traditional hunting brotherhood, which predated griots by many thousands of years. According to Téreba Togola, who headed Mali's Department of Heritage in the culture ministry, the traditional hunters or *dossos* could trace their roots back into the earliest of Palaeolithic human societies in West Africa.

The other group with a right to sing and talk and play instruments was the griots. Tradition had always prohibited people of noble birth from singing or making music; this being the exclusive birthright of griots and others of caste. People of noble birth who bore noble names, Keita for example, had simply never been permitted to raise their voice in song or raise an instrument to make music. But in recent decades, talented Malian nobles such as Salif Keita and Rokia Traoré had challenged the old taboos, become international stars and turned music into a profession open to nobles and griots alike, despite lingering disapproval in some traditional quarters.

As for griots being the nation's conscience, I wasn't so sure this one always held either. Many Malians – particularly friends who claimed to be of noble birth – told me that as far as they were concerned, the griots had become thorns in the nation's side, expensive to remove and causing much pain and annoyance.

As in olden days, griots still flocked to all public events and ceremonies, to family gatherings such as naming ceremonies and marriages, to ensure no separation of the past and present, and to sing
praise of nobles and their ancestors. And, just as in olden days, in
return for their words and song and music, nobles were supposed to
reward the griots with gifts and food, everything they needed to live.
Griots would be fed and cared for in exchange for their loyalty and
their knowledge and their song. It was supposed to be a complementary relationship. The taciturn, thoughtful noble looking after the
needs of their griots, while the talkative griot kept the noble in line,
obeying the life path laid out for them by their noble ancestors.

At least, that was the theory. The way it used to be. The way
Malians such as Amadou wishfully thought it still was.

But nowadays "to take care of" a griot usually meant paying them.
Money had altered the ancient social equation, and griots were making the best of it – and certainly the very most they could of it.

It was not unusual to see nobles slogging their way to social occasions or major events on foot, or in the ignominious crush in the rear
of a battered green *Sotrama* van, while griots cruised up to a baptism
or naming ceremony in their Mercedes or BMW.

Some griots were themselves very wealthy these days, especially
with the advent of democracy – multi-party politics and elections –
that had opened up a whole new lucrative arena for enterprising griots. Politicians, naturally, would pay vast amounts to have their praises sung. Some politicians – including presidents – covered all the
bases by engaging both griots and American public relations firms to
do the spinning for them.

Griots were also useful to incredibly wealthy people of griot origins, such as the infamous Babani Sissoko. Sissoko, now an MP in
Mali, is still on an Interpol arrest list for allegedly swindling, using a
deep "satanic voice" and "magical potions," 270 million US dollars
from the director of the Islamic Bank of Dubai. At least that's what it
says on the copy of the Interpol arrest warrant I was able to obtain.

Sissoko had spent time in a US prison for attempting to bribe
customs officials in Florida to facilitate the export of two military hel-
icopters. After his release in 1998, he returned to his country and did
so with a fleet of aircraft belonging to his own airline registered in

The Gambia, Air Dabia, which included three jumbo jets and several smaller Boeings. These would later be impounded by various creditors, but at that point Sissoko was still flush with his vast new fortune and he handed out hundred dollar bills to the police who lined the roadside to assure his passage through the multitudes that had turned out to see the homecoming of their super-rich, super-griot. He also doled out custom-made luxury cars (Hummers, BMWs and Jaguars) to various political figures and prominent Malian journalists, and sums of up to 100 thousand US dollars apiece to griots who sang his praises.

Traditionalists shook their heads in dismay – the end must be near, they told me, now that griots were singing praises of griots. You no longer had to be noble to earn praise from griots; you just had to be rich enough to afford it. All sacrilege, as far as my Malian friends of noble birth were concerned. Like many of Africa's greatest traditions, good griots – the ones who respected the rules and still behaved as the nation's conscience – seemed to be rapidly disappearing, giving way to griots who would sing the praises of anyone with enough money to pay them handsomely. And increasingly, the *noblesse* no longer wanted to *oblige*.

16

The library is burning

In Africa, whenever an elder dies, a library goes up in flames.

Malian author and philosopher,
Amadou Hampate Bâ

October was named officially the "month of social solidarity" in Mali. To me this sounded as useful as a declaration from Ottawa that February had been officially named a month of snow and cold in Canada.

I did not get it – but I often didn't.

I had never lived in any country – and I had lived in quite a few by the time we washed up there in 1997 – that stuck together the way Mali did. Everyone appeared to be related to everyone else, at least if you went back far enough, and Malians did indeed go back far enough. I rarely met an adult who couldn't trace his or her ancestry back many generations, over hundreds of years.

But there is no news in peace and understanding among peoples, which is one reason that the mainstream media have seriously skewed the picture of Africa, creating terrible stereotypes of people on the continent as bloodthirsty and anxious to fight rather than talk. Sometimes when I was faced with African tolerance of what I, in my impetuous Western way, decided were intolerable injustices at the hands of their authorities, I would ask them why they didn't just rebel, take to the streets, knock on the doors or knock down the doors, of those who abused their rights.

When we were living in northern Ghana in the early 1990s, the local officials of the Water and Sewerage Corporation regularly cut town water supplies, or didn't bother to repair pipes needed to keep them flowing. There was a lot more money to be made selling people water by the bucket from road tankers, although that water was often unsafe and full of guinea worm parasites. Because I had a large water tank behind the house, each time this happened women from neighbouring villages would line up at my door asking if they could fill their buckets. At first I always said yes, until I realized that there was an endless ocean of need coming through my gates. I would ask them why they didn't protest to the authorities. They told me they had, but several of the protestors who broke down doors and windows at the Regional Administration had disappeared, never to be seen again.

One elderly woman stared at me balefully for a moment or two, before announcing with a sigh, as if addressing an ill-behaved child (which is certainly how I must have appeared to her), "Madam," she said. "Dis one be fo' God. When God give too much, we want mo' and mo'. So sometime God He do take some ting back, make remember us be grateful fo' blessings we do have. Dat how it be."

In Cameroon, as I listened for hours to friends openly cursing (in the privacy of their homes), President Paul Biya and corruption in their country, I often asked why they sat back and took it, why they didn't, well, "do something."

"We look around us where people 'do something,'" replied one particularly articulate and politically astute young man in the western town of Foumban. "What can we do? Biya's foreign friends would come in to save him if we tried to overthrow him. So we have a choice. We can live in peace and keep our heads low and accept it. Or, we can start a war. Look around Africa. Has war ever solved a problem? If we start a war, we do not know how to end it. We prefer to remain as we are, poor but at peace."

Mali has a huge advantage over many other African countries that were drawn on a map in Europe during the scramble for Africa that brought together dozens of ethnic groups, divided up others, and that led to colonial powers favouring a handful of those over others, creating deep and powerful competition and ethnic tension. Mali has some historical integrity, having been part of many ancient empires. It comprises a dozen ethnic groups whom history binds together rather than dividing. In the last century the only overtly ethnic strife in the country was the six-year rebellion against the Malian government by the nomadic Berber people in the north, the Tuareg.

The Tuareg were seeking self-determination and a separate nation for themselves in the Sahara Desert to link the Berber peoples from Mauritania right across to Chad. They did this with logistical, financial and military support from the man who loved – in the 1970s, 80s and 90s – to challenge French, British and American interests in West Africa: Libya's Muammar Gaddafi.

Like the Moors in northern Mali and Mauritania, the Tuareg tended to view themselves as more Arab and 'white' than sub-Sahara Africans, which unfortunately also meant that some believed themselves superior to their fellow Malians who were darker in complexion, particularly the Songhay people with whom they shared northern cities such as Gao and Timbuktu. The Tuareg also felt, legitimately, that they had been neglected by the government in Bamako.

Any ethnic tension there might be among the other dozen ethnic groups in Mali is precluded or diffused by their shared history. Everyone seems bound by an extensive and extremely complex set of social ties. These begin with the family. And families are already complex and large in a polygamous society in which a man may have several wives, and where siblings, half-siblings, first cousins, second-cousins, third-cousins-twice-removed, are all considered brothers or sisters; and all aunts and uncles are considered mothers and fathers; all grandparents and relatives thereof are considered "parents." The adage "it takes a community to raise a child" applies beautifully.

There are also religious ties – most Malians are Muslim and so pray together. There are others who adhere to ancient traditional faiths and a small minority – between 3 and 10 percent depending on who's doing the counting – who are Christian. But any divisions that religion might have caused tend to be overridden by historical ties and the culture of tolerance and mutual respect that prevails, and which, despite common Western misconceptions to the contrary, is promoted in most of West Africa by Islamic leaders.

Religious faith is often inextricably linked to and mixed up with pre-Islamic or pre-Christian traditions. The origins of the traditional hunting societies in West Africa – known as *dossos* in much of Mali – go back millennia. They are said to possess mystical powers that allow them to commune with wild animals. At a festival of traditional hunters in Bamako I saw them strolling about with hyenas on leashes as if they were tame puppies and pythons slithered obediently behind them as if they had been hypnotized into submission. While some accuse the hunting societies of decimating remaining wildlife populations, the hunters gathered in Mali from all over the region said their respect for and knowledge of animals made them conservationists, and they attributed the loss of wildlife to the loss of woodlands for farming and livestock and to big-game hunters from abroad. They have intimate knowledge of the heavens that give them great orientation and trekking skills. Their mastery of traditional medicines affords them healing prowess. They are also considered protectors of their communities, which is why they are sometimes co-opted into civil conflicts as they were in Sierra Leone to fight the rebel forces and in Côte d'Ivoire, where they joined the rebels in the north of the country. The traditional hunting societies are highly secretive, and they create another important block of solidarity that is almost impenetrable and largely invisible to outsiders, even when they actively seek to understand and appreciate these ancient societies.

Then there are clans, linked by common ancestors way back, sharing names or related names. The ethnic groups, people who speak different languages and have different histories and cultures, are linked forever by those inherited social groups that crosscut the different ethnicities – the nobles and the rest, those people of caste descended from griots, cobblers, blacksmiths and weavers.

There are also groups of people descended from former slaves, who have long since been given the names of their long-ago owners, and who tend not to own up to their socially unenviable origins. In Mali's north among the Tuareg, there are the Bella people who were still considered slaves because they do the menial work for a noble family and in return are fed and clothed by their masters – although there is no such thing as buying or selling of these slaves.

Top that all off with that social glue known in French as *cousinage*, a feeble translation for the Bamanankan term, *sinankunya*, a relationship that doesn't exist in any European society. It means that if your ancestors have made an agreement to bind your family or clan to another family or clan – probably a few centuries ago and usually by exchanging vows in a complex ceremony – you are obliged to respect these ancient bonds. They are akin to blood oaths that can forbid you from marrying between ethnic groups or castes within them, but also and more importantly, from feuding or fighting with anyone from those families or clans.[372] It is so complex that few of us foreigners ever really grasped it, even if we witnessed *sinankunya* at work and keeping the peace in Mali.

The best example I ever witnessed was on the streets, when a man ran his moped into the back of a shining French sedan. The two drivers were not injured, at least not physically, but their vehicles were and they were blaming each other, shouting in fury that the other would have to pay. Until, that is, they paused in their argument long enough to find out the other person's family name. Suddenly they were shaking hands and making peace with their body language and exchanging friendly quips. One driver climbed back on his damaged moped and the other back in his damaged Peugeot and off they drove.

One day a seasoned American development expert who had spent 20 years in West Africa told me that "the problem with Mali" was that "the people don't want to change" and that they were "backward."

Not long after hearing this, I attended a conference of African historians in Bamako, who had gathered to look at the fate of African culture in the 21st century. Attending that conference was Pierre Claver Hien, the history professor at the University of Ouagadougou in neighbouring Burkina Faso who had spoken to me at length about the issue of caste in Mali. Hien described himself as "a child of the revolution of the late Thomas Sankara" and also a survivor of that era. He said he continued to support most of the ideals espoused by Thomas Sankara, but not the methods and the haste of change. He did not believe that Burkina Faso, or Mali, or any other African country could afford to reject its own traditions without a slow transition that would allow those old ways to evolve into something distinctively African, and not just a poor carbon copy of the West.

"We must use our wisdom," he told me. "I love tradition, I am an historian, and if you suppress tradition, you will get the opposite of what you want. In Burkina Faso, Sankara tried to suppress tradition too quickly, and many good sides of that tradition broke down. Children replaced traditional values with things they learn on European television and in schools teaching European subjects. Sankara said female circumcision was bad and laws were passed to forbid it. That made all the circumcised women – that's the vast majority of the women in Burkina Faso – feel dirty and sad, very, very sad. Today, in my country, we have a social crisis; there is no reference, only money. Tradition protects us from many bad influences, what you see in our cities at night, the broken society where the young will do anything for money."

I often listened to African friends explaining how they had to give their very last pennies to some very distant relative, in that loose, open African definition of "relative." This might be for a marriage or to pay school fees or to help buy a ticket to Europe (or sometimes a fake visa and fake passport to get a relative to Europe or North America) or just because they were asked for money by a needy friend or relative and *could not refuse* because to do so was unthinkable given traditional social rules. I sometimes imagined all the social glue that bound Malians together as a strait jacket woven from so many strands that everyone's hands were tied and individual freedom was strangled, non-existent.

This certainly didn't jive with the world I had grown up knowing, and thus accepting as the "norm" – which of course seemed "normal" only because I grew up knowing it. But now, from an African perspective reflecting back on my own Western world, I am not nearly so sure we have it all that right.

From this new vantage point afforded by years away from home, our modern world of material well-being that praises individual achievement, smiles upon wealth and the individual freedom to accumulate it in vast quantities, seems to stroke unpleasant human tendencies such as greed, selfishness and self-indulgence, doesn't look quite as civilized as I once assumed it was.

In the West we generally urge kids to be nice and sociable but often qualify this advice with warnings that they let no one "take advantage of them" and that they watch out for number one – one-self and maybe the nuclear family too, and success in life is often equated with accumulation of assets and money.

In this sense, Mali and many other countries in Africa are not yet modern societies and states. They may have joined the modern world in the sense that money now matters enormously; the problem is that most people in Mali (and many other African countries) don't have much money to matter. The tax system is in its infancy, the state social welfare is more holes than net itself and the average per capita income hovers at around 260 (US) dollars, or less, a year.

Despite – or partly because of – the low per capita incomes, the lack of modern infrastructure, and the very unhappy statistics on infant mortality and life expectancy, many Malians and people across the continent take time for each other and to a remarkable extent share with each other. Not always because they really want to in these changing times, but because social rules, moral norms and historical obligations still oblige them to do so.

Cheibane Coulibaly, a Malian professor of political science and one-time representative in Mali of the international watchdog group, Transparency International, recalled for me his memories of growing up in a village in the west of the country. At that time, in the 1950s and early 1960s, equality and equity were the ideals drummed into Coulibaly by his parents. Being slightly better off than others in the village was not something to be smug about or to show off; it was something shameful. As miniscule as the disparities may have been within rural farming communities – one family owning a radio or a bicycle when others did not – Coulibaly told me he had earned more than one punishment when his father learned that he had been bragging about the radio they had in their home. And his mother always prepared meals with the expectation that hungry visitors would show up; if they didn't, the food was quietly delivered to poorer families who may have suffered a poor harvest or illness in the family.

Coulibaly said these are the traditional values that Mali needs to protect, and where they have disappeared, to try to resurrect.

Tradition – which is still alive but definitely disappearing in much of Africa – puts the well-being of the extended family, the clan, the ethnic group and the social collective first. In fact, little of what many people in Africa do each day, has anything to do with what they *want* to do. What they, as individuals, want to do is not the point. The idea is to find happiness in being part of the community, putting the collective good above individual desires, to maintain social order, peace and happiness.

A few months before the Malian government declared October the Month of Solidarity, I had prepared a documentary for BBC about begging and the notion of charity in a country where so many people have so little money. I was in the habit of handing a few coins, which meant little to me, out my car window to people for whom they represented a meal or two, people who thronged the roadsides and surrounded the mosques seeking alms: maimed men, toddlers in rags, elderly blind women, a pair of twins with no legs who scrambled along the ground crablike using their arms to propel their torsos.

But my willingness to give paled next to that of Malians, many not wealthy enough to be riding about in cars, some who looked in need of alms themselves, who also tossed coins, and even bills the way of disabled beggars. I recalled what I had been told by the Minister of Social Development in Burkina Faso about not encouraging dependency and begging among garibouts and others on the roadside, wondering how to deal with the issue.

For some insights on how charity worked within the country, I went to see Mahamane Baby, from Timbuktu, who worked with a UN volunteer agency to combat poverty in Mali. He pointed out that according to official figures and standards, 70 percent of all Malians lived below the poverty line. And what a line *that* was. In Mali, you were officially considered poor if you earned less than 180 dollars *in an entire year*.

That is about half what the BBC paid me for the eight-minute report I did on begging, poverty and charity in Mali.

"I'm always surprised how generous poor people are," Mahamane Baby told me. "We work on a program which does poverty alleviation and you go see people you're supposed to help and when you go to visit them, they're ready to kill their last goat for you. You say, 'no, if you kill your last goat, you'll die.' Still, they're ready to do it. I think it's something which shows the level of the social cohesion and also it's something that we gain from our ancestors, and if there's anything we have to keep in our culture, it's this solidarity."

"If culture had a dollar value," said Mahamane with a smile, "Malians would all be billionaires."

Despite all this, each year Mali's Ministry of Social Development, Solidarity and Elderly Persons dedicated an entire month to social solidarity. Perplexed and curious, I went to the ministry and listened while the officials there heaped criticism on their own society, right in front of my microphone. Very solemnly, they told me that despite my impression to the contrary, the country's traditional and legendary solidarity was breaking down, was nothing compared with what it had once been. New imported values were turning ancient relationships on their heads, shredding old alliances and obligations until they had no more cohesion than confetti.

A miniscule minority of people, the political class close the reins of the new democratic powers in the country, were amassing vast private fortunes and were showing them off. They were building palaces, jetting off to Paris to consult doctors there or just to shop and sending their own children abroad for private education. The vast majority of Malian youngsters still didn't have the means to pay for anything but a few years of inferior elementary education in public schools devoid of teaching materials, seating, electric light, running water and sometimes even teachers.

This new elite, said the social workers, were ignoring ancient rules about sharing and caring, turning their backs on tradition that once conferred "Big Man" status on those who gave away rather than on those who hoarded their wealth.

So, they explained, their ministry declared October a month of drawing attention to all the citizens being marginalized in the new Mali – a meaner, leaner and more modern country than it was before the advent of foreign debt, foreign aid and modern values. The idea was to warn Malians not to succumb so readily to the pressures of the 21st century. Not to steep themselves in imported culture as viewed on American soap operas and satellite television, which they believed spread a mania for financial gain and the sense of false security it brings, and for eternal youth and beauty. They said the young people no longer respected the elders as they once did and still should. The resulting unhealthy hybrid of imported pop culture and watered-down tradition, they told me, led to the neglect of groups such as the elderly, the disabled and diseased.

Very noble and very good, I granted them. But alas, it didn't look like a story I could sell. No matter how many ways I tried twisting it about in my mind, I couldn't see that a story about Africans helping Africans in a country that many people in North America had never heard of, was going to fly in the mainstream media there. Furthermore, it didn't conform at all to prevailing pre-conceived editorial opinion off the continent that mostly sought news from Africa that focussed on disease and suffering, social tension and discord, conflict and death – or how Western aid or development people were working to solve these problems.

So I headed back home from the ministry and put the issue out of my mind. Until, that is, a few evenings later when I saw on the evening television news that as part of Solidarity Month, the minister herself had been visiting with some of Mali's most senior of senior citizens. A dozen of them lived right in Bamako and happened to be well over one hundred years of age.

Just the jolt – and the hook – I needed to find a way to report on social solidarity in Mali. As a journalist, I was used to tossing about and dishing up dismal statistics on average life expectancies in Africa, which rarely surpassed 50, and which these days were falling again as a result of the HIV/AIDS pandemic. But of course not everyone dies young in Africa – once a child has made it through those extremely fragile first few days, months and years, having already dealt with more infectious diseases than most Western immune systems would have to confront in a lifetime, they can often live a good long time. At least that was the case before the advent of HIV. To report on

extremely elderly people who defied all the statistics must be newsworthy, I reasoned.

Early next morning I was on the phone, calling up the ministry
again to see if I could arrange my own courtesy call on Hawa Sacko,
officially Mali's oldest woman. The social workers quickly agreed to
oblige by taking me to see her, or rather, by accompanying me
because as civil servants on dismal salaries, they had no vehicles at
their disposition.

Following narrow rutted mud tracks, we drove deep into the maze of
mud walls that constituted the neighbourhood on the northern outskirts of the Malian capital where Hawa Sacko lived. We then settled
ourselves in the shade of a large neem tree, the only bit of green left
in the area, to wait while the neighbours went to alert her of our
arrival. It was another blistering morning in Bamako, but my mind
was not on the heat. I was thrilled to be exactly where I was, seated
on a cloth spread on the baked earth of this small enclave of mud
houses, listening to the social workers from the ministry tell me what
they knew about the woman we had come to see. A woman whose
beauty was her age, which had always been venerated in Mali.

They told me they had calculated Hawa Sacko's age based on her
own vivid memories from the late 1800s. She also had a belated birth
certificate issued to her at the turn of the century by the French colonial administration, when she had been interrogated at length about
what she remembered first-hand of historical events in the last quarter of the 19th century. If the French who issued the birth certificate
had it right, Hawa Sacko's life spanned three centuries. On the bright
and sunny October morning when I came to see her, she was 125
years old, going on 126.

That made her the oldest person on earth by a full ten years. But
of course the world's record-keepers at Guinness would not recognize
this because the title is reserved for people with birth certificates that
Guinness recognizes. That means nearly every elderly person in
Africa – and much of the world where states have begun only recently to record vital statistics – is excluded.

With the help of one of her great-great grandsons, Hawa Sacko's only surviving son, who was a mere 95 years of age, carried her across the threshold and out of her small mud home. They placed her gently on the cloth spread out at the base of the neem tree, where a couple of dozen neighbours and friends had gathered.

To receive us, Hawa Sacko had donned a bright green and orange print robe and covered her head with a shawl of white lace. She was petite and frail, no longer able to get about on her own. Once she was comfortably settled against the tree and the long rounds of morning greetings were finished, I asked my first question. I wanted to know how she felt about being the oldest person in Mali, maybe even the world.

Getting this question across to her was complicated. Her hearing was not what it once was, and Hawa Sacko spoke Bamanankan and no French, the official language of the country. So I had to pose my question first in English for the sake of the minidisk onto which the conversation was being recorded, then quickly rephrase it in French for the social worker, who then translated it into Bamanankan for Hawa Sacko's son, seated right next to her on the cloth. He then relayed the question, much more loudly, directly into his mother's ear.

I wondered what on earth had happened to my question in the translation because when it reached her ears, Hawa Sacko, bless her soul, started to laugh. Her whole body shook with the wheezing laughter and soon all of us – the social workers and her extended family and neighbours who had crowded in to see what was happening – were laughing too.

When she finally did speak, and her words were relayed back to me in French via that long circuitous linguistic dance, her reply was: "I can't be older than my mother!" This made everyone laugh some more. "But as far as my being older than other living people, it's true that I'm older than all the other living people I know. But I can't say anything about all those people I don't know, whether I'm really older than them or not."

Next, I zeroed in on the numbers and facts that no journalist can ever live without. I wanted to know about her own offspring, how many, their ages, that sort of thing. This took a great deal of time because quantifying people is not an African tradition and rural

Africans often have to stop and count aloud to come up with the numbers we foreigners seem condemned to spend our lives seeking. She said that she had outlived all but one of her seven children, and that one surviving son was the one talking to me now. She had three grandsons and ten great-grandchildren. She couldn't count all her great-great grandchildren, but she did know that she had one *great-great-great* granddaughter.

All those statistics out of the way, I now wanted to know what she recalled of her youth, a turbulent time in West Africa when the French were conquering; bludgeoning the population into submission and capturing territory that would form a huge colony stretching from the West African coast all the way to Lake Chad. Contrary to popular belief, or rather to the history textbooks written by the French that had the Africans capitulating to them without a whimper, there were several African leaders and groups that fought tooth and nail to try to keep the colonists out.[373]

One of these was King Babemba Traoré in the Malian town of Kénédougou, who built an enormous wall around his town, the capital of the Senoufou Kingdom of Kénédougou, as a last bastion of African resistance to French invasion. In 1898, with 40 thousand residents, Kénédougou, (known today as Sikasso) was the second largest city in West Africa, after Kano in present-day Nigeria. The wall, remains of which still stand today, was twelve kilometres long, six metres thick at the base, five metres tall and one metre thick at the top. But it was still not enough to stop French cannonballs and the French conquerors that attacked and took the city in May 1898.

King Babemba had pledged that the French would take his kingdom only over his dead body, so when his wall fell, he had his aide-de-camp shoot him and his wife, rather than submit to a humiliating capture. At least that is the Malian version. Not surprisingly, the French history books claim the French shot him themselves.

That left only one other African resistance fighter in the region, Almamy Samory Touré, who had been battling the colonists for years. According to the French history books, Touré was a bloodthirsty tyrant. According to Mali's oral historians, he was a freedom fighter and African hero, who in the late 1800s controlled an empire stretching across much of present-day Mali, Guinea, Côte d'Ivoire,

Burkina Faso and Ghana. He headed an army of 60 thousand men, with an elite cavalry and a network of spies throughout West Africa where he led the struggle against French and British colonialism.

Malian historian Bakary Kamian told me that Samory makes nonsense of "the French myth that Africans went running every time a gun was pointed at them." Not only did he never run away from French rifles but he had his own blacksmiths copy and manufacture facsimiles of them – a first in Africa. Eventually, he was captured by the French and shipped to Gabon where he lived out his days in captivity until he died in 1900.

The Malian historians agree that Samory was ruthless. It is said he executed three of his own ill-behaved children to drive home his point to his people that no one was above the law. And it is that terrifying side of Almamy Samory Touré that Hawa Sacko recalled for me in October 2002 – in memories more than a century old.

"I remember so clearly when Almamy Touré was advancing," she said, in her quiet and raspy voice. "When they told us Touré was coming, I was terrified. It was said he opened the stomachs of pregnant women to see what was inside; he killed his own child for disobeying him, and it was said that he burned children over a grill if they did not go with him; he called them 'grilled groundnuts.'"

Then she went on to speak about the French.

"When the white man came, they were even worse," she says. "They captured our men and took them to the other bank of the river to kill them. To capture you they came right up to your house and even broke down your wall. We gave them food to eat and they gave it to their horses. We even sacrificed a sheep and gave the meat to them, and they gave it to their horses instead of sharing with us."

Sacko recalls aloud how straightforward life was back then. Women sewed their own clothes and worked in the fields or walked to market or cooked with the baby always on their backs.

"Money didn't even exist," she said. "We all lived together."

She told me that her eyes and ears were not what they once were, but that she was still in good overall health. In her long life she had been to see a doctor in a hospital only once, and then only because, as she put it, "someone cast a bad spell on me; it wasn't any physical illness."

When I asked her to share with me the secrets to her long and healthy life, what I should do to live as long and as well as she had, she laughed long and hard before replying.

"There are no secrets," she said. "I didn't do anything special. I ate normally. But I kept my faith in Allah, and He granted me a long and healthy life."

By almost any modern definition, Hawa Sacko was poor. She lived extremely modestly in a mud dwelling with a few members of her extended family in a larger neighbourhood of mud dwellings and mud paths. No running water, no electricity. A small cloth to sit on when she received visitors.

But could that dignified, spry and humorous woman who had lived a full and healthy life that spanned three centuries really be considered poor?

I was beginning – at long last – to see that it was a terrible mistake to equate the lack of material goods and money in much of Africa with true poverty and its related social ills. The drugs, prostitution, violent gang warfare, the crime, alcoholism and physical or emotional abuse within families that are often found in city slums in rich and poor parts of the world. The poverty that I saw in Kibera, Nairobi's immense never-ending slum rife with suffering, crime, filth and all the urban social ills of drug abuse and murder, cannot be compared with the lack of money and amenities one finds in more rural areas, and in urban neighbourhoods that are really just transplanted villages and functioned like them.

Even if I could see it was a mistake to assume physical squalor equals misery, that didn't mean I still didn't make the mistake almost daily in West Africa. I surrendered frequently to bleak moods, when my vision was blurred by memories of life in North America. Looking only at the physical surroundings in Bamako often blinded me to the incredible wealth there in the minds and souls of people who were steeped in their own rich history and culture.

Newcomers from other parts of the planet often assume that cities such as Bamako are dens of abject suffering and misery. But inside many of those crumbling walls are mostly reasonable healthy and apparently happy people living difficult, but dignified lives. Yes, they have to deal with many big problems that would send me down a rabbit-hole of despair and depression. But for all the problems and hardships they have to confront every day, many of them matters of life and death, many Malians – like most Africans – remain stoic and cheerful, full of humour. They are both resigned to whatever fate God or Allah has in store for them and also ready to leap at any opportunity that comes their way to better their lot in life. It certainly helps that in some countries or parts of countries they still have their rich culture to fall back on.

Many Africans I know are intensely religious, believing that if they are unable to get their hands on any money – or a visa to a country where they could earn some – then this is God's (or Allah's) will. There is no point in complaining. Indeed, to complain would be to question why God made some rich and some poor.

Some newly landed strangers (and also longer-term visitors such as I) can be so bothered by the squalor – the appalling state of the mud roads that have no gutters and double as sewers, the mountains of rubbish and plastic that threaten to bury the whole country, the toxic clouds of smoke created when local people burn these garbage heaps for lack of any other form of disposal, the beggars with what can be alarming deformities and handicaps, the sheer mess of a city like Bamako or Freetown where markets, roadways and housing merge into each other in one enormous and daunting chaotic jumble – that they are overwhelmed and completely miss the subtle beauty of the crush of humanity, and the cultural riches all around them.

An adage in Ghana states that "strangers are like children," strangers being visitors from other places. Like children, we foreigners often do not know how to behave in the places we find ourselves in Africa. My experience showed me that it is treacherous to try to interpret what we see and hear without some grounding and time to learn.

Nick, an Irish agricultural researcher who had grown up in West Africa and was working in Kenya, described for me the visit of one of his bosses from the UK, one of those who made decisions about which important agricultural research projects would or would not be funded. They had been driving for some time, and Nick had been describing the pressing poverty of farmers in western Kenya, where land-holdings were miniscule and farming to feed a family was extremely difficult. As they cruised along in their Land Rover, a new model with all the comforts, his boss from the UK turned to Nick and said he didn't understand what he was on about. "Look at all these people smiling and waving at us. They don't look like they're suffering."

I had travelled myself in West Africa with some fly-in experts from Europe and North America, who after a few hours of waving back to people on the side of the long hot ribbon of Sahelian pavement, piped up with the remark that the people out here were very friendly. "They're all waving at us!" said one, clearly pleased. "They are trying to wave us down for a lift," retorted my husband. "They wait there all day for a vehicle to pass."

Lacking so much in infrastructure and comforts, Africa's charms and graces are not always immediately apparent to those of us jetting in from more regulated, richer – and usually cooler – parts of the world.

The prevailing good manners and smiles in Mali – as elsewhere in Africa – hint at something quite remarkable and something surely worth copying for export. Once you penetrate the surface, you begin to uncover an endless treasure trove, a social maze of unwritten social rules and etiquette, social roles and cohesion that defies easy description, let alone explanation.

In Mali, there is very little serious crime, no fear on the streets and there is a very strong moral bent. What makes Mali and other countries in the region that were once part of the Mali Empire such beacons of peace, if not *material* prosperity?

These are the secrets I wish Africa could share with the outside world. But for that to happen, the outside world has to be listening.

17

View from Timbuktu

For some people, when you say "Timbuktu" it is like the end of the world, but that is not true. I am from Timbuktu, and I can tell you we are right at the heart of the world.

The late Ali Farka Touré

In February 2003, with the war drums already pounding out warnings in Washington, I attended a "hostile environment" training course in the UK. Major media houses make such courses mandatory for journalists heading into war zones. The former military and special services personnel who run these companies train not just journalists but also aid workers and corporate CEOs sending their people out to places deemed dangerous. The courses involve a lot of extremely useful first-aid training. There are lengthy sessions learning about the macabre ingenuity that goes into making landmines so that – hopefully – we journalists can escape the diabolical effects of the dozens of kinds of landmines, each designed to kill or maim in a slightly different way. Unfortunately, innocent civilians caught in conflicts where landmines are laid are never given this same training.

The training also includes orienteering, how to negotiate successfully through hostile military checkpoints, how to survive in a mock battle and how to avoid being trampled in a riot. The finale of the course was a horrendous half-day experience as a hostage, where participants undergo a mock kidnapping at gunpoint and then spend several hours learning how to put up with vicious and provocative interrogation (with a sack over one's head) and how to use charm and quick wit to avoid – hopefully – being shot in the head at the end of the exercise. I came up short on both counts and at the end of the session; the man in the balaclava did not release me but pulled the trigger of the pistol pressed against my temple. Only the loud explosion was real. Many of us ended that exercise in tears, including tough television camera-men from major networks, who made their living filming wars.

Of the dozens of journalists and camera-men attending the course, I was the only one *not* preparing to go to Iraq, where war had not yet even begun.

I was on my way back to northern Côte d'Ivoire to report for the BBC on the on-going civil war that had divided the country in half since September 2002. In the south of that country, President Laurent Gbagbo (who had not actually won the dubious elections of 2000, but who had orchestrated a popular uprising to put himself in office) had been whipping up xenophobia and genocidal fervour, particularly among the group of unemployed zealots he had set up called Young Patriots. In the north, the New Forces rebel groups had been mobilizing and arming hundreds of thousands of young people, as well as the *dossos*, the traditional hunters. The New Forces rebel leaders needed to do little to stir up animosity towards President Gbagbo and southern ethnic groups that had dominated, marginalized and exploited northerners and immigrants for years. This distorted system had been established by the French before Côte d'Ivoire's independence and then perpetuated by its first president, President Houphouët-Boigny, for more than three decades.

The Ivorian conflict had already resulted in thousands of deaths, horrendous mass graves, and mass evacuation of hundreds of thousands – if not millions – of people not originally of Ivorian descent. These included Malians, Burkinabé, Guineans, Nigeriens and other West Africans who had migrated south to Côte d'Ivoire over the decades to work on cocoa and coffee plantations. Some were already third generation, but were being denied Ivorian citizenship, the right to run in elections and also the vote. This was because of the ethnist concept of *Ivoirété* promoted by President Gbagbo and his two predecessors. If you were not descended from Ivorian parents, grandparents, and so on, you could not call yourself an Ivorian. Given that the country was not even a half century old, the idea was deadly lunacy. The kind of thing any African president ruling an independent nation the borders of which were drawn by former colonial powers should be deeply ashamed of.

All of the descendants of immigrants, who had helped build the country and its once thriving economy, were tired of the exclusion. As many as four million people of Burkinabé and three million of Malian descent worked in Côte d'Ivoire, many of them in virtual bondage on cocoa plantations.[374] I had interviewed trafficked children who had been rescued from cocoa plantations there, who spoke of being chained up at night, sleeping in their own urine, after days of carrying 50-kilogram sacks on their heads and being whipped if they fell down.

The migrants and descendants of migrants contributed greatly to the Ivorian economy and many still sent revenue back regularly to members of their extended families in other West African countries. With their labour over the decades, Côte d'Ivoire had become the world's largest cocoa producer, and as many Western pundits had liked to say, "the economic motor" and "a bastion of political stability" in West Africa. This isn't the first time that the West has been wrong about stability and prosperity in Africa, equating it with luxury hotels in capital cities with modern amenities that can shield visitors from realities on the ground – injustice, inequity and disparities – which are hardly firm foundations for political stability, not in Côte d'Ivoire or any other country.

Predictably, it took the conflict to reveal the longstanding imbalance in the country and the grievances it caused. The rebels claimed to be championing the rights of millions of northerners and immigrants, and descendants thereof, who still lived the unenviable lives of migrant workers anywhere. The untenable situation in Côte d'Ivoire had exploded in a failed coup in 2002, rapidly put down by President Laurent Gbagbo with French military help, which then led to bloody conflict and the stand-off between north and south that left the country as divided as Berlin during the Cold War.

When I was asked during the hostile environment training in the UK which war I was heading off to cover and I said I was going to

Côte d'Ivoire, several prominent European and British journalists admitted they had not heard of it – or of the war there.

That was hardly surprising. The only time the mainstream North American media had really spoken of the conflict was in the very first few days, when a missionary school full of Canadian and American children in the city of Bouake had been caught in the crossfire, and then evacuated en masse by the French military with the assistance of the rebel leaders, who had taken that city as their base. Shortly afterwards, I overheard a conversation over high-frequency radio between one of the Canadian boys there and some missionary friends in Mali; he was upset because he feared that the Sea-Doo and other playthings he had left behind in the school when he was safely evacuated to Senegal would be taken by the rebels.

A little-known war in Africa wasn't of much interest to some of the high-powered international war correspondents who were heading to Iraq. Too many of them – in my mind – also didn't seem to be paying much attention to the trumped up justification for or faulty rationale behind the imminent US-led attack on Iraq. A very few seemed downright happy to have this big war with unlimited news potential to go to. Next to that, the Ivorian war never really counted at all. It certainly wasn't very newsworthy, if newsworthy means being carried live and round-the-clock on CNN. There would be no "shock and awe."

Actually, there was plenty to be shocked about. From Côte d'Ivoire I reported on what looked like a never-ending crisis that the media and thus the non-African public had all but forgotten. I reported about the millions of school children who had not set foot in school for a year, about the lack of health care, the outbreaks of disease, about the child soldiers being trained by both the rebels and President Gbagbo as his Young Pioneers. I covered the horrific slaughters in the Wild West of the country, where ex-Liberian rebels and soldiers were joining the fray. On my computer I have a huge collection of photographs from that time, some of them gruesome shots of mass graves and human corpses, which I cannot make myself even open long enough to identify and delete.

It was a complex and tragic mess, and despite the presence of UN peacekeepers, it persisted for four years before negotiations, due to more good work by the UN, finally forced Gbagbo to integrate leaders of the New Forces (as the rebels renamed themselves during the stand-off) into the government and its leader became prime minister. The major powers – like their media – just didn't seem particularly interested in the conflict.[375]

It was after this final and deeply disturbing trip to the war zones of northern and western Côte d'Ivoire that I headed back to Mali and then northeast along the River Niger for a respite. The first stop was the visit to Niafunké with Ali Farka Touré. From there, I continued to Timbuktu, which is a fitting example of just how wrong Europeans and those of us of European descent can be when it comes to Africa.

Contrary to what I grew up believing and hearing, Timbuktu is not even close to the end of the earth – at least it's no closer than any other place that human beings call home and live out their lives on this fragile little sphere called earth. Some religious doctrines eschew all relativism and instead seek absolutes. My long sojourn in Africa and the forays I made to Timbuktu over the years showed me that absolutes crumble quickly when one is offered the immense privilege of different vantage points and perspectives.

Timbuktu may be known far and wide as a mythical destination, the place parents threaten to send children if they strike their siblings or misbehave. But to those who live there, of course, it is the centre of their universe. For many in West Africa and for Islamic scholars around the world, Timbuktu is a very holy place. It is said to be the "city of 333 saints," and is known in Mali as the "ville mysterieuse" – protected by El Farouk, a phantom rider on a white horse that patrols its alleyways at night.

Timbuktu is said to have developed around a simple source of water in about 1000 AD. That well (or "Tom" in the Songhay language) was run by a woman called Bouctou, and when thirsty travellers arrived at her well, she allowed them to drink, as long as they wore the Muslim cross. So the name, Timbuktu, or as it is spelled in French, Tombouctou, means quite simply, "Bouctou's well." That deep well still exists in the centre of the small sandy compound in front of the town's plucky little museum.

In the early centuries of the second millennium, Timbuktu developed into an extremely wealthy city, a bustling port on the River Niger and the meeting place for people of the desert and people of the coastal forests in sub-Sahara Africa. Like Venice, it was criss-crossed by canals. These were long fingers of the river plied by boats laden with gold, wood, kola nuts, spices and slaves coming from the forested regions of sub-Sahara Africa, or with salt and textiles being shipped south.[376] Caravans of camels set out from Timbuktu, filled with goods heading north to cross the Sahara Desert, bound for the Middle East and Europe. In the early 1500s, the city inspired the Spanish explorer, Leo Africanus, to paint a picture of a learned, cultured and peaceful place where books were the main industry, a city full of 'gold.'

This metaphor escaped other European explorers. For them, gold meant only one thing, and it captured their imaginations. For centuries they tried unsuccessfully to find and reach Timbuktu, many perishing along the way.[377] By the time the first ones did make it there in the 1800s, the city had long since been conquered by Moroccan armies and mercenaries and fallen on hard times. The first European explorers were roundly chastised or even disbelieved by their financiers back home when they reported that they had found a desolate desert outpost not all that different from the sand-swept town of today, with little evidence of all the fabled wealth and precious yellow metal. Hence the long-standing tendency among Westerners to view Timbuktu as not being of this earth.

It is a magical and mystical place, but it is very much of this earth. Timbuktu never failed to beguile and delight me, to fill me with the awe that no battle scenes ever will. Today it suffers from an abundance of self-made and self-proclaimed tour guides, a by-product of tourism in any impoverished part of the world. The guides often fall into step beside visitors wandering through the narrow sandy paths of the fabled town. They can be very impertinent, often a third my age and half my height, but that didn't stop them from trying to con, cajole and flirt their way into my good books – or rather, my pocket book – by hook or by crooked declaration of love in a dozen languages they had mastered. One engaging young Timbuktu guide who called himself George Washington Ali Baba had even mastered American "gangsta-rap" that he used on tourists who failed to respond to his greetings in French, German, English, Italian, Japanese, Arabic or Chinese.

I generally sent them packing, preferring to tour the mystical town with local journalists or historians. Over the years I spent many days traipsing the labyrinth of narrow sandy lanes lined with impos-ing stone or mud-brick houses, many of which date back centuries. Much to the amusement of the people who dwell there, I would kneel and fill my palms with the fine, satiny, white sand of the roadways, let it run through my fingers like liquid satin, lost in a reverie about the inexorable passage of time and the shifting sands of the desert, the shifting fortunes of the human race.

As the sun set on the eve of the American-led invasion of Iraq in March 2003, I sat with eminent Malian historian Salem Ould Elhaj on the balcony of the Hotel Bouctou, overlooking a valley of sand, where riverboats loaded with riches once came to dock.

"Timbuktu is a city known around the world because it was a city that knew great cultures," he said. "In the 16th century, more than 100 thousand people lived here, 25 thousand of them were students, and there were many great scholars. Just to name one, there was Ahmed Baba, a contemporary of Shakespeare." He glanced at me and smiled. "Ahmed Baba wrote 50 books; Shakespeare wrote only 40."

Today, suffering from drought, silt and the deforestation of its watershed and its valleys, the River Niger is a pale shadow of its for-mer self. The last narrow inlet from the river that reached Timbuktu dried up in 1981, at the onset of a great drought that caused enor-mous suffering and hunger from Senegal in the west to Ethiopia in the east of Africa. A study by scientists from the Massachusetts Institute of Technology shows that prolonged drought – diminished rainfall and shorter rainy seasons – and desertification in the Sahel can be attributed to the loss of rainforest cover to the south, along the coast of West Africa where forests have been felled for logging and for large monoculture plantations of cash crops such as cocoa, pineapples and oil palm.[378] With the added impact now of renewed interest in a Green Revolution and industrial farming in Africa, and of climate change caused by carbon emissions coming mostly from non-African nations, the health of the River Niger and millions of people in West Africa's Sahel is increasingly threatened. Already, the river has retreated from Timbuktu, 14 kilometres away, leaving behind valleys of sand.

For almost a decade in the late 1980s and 1990s, Timbuktu was off-limits to visitors because of the Tuareg rebellion that pitted the northern desert people against the government in Bamako and the Songhay population in the north of Mali. A peace treaty signed in 1996 put an end to that conflict. In 2002, an expensive monument, adorned with the remains of a large pile of weapons burned at the peace ceremony, was unveiled on a sandy square on the edge of town that is often filled with snorting and grunting camels. With the return of peace, Timbuktu once again became a popular destination for adventurous travellers eager to take a camel ride, spend a glorious night sleeping in Tuareg tents on sand dunes or listen to historians eager to explore the ancient city of learning. Some former rebels have turned their energy and talents to music and tourism.

Tuareg chief and tour guide Mohamed Lamine Ould Najim, better known simply as Shindouk, together with his wife Miranda Dodd from Cape Breton in Nova Scotia, have turned their home into the Sahara Passion hotel. They offer tourists a fantastic place to stay on the outskirts of Timbuktu with a view of camel caravans heading off to the salt mines far to the north and the chance to join one for the trek. When Miranda said to her friends back in North America that she was going to marry a Tuareg, some laughed and asked her if that wasn't the name of a car (the name Volkswagen appropriated for its SUV), "How can you marry a car?" This has given her added ambition to help people back home learn more about the desert people she lives with, and get more visitors to come to Timbuktu.

Some tourists who make their way there aren't so much interested in learning or in the adventures on camel-back offered by guides like Shindouk and prefer just to fly in and out of Timbuktu so they can mail a postcard or send an email from a cybercafé at the proverbial "end of the earth."

Left high and dry by the river that once nourished it, the centre of an empire that has long since crumbled, Timbuktu has fallen on tough times. However, there are still hints of the ancient grandeur, reminders of that bygone era when Timbuktu was a world capital of scholarship, faith and wealth, from the 14th century right through to the end of the 16th when Moroccans invaded and took over the town from the Songhay and the scholars.

There are two fabulous mosques. First is the Djingereber (literally "Big Mosque") that dates back to 1325, built on the orders of Emperor Kanku Musa when he passed through Timbuktu on his way home from a pilgrimage to Mecca. Another, the Sankoré, once housed a university and tens of thousands of Islamic scholars from all over the world.

But perhaps most momentous of all is the written legacy in Timbuktu, the hand-inscribed manuscripts, a few dating back to the 12th century, and most to the heyday of the Songhay Empire in the 15th and 16th centuries, when writing and learning were the most cherished activities in the city. The manuscripts explode the myth that Africa had only an oral history.

These written treasures are called the Timbuktu manuscripts and there are hundreds of thousands of them hidden away in deep wells or in mud-walled storerooms in northern Mali. They have been passed down in families over many generations, kept out of sight for centuries in fear that French colonists and European explorers would abscond with them. Their 'discovery' by American and European scholars is being touted as one of the most significant historical events in the last half century.[379]

"Before, all the manuscripts were kept in our homes," Abdelkader Haidara told me when I made my way to his private library, the Mamma Haidara, tucked away on a street of sand in Timbuktu. In it, he had his family's collection of 9,000 manuscripts dating back to the 16th century. "Then in 1993, I had an idea to open a private and modern library that would be open to everyone." One of those who happened by to visit his library was Professor Henry Louis Gates Jr., chair of Harvard University's African and African American Studies department, who travelled through Mali in 1998 to make a television series on the wonders of the African world.

"When Professor Gates came here and saw the storeroom full of these manuscripts written by African scholars centuries ago, he started to cry," Haidara said to me. "He wept like a child, and when I asked him why, he said that he had been taught at school that Africa had only oral culture and that he had been teaching the same thing at Harvard for years and that now he knew all that was wrong."

"When I held those books in my hands, tears rolled down my face," Henry Louis Gates recalled for me in 2005. "It is unquestionably true that I was moved to tears by the feel of these books, of this history, in my hands. It was one of the greatest moments of my life."

In the 1960s, in an attempt to preserve and promote some of Africa's great treasures, the Ahmed Baba Centre was opened in Timbuktu, named after the scholar who had written so many monumental works in the 16th century. It now houses 30 thousand manuscripts, all fantastically scripted and some adorned with gold. They deal not just with Islamic law and theology but also with astronomy, mathematics, geography, herbal medicine, conflict prevention, democracy and good governance, all of which were written centuries ago. Books known as the *Searchers' Chronicles* are comprehensive historical accounts of empires in West and North Africa up to the 16th century, written by African scholars in African languages using Arabic script.

One of the authors of the *Searchers' Chronicles* was a scholar named Mahmud Kati, whose father immigrated to Timbuktu from Spain in the 15th century, when Muslims were forced to flee crusading Christians in the southern province of Andalucia. Mahmud Kati's mother was Songhay royalty, sister of the Askia Mohamed who ruled the flourishing Songhay Empire that controlled Timbuktu at the time. In recent years Ismaël Haidara, one of Mahmud Kati's direct descendents, has received Spanish funding to develop the Fondo Kati Library in Timbuktu, in which thousands of his forefathers' invaluable manuscripts are stored.

But it's a struggle. Hawa Haidara, who co-manages the library with her husband, explained how difficult it is. "The problem is that the manuscripts need to be preserved, and that is very expensive. You can't handle them or words fall literally right off the pages, because the paper is old and so fragile."

The manuscripts are stored in open-cage shelves in a dark room, but every time Hawa Haidara attempted to remove the dust that is abundant in Timbuktu, bits of paper broke off. To illustrate, she led me to a corner where bits of brittle paper lay piled like fallen leaves. "The other problem is that all these manuscripts are written in Arabic scripts," she said. "The authors were sometimes writing in African languages, so even if we get funds to restore them, the manuscripts must also be digitized, translated and studied to see what all is in them."

Soft-spoken Ismaël Haidara said that there is "great symbolism" in the manuscript collections of Timbuktu and in his family's library; his ancestors include black Muslims, white European Christians who converted to Islam and also black Jewish merchants who settled in Timbuktu centuries ago. "Timbuktu may be one of the poorest places on earth," he said. "But it is important not to forget that every citizen of Timbuktu has in his eyes and in his blood a thousand years of history and a thousand years of different cultures, and that is our wealth."

Another person who spoke to me on the day before the US-led "coalition of the willing" invaded Iraq in 2003 was Abdramane Ben Essayouti, the scholarly Imam at the Djingereber Mosque in Timbuktu. Looking regal, poised and dignified in a pale blue *boubou* and matching turban, he sat on a long padded bench at one end of a large room on the second floor of a large building of stone bricks, listening to my questions about Timbuktu, Islam and world events, and then weighing his words as he cautiously replied. He said Timbuktu occupied a very important place among Islamic centres around the world. "After Mecca, Medina and Al-Aqsa in Jerusalem, it is Timbuktu that is cited among holy Islamic sites ... Islam rules in the four corners of Timbuktu."

But did it?

In the past few years the Assemblies of God missionaries had set themselves up in Timbuktu to save what they consider the unsaved souls of Muslims in West Africa. Baptists had also moved in. The American military were increasingly visible in the ancient town, flying in regularly from their European Command in Germany while waiting to decide where to put their new African Command, running what was originally called the Pan-Sahel Initiative and later the Trans-Sahara Counter-Terrorism Initiative to fight the war on terror in a whole swath of Africa, west to east.

I had heard numerous reports from American and German aid workers living in Timbuktu about the frequent visits of US generals to the region, how they seconded vehicles from American NGOs and headed out into the desert. Diplomatic sources had told me that when Liberia imploded under Charles Taylor, the US moved its major West African "listening post" to northern Mali. UN officials said, in whispers and with warnings to avoid the region, that the Americans had set up their spy centre in Tessalit in Mali's Sahara Desert, which offered them a camel's eye view of Islamic activities in neighbouring Algeria, Mauritania and even as far as Libya.

"You can go there, but you will not come back. They will hire bandits to eliminate you," said one UN diplomat in Bamako.

When I asked the Public Diplomacy Officer at the US embassy in Bamako about Tessalit, he at first scoffed. "Oh, our UFO centre up there? Ha ha ha." I took out my notebook and pen (all I was allowed to take into the embassy with me) and asked if that was how he wished to be quoted. He then explained that any American military activities in Mali's north were related to the Pan-Sahel Initiative. He would not confirm or deny that Tessalit was a major American listening centre.

So I took this opportunity to ask the Imam in Timbuktu if he was bothered by all the foreign activities and influences in Timbuktu.

"I don't pay attention to those things," he replied. "I am a religious leader; I have nothing to do with espionage."

Did he have any fears that with their military presence in Mali's north and throughout the African countries where they run their counter-terrorism activities, that the US interventions could increase religious tensions?

"A city like Timbuktu was born with Islam," he replied. "Countless generations have followed the Islamic path here. How can anyone pervert us?"

I wanted to know what he thought about the American-led "war on terror" and the imminent attack on Iraq. "We in Timbuktu have the same reaction to that war as does the whole world; we share the views of our Muslim brothers. The whole world is against that war; people are demonstrating everywhere, saying that war is not worth it.

We consider it a kind of war against Islam, and that's dangerous. Something small can become very big. It can become a religious war."

He said that one of his own forefathers, Islamic scholar Mohamed El Iraqi, came to Timbuktu in the 18th century from Iraq, and added, "We have an adage that says, even if you have the power to do something, it's at that moment that you should stop yourself; never react in anger or you will regret it."

"They say they're fighting against terrorism," he continued. "But what is terrorism but the arm of despair? People who will strap bombs to themselves to kill themselves and others, I say that's despair, and all this starts with the problem of Palestine that we've all ignored. We've always regarded the United States as the model of democracy, but with this war, where should we classify that democracy?"

Later that day, in the relative cool and reverential silence of the archives at the Ahmed Baba Centre in Timbuktu, researcher Chirfi Alpha Sane showed me just a few of the fragile manuscripts that he helped to preserve. "There is everything here in these manuscripts," he said. "Islamic law with lessons for peace through dialogue, as well as science, astronomy, medicine. In Timbuktu these scholars said that gold came from the south, salt came from the north, and money came from the lands of the white men. But they believed that wisdom and the word of God were to be found only in Timbuktu. That wisdom is here, in these manuscripts."

"In the Middle Ages this was almost the centre of the world," he said. "Then one day God turned it all around and many people started viewing Timbuktu as the end of the world. One day God may turn it all around again, and Timbuktu will once again find its rightful place and regain its glory."

For the time-being, however, Timbuktu – like much of Africa – remains off the beaten path, off the map altogether for many around the world. Then again, what do we mean when we speak of beaten paths? There are many very well-beaten paths in Africa that I, as a Westerner, hardly recognized as such, as I learned over two and a half decades on the continent. Beaten paths in Africa are rarely paved, or marked with road signs or speed limits, but that doesn't mean they are not beaten. Who needs speed limit signs for people on foot, often barefoot or in flimsy plastic flip-flops, or for donkeys or camels making their way along sand or mud tracks?

On a river journey to find the village of BBC in Ghana many years earlier, I had come equipped with two metal cases, filled with everything I might ever need for an overnight stay in the bush or for any other eventuality. They held a portable water filter lest my bottled water run out, books to stave off boredom lest our motorboat break down, sunscreen, a sunhat, a shortwave radio with the extra batteries to run it and two flashlights as well as my first aid kit. Like a boy scout, I had come prepared. The nine men who shared that river journey with me had come with nothing except the trousers they wore, not even shirts on their backs. They watched me taking an inventory of my precious worldly belongings intended to protect me against any eventuality, asking me to tell them what each gadget was for, and why I carried it. I performed a little show and tell. Eventually, when they had stopped laughing, one man explained to me what he found so funny. "You Whites," he said, "you think you can outsmart God Himself!"

In Africa I have come to accept that life is not predictable and no matter how much one prepares or plans, well-laid plans rarely go very far. There's precious little rhyme to or reason in much of what we do while on this earth. Especially if, as is the case for our Western society, so much of what we spend our time doing is completely divorced from the things we once did to survive. Most of us no longer grow our own food or even prepare our own food, make our own textiles and clothing, build our own houses with tools we fashion ourselves, get about using draught power, animals we rear ourselves, or just on the two good feet the gods gave us.

And even as the main currents in our Western industrial world and increasingly the currents in booming Asian countries carry us further and further from these basics, the things that are truly issues of life (in the fullest sense) and death, the more we seem inclined to view any people who still pretty much fend for themselves, without the benefit of any modern amenities, as backward. I often ask myself, now that I have had my own deep-rooted cultural biases severely challenged and even overturned over so many years of living, working and blundering about in Africa, how it is that we in the West can be so sure that our way is the right way? Not just for us, but for everyone else on the planet too. It starts to look increasingly like blinkered nonsense.

I've always found it perplexing that a Westerner who adopts African dress, or mannerisms and perspectives risks being labelled disparagingly by a few other expatriates as "bushed" or "gone native," as if to embrace and accept African ways of thinking and doing things are considered somehow inferior at best, a sign of insanity at worst. A cliché I've heard many times from European experts and others like them working in Africa goes like this: "We're here to bring them up to our level, not to lower ourselves to theirs." An African sporting a tailored suit, a tie, a Parisian or London accent, and criticizing the people of Africa or a particular African country as "lazy" (I can't count the number of times I've heard this) may be admired and praised by some Westerners and like-minded Africans as "enlightened" and "sophisticated." Those who stick to the old African ways of thinking and living risk being labelled primitive, savage, stone-age. But as columnist George Monbiot puts it so succinctly: "Stone-aged and primitive are what you call people when you want their land."[380]

Africa has taught me to question absolute truths about progress and development. 'Advanced,' 'modern' and 'technologically superior' now seem to me to be words that describe, increasingly, a way of living and thinking for a minority on the planet, which may lead to the extinction of the entire human race (not to mention much of the plant and animal kingdom as we know it), sooner rather than later.

Education is not necessarily something obtained *only* in a formal school where children sit in neat rows watching a teacher making little scribbles on a blackboard so that one day they can get a 'good job.' Africans have taught me that education is something much broader; it includes social responsibility, respect for others and elders, tolerance of differences, good manners, all of which can be taught at home and by the community.

Uneducated, to me, applies far less to an African farmer who has never set foot in a school and who welcomes visitors and new ideas with curiosity and an open mind, as much as it does, say, to a selfish and ill-mannered teenager in an elite private school who has no respect for those without the same money and privileges.

It is not easy to shed the Western mindset, because it is so deeply engrained and we have been so busy patting ourselves on the backs for too long, saying *ours* is the age of enlightenment and we can lead the rest of the world. This Western hubris is what first led Europeans to annex the entire continent of Africa (and a good part of the several other continents) as their colonial territories, led missionaries to believe they had a moral obligation to rid Africa of her traditional religions and reveal to the 'truth' of their version of God. God, in the literal translation of some languages in Sierra Leone, is "Something You Meet" here on earth, something that was here long before you and will be here long after you are gone. In other words, your individual life is beholden to those who went before you and will shape life – something they meet – of those who come after you. This perspective, which is now disappearing, creates humility.

The 20th century brought us great horrors, genocides on an unprecedented scale; but it also brought great advances in humanity's attempt to establish reason and justice. Among them, the Universal Declaration of Human Rights, the Geneva Conventions, the UN Convention on Torture, which, if applied by everyone for everyone on this little world of ours, could indeed mark human progress. Alas, in this new age, even those are being trampled by the same West that continues to preach about democracy and human rights to the rest of the world.

Viewed from Timbuktu, surrounded by magnificent sand dunes carved by the wind and glinting in the sun, the voices of reason of the local philosophers drawing on the ancient wisdom of the many manuscripts in their collections, the world looks very different than it does, say, from a parking lot of a North American shopping mall.

It dawns on me, perhaps belatedly, that no wealth is eternal. No people or culture or civilization is infallible. As they love to write on bush taxis from Nigeria across to Sierra Leone: No Condition is Permanent.

Civilizations may fancy themselves superior to others and believe that only their way of life and thinking is God-blessed, but civilizations come and go, rise and fall, and so do great and powerful centres of wealth and learning. Everyone on earth has something to teach others and something to learn from others.

I believe that is the lesson of Timbuktu – and of Africa.

April 2008, Freetown, Sierra Leone

Acknowledgments

I lived for almost a quarter of a century in Africa – in Niger, Cameroon, Burkina Faso, Ghana, Kenya, Mali, Sierra Leone – travelling in another 27 countries. The continent is so vast, complex and diverse that it defies in-depth coverage in a whole library, let alone a single book. And this one does not even pretend to do justice to that diversity and complexity, and to all the wonderful, insightful people I've met along the way. I could not have written this book, comprehended what I was seeing and hearing, learned what Africa had to teach, without years and years of schooling from people all over the continent, both friends and those whom I met and interviewed as a journalist, science writer or development consultant. Inspiration came from the countless memories of smiling, singing, laughing, insightful, thoughtful, stalwart, suffering and sharing people in Africa who have greeted me, put up with my questions, taught me, befriended me and offered freely – often along with gifts they could ill afford to give me – their wisdom, insights and stories. I thank all those people, too many to mention, who helped me see their world – and mine – from the other side of the looking glass. Countless people provided me with information for this book, but none is responsible for the way it is interpreted in this book. I take full responsibility for the way the material is presented here, and for any inadvertent errors that appear.

I am greatly indebted to those who read and commented on the book or parts of the book in various stages, among them Ian Smillie, Christiane Kayser, Flaubert Djateng, David Baxter, Andreas Massing, Gary Blackwood, Anna Gyorgy. I wish to thank many people at BBC World Service who kindly allowed me great latitude in pursuing stories that might not be construed as newsworthy in other large media, and special thanks to Iain Croft of BBC News and Ann McKeigan of CBC's wonderful erstwhile program, *Global Village*, who supported my trip to Niafunké to meet Ali Farka Touré.

I would also like to thank all those who were took me under their wings and were, often involuntarily, my mentors over many years in Africa, among them Saïd Penda, Dali Mwagore, Helen van Houten, Mary Fukuo, Asseta Zango, Iliasu Adam, the late Iddrissu Issah and William Umbima, Abi Camara, the Tinorgah family, Brigitte Sodatanou and many others who patiently allowed me to pick their brains repeatedly when I sought information and enlightenment, among them: Aminata Dramane Traoré, the late Mohamed Lamine Traoré, and a host of intellectuals in many countries. My thanks also to the courageous and hard-working civil society groups in Mali and Sierra Leone who are working so hard to bring justice and environmental sanity to the mining and agricultural sectors in their countries and who shared freely with me their knowledge and sometimes also their frustrations, including Mamadou Goïta, Theophilius Gbenda, Abu Brima, Cicilia Mattia, Kadi Julia Jumu, Leslie M'boka, Musa Kamara, to name just a few. I wish to thank all the people who have been dear friends over the years in all the African countries we lived in, who made our lives rich and each country feel like home. They are too many to name here, but they know who they are. And I want to thank the staff and friends of NSGA for their gracious support while I worked with them.

I also wish to offer heartfelt thanks to Vivan Godfree for her kind support and encouragement right from the start, to Lesley Choyce of Pottersfield Press for allowing the use of some material that has appeared previously in a different form in my earlier books. I am grateful to Robert Lecker, my supportive agent, to Simone Saunders and all the hard-working staff at Wolsak & Wynn, who helped hammer this book into shape and promote it. And to Noelle Allen, my publisher, I can only express my deepest gratitude and admiration for her support and professional advice, without which this book might never have taken shape at all. My gratitude to my parents for their interest and encouragement, and to Karlheinz, Anna and Bobo, Deb and David who lived through it all whether they wanted to or not. I wish to thank the Canada Council for its support that made the writing of this book possible. And I remain eternally grateful to the elderly woman who asked me the crucial question: Why do you bring your mistakes here?

Endnotes

Introduction

[1] Binyavanga Wainana. 2005. "How to write about Africa." *Granta 92*, Winter 2005: 93.

[2] Caplan, Gerald. 2008. *The Betrayal of Africa.* Toronto: Groundwood Books / House of Anansi Press. p 16.

[3] Aligiah, George. 3 May 1999. "The 20th century view of Africa infected with the prevailing wisdom of the 19th century." *The Guardian.*

[4] Nolen, Stephanie. 2007. *28: stories of AIDS in Africa.* Toronto: Knopf Canada

[5] Ankomah, Baffour. June 2008. "Reporting Africa." *New African.* No. 474: 14.

[6] Always Canada says its Protecting Futures project is part of the so-called HERO campaign of the United Nations Association of the United States of America [distinct and separate from the actual UN], together with the Business Council for the United Nations. HERO works with the US Agency for International Development (USAID) as "an awareness-building and fundraising initiative dedicated to providing comprehensive, school-based support to orphans and vulnerable children living in HIV/AIDS-affected communities in Africa." [http://www.unausa.org/site/pp.asp?c=fvKRI8MPJpF&b=260414] Sounds noble. But HERO partners such as Always Canada to push sanitary projects on African women does not. Proctor & Gamble's Always Canada would have the well-intentioned woman consumer believe that they "discovered" an urgent need in Africa for their feminine sanitation products. African women have survived quite well without those products for countless millennia, as they have their own ways to absorb their monthly flows. One is re-usable pieces of cloth. But, this doesn't expand markets for pads and tampons, with those environmentally disastrous plastic inserters. [Protecting Futures http://www.alwayscanada.com/ca_en/protectingfutures/youcan.php?id=wycd]

[7] Klein, Naomi. 2007. *The Shock Doctrine — the rise of disaster capitalism.* Toronto: Alfred A. Knopf Canada. p 18.

[8] United Nations University. 5 Dec. 2006. *Pioneering Study Shows Richest Two Percent Own Half World Wealth.* http://www.wider.unu.edu/.../_files/78204611177480527/

[9] Hochschild, Adam. 1998. *King Leopold's Ghost – a story of greed, terror, and heroism in colonial Africa.* New York: Houghton Mifflin.

[10] Caplan, 2008 p. 127.

[11] Sharife, Khadija. June 2008. "Whose reality are we living in?" *New African.* No. 474: 22.

[12] See: Lewis, Stephen. 2005. *Race Against Time.* Toronto: House of Anansi.

[13] Frei, Matt. 14 Feb. 2008. "George W. Bush's BBC interview." BBC News. http://news.bbc.co.uk/2/hi/americas/7245670.stm

[14] EURODAD (European Network on Debt and Development). 18 Jan. 2008. *Old Habits Die Hard: aid and accountability.* EURODAD with Campaign for Good Governance. p 8. http://www.eurodad.org/whatsnew/reports.aspx?id=2038

[15] "Donor" is the vague term widely used for developed countries that send development assistance and emergency aid to developing countries through bilateral and multilateral programs, including those administered by the United Nations and the Bretton Woods institutions (World Bank and the International Monetary Fund). Mali's former Minister of Culture, sociologist Aminata Dramane Traoré, and many African intellectuals and activists insist these countries and institutions are not donors so much as they are creditors, maintaining that they take more out of Africa in debt servicing, contract spin-offs, overheads for their own administration of development programs and consultants' fees, and profits from natural resource exploitation, than they actually put in through donations. Traoré also points out that the World Bank and IMF cannot be considered members of the "donor community" because they are profit-making financial lending institutions. For the purposes of this book, however, I will refer to them as "donors." [Traoré, Aminata Dramane. 1999. *L'étau: L'Afrique dans un monde sans frontiers.* Paris: Actes Sud.]

[16] Gupta, Shyamal. 18 Mar. 2008. "Reach out to Africa." *The Times of India.* http://timesofindia.indiatimes.com/Reach_out_to_Africa/articleshow/2875380.cms

---

Part I: Breaking the heart-shaped continent

1   Who's crazy?

[17] Thoreau, Henry David. *n.d. Walden.* p 7.

[18] Naipaul, V.S. 1984. *Finding the Centre: two narratives.* London: André Deutsch. p 103.

[19] In 2006, Ali Farka Touré won a second Grammy award for his album, *Heart of the Moon,* done together with Mali's renowned Kora player, Toumani Diabité. By then, he had also become mayor of Niafunké.

[20] Like many Africans of his generation, Ali Farka Touré did not know his exact birth date.

[21] "Poor" in this book describes people who have very little money or resources needed to provide for the well-being of themselves and their families with basic necessities — access to clean water, shelter from the elements, schooling, basic heath care. It does not imply that they are in any way "less developed" socially, intellectually or spiritually and it may often be no indicator of satisfaction levels with their lives. For this reason, I often use the term "monetarily poor" to clarify what kind of poverty I am describing.

[22] Bush, George W. 1 June 2002. President George W. Bush's Speech to the 2002 Graduating Class at the United States Military Academy, West Point, New York. http://www.ashbrook.org/articles/bush_02-06-01.html

[23] Diamond, Jared. 2005. *Collapse: how societies choose to fail or succeed.* New York: Penguin.

[24] Wright, Ronald. 2004. *A Short History of Progress.* 2004. Toronto: Anansi Press.

2   No longer ourselves

[25] Thomas Sankara, President of Burkina Faso, 1983–1987.

[26] Francis Bebey, from "The coffee-cola song" on his 1991 Sonodisc album, *La Condition Masculine.*

[27] Bolton, Giles. 2007. *Poor Story — an insider discovers how globalisation and good intentions have failed the world's poor.* Toronto: Key Porter Books. p 76.

[28] Hochschild, 1998.

[29] Conrad, Joseph. 1902. *Heart of Darkness.* 1973 edition New York, NY: Penguin. p 52,43.

[30] Least Developed Countries or LDCs are those designated as such by the United Nations, according to its Human Development Index, which ranks the development levels of nations around the world according to a complex set of criteria. LDCs are sometimes also known as "Fourth World" nations.

[31] Fula (also Fulani, Fullah, Peul, Peuhl) is the name of a very large ethnic group stretching from Cameroon across to the West African coast, speaking a language known as Fulbe or Fulfulde.

[32] Mandé people — comprising many smaller ethnic groups — are found in Burkina Faso, Côte d'Ivoire, Ghana, Guinea, Guinea-Bissau, Liberia, Mali, Sierra Leone and The Gambia; the Mandé languages belong to a branch of the Niger–Congo family.

[33] See, for example: Edney, Julian. 2002-2004. *Theory and debate: greed.* http://www.g-r-e-e-d.com/GREED.htm

3   The case there for God

[34] Eventually, young desperate African men may have another option, at least if retired US Colonel Wayne Long has his way. In March 2006, Colonel Long penned an editorial in *The International Herald Tribune,* calling for an American foreign legion, which would be made up largely of young men now flocking to US embassies in Africa. In an interview on CBC radio on 7 March 2006, Col Long pointed out that he lived in Africa and saw the numbers lining up at embassies. His idea was to fill the military ranks not with young men from what he termed "advanced countries," but from developing countries where young people are desperate for visas to the developed world. Wrote Col. Long, "The good news is that there is a large untapped resource of potential manpower that has not ever been considered by the army: huge numbers of young foreign military age males who have green cards and are eagerly seeking U.S citizenship, or are awaiting visas in their homeland. In exchange for U.S. citizenship at the end of enlistment, these young men could be vetted and recruited by the army on five-year terms at recruiting stations in the United States and around the world." This proposal is as cynical an exploitation of desperate young men in impoverished countries that I could imagine ? it would offer young Africans a chance to fight and die for a country in which they had never set foot. [Long, Wayne. 1 Mar. 2006. "It's time for an American foreign legion." *International Herald Tribune.* Opinion.]

[35] See: IRIN news. 21 Mar. 2008. WEST AFRICA: "Bad economic policies driving migration." United Nations humanitarian news and information service (IRIN). http://www.irinnews.org/Report.aspx IRIN news (Integrated Regional Information Network) is a United Nations humanitarian news and information service. It is a project of the UN Office for the Coordination of Humanitarian Affairs (OCHA), and its reports may not reflect the views of the United Nations or its agencies. IRIN reports can be found be searching the website: http://www.IRINnews.org and the caveat on their not reflecting the views of the United Nations or its agencies applies to all IRIN reports cited in this book.

[36] In northern Ghana, people asked me if the British and Canadian volunteers who worked there and who broke this stereotype — moving about on foot or bicycle or in public transport, dressing down and paying little or no attention to personal appearance and sometimes hygiene — were sent out to work in Africa because they were social rejects and of no use in their own societies. They were generally looked down upon, partly because their inattention to their appearance (and sometimes hygiene) was viewed locally as disrespectful to local people who paid enormous attention to both hygiene and dress, no matter how little money they had, and partly because these volunteers were an unfamiliar breed on a continent that had come to have a distorted view of white people as naturally wealthy and disinterested in much that was local.

[37] In March 2006, the Canadian embassy in Pretoria, South Africa, refused a visa for renowned South African ex-political prisoner, Ahmed Kathrada, saying he needed police clearance first. Kathrada spent 26 years in Robben

Island and is a close confidant of Nelson Mandela. When a Canadian diplomat noticed the political mistake that had been made and called Mr. Kathrada to explain that they didn't realize "who he was," Kathrada replied that he didn't want any special treatment and cancelled his trip to Canada to promote his book, *Memoirs,* limiting his tour only to the United States where he had no visa problems. A Sudanese friend who also had troubles acquiring a visa for Canada even though he had been invited by universities working in partnership with the international research institution for which he worked, told me "Canada seems to prefer giving visas to rich African criminals to ordinary and honest Africans." [*Mail & Guardian Online.* 7 Mar. 2006. "Kathrada cancels trip to Canada over visa flap." SAPA and AP http://www.mg.co.za/articlePage.aspx?articleid=265999&area=/breaking_n ews/breaking_news__national/]

[38] In most of Africa, tradition demanded that visitors – invited or not – be offered food and drink, no questions asked. Often they were given a place to sleep as well, and water for washing. Today, like many traditional practices, these rules of hospitality are breaking down and being perverted under modern pressures. Increasing poverty and escalating food prices in urban areas make it difficult for many people to eat more than one or two meals a day, making it difficult to share scarce food with visitors, who at the same time become more numerous as they seek out extended family or distant relatives or friends who might be able to feed them. The generosity among family members or people related only by ethnicity has also traditionally extended to gifts of money, when desperately needed, and to sleeping room in homes. Today, the obligation to be one's distant relative's keeper has become an irritant, causing enormous resentment among those who have paying work and are trying to 'get ahead,' in the face of the weighty burden of looking out for, feeding and sustaining unemployed relatives. And yet, when disaster strikes, as it did in Côte d'Ivoire in 2002 when a civil conflict erupted, it is this social elasticity that serves as Africa's greatest strength and safety net. Hundreds of thousands of people with Malian roots who had been living in Côte d'Ivoire for generations came north to Mali and found refuge and sustenance in the homes of distant relatives. In some cases, these were people who had been sending money back to impoverished Malian relatives for many years, and now found their generosity over the years repaid.

[39] "419" refers to the article of the Nigerian Criminal Code that deals with fraud and obtaining property on false pretences.

[40] Maphosa, Tendai. 11 Jan. 2008. "Study: More African doctors, nurses working abroad than at home." VOA News. http://www.voanews.com/english/2008-01-11-voa66.cfm.

[41] Warnica, Richard. 22 Feb. 2008. "Poaching African doctors a crime, says international MDs group. 13,000 sub-Sahara physicians work in Canada, the U.K., U.S. and Australia." Canwest News Service. http://www.canada.com/edmontonjournal/news/story.html?id=ced619cb-65d3-4eef-8e53-fd7404e8ff5e AND: Attaran, Amir and Walker, Roderick B. 29 Jan. 2008. "Shoppers Drug Mart or Poachers Drug Mart?" *Canadian*

Medical Association Journal (CMAJ): 178(3)
http://www.cmaj.ca/cgi/content/full/178/3/265

[42] See: Findley, Sally E. Sept. 2004. "Mali: seeking opportunity abroad." *Migration Information Source.*
http://www.migrationinformation.org/Profiles/display.cfm?ID=247 AND: Migration News. 2003. Cooperative efforts to manage emigration (CEME). http://migration.ucdavis.edu/ceme/more.php?id=96_0_6_0

[43] Gerald Caplan points out that Africans contributed enormously to the Allies' war against Nazi racism; 374,000 Africans served in the British army during World War II, and 80,000 in the French. [Caplan, 2008. p 25.]

[44] Ibid. p 93.

[45] French, Howard W. 2004. *A Continent for the Taking: the tragedy and hope of Africa.* New York: Random House. p XV.

[46] The Salafist Group for Call and Combat with its base in Algeria is designated a terrorist group by the US State Department. [US Department of State, Office of Counterterrorism. 29 Dec 2004. Terrorist Exclusion List. http://www.state.gov/s/ct/rls/fs/2004/32678.htm]

4   Miracles, marabouts and magic

[47] See, for example, the effect of the crusades by German Evangelist Reinhard "Bonnke in Nigeria: Cutrer, Connie 11 Aug. 2000. "Bonnke returns to Nigeria one year after tragedy." *Christianity Today.* http://www.christianitytoday.com/ct/2000/145/34.0.html

[48] Bambara is the common term for the Bamana people of Mali, and also for their language, Bamanankan.

[49] NGO is the acronym for non-governmental organization, a catch-all name used to describe the myriad development and charitable agencies working around the world, with no official governmental connections.

[50] Shea or shea nut is the English for the tree that in French is called *karité* (there are as many names for this tree and for the oil derived from its nut as there are languages in the Sahelian zone of West Africa). Shea trees produce a high-quality edible and medicinal oil product derived from a tree indigenous to the Sahelian region of Africa, with the Latin name, *Vitellaria paradoxa.* It has become a valuable commodity on the international market.

5   Burying African hopes

[51] Amnesty International has documented massive abuses of human rights over the years in Togo under General Eyadéma. In 1998, Amnesty reported that the Togolese security forces murdered hundreds of opponents before and after presidential elections. President Eyadéma changed the constitution to allow himself to run — and win — presidential elections in 2003. He died in power in 2005. His son succeeded him, and then won elections widely denounced as fraudulent, to perpetuate his father's dynasty.

[52] French investigative journalist, Pascal Kopp, alleges that this first coup–assassination in Africa was done as a covert French military operation, orchestrated by French president General Charles de Gaulle, incensed that Togolese President Sylvanus Olympio had publicly defied him, and was no longer serving the interests of France, having visited both Germany and the US without French "permission." When Gnassingbé Eyadéma and his two accomplices showed their willingness to confront President Olympio to demand admission to the Togolese army, Kopp reports that French officers then convinced them that Olympio would kill them if they requested such a thing, and that the only solution was to eliminate the president. [Krop, Pascal. 1994. *Le genocide franco-africain: faut-il juger les Mitterrand?* Paris: Editions Jean-Clause Lattès.]

[53] Among the groups that Libya helped train to counter Western influence in West Africa were the Tuareg desert peoples of the Sahara Desert, and the rebels who would later become the Revolutionary United Front who caused such mayhem and suffering in Sierra Leone.

[54] In 2006, South African president, Thabo Mbeki announced that it was time to re-open the investigation into Samora Michel's death in 1986. There had long been suspicion in Africa that the Apartheid regime in South Africa and its security forces had been responsible for his death.

[55] Niamey is the capital of Niger, Yaoundé the capital of Cameroon, Cotonou the largest commercial city in Benin, Lomé the capital of Togo, and Kano is the largest city in the north of Nigeria.

[56] Jonas Savimbi founded the Maoist UNITA movement in Angola in 1966, and from then till the early 1990s, he was supported – with arms and training – by apartheid South Africa. In the 1980s he was championed by the American right-wing think tank, the Heritage Foundation, and supported by the United States under President Ronald Reagan (whom Savimbi visited in Washington) and Vice President George H.W. Bush, who had headed the CIA in the 1970s. After its independence from Portugal in 1974, previous nationalist movements within Angola continued their struggle. On one side was the People's Movement for the Liberation of Angola (MPLA) backed by Cuba; on the other were the South African- and US-backed FNLA and UNITA under Savimbi. Savimbi was close to two of the West's favourite and key African leaders, Côte d'Ivoire's Félix Houphouët-Boigny and Zaire's Mobutu Sese Seko. In later years, when the Cold War ended, Savimbi fell out of favour with his former friends in Washington, and was accused of being involved in drug, arms and diamond trafficking throughout Africa. Savimbi was killed by Angolan government troops in February 2002. The decades of fighting in oil- and diamond-rich Angola decimated the country, causing repeated famines, untold numbers of civilian deaths and atrocious maiming and death tolls from landmines throughout the country. See: Simpson, Chris. 25 Feb 2002. "*Obituary: Jonas Savimbi, Unita's local boy.*" BBC News. http://news.bbc.co.uk/2/hi/africa/264094.stm

[57] PW Botha was prime minister of apartheid South Africa from 1978 to 1984, when he became its first state president, governing until 1989.

[58] Female circumcision comes in many forms and is widespread in parts of Africa. The UN and many Western agencies call all of these "Female Genital Mutilation" or FGM, and are trying to eliminate the practise. This campaign is widely and hotly debated in Africa, with many in favour of the elimination of the practise and others who defend it. Dr. Fuambai Ahmadu, a Sierra Leonean / American scholar and Associate Professor at the Department of Comparative Human Development at the University of Chicago, is one of those that denounces the campaign led by UN agencies as an "alarming multi-million dollar 'development' industry." [Ahmadu, Fuambai. 4 Mar. 2008. "Hurray for Bondo women in Kailahun: Commentary." *The Patriotic Vanguard: Sierra Leone Portal.* http://www.thepatrioticvanguard.com/article.php3?id_article=2403] Another Sierra Leonean scholar, Aisha Fofanah Abrahim, says the WHO is right to call the removal of a woman's health organ "mutilation" but notes that aesthetic bodily modifications in the West such as breast augmentations, face lifts, liposuctions, etc, acquire a "neutral coinage," becoming "choices," not mutilation. She says that to argue that these are performed by consent in the West, is to assume, incorrectly, that there is no consent in much of the female circumcision ceremony in Africa. [Abrahim, Aisha Fofana. 25 Mar. 2008. "Female genital mutilation crisis: a response." *Standard Times* (Sierra Leone).]

[59] The second-hand clothes that flood every market in Africa today come primarily from Europe and North America, where individuals give them away to charities. Charities sell them to wholesale dealers for whom frippery is very big business. They then bundle them up in bales that are sent off to Africa by the container-load. Dealers also buy bulk the unsold clothes from major clothing retailers for this burgeoning and lucrative trade that so undermines and greatly harms local textile and tailoring industries on the continent. Today, in much of Africa, people are clad primarily in these cast-off clothes, abandoning their own magnificent textiles and styles.

[60] *Almudos* is the term for them in The Gambia; they are known as *talibes* in Senegal and *al manjeri* in northern Nigeria.

[61] Church Committee.1975. *Interim Report: alleged assassination plots to kill foreign leaders.* p 14. http://history-matters.com/archive/church/reports/ir/contents.htm

[62] Blaise Compaoré, Sankara's right-hand man and friend in the Revolutionary Council, who later became president of Burkina Faso, stepped in and did arrange for Joseph Sankara to get to France for medical care. He also bought him a moped. Compaoré's own father had died when he was a child, something that one of his friends told me had "deeply marked" him. Until the coup in 1987, Sankara's parents viewed Compaoré as a son who visited far more often than did their son, Thomas. Their walls were filled with photographs of Compaoré and members of the Sankara family. After the coup, Compaoré never came back and those photographs of Compaoré came down, leaving the walls almost empty but marked by pale squares where they had once hung on the dusty walls.

[63] In a candid conversation with a UNICEF official, he also worried about the impact of universal childhood vaccinations without a parallel campaign on

family planning. The UNICEF official told me that Sankara was saying what no one else dared to even contemplate: in his country mothers produced many children assuming that half of them would die very young, that only the strong children would survive the harsh realities of rural life. Traditional methods of spacing births, with young mothers going back to their mothers' homes after the birth of a child until that child was weaned, were disappearing. Without a concomitant emphasis on family planning, vaccinating children would result in rapid population growth that would outstrip resources available for national development. The population of the country has doubled since then, and Berkina Faso remains one of the world's very least developed countries.

[64] For more on Thomas Sankara, see: Andriamirado, Sennen. 1987. *Sankara le Rebelle.* Paris: Jeune Afrique Livres "Collection Destins"; Andriamirado, Sennen. 1989. *Il s'appelait Sankara: chronique d'une mort violente.* Paris: Jeune Afrique Livres; Ray, Carina. 2007. True visionary: Thomas Sankara (1949–1987) *New African,* December 2007: 8–9; Sankara, Thomas. 1988. *Thomas Sankara speaks – the Burkina Faso Revolution: 1983–87.* New York: Pathfinder Press; Wa Ngugi, Mukoma. 2007. Future imperfect. *BBC Focus on Africa Magazine,* Oct–Dec 2007: 19; AND : Ziegler, Jean (entretiens avec Jean-Philippe Rapp). 1986. *Thomas Sankara: un nouveau pouvoir africain.* Lausanne, Suisse: Editions Pierre-Marcel Favre. Collection: Les Grands Entretiens.

[65] Ellis, Stephen. *The Mask of Anarchy: the destruction of Liberia and the religious dimension of an African civil war.* London: Hurst. p 68.

[66] Mariam Sankara and her two sons were flown to Libreville, Gabon, on a plane sent by Gabonese president Omar Bongo, who offered them a safe haven in his palace. Eventually, after Mariam Sankara complained about being treated as a prisoner rather than a guest by President Bongo, Danielle Mitterrand, wife of the French president and a human rights activist, arranged for Sankara's widow and her two sons, Philippe and Auguste, to go to France to live. There Mariam Sankara completed a PhD in agronomy. She has worked with the Group for Research and Initiative for the Liberation of Africa, the International Campaign for Justice for Sankara and a team of international lawyers to mount a legal case to force Compaoré's government to shed light on the assassination of his predecessor. In March 2006, the UN Human Rights Committee (UNHRC) ruled that the Sankara family had "the right to know the circumstances of his death." But to date, not surprisingly, the government has not complied.

[67] Personal communication with Marco Werman. What the American role in the coup may have been is impossible to determine unless CIA archives on its work in Burkina Faso are opened for public scrutiny. However, it is worth noting that following the exposure of CIA assassinations in the 1960s, President Gerald Ford enacted Executive Order 12333 in 1976, banning assassinations by the CIA. President Ronald Reagan renewed the ban, but it had become ambiguous: did it cover just targeting a head of state or just the way the assassination was carried out? If the coup or assassination was not actually carried out by US agents, was it legal for the CIA to be

involved? In any case, if such covert support is never revealed, if the agents are special forces involved in "deniable operations," there is little way to find out just how much the CIA are involved, especially in out-of-the-way countries in Africa. This is problematic for democratic countries, where the public is not permitted to know what crimes may be committed "in their interests" by their secret service agents around the world. The Church Committee interim report into CIA covert operations and alleged assassinations issued in 1975 reveals that crimes were indeed committed. Other publications that provide ample evidence that these denial ops have continued around the world include: Coll, Steve. 2004. *Ghost Wars – the secret history of the CIA, Afghanistan, and Bin Laden, from the Soviet Invasion to September 10, 2000.* Toronto: Penguin Group (Canada), AND: Blum, William. *Killing Hope: U.S. military and C.I.A. interventions since World War II.* Monroe, Maine: Common Courage Press.

[68] Thomas Sankara website:
http://www.thomassankara.net/article.php3?id_article=0419

[69] On 25 January 2008, *The News* in Sierra Leone carried a report on the decisions made by West Africa's leaders at the annual ECOWAS (Economic Community of West African States) summit, held in Ouagadougou, Burkina Faso a few days earlier. In the article entitled "West African leaders approve framework to combat poverty," it was reported that the presidents "praised President Blaise Compaoré of Burkina Faso for his untiring efforts towards the restoration of sustainable peace to that country." In April 2008, the United Nations Secretary-General, Ban Ki-moon visited Ouagadougou and praised the "noble" efforts of Compaoré in promoting "peace and stability."

6   Greasing the political gears

[70] Kaplan, Robert. 1997. "Was democracy just a moment?" *Atlantic Monthly,* Vol 280 (6): 55–80 http://www.theatlantic.com/issues/97dec/democ.htm

[71] Buckoke, Andrew. 1990. *Fishing in Africa: a guide to war and corruption.* London, UK: Picador, p 221.

[72] Meredith, Martin. 2005. *The Fate of Africa: from the hopes of freedom to the heart of despair. A history of 50 years of independence.* New York: Public Affairs.

[73] Ayittey, George B.N. 2005. *Africa Unchained: the blueprint for Africa's future.* New York, NY: Palgrave MacMillan.

[74] See: Sourcewatch (Center for Media and Democracy): The Free Africa Foundation [http://www.sourcewatch.org/index.php?title=The_Free_Africa_ Foundation] Neo-conservative, hawkish and pro-business ideology is today being propagated all over the world by hundreds of "think tanks," many intertwined, which exert a disproportional influence on public policy making in North America and other industrialized countries, through the media and by securing powerful positions for their hired 'fellows' in government and on committees that influence government or drawing on formerly powerful government figures as fellows. Their influence spreads around the

world through think tanks such as the Free Africa Foundation, affiliated with right-wing American think tanks and funded by the same right-wing Foundations and corporate lobbies. Sharon Beder has written extensively on corporate influence on public policy and opinion through global spin [See: Beder, Sharon. 2002. *Global Spin: the corporate assault on environmentalism. Vermont: Chelsea Green Publishing Company,* AND: Beder, Sharon. 2000. The corporate assault on democracy. *Australian Rationalist* 52: 4–11]. She says there is "a revolving door between these think tanks and governments, bureaucracies, and politicians." Such think tanks often state that to maintain their "independence" they receive no funding from governments, as if governments that represent the people are somehow biased or sinister, while their private funding bodies that generally represent specific corporate lobbies with a vested interest in diminishing government powers and increasing the freedom of corporations to act without regulation, might somehow be seen as "independent." Such think tanks are funded by corporations and by private foundations, endowed with capital generally accrued over the last century by corporations in oil, munitions, tobacco, chemical or agrochemical businesses, pharmaceuticals, including the John M. Olin Foundation, Scaife Foundations (Scaife Family, Sarah Mellon Scaife, Carthage), Lynde and Harry Bradley Foundation, The Earhart Foundation, and others. The Center for Media and Democracy (Sourcewatch) offers invaluable insight into the think tanks and their funders. Unfettered by the need for peer reviews required for scholarly publications, the studies performed by 'fellows' and 'scholars' of the tangled, interlocking web of think tanks are unlikely to be objective, intended as they are to promote a product or a point of view favourable to the corporate interests that fund their work. The subjective studies, info-mercials, 'educational' materials and Op Eds they pump out often generate an undue amount of uncritical media publicity and shape public policy by shaping public opinion to suit large corporate interests and business lobbies — often (in my mind) against the public good.

[75] Calderisi, Robert. 2006. *The Trouble with Africa: why foreign aid isn't working.* New York, NY: Palgrave MacMillan. p. 3

[76] Pascal Krop, who has made a career of examining French foreign policy in Africa and France's secret operations, notes that before granting 'independence' to its African colonies, French President Charles de Gaulle ensured that the new leaders would be his "reliable friends" – Léopold Sédar Senghor in Senegal, Félix Houphouët-Boigny in Côte d'Ivoire, Philibert Tsniranana in Madagascar, Léon M'Ba and then Omar Bongo in Gabon, Ahmadou Ahidjo in Cameroon. De Gaulle would tolerate no political or economic intrusion in these French neo-colonies by the Soviets, China or the Americans. Secret military agreements were set up with these countries, monitored by De Gaulle himself, who met each evening with his Secretary for African and Madagascan Affairs, Jacques Foccart. Foccart instilled fear in Africa, where he was known as De Gaulle's eminence grise, or the "grey eminence." [Krop, Pascal. 1994. *Le genocide franco-africain: faut-il juger les Mitterrand?* Paris: Editions Jean-Clause Lattès.]

[77] Caplan, 2008. p 73.

[78] In 1997, Mali's Constitutional Court annulled the first round of the presidential election because of the lack of viable electoral lists. Without rectifying the lists, incumbent Alpha Oumar Konaré went ahead and scheduled another vote, which was boycotted by the opposition parties. Konaré was able to convince a straw candidate – a political buffoon – to run against him in the election to make it look as if he had some opposition. Naturally, he won, and was then feted as a model democrat. In the 2002 elections, there were serious concerns about the counting process, which was put on hold for an entire night when the man who held the key to the computer headquarters for the counting process suffered a strange late-night car accident. Later, Mali's Constitutional Court inexplicably annulled a quarter of the votes cast, coincidentally in the areas where the main opponent, Ibrahim Boubakar Keita, had the most support. That election brought Amadou Toumani Touré to power. While Touré was undoubtedly popular in Mali, where he had led the coup that overthrew dictator Moussa Traoré in 1991 and ushered in an era of democratic reform before stepping back a year later, observers in Mali also noted that he was the clear favourite of the US and European nations.

[79] See: Mwakugu, Noel. 18 Jan. 2008. "Outrage at police tactics." BBC News. http://news.bbc.co.uk/2/hi/africa/7194832.stm; AND: Allen, Karen. 9 Jan. 2008. BBC News. "Tough task for Kenyan diplomacy." http://news.bbc.co.uk/2/hi/africa/7179475.stm; AND: BBC News. 22 Jan. 2008. "US dismisses Kenyan propaganda." http://news.bbc.co.uk/2/hi/africa/7201954.stm; AND: BBC News. 8 Jan. 2008. Kenya's dubious election. http://news.bbc.co.uk/2/hi/africa/7175694.stm

[80] Canada refused to join this group of observers. A lone Canadian observer, sent by the Foreign Minister to submit a confidential report for "internal purposes," told me that the Commonwealth team was not considered "credible."

[81] Benramdane, Djamel. Mar. 2004. "Algeria: a long and dirty war. Looking back at the extent of the nightmare." *Le Monde Diplomatique*. http://mondediplo.com/2004/03/08algeriawar

[82] Global Witness is a London-based watchdog group focussing on human rights and natural resources. Global Witness. 25 Mar. 2004. *Time for Transparency — revenue transparency: a priority for good governance and energy security.* p 1. http://www.globalwitness.org/media_library_detail.php/115/en/time_for_transparency

See also: Global Witness. Dec. 2005. *The Riddle of the Sphynx: where has Congo's oil money gone?* http://www.globalwitness.org/media_library_detail.php/145/en/the_riddle_of_the_sphynx_where_has_congos_oil_mone

[83] The full extent to which Elf damaged democracy – not just in Africa but also in France itself – is dealt with in detail, as is the courageous investigation into the immense oil scandal by legal and financial investigator Eva Joly,

in the book by Nicholas Shaxson. 2007. *Poisoned Wells — the dirty politics of African oil.* New York: Palgrave MacMillan.

[84] Gidley-Kitchin, Virginia. 24 Dec. 1997. "Africa: US And France vie for influence." BBC News. http://news.bbc.co.uk/2/hi/world/analysis/42341.stm

[85] "Common knowledge" in countries such as Cameroon is often all there is to go on, and it refers to information regularly offered by everyone from taxi drivers to journalists to scientists. Analysis of covert operations to trick an African president out of office has to be limited to such "common knowledge," which often has as its basis well-founded insider information gathered by those with close connections (family member who work close) to inner circles of power. Any serious or credible inquiry to illuminate the truth in a country that has never known true democracy is unrealistic, and one of the greatest impediments to journalistic or even scholarly accounts of recent history in much of Africa. (A recent survey in Sierra Leone showed that one third of the populace relies on rumour as the primary information source.)

Ahidjo lived several more years after being told his life was in danger in 1982. He passed away in exile in France in 1989. He had been branded a traitor after the armed insurrection and coup attempt of 1984, and was condemned to death in his absence. He was buried not in Cameroon, but in Senegal.

[86] Jean-Christophe Mitterrand became known in Africa as *"Papamadit"* because his father the French president put him in charge of a shadowy *"cellule Africain"* that handled all sorts of highly suspect activities on the continent – filming African opposition politicians for 'friendly' African presidents and secret services, negotiating arms and business deals involving oil, diamonds and timber, and dishing out enormous amounts of money to African leaders in need of it to maintain control – for the French – of their countries, viciously putting down demonstrations and movements either covertly or sometimes openly with French troops. Among those who received such gifts from France from the hands of Jean-Christophe Mitterrand were: Togo's Gnassingbé Eyadéma; Rwanda's Juvénal Habyarimana who represented growing Hutu power long before dying in a mysterious plane crash that sparked the genocide in 1994 and whom the French supported simply because he opposed the anglophone influence of Uganda and Rwandan Tutsi dissidents; Côte d'Ivoire's Houphouët-Boigny; Congo's Denis Sassou-Nguesso; Chad's Hissan Habré; Cameroon's Paul Biya; Benin's Mathieu Kérékou. [Krop, 1994.]

I saw Jean-Christophe Mitterrand at an inaugural ceremony for the king of the Bamoun people in Foumban, western Cameroon, in January 1985, where he was already representing his father in Africa, in places and with people that counted.

[87] Brown, Paul. 27 Sept. 2002. "Chad oil pipeline under attack for harming the poor." *The Guardian.* http://www.guardian.co.uk/environment/2002/sep/27/internationalnews

[88] Open Letter to Mr. James D. Wolfensohn, President of the World Bank, from 86 NGOs in 28 countries concerning the Chad/Cameroon Oil & Pipeline Project. 9 July 1998. http://www.africa.upenn.edu/Urgent_Action/apic_8198.html

[89] In January 2008, ExxonMobil – the world's largest oil corporation – announced its annual profit at 40.6 billion US dollars, beating its own profit records and the highest profit in history for any company. [Mouawad, Jad. 1 Feb. 2008. "ExxonMobil profit sets record again." *The New York Times.* http://www.nytimes.com/2008/02/01/business/01cnd-exxon.html?_r= 1&em&ex=1202101200&en=575e77c5fd8688b0&ei=5087%0A&oref= slogin]

[90] Calderisi. 2006. p. 184.

[91] Shaxson, 2007. p 3.

[92] World Bank. 27 Sept. 2004. *Today's Challenges on the Chad-Cameroon Pipeline: An interview with Ali Mahmoud Khadr, World Bank Country Director for Chad.* http://web.worldbank.org/WBSITE/EXTERNAL/NEWS/0,, contentMDK:20261758~pagePK:64257043~piPK:437376~theSitePK: 4607,00.html

[93] IRIN news. 8 Oct. 2004. "Kome, Chad: Trying to make oil wealth work for the people." United Nations humanitarian news and information service (IRIN). http://www.irinnews.org/report.asp?ReportID=43576&SelectRegion =West_Africa&SelectCountry=CHAD See also: IRIN news. 6 Feb. 2006. "Chad: Government and World Bank struggle to save face in oil row." United Nations humanitarian news and information service (IRIN). http://www.irinnews.org/report.asp?ReportID=51565&SelectRegion=West_A frica&SelectCountry=CHAD; AND: IRIN news. 20 Oct. 2003. "Doba, Chad: oil boom raises expectations, but fails to meet them." United Nations humanitarian news and information service (IRIN). http://www.irinnews.org/report.asp?ReportID=37324

[94] BBC News. 27 Aug. 2006. "Chad orders foreign oil firms out." http://news.co.uk/2/hi/africa/5289580.htm

[95] Freedom House. *Map of freedom in the world.* Map of freedom 2008. http://www.freedomhouse.org/template.cfm?page=363&year=2008

[96] IRIN news. 18 Oct. 2004. "Cameroon: presidential election lacked credibility – Commonwealth." http://www.irinnews.org/report.aspx?reportid=51730

[97] BBC News. 28 Feb. 2008. "Cameroon head blames opposition." http://news.bbc.co.uk/2/hi/africa/7267731.stm

[98] Sachs, Jeffrey D. and Warner, Andrew M. 1995. "Natural resource abundance and economic growth." Harvard University Development Discussion Paper No. 517a. http://www.earthinstitute.columbia.edu/about/director/pubs/517.pdf

[99] Jeffrey Sachs defines extreme or absolute poverty as that preventing a household from meeting basic needs for survival – they are "chronically hungry, unable to access health care, lack the amenities of safe drinking

water and sanitation, cannot afford education for some or all of the children, and perhaps lack rudimentary shelter ... and basic articles of clothing, such as shoes." He notes that the World Bank estimates the purchasing power of the extreme poor as [US] $1 a day, that of the "moderate poor" as $1 to $2 a day. Sachs believes that endemic diseases such as malaria and now the HIV/AIDS pandemic are major causes of Africa's persistent and extreme poverty, saying that those who believe Africa's poverty can be attributed to African governance or to Western violence and meddling "have it wrong." Then he seems to contradict his own conclusion, saying, "Indeed, almost every African political crisis – Sudan, Somalia, and a host of others – has a long history of Western meddling among its many causes." In his book he also acknowledges the devastating effects of the budget policies of the IMF and World Bank through the 1980s and 1990s, that Africa became a pawn in the Cold War after the colonial period ended, and that the CIA helped assassinate or overthrow nationalist leaders. [Sachs, Jeffrey D. 2005. *The End of Poverty – economic possibilities for our time.* New York, NY: Penguin p 190.]

7   You are a good friend and we welcome you

[100] Lapham, Lewis H. 2004. *Gag Rule – on the suppression of dissent and the stifling of democracy.* London: Penguin Books. p 158.

[101] Baker, Raymond. 18 July 2006. *Presentation by Raymond Baker at the Brown Bag Lunch on Corruption.* New rules for global finance. http://www.new-rules.org/docs/bakerpresentation071806.htm

[102] Jean-Bédél Bokassa, president of the Central African Republic from 1966 to 1979, had himself crowned an "emperor" in 1976 at a lavish ceremony paid for in part by France. French president Valéry Giscard D'Estaing was a close friend to Bokassa at the time, receiving diamonds from him and enjoying big game hunting trips in the former French colony. When the French learned he had been forging links with Libya's Muammar Gaddafi, and of his excesses in opening fire on demonstrating schoolchildren and allegations of cannibalism made media headlines, French support for Bokassa ended. He was overthrown in a French-orchestrated coup. It should be noted that Bokassa himself was deeply marked by colonial events: his father had been beaten to death for resisting forced labour in French camps and his mother committed suicide out of sheer grief. Bokassa had also fought for the French in Europe during World War II.

[103] In the mid-1990s, Baroness Lynda Chalker, British Minister of State for Overseas Development at the Foreign Office, made an official visit to Kenya. On her arrival at the airport in Nairobi, she made a quick statement to the press expressing her concern over the corruption and human rights violations in the country. The reaction of then President Daniel arap Moi was swift, angry – and telling. He said it was unacceptable that this woman would come to Kenya behaving like a "schoolmistress" to lecture on how the country should be run. He went on to threaten British interests in Kenya, noting the many millions of British pounds of profits that Barclays

Bank had made the previous year, its immense land holdings in the Rift Valley and pointedly remarked on the recent military agreements that Britain and Kenya had signed. The following week, the French ambassador to Kenya made an official and much-publicized visit to President Moi, reiterating France's "friendship" with Kenya. After that, the British were very quiet and the corruption continued unabated in Kenya.

[104] The Multilateral Investment Guarantee Agency (MIGA) is a member of the World Bank Group, set up to promote foreign investment in developing countries by offering investors insurance, technical input and information on risks to their investments. [http://www.miga.org/guarantees/index_sv.cfm?stid=1549] In effect, it makes the government of the host country responsible for ensuring the investor profits and does not lose from the investment, ensure that labour strife, protests about environmental destruction, etc, do not impinge on the investor's business and profits. This automatically forces the president of the country to serve the foreign (investor's) interests first. "An investor that has a MIGA guarantee can claim a payment to MIGA for the loss covered by the guarantee. In return, MIGA will request that the host country — which must be a MIGA member – reimburses the amount. If the host country refuses to pay, MIGA will suspend their coverage for projects in that country. With such an arrangement, governments are unlikely to take or promote actions that would require that a claim be paid. Countries are very careful to not damage their reputation with other investors, cause problems with the Bank, or threaten Bank loans to their countries." [Down to Earth IFI (International Financial Institutions) Factsheet Series, No 16, 2001. http://dte.gn.apc.org/Af16.htm]

[105] The National Endowment for Democracy has many of the same members as does the Project for the New American Century (PNAC), which grew out of the New Citizenship Project (NCP). The Center for Media & Democracy's project, Sourcewatch, says that the PNAC and the NCP share suites and even a telephone number, which is jointly used by the Philanthropy Roundtable, and the PNAC was one of the key behind-the-scenes architects of President George W. Bush's foreign policy. Funding is from far right-wing sources. These include: the John M. Olin Foundation Inc., which grew out of a family business of chemical and munitions industries and also funds other right-wing think tanks such as the American Enterprise Institute, where Vice President Dick Cheney's wife, Lynne Cheney is a Senior Fellow; the Heritage Foundation; the Manhattan Institute for Public Policy Change and the Hoover Institution on War, Revolution and Peace. See: Project for the New American Century. http://www.newamericancentury.org/aboutpnac.htm; http://www.newamericancentury.org/statementofprinciples.htm AND: Sourcewatch (a project of the Center for Media & Democracy). New Citizenship Project. http://www.sourcewatch.org/index.php?title=New_Citizenship_Project

[106] MacKinnon, Mark. 14 Apr. 2007. "Agent orange: our secret role in Ukraine." *The Globe and Mail* (Canada). MacKinnon says the US also played a leading role in the so-called Orange Revolution, "as it came to see the Ukrainian election standoff as a major battle in a new cold war that it was

fighting with a resurgent Kremlin for influence across Moscow's old empire. The Bush administration was particularly keen to see a pro-Western figure as president to ensure control over a key pipeline running from Odessa on the Black Sea to Brody on the Polish border."

[107] BBC News. 25 Jan. 2005. "Yushchenko seeks EU membership." http://news.bbc.co.uk/2/hi/europe/4204149.stm

[108] Roth, Kenneth. 2008. "Despots masquerading as democrats." *Human Rights Watch 2008 World Report* http://hrw.org/wr2k8/introduction/index.htm

[109] In recent years the Conservative Government of Canada has, for example, reneged on Canada's commitment to Kyoto, blocked the addition of asbestos to the Rotterdam Convention's list of toxins, opposed a UN moratorium on high seas bottom-trawling, and blocked a UN resolution that would have made water a basic human right.

[110] Ankomah, June 2008. p 12.

[111] Sasa, Mabasa. June 2008. "The Zimbabwe treatment." *New African.* No. 474: 34

[112] Touray, Saihou. June 2008. "The heart of the matter." *New African.* No. 474: 6

[113] Sasa. June 2008. p. 34–35.

[114] Freedom House. 2008. *Map of Freedom.*

[115] Museveni, Yoweri K. 1992. *What is Africa's Problem? Speeches and writings on Africa Vol. 1.* Kampala: NRM Publications. p 186.

[116] According to American journalist and author, Ken Silverstein, Herman Cohen is the "influence peddler of choice for African despots in need of a public relations buff-up" in Washington. Silverstein notes that the World Bank-affiliated Global Coalition for Africa "preaches orthodox pro-business recipes for the continent." [Silverstein, Ken. 8 Apr. 2001. *Good Press for Dictators.* http://www.prospect.org/cs/articles?articleId=5708]

[117] Ross, Will. 30 July 2008. "Outcry over China-Niger oil deal." BBC News. http://news.bbc.co.uk/2/hi/africa/7534315.stm

[118] See: Hilsum, Lindsey. 2005. "We love China." *Granta 92* (Winter 2005): 235–240; AND: IRIN news. 27 June 2006. "China and Africa – for better or for worse?" United Nations humanitarian news and information service (IRIN); IRIN news. 4 Nov. 2006. "AFRICA: China to double aid to Africa." http://www.irinnews.org/report.aspx?reportid=61487

[119] EURODAD. 18 Jan. 2008. *Old Habits Die Hard: aid accountability in Sierra Leone.* EURODAD with Campaign for Good Governance. p 4. http://www.eurodad.org/whatsnew/reports.aspx?id=2038

[120] See: Leigh, David and Pallister, David. 1 June 2005. "Revealed: the new scramble for Africa revealed." *The Guardian.* http://www.guardian.co.uk/uk/2005/jun/01/g8.development

[121] Jewelry, Judaica, Arts & Craft. 20 Nov. 2007. "Israel diamond industry signs bilateral cooperation MOU with Government of Liberia." The Israel

Export & International Cooperation Institute.
http://www.export.gov.il/Eng/_Articles/Article.asp?CategoryID=803&ArticleI
D=7237; AND: BBC News. 20 Nov. 2007. "Israel signs Liberia diamond
deal." http://news.bbc.co.uk/2/hi/africa/7104465.stm

[122] Weiner, Tim. 11 July 1998. "US aides say Nigeria leader might have been
poisoned." *New York Times.* http://query.nytimes.com/gst/fullpage.html?res
=9C03EFDB1431F932A25754C0A96E958260

[123] Apple Jr., R.W. 28 Mar. 1998. "Clinton in Africa: the policy; US stance
toward Nigeria and its ruler seems to shift." *New York Times.* http://query.
nytimes.com/gst/fullpage.html?res=9A01EFD8143BF93BA15750C0A96E958
260

[124] Baker, Raymond. *Money Laundering and Flight Capital: the impact on private banking.* Permanent Subcommittee on Investigations of the Committee
on Governmental Affairs, United States Senate. http://www.senate.gov/
~govt-aff/111099_baker.htm

[125] Pawson, Lara. 13 Mar. 2007. "Angola calls a halt to IMF talks." BBC
News. http://news.bbc.co.uk/2/hi/business/6446025.stm

[126] Colombant, Nico. 12 Nov. 2004. "São Tomé sparks American military
interest." Voice of America News. http://www.voanews.com/english/2004-
11-12-voa42.cfm

[127] A list of the CSIS Task Force members who signed on to the reports on
US interests in the Gulf of Guinea includes people affiliated with Halliburton,
PFC Energy, Marathon Oil Company, Chevron, ExxonMobil, BP, Shell,
Goldwyn International Strategies and the Office of Vice President, Dick
Cheney. Co-chairs of the Task Force are David L. Goldwyn, president of
Goldwyn International Strategies and former assistant secretary for interna-
tional affairs with the US Department of Energy, and J. Stephen Morrison,
director of the CSIS African Program. The honorary chair of the CSIS Task
Force is Republican Senator Chuck Hagel from Nebraska. Many of the prin-
cipals of CSIS were originally "Cold Warriors," including four former
Secretaries of State, one former National Security Adviser, two former
Secretaries for Defense, a former Secretary of the Treasury, a former
Secretary of the Department of Housing and Urban Development, a former
Director of the CIA, and three Senators. There is a good deal of overlap
between the scholars and fellows of CSIS, Republican administrations and
the American Enterprise Institute. See: Sourcewatch (a project of the Center
for Media and Democracy): Center for Strategic and International Studies.
http://www.sourcewatch.org/index.php?title=Center_for_Strategic_and_Inte
rnational_Studies

[128] Center for Strategic and International Studies (CSIS). 1 Mar. 2004.
*Promoting transparency in the African oil sector: a report of the CSIS Task Force
on rising U.S. energy stakes in Africa,* co-chaired by David L. Goldwyn and J.
Stephen Morrison. Washington, DC: CSIS. http://www.csis.org/africa/
GoldwynAfricanOilSector.pdf

[129] Center for Strategic and International Studies (CSIS). 1 July 2005. *A
strategic US approach to governance and security in the Gulf of Guinea: a*

report of the CSIS Task Force on Gulf of Guinea security, co-chaired by David L. Goldwyn and J. Stephen Morrison. Washington, DC: CSIS. p 9. http://www.csis.org/media/csis/pubs/0507_gulfofguinea.pdf

[130] Lake, Anthony and Todd Whitman, Christine (Chairs). 2006. *More than Humanitarianism: a strategic US approach toward Africa.* Washington DC: US Council on Foreign Relations. p xii. http://www.cfr.org/publication/9302/ more_than_humanitarianism.html Christine Todd Whitman, who chaired the Council on Foreign Relations in 2006 when the study was done, is a prominent Republican. She was the extremely controversial and pro-industry head of the US Environmental Protection Agency from 2001 until 2003. Since then she has worked as a consultant and lobbyest for corporate front groups promoting nuclear power.

[131] See: Tisdall, Simon. 9 Feb. 2007. "America moves in on Africa." *The Guardian.* http://www.guardian.co.uk/commentisfree/2007/feb/09/ world.tisdallbriefing

[132] Colombant, 12 Nov. 2004.

[133] Diego Garcia, a British Indian Ocean Territory off the southern tip of India, was set up as an important joint British and American military base and navy support facility during the Cold War, and has also served as a base for bombers and cruise missiles used in the Persian Gulf War, the attacks on Afghanistan in 2001 and in the Iraq invasion in 2003. Today a number of alleged al-Qaeda suspects are reportedly also being held and interrogated there. The indigenous population of Ilois or Chagossian people were forced to relocate between 1967 and 1973, despite protests from other islands in the Indian Ocean that did not want cruise missiles in their peaceful neighbourhood. Many were deported to Mauritius (1600 km from their island home) or to the Seychelles. See: Bomford, Andrew. 10 Jan. 2001. "Diego Garcia: remembering paradise lost." BBC News. http://news.bbc.co.uk/2/hi/ uk_news/835963.stm; AND: BBC News. 31 Oct. 2002. "Diego Garcia islanders battle to return." http://news.bbc.co.uk/2/hi/africa/2380013.stm; AND: "United States Navy Support Facility Diego Garcia." http://www.dg.navy.mil/web/

[134] See: IRIN news. 2 Feb. 2005. "São Tomé and Principe: Government nets $49m from signature of first oil exploration deal." United Nations humanitarian news and information service (IRIN). http://www.irinnews.org/ report.asp?ReportID=45346&SelectRegion=West_Africa&SelectCountry=SAO _TOME_AND_PRINCIPE

IRIN news. 28 Oct. 2003. "Nigeria-São Tomé and Principe: Oil companies bid over $500m for offshore exploration rights." United Nations humanitarian news and information service (IRIN). http://www.irinnews.org/ report.asp?ReportID=37513&SelectRegion=West_Africa&SelectCountry=NIG ERIA-SAO_TOME_AND_PRINCIPE

IRIN news. 16 Feb. 2004. "São Tomé and Principe: US funds study for airport expansion and deep-water port." United Nations humanitarian news and information service (IRIN), Abidjan.

http://www.irinnews.org/report.asp?ReportID=39516&SelectRegion=West_A
frica&SelectCountry=SAO_TOME_AND_PRINCIPE

[135] Klitgaard, Robert. 1990. *Tropical Gangsters.* New York: Basic Books.

[136] IRIN news. 18 Sept. 2003. "Equatorial Guinea: Oil and gas production
climbs, but where does the money go?" United Nations humanitarian news
and information service (IRIN). http://www.irinnews.org/Report.aspx?
ReportId=46231

[137] CIA. 2005. *The World Factbook – Equatorial Guinea.* Updated 10 Feb.
2005. http://www.cia.gov/cia/publications/factbook/print/ek.html

[138] BBC News. 10 Sept. 2004. "Profile: Simon Mann."
http://news.bbc.co.uk/go/pr/fr/-/2/hi/uk_news/3916465.stm

[139] Vally, Salim and Clarno, Andy. 6 Mar. 2005. "Privatised war: the South
African connection." *The Sunday Independent.* http://www.sundayindepen-
dent.co.za/index.php?fSectionId=1081&fSetId=453

[140] Roberts, Adam. 2006. *The Wonga Coup: guns, thugs and a ruthless determination to create mayhem in an oil-rich corner of Africa.* New York: Public
Affairs. See also: BBC News. "Timeline: E Guinea 'coup plot'."
http://newsvote.bbc.co.uk/mpapps/pagetools/print/news.bbc.co.uk/2/hi/afr
ica/4170589.stm; AND: Gidley-Kitchin, Virginia. 11 Mar. 2004. BBC News.
Equatorial Guinea: ripe for a coup. http://news.bbc.co.uk/2/hi/africa/
3500832.stm

[141] Roberts. 2006. p.

[142] Gove, Michael. 2004. "Why the world needs such men as Simon Mann."
TimesOnline. http://www.timesonline.co.uk/0,,1-152-1184969-152,00.html

[143] See: BBC News. 3 Apr. 2005. "Sir Mark Thatcher refused US visa."
http://news.bbc.co.uk/2/hi/uk_news/4405755.stm; AND: BBC News. 14
Jan. 2004. "Relieved Sir Mark set for US." http://news.bbc.co.uk/go/pr/fr/-
/2/hi/africa/4173151.stm; AND: Sylvester, Elliot, Associated Press Writer.
Mark Thatcher Pleads Guilty in Coup Plot. 13 Jan. 2005. http://news.yahoo.
com/news?tmpl=story&cid=515&u=/ap/20050113/ap_on_re_af/south_

[144] BBC News. 7 July 2007. "Mann sentenced for E Guinea plot."
http://news.bbc.co.uk/2/hi/africa/7493717.stm

[145] Pallister, David. 23 Feb. 2007. "Eight accused of Equatorial Guinea coup
plot walk free." *The Guardian.* http://www.guardian.co.uk/world/2007/feb/
23/southafrica.equatorialguinea

[146] Ross, Will. 7 July 2008. "Mann sings in E Guinea coup trial." BBC News.
http://news.bbc.co.uk/2/hi/africa/7470762.stm

[147] Silverstein, Ken. 18 Apr. 2006. "Our friend Teodoro: Equatorial Guinea's
leader visits the Beltway." *Harpers.* http://www.harpers.org/sb-obiang-
eg.html; AND: US State Department. 2006. "Secretary Condoleezza Rice:
Remarks with Equatorial Guinean President Teodoro Obiang Nguema
Mbasogo before their meeting." 12 Apr. 2006. http://www.state.gov/secre-
tary/rm/2006/64434.htm

148 Kairos (Canadian Ecumenical Justice Initiatives). 2004. *Africa's Blessing, Africa's curse: the legacy of resource extraction in Africa.* Toronto: Kairos.

149 The Extractive Industries Transparency Initiative summarizes its purpose this way: "3.5 billion people live in countries rich in oil, gas and minerals. With good governance the exploitation of these resources can generate large revenues to foster growth and reduce poverty. However when governance is weak, it may result in poverty, corruption, and conflict. The Extractive Industries Transparency Initiative (EITI) aims to strengthen governance by improving transparency and accountability in the extractives sector." [EITI (Extractive Industries Transparency Initiative). 2004. Factsheet: About Extractive Industries Transparency Initiative. http://www.eitransparency.org/about.htm; AND: EITI (Extractive Industries Transparency Initiative). EITI Summary. http://eitransparency.org/eiti/summary]

150 Baker, Raymond. 18 July 2006. *Presentation by Raymond Baker at the Brown Bag Lunch on Corruption.* New Rules for Global Finance. http://www.new-rules.org/docs/bakerpresentation071806.htm

151 Shaxson. 2007. p. 224.

152 Global Witness. 1 Dec. 1999. *A Crude Awakening.* http://www.globalwitness.org/media_library_detail.php/93/en/a_crude_awakening

153 According to the Publish What You Pay website, the campaign was founded by Global Witness, the Catholic Agency for Overseas Development (CAFOD), Oxfam, Save the Children UK, Transparency International UK, George Soros, chairman of the Open Society Institute. [Publish What You Pay website. http://www.publishwhatyoupay.org]

154 Those concerned about the potential negative effects of oil in Mali are resigning themselves to the inevitable. In late 2004, Mali's Authority for the Promotion of Oil Exploration signed an agreement with the Australian company, Baraka, for oil and gas exploration in the desert north in the Taoudeni area, site of the ancient salt mines that are still worked by artisanal Tuaregs. Baraka announced at a press conference in 2005 that the first well was expected to go into operation in 2008. In June 2006, the Malaysian company, Markmore, took out a concession for oil exploration in Mali's desert north, in the region of the ancient salt mines of Tauodeni.

See: Afribone. 21 June 2006. "Recherche pétrolière au Mali: la société malaisienne Markmore vient d'acquérir le bloc 6 du basin de Taoudénit pour une durée de quatres ans." http://www.afribone.com/article.php3?id_article=3833; AND: Touré, Birama. 31 Oct. 2005. "Premier forage au Mali – le rendez-vous est pris pour 2008." *Inter De Bamako.* http://www.mali-pages.com/presse/news¬_10_05/news_0052.asp

8   White elephants and 800-pound gorillas

155 Lewis, Stephen. 2005. *Race Against Time.* Toronto: House of Anansi. p 16.

156 Traoré, Aminata Dramane.1999. *L'etau: l'Afrique dans un monde sans frontières.* Paris: Actes Sud. p 12.

[157] Annan, Kofi, United Nations Secretary General. http://www.un.org/millenniumgoals/

[158] Sachs, Jeffrey D. 2005. *The End of Poverty: economic possibilities for our time.* New York, NY: Penguin. p 74. Paradoxically, Sachs himself was very active in promoting similar free market economic reforms in Bolivia and Russia, as documented by Naomi Klein in 2007, in *The Shock Doctrine.*

[159] Caplan, 2008.p 120.

[160] Ayuk, Elias and Marouani, Mohamed Ali. 2005. "An emerging continental consensus," *IN:* Ayuk E and MA Marouani (eds). *The Policy Paradox in Africa ? how to strengthen the links between economic research and policymaking on and for the continent.* Ottawa, Canada: Africa World Press/IDRC

[161] Mkandawire, Thandika and Soludo, Charles C. 1999. *Our Continent, Our Future – African perspectives on structural adjustment.* Trenton, NJ: Africa World Press. p xi.

[162] James Wolfensohn, an Australian-born American citizen, was president of the World Bank from 1995 until 2005. Like many powerful figures from the North American or European establishment, he has attended meetings of the highly secretive and highly influential Bilderberg Group that meets once a year, and that BBC describes as a "coterie of thinkers and power-brokers" and "perhaps the most powerful organisation in the world". [Duffy, Jonathan. 3 June 2004. "Bilderberg: the ultimate conspiracy theory." BBC News. http://news.bbc.co.uk/2/hi/uk_news/magazine/3773019.stm.]

[163] Horst Köhler was Managing Director of the IMF from May 2000 until March 2004, when he was appointed Bundespresident of his native Germany.

[164] Dogon Land, named after the Dogon people who inhabit it, is a spectacular region of cliffs in the southeast of Mali. The Dogon carve their homes into the rocky cliffs, and construct them of stones. Dogon Land has become a major tourist attraction, largely because of the magnificent landscape and the highly traditional Dogon people who have retained their ancient beliefs and faith. Ironically, the foreign intruders who come to witness the traditional people are the greatest threat to Dogon culture, and today Islamic and Christian influences are making deep inroads into Dogon tradition.

[165] Stiglitz, Joseph E. 2002. *Globalization and Its Discontents.* New York: W.W. Norton & Company Inc. p. 3.

[166] The advent of cell phones in Africa in the mid-1990s has been one of the most monumental changes on the continent. Over the past decade mobile phones have transformed communications — life — for tens of millions of people who would never have had access to a fixed phone line, making instant communication possible even to rural areas without electricity. Wireless communication has become a major local industry and an important source of economic growth as it spawns side industries — in advertising, retail sale of phones and accessories, "recharging" centres where phones can be plugged in to electrical outlets for a fee, new towers and telecommunications facilities.

[167] The International Finance Corporation (slogan: "reducing poverty, improving lives") says it "provides loans, equity, structured finance and risk management products, and advisory services to build the private sector in developing countries." http://www.ifc.org/about

[168] The now defunct West African airline, Air Afrique, was set up in 1961, co-founded by France and 11 former colonies: Benin; Burkina Faso (then Upper Volta); Central African Republic; Chad; Congo (Republic of); Côte d'Ivoire; Mali; Mauritania; Niger; Senegal; and Togo. Plagued by inefficiency and corruption, it nevertheless provided relatively safe, if sometimes unpunctual air service within the region. In the early 1990s, after years of mismanagement and debt, France (11 percent shareholder) imposed its own director on the airline, and he borrowed millions of dollars to upgrade the fleet with European Airbuses. This debt then doubled overnight in 1994, when France decided to devalue by 50 percent the CFA franc used in these former French colonies. In 2000, the African countries that owned Air France then turned to the World bank for a bail-out for a debt they saw as unfairly incurred by a French director, serving the interests of Air France and European aircraft industries. The World Bank provided 800 thousand US dollars to restructure Air Afrique, providing it would be run by the former boss of TWA, American executive, Jeffrey Erikson. Erikson proceeded to lay off half its 4,000 employees. A prolonged strike by protesting employees ensued. In Mali, gendarmes blocked a protest march by Air Afrique employees and labour unions. Spokesperson for the Air Afrique Union, Aïchata Haïdara, said she was shocked that African leaders who espoused regional integration did not support the cause of the airline and its workers, preferring to remain silent while the "World Bank tried to liquidate Air Afrique." In July 2001, that is exactly what happened. All Air Afrique assets were taken over by the French airline, Air France. A host of small airlines sprang up in the region, few of which passed any sort of safety standards, leaving West and Central Africa with reduced choices of safe and approved flights within the region, and leaving the lucrative field of long-haul flights between major African cities and Europe wide open for European companies.

[169] Klein, 2007.

[170] Probe Alert Fall 2000. *Canadian Government Defends More Aid for Disastrous Manantali Dam.* http://www.probeinternational.org/pi/print.cfm?ContentID=1310; AND Sevunts, Levon. "A river of disease: Canada-backed dam contributes to 8,500 African deaths a year." *Montreal Gazette:* 14 May 2001. http://www.probeinternational.org/pi/index.cfm?DSP=content&ContentID=2069

[171] This exclusive Club that has so much control over so many lives in Africa comprises Australia, Austria, Belgium, Canada, Denmark, Finland, France, Germany, Ireland, Italy, Japan, The Netherlands, Norway, Russia, Spain, Sweden, Switzerland, the UK and the US.

[172] Ayuk and Marouani, 2005.

[173] Easterly, William. 2006. *The White Man's Burden: why the West's efforts to aid the rest have done so much ill and so little good.* New York: The Penguin Press.

[174] EURODAD. 18 Jan. 2008.

[175] Marphatia, Akanksha and Archer, David. Apr. 2007. *Confronting the Contradictions: the IMF, wage bill caps and the case for teachers.* ActionAid International. http://www.actionaidusa.org/imf_africa.php
See also: Marphatia, Akanksha. 14 June 2007. Letter to Calvin McDonald, IMF. http://www.actionaidusa.org/imf_africa.php; AND: McDonald, Calvin. 17 May 2007. "A Response to ActionAid International." IMF. http://www.imf.org/external/np/vc/2007/051707.htm

[176] BBCNews. 26 June 2006. "Blair promises new Africa focus." http://news.bbc.co.uk/2/hi/business/5115806.stm

[177] Reynolds, Paul. 17 Mar. 2005. "Wolfowitz to spread neo-con gospel." BBC News. http://news.bbc.co.uk/2/hi/business/4358045.stm; AND: Tyler, Patrick E. 8 Mar. 1992. "US strategy plan calls for insuring no rivals develop — a one-superpower world: Pentagon's document outlines ways to thwart challenges to primacy of America." *The New York Times.* http://work.colum.edu/~amiller/wolfowitz1992.htm

[178] BBCNews. 1 Apr. 2005. "Wolfowitz sets Africa poverty aim."
http://news.bbc.co.uk/2/hi/business/4399667.stm

[179] Atkinson, Simon. 25 June 2007. "Profile: Robert Zoellick." BBC News. http://news.bbc.co.uk/2/hi/business/6702943.stm

[180] Project for a New American Century (PNAC). 26 Jan. 1998. "Letter to President William J. Clinton." http://www.newamericancentury.org/iraqclin-tonletter.htm

[181] *The Wall Street Journal.* 3 May 2007. "World Bank rolls: nearly 1,400 employees make more than Condi Rice." http://opinionjournal.com/editori-al/?id=110010018

[182] CATO Institute Handbook for Congress. 51. The United Nations. http://www.cato.org/pubs/handbook/hb105-51.html

Part II: The inevitable curse

9   Coffin of Gold

[183] Davidson, Basil. 1991. *Africa in History* (Revised and expanded edition).New York: Collier Books. p 3.

[184] In recent years in Canada there have been efforts to introduce Afrocentric curricula into the school system, but these would be used primarily in schools with a large African-Canadian population, and would not bring this knowledge to the wider populace.

[185] Von Däniken, Erich. 1970. *Chariots of the Gods.* London: Book Club Associates. In his film Chariots of the Gods, von Däniken rotated by 90 degrees the image of the burial tablet in Palenque that marked the tomb of a Mayan ruler and portrayed the ruler depicted on it as a space-person in a spacecraft sitting upright, presumably one of the extra-terrestrials credited with constructing the Mayan temples and tombs.

[186] This demeaning and distorted assumption pervades many historical accounts of Africa. "Even the stone remains of Great Zimbabwe could not be accepted unless they were attributed to King Solomon – Africans are considered to be 'just not capable' of that sort of thing unless they have outside assistance." [Goodwin, Clayton. June 2008. "Bad reporting on fertile soil." *New African.* No. 474:30-31.]

[187] Welcome to the World of Mysteries of Erich von Däniken. http://www.daniken.com/e/index.html

[188] Fage, JD. 1969. *A History of West Africa – an introductory survey.* London: Cambridge University Press. Fourth edition. p 199.

[189] Malinowski, Bronislaw. 1948. "Primitive man and his religion." *IN: Malinowski, B. Magic, science and religion and other essays.* Waveland Press, Inc.

[190] Shipman, Pat. 2004. *To the Heart of the Nile – Lade Florence Baker and the exploration of Central Africa.* New York: HarperCollins. p 161.

[191] Michels, Spencer. 2 Apr. 1998. "Spencer Michels reports on Clinton's last day in Africa and reviews the highlights of the President's trip." PBS Online Newshour. http://www.pbs.org/newshour/bb/africa/jan-june98/lastday_4-2.html

[192] From 2001 until 2005, the village of Siby in Mali was the site for an annual meeting of West Africans and activists from all over the world protesting globalization and the policies of the world's industrial powers, the G8. The Africans called theirs the "Poor People's Summit," and held it simultaneously with and to counter the annual meeting of leaders from the G8, which was invariably held in utmost luxurious and highly secured settings in one of its rich member countries. At the Poor People's Summit in Siby, with neither running water nor electricity, people slept in simple mud huts on mattresses on the floors, and villagers prepared large bowls of rice and sauce to feed the teachers, students, farmers and activists meeting to protest what they saw as unfair economic policies of the G8. In 2003, Fanta Coulibaly, who regularly cooked enormous pots of rice to feed the participants in Siby, used my microphone to extend an invitation to the leaders of the world's richest countries, saying, "Instead of staying in air-conditioned comforts and drinking champagne, the G8 leaders should come to Siby and have a look at the reality."

[193] Sharife, June 2008. p 22.

[194] United Nations Human Development Report, 2007/2008 http://hdr.undp.org/en/media/hdr_20072008_en_complete.pdf

[195] George Bush Foundation Presidential Library website. Brian Mulroney. http://www.georgebushfoundation.org/articles/Brian%20Mulroney

[196] Where to begin to try to counter that bizarre and far-fetched conspiracy theory? The murky CIA record didn't really help on this. In 1973, concerns about CIA involvement in unsavory intelligence activities and assassinations abroad led to the setting up of the US Senate Select Committee to be headed by Senator Frank Church on alleged assassination plots of former leaders by the CIA. One of the star witnesses at the Church Committee hearings was the late Sidney Gottlieb (appearing under the pseudonym Schieder), a former senior CIA scientist sometimes called the "Black Sorcerer" or "Dirty Trickster" because of his work with toxins and drugs to try breaking the human mind and psyche. He admitted to the Church Committee in 1973 that he had put together an assassination kit – actually a lethal toothpaste – for Congo's prime minister, Patrice Lumumba, after US President Eisenhower ordered Lumumba's elimination in 1960. In its interim report issued in 1975, the Church Committee says that Gottlieb included in this assassination kit intended for Lumumba in Central Africa, a poison designed "to produce a disease indigenous to that area of Africa and that could be fatal." [Church Committee. 1975. *Interim Report: alleged assassination plots to kill foreign leaders.* p 21. http://history-matters.com/archive/church/reports/ir/contents.htm] Nor does it help that the Project for the New American Century, with its proponents moving in and out of some of the highest positions in Washington under President George W. Bush and including his brother, Jeb, proposed in September 2000 that the US develop "advanced forms of biological warfare to target specific genotypes that can transform biological warfare from the realm of terror to a politically useful tool." [Project for the New American Century. Sept. 2001. *Rebuilding America's Defenses: strategy, forces and resources for a new century.* p 60. http://www.newamericancentury.org/RebuildingAmericasDefenses.pdf.] None of this information is helpful in trying to convince conspiracy theorists in Africa that the CIA and secret US defence research programs have nothing to do with epidemics and new diseases that arise on their continent.

[197] BBC News. 26 Sept. 2007. "Shock at archbishop condom claim." http://news.bbc.co.uk/2/hi/africa/7014335.stm

[198] Naipaul, V.S. 1984. *Finding the Centre: two narratives.* London: Andre Deutsch. p. 109.

[199] Madelaine Drohan writes extensively about the unsavory and poorly publicized business of using mercenaries to secure large foreign investments in Africa. [Drohan, Madelaine. 2003. *Making a Killing – how and why corporations use armed force to do business.* Toronto: Random House.]

[200] A South African diplomatic mission in Bamako would be opened in 2002, following promises made by South African President, Thabo Mbeki, during a state visit to Mali in November 2001.

10 All that glitters is ... taken away

201 Caplan, 2008. p 92.

202 For Valentine's Day 2006, eight of the world's major jewelry companies pledged to move away from what Resource Media, Oxfam America and the NGO Earthworks called "dirty" gold, by joining the NGOs in calling for mining corporations to ensure gold be produced in more socially and environmentally friendly ways. The "No Dirty Gold" campaign lauded the retailers Sale Corp, the Signet Group, Tiffany & Co, Helzberg Diamonds, Fortunoff, Cartier, Piaget and Van Cleef & Arpels for joining the campaign. In a full-page advertisement in the New York Times, they identified the "laggard" retailers as Rolex, JCPenney, Wal-Mart, Fre Meyers Jewellers, Whitehall Jewellers, Jostens, QVC and Sears/Kmart. [No Dirty Gold. 13 Feb. 2006. *Eight of the world's leading jewelry retailers urge mining industry to clean up "dirty gold."* Earthworks and Oxfam America. http://www.nodirtygold.org/PRleaderslaggards.cfm]

203 In the 1990s, the European Union, American and Canadian development programs in many African countries began pouring a good portion of their development budgets into decentralization programs, intended to promote local government by creating municipal divisions and holding elections. In Mali, this costly program led to great tension over new municipal boundaries and confusion over the role of traditional political structures and leaders and new, elected ones. Mali's former minister of mines and energy suggested to me in an interview that decentralization allowed foreign investors and interests easier access to natural resources on the continent; rather than dealing with highly educated and politically astute national governments, this would eventually allow them to deal directly with less worldly and often illiterate elected officials in rural areas who would demand less for, say, a mining concession. He also suggested that the only two countries in the world that could truly be called federal and decentralized were Canada and Germany, two of the wealthiest nations on earth. Others criticized the whole decentralization effort because it completely ignored and undermined highly sophisticated and developed local traditional governing structures in African societies.

204 In August 2005, 300 workers at Morila, employed by the Malian firm, SOMADEX *(Société Malienne d'Exploitation)* that is sub-contracted by the foreign mining companies, were laid off without any benefits, following a strike. Five members of the miners' union were imprisoned. SOMADEX maintained that the action was justified because the sacked workers were on six-month trial period contracts. The workers claimed that these contracts were falsified and that many of them had worked at the mine for more than four years. The leader of an opposition party, *Solidarité Africaine pour la Démocratie et l'Independence* (SADI), asked the question: "How is it possible that at Morila gold mine, the second largest reserve of gold in the world, there are no measures to protect against cyanide, no potable water, electricity, and infrastructure, and that the mining officials have the right to sack 300 people who were merely exercising their rights? ... In addition, the village of Domba where the gold reserves are found, was sold to

Randgold for peanuts ... Today, we don't have enough to eat, there is no work, health is a mess. UNESCO has just classified our education system as the worst on earth ... the country is ailing and the government has to act." ["Nos dirigeants sont insouciants de ce qui se passé." 16 Aug. 2005. Les Echos http://www.afribone.com/article.php3?id_article=1539]

[205] Jul-Larsen E, Kassibo B, Lange S and Samset I. 2006. "The economic and social impacts of the gold mining industry in Mali." Bergen: Chr. Michelsen Institute (CMI Report R 2006: 4).

[206] See: Bakan, Joel. 2004. *The Corporation: the pathological pursuit of profit and power.* Toronto: Penguin Canada.

11 Washing the blood from the diamonds

[207] Conrad. 1902. p 61

[208] This has been documented not just by concerned NGOs (Global Witness and others), but also by the World Bank: Bannon, Ian and Collier, Paul. 2003. *Natural Resources and Violent Conflict – options and actions.* Washington, DC: World Bank.

[209] Chavis, Rod. 2 Oct. 1998. "Africa in the Western media," Paper presented at the Sixth Annual African Studies Consortium Workshop. University of Pennsylvania, African Studies Center. http://www.africa.upenn.edu/ Workshop/chavis98.html

[210] Gum arabic is used in many processed foods and soft drinks, such as Coca-Cola. It comes from two species of acacia trees in sub-Sahara Africa, and has been exempted from the trade sanctions the US imposed on Sudan. Such is its importance to major food and drink companies.

[211] Tegera, Aloysa and Johnson, Dominic. 2007. "Ressources naturelles et flux du commerce transfrontaliers dans la région des grands lacs." Etude de Pole Institute. *Regards Croisés* (19): juil. 2007. p 3. The Pole Institute is an inter-cultural organization working in the Great Lakes Region of Central Africa. http://www.pole-institute.org/documents/regard%2019_RN.pdf

[212] Hochschild, 1998.

[213] See: IRIN news. 21 Oct. 2002. "DRC: Focus on UN Panel report on the plunder of the Congo." http://www.irinnews.org/report.asp?ReportID= 30525&SelectRegion=Great_Lakes; AND: Dodd, Benjamin. Congo, Coltan, Conflict. The Heinz School Review. http://journal.heinz.cmu.edu/Current/ CongoPages/congo.html

[214] Oxfam International. 2003. "UN must address corporate involvement in Congo conflict." Press release. 27 Oct. 2003. The group of international human rights, environmental and aid organizations quoted includes: Christian-Aid; Fatal Transactions; Friends of the Earth United States, Friends of the Earth England, Wales and Northern Island; Global Witness; Human Rights Watch; International Peace Information Services (IPIS); International Rescue Committee; OECD Watch; Oxfam International; Pax Christi Netherlands; Save the Children UK, 11.11.11; CENADEP platform of

Congolese organizations. http://www.oxfam.org/eng/pr031027_drc_corporate.htm

[215] By 2003, 3.3 million people had already died because of the conflict and 2.25 million had been driven from their homes. [Shah, Anup. 1999. *Conflicts in Africa: The Democratic Republic of Congo.* Global Issues: updated 31 Oct. 2003. Conflicts in Africa: The Democratic Republic of Congo. http://www.globalissues.org/Geopolitics/Africa/DRC.asp]

[216] Caplan, 2008. p 76.

[217] Blondel, Alice (Global Witness), Paul, James (Global Policy Forum) and Scott, Matt (World Vision). *NGO Letter to the UN Secretary General's High Level Panel on Threats, Challenges and Change On Natural Resources and Conflict.* 11 Oct. 2004. http://www.globalpolicy.org/security/natres/generaldebate/2004/1011highlevel.htm

[218] Caplan, 2008. p 76.

[219] International Rescue Committee (IRC). 22 Jan. 2008. IRC Study shows Congo's neglected crisis leaves 5.4 million dead. http://www.theirc.org/news/irc-study-shows-congos0122.html

[220] The average consumer's inadvertent complicity in the vicious conflict and plundering of Congo's resources today is insignificant next to the First Degree involvement of men such as Frank Carlucci, Chairman Emeritus of the Carlyle Group and Nortel Networks, ex-deputy director of the CIA and also part of the Project for the New American Century that seeks to promote a world led by Washington. In 1960, Carlucci was second secretary in the US embassy in Kinshasa, in the newly independent Congo, led by Prime Minister Patrice Lumumba. Lumumba was a popular leader and determined that his country's resources would be used for the benefit of his people. This, the US and former colonial power in Congo, Belgium, interpreted as a "communist threat" and so a plot was hatched to remove Lumumba and replace him with Joseph-Désiré Mobutu (later Mobutu Sese Seko). Carlucci was allegedly instrumental in the plot, something he denies, but the CIA bureau chief in Kinshasa at the time has admitted on camera to the US role in the overthrow and death of Lumumba and there are allegations that Carlucci also had a hand in passing information on Lumumba's whereabouts in captivity to assassins who killed him. The CIA successfully installed Mobutu as president of Congo, which he renamed Zaire. Mobutu went on to become one of Africa's most despotic and oppressive dictators, synonymous with kleptocracy, allegedly stashing away billions of dollars in offshore numbered accounts. But he remained very close to the Bush family in the US, visiting the family more than two dozen times over the years. In the late 1990s, with the end of the Cold War, he fell out of favour (was no longer useful to the US) and was abandoned. He was overthrown by Laurent Kabila who was funded in part by Western mining magnates close to the reins of power in Washington, and he died ignominiously of prostate cancer in Morocco in 1997. Conflict simmered on in the country, fuelled by arms and influence-peddling from abroad, and millions of innocent civilians died

in those conflicts. Carlucci, on the other hand, has enjoyed a stellar career in the corridors of US power and high-flying wealth atop the Carlyle Group.

See: Komisar, Lucy. 18 Oct. 2002. "Carlucci can't hide his role in 'Lumumba'." Pacific News Service. http://news.pacificnews.org/news/view_ article.html?article_id=882; AND: Partial list of people associated with the Project for the New American Century. http://www.reasoned.org/e_PNAC2.htm

[221] The Global Policy Forum, a non-profit consultative group that advises at the United Nations, says: "Natural resources often lie at the heart of wars and civil strife. Huge mining and resource companies, including giants like ExxonMobil and Anglo American/De Beers, do not hesitate to use force in pursuit of their corporate interests. There are many players in this bloody nexus of natural resources and conflict, including shadowy resource traders, smugglers, corrupt local officials, arms dealers, transport operators and mercenary companies. Increasing scarcity of resources, driven by rising world population and the spread of unsustainable consumption, further sharpen such conflicts. NGOs, investigative journalists and UN expert panels have revealed some of the players in these clandestine networks and spotlighted governments that give them comfort, in the North as well as the South." [Global Policy Forum. *The Dark Side of Natural Resources.* http://www.globalpolicy.org/security/docs/minindx.htm AND: Global Policy Forum. Nov. 2003. *NGO Proposals on Natural Resources and Conflict.* http://www.globalpolicy.org/security/natres/generaldebate/2003/11proposals.htm]

[222] The conflict in the Democratic Republic of Congo which resulted in 5.4 million deaths was never seriously debated or denounced by the US government, while it was quick to describe the Darfur crisis as "genocide." This has been attributed by some sceptics to the US frustration with the Sudan-Sino alliance with China receiving South Sudanese oil which American companies have been trying for years to get their hands on. See: Sharife, June 2008. p 23.

[223] Shaxson, 2007: 223.

[224] Two rebel groups, UNITA and the MPLA, fought first for 14 years for independence from Portugal. When independence came in 1974, they then turned on each other and continued to fight. During the Cold War, UNITA led by Jonas Savimbi had backing from South Africa and the United States, financing their side in the conflict from the sale of diamonds, while the MPLA were backed by Cuba and the Soviet Union and financed their forces from the sale of oil. When the Cold War ended, foreign troops pulled out, elections were held in 1992, and the MPLA won the first round. The second round was never held because UNITA under Jonas Savimbi – backed by the CIA for many years – relaunched the war, which lasted until his death in 2002. Oil continued to fund the MPLA government military operations. The UN Security Council slapped sanctions on UNITA in 1998 to try to halt the diamond exports that financed UNITA, but it was only later, when NGO campaigns got going on the issue, that the flow of diamonds was slowed and then halted just before Savimbi's death. Both sides committed atrocities.

[225] This link between Ranger Oil and Executive Outcomes is dealt with in depth in the book by Madelaine Drohan, 2003.

[226] The Canadian Broadcasting Corporation (CBC) did an in-depth investigation into these murky companies and their relationships in its *Fifth Estate* television program on 3 Nov. 1999.

[227] Abrams Fran, Buncombe Andrew and Boggan Steve. 1998. "Who is Tony Buckingham? And why does everyone want to talk to him?" 13 May 1998. *The Independent* (London).

[228] Canadian author and investigative journalist, Madelaine Drohan, points out that the residence for the chairman and chief executive officer of Heritage Oil and Gas is Switzerland, as it is for Buckingham, who is director and the major shareholder. She notes that all of its operations are overseas – Oman, Uganda, and the Democratic Republic of Congo – and they are owned through a series of companies registered in the offshore tax havens of Barbados and the Bahamas. This means that while such companies are registered in Canada and benefit from free Canadian diplomatic services in countries in which they work, they are exempt from paying Canadian tax. See: Drohan, Madelaine. March 2005. "Open for business: how international corporations are exploiting our nation's positive image with little more than a postal box." *Walrus Magazine.* http://www.walrusmagazine.com/articles/2005.03-business-international-corporations-canada/1/

[229] The landmark report on how blood diamonds fuelled the conflict in Sierra Leone and the sinister complicity of diamond dealers, mining companies and diamond interests worldwide that profited from blood or conflict diamonds was put out by Partnership Africa Canada: Smillie, Ian; Gberie, Lansana and Hazleton, Ralph. 2000. *The Heart of the Matter: Sierra Leone, diamonds and human security.* Ottawa: Partnership Africa Canada. Other key sources on the conflict in Sierra Leone include: Smillie, Ian. 2002. *Conflict Diamonds – unfinished business.* Ottawa: International Development Research Centre (IDRC). http://www.idrc.ca/en/ev-5505-201-1-DO_TOPIC.html; Gberie, Lansana. 2006. *A Dirty War in West Africa – the R.U.F. and the destruction of Sierra Leone.* London: Hurst & Company; Hirsh, John. L. 2001. Sierra Leone – diamonds and the struggle for democracy. International Academy Occasional Papers Series. Boulder, Colorado: Lynne Renner Publishers, Inc.; Keen, David. 2005. *Conflict and Collusion in Sierra Leone.* Oxford: James Currey; Reno, William. 1995. *Corruption and State Politics in Sierra Leone.* Cambridge: Cambridge University Press; Reno, William. 1998. *Warlord Politics and African States.* Boulder: Lynne Reinner; Richards, Paul. 1996. *Fighting for the Rain Forest: war, youth and resources in Sierra Leone.* London: Villiers Publications.

[230] The use of amputations as a particularly sadistic battle tactic to terrorize the population did not originate in Sierra Leone in the 1990s. Already in the 1980s in Mozambique, the brutal Renamo mercenary force (supported by South Africa, the Rhodesian secret service and the CIA) had practised mutilations. And before that, in the late 1800s, rubber plunderers in Belgian King Leopold's Congo carried out orders to amputate hands. Foday Sankoh, who headed the RUF rebels in Sierra Leone, may have learned of this partic-

ularly depraved but effective terror tactic in the Congo when he spent some time there as a UN peacekeeper in the 1960s. [Gberie, Lansana. 2005. *A Dirty War in West Africa – the R.U.F. and the destruction of Sierra Leone.* London: Hurst & Company. p 17.]

[231] The Kimberley Process Certification Scheme involves industry and civil society working together to end the trade in conflict diamonds, to "ensure that the horrors caused by conflict diamonds may one day come to an end." However, those involved admit on their web site that "there remains much to be done." The certification process, a condition to which members of the Jewelers of America agreed in 2002, stipulated "Each time diamonds change hands, the seller must attest to their legitimacy by means of a warranty." See: Kimberley Process, Background http://www.kimberleyprocess.com:8080/site/?name=background

[232] An unpublished World Bank study found that 75 percent of the dramatic rise in food prices in 2007-2008 could be attributed to the conversion of food crops to biofuels. It is believed that the World Bank did not publish the report because it would embarrass President Bush and the White House. President of the World Bank, Robert Zoellick, was a close associate of George W. Bush. [Chakrabortty, Aditya. 4 July 2008. "Secret report: biofuel caused food crisis – internal World Bank study delivers blow to plant energy drive." *The Guardian.* http://www.guardian.co.uk/environment/2008/jul/03/biofuels.renewableenergy]

[233] Many Sierra Leoneans are happy to see the Special Court trying former Liberian president Charles Taylor for his role in the war. But some also told me they feel that with Foday Sankoh (former RUF commander) and other chief protagonists in the war either now dead or mysteriously disappeared and Charles Taylor being tried in The Hague, while "lesser" war criminals – many from the Civil Defence Force that was formed to combat the rebels – are tried in Freetown, the Court is not a priority for them and a "waste of money." There is also the extremely delicate issue of where those convicted war criminals are sent to serve their terms. Prisons that meet international standards in Europe are on offer to those convicted of war crimes, which American Chief Prosecutor Stephen Rapp described as some of the worst crimes "in human history" (apparently he has not been made aware of the torture techniques promulgated by the CIA in Latin America or the Holocausts in Germany and the DRC). The conditions, amenities and assured food supplies in such detention facilities might seem like a reward to many Sierra Leoneans today struggling to feed themselves once a day. Others say that the Truth and Reconciliation Commission (TRC) which was set up as part of the peace accord should have had its recommendations implemented and done far more work. The TRC public testimony was curtailed by the setting up of the Special Court, encouraged by the US, which refuses to support an International Criminal Court that could have tried suspected war criminals. People also told me that some extremely powerful people – actual and former African presidents- whom they suspect of involvement in the trade of blood diamonds and supporting the rebels during the conflict have been conspicuously absent from the list of those called

to appear before the Special Court. This, they said, casts doubt on just how high the Court has been willing to cast its net. Many recall that Charles Taylor was a good friend of President Blaise Compaoré of Burkina Faso (now feted as a peace-maker and statesman) and Libya's Muammar Gaddafi. Many said the Court should investigate how Taylor mysteriously escaped detention in the US to return to West Africa to launch his rebellion to unseat, Liberian President Samuel Doe, who had been helped to power by the US in the first place. However, others defend the court and Taylor's trial, hoping it will help eliminate impunity for war criminals and also bring some closure.

[234] The official amount of aid money that Sierra Leone receives from outside may be deceptive for the simple reason that much of it goes to pay for foreign "technical experts" and for overheads; in 2006, for example, the official amount of aid to Sierra Leone that could be documented because it was officially declared by bilateral and multilateral agencies (NGOs often bring their own funds and these may not show up on official government budget documents), was 361.3 million US dollars. That meant the equivalent of 67 US dollars per person. But hefty percentages of aid money from the European Union and the British development agency DFID, as two examples, are used up to pay for "technical assistance," namely their own experts and their expenses. So how much of the 67 US dollars per person actually "trickles down" to the average Sierra Leonean may be precious little, or nothing at all. EURODAD. 18 Jan. 2008.

[235] Gberie, 2005. p 196.

[236] A 2006 study found that even more alarming is the continued use of child labour in the mines themselves. During the long civil war, children were forced into combat and diamond mining by rebels. But even five years after peace returned to Sierra Leone, a national survey found that more children worked in the mines doing either heavy work of shovelling or lighter work doing errands or carrying supplies and food, than attend school. The ratio of child labourers to children in school is by far the highest in the epicentre of Koidu, the capital of the nation's diamond-mining district of Kono. [Network Movement for Justice and Development Sierra Leone. Oct. 2006. *Report on the Situation of Child Miners in Sierra Leone: case study of four districts.*]

[237] It is a sad comment on African appreciation of their own products that the well-heeled and many expatriates never consume local drinks. Sierra Leonean Star beer, at half the price of the imported brews, is not often the choice of rich Sierra Leoneans and expatriates.

[238] According to Ian Smillie of Partnership Africa Canada [personal communication], sooner or later the diamonds will have to go into the legitimate stream, and someone then has to pay the right price. Sierra Leone exported one million dollars worth of diamonds officially in 2000; in 2007 it was around 140 million. That means that the Kimberley Process has had a major impact on forcing people to go legitimate, including, hopefully this vagabond Canadian who finds it all "fun." See also: Partnership Africa Canada and Global Witness. 2004. "Rich man, poor man: development dia-

monds and poverty diamonds. The potential for change in the artisanal alluvial diamond fields of Africa." http://blooddiamond.pacweb.org/docs/rich_eng.pdf; AND: Smillie, Ian. 2002. *Conflict Diamonds – unfinished business.* Ottawa: International Development Research Centre (IDRC). http://www.idrc.ca/en/ev-5505-201-1-DO_TOPIC.html; AND: Partnership Africa Canada and Network Movement for Justice and Development. 2006. "The miners: less than a dollar a day?" Diamond Industry Annual Review, Sierra Leone 2006: 3-5. http://www.pacweb.org/e/images/stories/documents/annual%20review%20sl%202006.pdf

[239] The Diamond Development Initiative. http://blooddiamond.pacweb.org/ddi/

[240] Network Movement For Justice and Development Sierra Leone and the Campaign for Just Mining. June 2007. *Profiles of small to large-scale mining companies operating in Kono District: Paradise lost?* p IV.

[241] Much more information on Timis and his controversial past and present business dealings can be found on Wikipedia: http://en.wikipedia.org/wiki/Frank_Timi%C5%9F

[242] African Minerals Limited. http://www.african-minerals.com/Corporate/Home.aspx?id=2

[243] Tumoe, Tatafway. 2008. "Koidu Holdings versus the truth". *For Di People (FDP) newspaper.* p 8.

[244] Tim Spicer, alleged to have close links to former UK Prime Minister Tony Blair (among others in powerful positions), appeared to own Sandline (although who owned what in the shifting sands of the nexus of mercenary and resource companies it was part of, is never set in concrete). When Sandline closed, it appears to have set out tentacles, one of which is Aegis Defense Systems with Tim Spicer as CEO and Chair, which in 2004 won the lucrative (292 million US dollar) contract from the US to protect the Green Zone in Baghdad. More on Aegis can be found on the Public Broadcasting Service (PBS) web site devoted to the contractors in Iraq, "Who are the contractors?" http://www.pbs.org/wgbh/pages/frontline/shows/warriors/contractors/companies.html

See also: Wrigley, Christopher. 1999. "The Privatisation of violence: new mercenaries and the state." Campaign Against Arms Trade (CAAT). http://www.caat.org.uk/publications/government/mercenaries-1999.php; AND: Bowles, William. 18 Aug. 2004. *Tony Blair's pet bulldog? The curious case of Tim Spicer.* http://www.williambowles.info/ini/ini-0266.html

[245] Drohan, Mar. 2005.

[246] I recently met a Canadian woman who was working in Guatemala and found herself in the midst of a protest against the gold mining company that had set up there; she was told she should say to Guatemalans she was American, and never admit she was Canadian because Canada has become synonymous with bullying companies after gold in that country. This may be increasingly the case around the world, as 60 percent of the world's resource-based companies are registered in Canada, and working well out of sight of the average Canadian citizen or investor. It may be time

Canadians seeking a safe and respectable "flag of convenience" for their t-shirts and backpacks reconsidered using the maple leaf; it is losing its lustre.

[247] Energem owned 40 percent of Koidu Holdings until May 2007, when it sold its shares to Geneva-based Beny Steinmetz Group Resources, led by Israeli-American Beny Steinmetz, with the remaining shares in the hands of Magma Diamond Resources, also part of the Steinmetz Group. See: MiningWatch Canada. http://www.miningwatch.ca/index.php?/Diamondworks; AND: Purcell, Will. *DiamondWorks Remembers its Dead, in Silence.* Stockwatch Street Wire (Canada), 11 Nov. 2003. http://www.mine-sandcommunities.org/Action/press213.htm

[248] Tumoe, Tatafway. 13 Feb. 2008. "Koidu Holdings versus the truth." *For Di People (FDP) newspaper.* p 8.

[249] The senseless destruction of every form of infrastructure and building in the country did not extend to most of the mosques and churches. Sierra Leone is about half Muslim and half Christian, with some traditional faiths still mixed in in places, but it could teach the world an enormous amount about religious tolerance. Christians share Muslim festivals; Muslims share Christian festivals, and throughout the war in which history, injustice, economic disparity, political mismanagement and foreign meddling and diamonds were all major factors – religion was not.

12 Strategic Minerals, strategic games

[250] Beah, Ishmael. 2007. *A Long Way Gone – memoirs of a boy soldier.* New York, NY: Sarah Crichton Books / Farrar, Straus and Giroux.

[251] *Strategic Materials, Final Report.* Spring 2007. Industrial Study. The Industrial College of the Armed Forces, National Defense University, Fort McNair, Washington, DC. 20319-5062.

[252] Comment by: "I hate Tofu". 11 Apr. 2006. Investors' Pages: Titanium supply will be tight through 2010. Capacity expansions won't help supply until next decade http://www.purchasing.com/article/CA6482987.html?title=Article&spacedesc=news&nid=2520

[253] Pye, Daniel. 2 May 2008. "Shadow networks: violence, war and plunder in the Great Lakes Region of Africa." Diaries of Dissent. *London Progressive Journal:* Issue 17. http://londonprogressivejournal.com/issue/show/17#article126

[254] TRG website. Management Team. http://www.titaniumresources.com/site/en-GB/Page_10.aspx

[255] Ismi, Asad. Oct. 2001. "The Western heart of darkness: mineral-rich Congo ravaged by genocide and Western plunder." *Canadian Centre for Policy Alternatives.* http://www.policyalternatives.ca/MonitorIssues/2001/10/MonitorIssue1686/

[256] Innes, William I. 1 Nov. 2006. "Tax planning for possible future events does not attract GAAR: MIL (Investments) S.A. v. The Queen (General Anti-

Avoidance Rule)." *Tax Executive.* http://goliath.ecnext.com/coms2/gi_0199-6248766/Tax-planning-for-possible-future.html

[257] Waldie, Paul. 8 May 2006. "Mining promoter Boulle hit with huge tax bill; Ottawa demands $190-million." *The Globe and Mail.* http://www.globeadvisor.com/servlet/ArticleNews/story/gam/20060508/RTAX08

[258] World Trade Organization. "Trade Policy Review." Sierra Leone. p 64. HTTP://WWW.WTO.ORG/ENGLISH/TRATOP_E/TPR_E/S143-4_E.DOC

[259] Sierra Leoneans told me that Boulle got his start in African mining in Sierra Leone in the 1960s, working for De Beers, and that John Sisay's father was an agent for Boulle, who asked his boss to "adopt" his son and send him to Europe for his education.

[260] Knight, James and Manson, Katrina. 4 Apr. 2007. "INTERVIEW-Sierra Rutile aims to be world No. 1 in three years." Thomsons Reuters. http://uk.reuters.com/article/oilRpt/idUKL0472258020070404?sp=true

[261] http://www.titaniumresources.com/site/en-GB/Page_10.aspx

[262] Seibure, Ibrahim and Hill, Kevin. 26 May 2008. Sierra Rutile tops government mining review. *Concord Times.* pp 1 and 8.

[263] Kamara, Sullay. Apr. 1997. "Mined out: the environmental and social implications of development finance to rutile mining in Sierra Leone." Friends of the Earth, Briefings. http://www.foe.co.uk/pubsinfo/briefings/html/19971215144610.html

[264] *Dredging News Online.* 29 July 2008. "Joint statement issued about Sierra Rutile dredge incident." http://www.sandandgravel.com/news/article.asp?v1=11183; AND: Koroma, Pel and Hill, Kevin. 28 July 2008. "Sierra Leone: Rutile dredge disaster – dozens injured, two feared dead." Concord Times (Freetown). http://allafrica.com/stories/200807281480.html

[265] Raj Patel writes that today the United Fruit Company has been "rebranded as the warmer, fuzzier 'Chiquita Brands,' through public relations and fair trade schemes, but that it doesn't deserve this improved reputation. [Patel, Raj. 2008. *Stuffed and Starved – markets, power and the hidden battle for the world's food system.* Toronto: HarperCollins Ltd. pp 100-102.]

[266] Ankomah, Baffour. June 2008. "Reporting Africa." *New African.* No. 474: 11.

[267] Duodo, Cameron. June 2008. "Beware the propaganda." *New African.* No. 474: 20.

[268] Ankomah, 2008. p 13.

[269] CBC News. 29 Oct. 2007. "Canada's military exports soar as numbers go unreported: CBC investigation." http://www.cbc.ca/canada/story/2007/10/29/military-exports.html

[270] The Ottawa Treaty to ban landmines was never signed by the US, China or Russia, along with 37 other nations including Israel, Cuba, Iran and Iraq.

[271] The Canadian public is not to blame for this illusion; in 2007 the government had not released detailed reports on military exports to Parliament since 2003, when a report from 2002 was tabled.

[272] Pilger, John. 14 Apr. 2006. "War by media." Address at Columbia University, New York. http://www.johnpilger.com/page.asp?partid=267

[273] CNN. 23 May 1996. "House bill forbids CIA from using U.S. journalists as spies." http://www.cnn.com/US/9605/23/journalists.cia/index.html

[274] CNN (Anthony Collings). 18 July 1996. "Journalists tell Senate they want no CIA ties." http://www.cnn.com/US/9607/18/spies.journalists/

[275] Anonymous. 15 June 2004. *On Her Majesty's Secret Service – uncensored.* Information censored by the British Government from Chapter 36 of MI6: *Inside the covert world of Her Majesty's secret intelligence service,* by Stephen Dorril.http://cryptome.sabotage.org/mi6-sd36.htm

[276] Arzouni, David and Linda. Missionaries to West Africa. 2000. http://www.arzouni.com/

[277] Jones, Shannon. 2002. *US Attorney General Invokes God in "War on Terrorism".* World Socialist Web Site, International Committee of the Fourth International: 15 May 2002. http://www.wsws.org/articles/2002/may2002/ashc-m15.shtml

[278] In the early 1990s, on his Christian Broadcasting Network's (CBN) talk show *The 700 Club,* Pat Robertson solicited donations for the work of the CBN international charity, Operation Blessing, which was working in Zaire (now the Democratic Republic of Congo), then ruled by Mobutu Sese Seko, human rights abuser and infamous for his megolomania. In 1997, two pilots working in Zaire revealed that the cargo planes (tax exempt) used by Operation Blessing were actually working for Robertson's company, African Development Co, which was doing diamond exploration in Zaire. Robertson reportedly lost as much as $10 million from this venture. Revealing his indefatigable imperial attitude, speaking again on his *700 Club* radio show on CBN, in August 2005 Pat Robertson called for the assassination of Venezuelan president, Hugo Chavez. "We have the ability to take him out, and I think the time has come that we exercise that ability. We don't need another $200 billion war to get rid of one, you know, strong-arm dictator. It's a whole lot easier to have some of the covert operatives do the job and then get it over with … It's a whole lot cheaper than starting a war … and I don't think any oil shipments will stop." [Sizemore, Bill. Sept. 2003. "Pat Robertson's right-wing gold mine: the little-known tale of the evangelist and the dictator." *Ms. Magazine.* http://www.msmagazine.com/sept03/sizemore.asp]

[279] Freedom Gold Limited, an offshore company registered in the Cayman Islands, is based at the headquarters of Pat Robertson's Christian Broadcasting Network (CBN) headquarters in Virginia Beach and Robertson is the company's president and only director. In 1999, on behalf of Freedom Gold, Robertson signed an agreement with Charles Taylor and some members of his cabinet for mining rights in southeast Liberia. When this venture looked set to fail with the removal of Charles Taylor from power, Robertson defended the Liberian president on his CBN. In 2002, during a three-day "Liberia for Jesus" rally in Monrovia, sponsored by the CBN, Taylor was centre-stage. Robertson claimed Taylor was a defender of Christianity against

Islam in the region. Robertson later claimed he had never met Taylor, while Taylor would be called up on 11 war crime charges by the UN-backed Special Court for Sierra Leone, and be tried at the International Criminal Court in The Hague. [King, Colbert I. 22 Sept. 2001. "Pat Robertson's gold." *Washington Post* (A29). http://www.washingtonpost.com/ac2/wp-dyn?pagename=article&node=&contentId=A7124-2001Sep21]

[280] Jones, 2002.

[281] See: Arzouni, David and Linda. 2000. AND: http://www.arzouni.com/index.php/search/results/03be09f50e8e3400b13985c92152f2e0/; AND: http://www.jesusfilm.org/

[282] See also, for example, Kawato, Wesley. May 2003. *The hour has come for Mali to find her savior!* http://global-prayer-digest.org/monthdetails/2003/md-May-2003.asp

[283] Klein, 2007. p 498.

[284] GlobalSecurity.org. Operation Enduring Freedom – Chad. http://www.globalsecurity.org/military/ops/oef-chad.htm; GlobalSecurity.org. Operation Enduring Freedom – Trans Sahara (OEF-TS). http://www.globalsecurity.org/military/ops/oef-ts.htm; GlobalSecurity.org. Trans-Sahara Counterterrorism Initiative (TSCTI) http://www.globalsecurity.org/military/ops/tscti.htm

[285] US embassy Freetown. 7 July 2004. Press Release: *RSLAF to Niger: Sierra Leone soldiers assist in Global War on Terrorism* http://freetown.usembassy.gov/pr070704.html; AND: PAE A Lockheed Martin Company. http://www.paegroup.com/. Sourcewatch (a project of the Center for Media and Democracy) notes, that "War, and the threat of war, has always been lucrative for PA&E. They have an extensive transport system which enables them to ship equipment and personnel anywhere in the world. ... in the spring of 2004, in a partnership with SNC-Lavalin of Montreal, PA&E won a $400 million (Cdn. $) contract to build and maintain 'distant Canadian bases for the next decade'." http://www.source-watch.org/index.php?title=Pacific_Architects_and_Engineers%2C_Inc.

[286] IRIN news. 14 Oct. 2004. "WEST AFRICA: Famine not fanaticism poses greatest terror threat in Sahel." Integrated Regional Information Network (IRIN). UN Office for the Coordination of Humanitarian Affairs http://www.irinnews.org/Report.aspx?ReportId=51706

[287] The website [http://www.hoa.centcom.mil/factsheet.asp] of the Combined Joint Task Force in the Horn of Africa says it "conducts unified action in the combined joint operations area of the Horn of Africa to prevent conflict, promote regional stability, and protect Coalition interests in order to prevail against extremism ... The people of CJTF-HOA focus on military-to-military training, civil-military operations, and engagement to fulfill the CJTF-HOA mission." Its website offers heart-warming stories about US military personnel doing charitable work, alongside photos of American warships visiting the Horn. What is conspicuously absent on the site is any identification of the CJTF-HOA as being an American-led mission; and says only "The area of responsibility for CJTF-HOA includes the countries of

Djibouti, Ethiopia, Eritrea, Kenya, Seychelles, Somalia, Sudan, Tanzania, Uganda and Yemen. Other areas of interest are Comoros, Mauritius, and Madagascar." This mission for the Horn of Africa was established on October 19, 2002 not in Africa, but at Camp Lejeune, North Carolina, USA.

[288] Wax, Emily and DeYoung, Karen. 17 May 2006. "US secretly backing warlords in Somalia." *Washington Post Foreign Service,* p A01.

[289] Cawthorne, Andrew. 17 June 2006. "Somali warlords flee to US boat: Islamists." Reuters News. http://go.reuters.com/newsArticle.jhtml? type=worldNews&storyID=12559197&src=rss/worldNews

[290] Barnett, Anthony and Smith, Patrick. 10 Sept. 2006. "Emails suggest that the CIA knew of plans by private military companies to breach UN rules." *The Observer.* http://observer.guardian.co.uk/world/story/0,,1868920,00.html

[291] BBC News. 11 Jan. 2008. "Somali raids miss terror suspects." http://news.bbc.co.uk/2/hi/africa/6251077.stm; AND: BBC News. 9 Jan. 2007. "US Somali air strikes 'kill many'." http://news.bbc.co.uk/2/hi/africa/6243459.stm; AND: BBC News. 7 June 2006. "Somali Islamic state ruled out." http://news.bbc.co.uk/2/hi/africa/5051220.stm

[292] Gellman, Barton. 23 Jan. 2005. "Secret unit expands Rumsfeld's domain." *Washington Post.* p A01. http://www.washingtonpost.com/ac2/ wp-dyn/A29414-2005Jan22?language=printer

[293] Miller, Greg. 31 Oct. 2004. "Special forces enter CIA territory with a new weapon." *Los Angeles Times.*

13 Cotton-pickin' hypocrisy

[294] Stiglitz, 2002. p 6.

[295] Watkins, Kevin and Sul Jung-ui. 2002. *Cultivating Poverty: the impact of US cotton subsidies on Africa.* Oxfam Briefing Paper 30. Washington: Oxfam International: advocacy@oxfaminternational.org

[296] Given that ActionAid International says that 90 percent of American "aid" funds never reach the poor because of a range of factors – expensive technical assistance from the donor, high administrative costs among them – it is unclear how much of the 37.7 million dollars of US aid money budgeted in 2001 for the country actually landed in Mali to serve the needs of the poor people there. ActionAid International. 2005. *Real Aid.* http://www.actionaidusa.org/Action Aid Real Aid.pdf

[297] Easterly, William. 2006. *The White Man's Burden: why the West's efforts to aid the rest have done so much ill and so little good.* New York: The Penguin Press. p 5.

[298] BBC News. 29 July 2008. "Q&A: Crunch trade talks." http://news.bbc.co.uk/2/hi/business/7517028.stm

[299] Bush, George W. 13 May 2002. "President signs farm bill: Remarks by the President upon signing the Farm Bill." Press Release. Washington: The White House.

[300] See: Blustein, Paul. 2002. "Who really pays to help US farmers?" Washington: *Washington Post:* 6 May 2002.

[301] Environmental Working Group's Farm Subsidy Database. http://farm.ewg.org/farm/persondetail.php?custnumber=009270251

[302] Watkins and Jung-ui. 2002.

[303] BBC News. 4 Mar. 2005. "US must act "quickly" on cotton." http://news.bbc.co.uk/2/hi/business/4317235.stm

[304] BBC News. 2 June 2008. "US loses in cotton dispute at WTO." http://news.bbc.co.uk/2/hi/business/7432021.stm

[305] UNICEF Press release.19 Jan. 2005. *UNICEF Welcomes Appointment of next Executive Director – Ann Veneman will succeed Carol Bellamy in May 2005.* United Nations. http://www.unicef.org/media/media_24885.html. In January 2005, Ann Veneman was named as the new Executive Director of UNICEF, the United Nations organization devoted to children, and working under the banner: "For every child, health, education, equality, protection – Advance Humanity." She had been put forward by US President George W. Bush, presumably in appreciation of her hard work to protect the interests of American agribusinesses in her time as Agriculture Secretary. The tragic and dark irony of this cynical appointment of such a champion of big business in the wealthy world to the global organization supposed to be the most compassionate of all, with a mandate to look out for the downtrodden children and women of the world, didn't make a ripple in the mainstream media in North America. This looked like another indication of how those media have been co-opted by corporate ownership or perhaps they have just lost interest in the United Nations, which they themselves along with the Bush regime have disparaged into disrepute. With Veneman heading UNICEF, and another member of the US neo-conservative juggernaut, John Bolton (another member of the Project for the New American Century) subsequently the US ambassador to the United Nations in New York until late 2006, Washington was well-placed to exert its influence and restructure the world body that in the past has occasionally challenged US administrations' rights to global supremacy.

[306] In 2005, Monsanto had admitted that one of its former senior managers had in 2002 directed an Indonesian consulting firm to give a 50,000-US-dollar bribe to a senior Indonesian official to avoid carrying out environmental impact studies on its cotton. The giant agrochemical company agreed to pay a 1.5 million dollar fine for corrupting the official, which it said it did because it was facing stiff competition from activists and farmers who were campaigning against the introduction of genetically modified cotton in Indonesia. [BBC News 1 July 2005. "Monsanto fined $1.5 m for bribery." http://news.bbc.co.uk/2/hi/business/4153635.stm]

[307] ENS. 22 June 2004. "West African leaders embrace US biotechnology." http://www.ens-newswire.com/ens/jun2004/2004-06-22-02.asp

[308] Kelly Valerie, Carpenter Janet, Diall Oumar, Easterling Tom, Koné Moctar, McCornick Peter and McGaguey Mike. 2005. *Options for Economic Growth in Mali through the Application of Science and Technology to Agriculture.*

Washington: USAID. This study was commissioned by USAID as part of its "Initiative to end hunger in Africa." It may also have helped combat hunger at the American universities and consulting firms engaged to carry out the research, including Michigan State University and Weidemann Associates. Perhaps not surprisingly, given that USAID commissioned the study and USAID was working closely with biotechnology and agrochemical multinationals, it recommended that Mali exploit the potential use for Bt cotton, Bt maize, and transgenic tomatoes and potatoes.

[309] Agricultural Biotechnology Support Project II; http://www.absp2.cornell.edu/

[310] African Centre for Biosafety. http://www.biosafetyafrica.net/portal/

[311] Ivins, Molly and Dubose, Lou. 2003. *Bushwhacked: life in George W. Bush's America.* New York: Random House.

[312] Cohen, Robert. 2001. "Monsanto and G.W. Bush administration: who will own the store?" *The Notmilk Newsletter.* 21 Jan. 2001. http://www.pure-food.org/Monsanto/MonBushAdmin.cfm

[313] Ghanaian journalist Cameron Duodu asks how Taylor could have escaped a US prison (where he was being held on extradition charges laid by then-Liberian president Samuel Doe) and managed to get out of the US to return to West Africa and garner funds and military backing enabling him to overthrow Samuel Doe. Duodu says that many Liberians believe Taylor had to have help, perhaps from the CIA. Duodu, Cameron. 30 Mar. 2006. "The nine lives of Charles Taylor." *The Guardian.* http://commentisfree.guardian.co.uk/cameron_duodu/2006/03/why_should_charles_taylor_be_t.html

[314] Under US pressure, in 1992 the UN Security Council imposed sanctions on Libya, to press Tripoli to hand over suspects in the 1988 bombing of a Pan American airliner over Lockerbie, Scotland, and would not agree to the removal of the sanctions until 2003, when Libya accepted responsibility for the bombing and agreed to pay 2.7 billion US dollars in compensation. [Libya: Sanctions. http://www.globalpolicy.org/security/sanction/libya/indxirlb.htm] However, Halliburton, under then CEO Dick Cheney, and formerly Secretary of Defense under George Bush (Senior) and later Vice President to George Bush (Junior), allegedly did brisk business with Libya throughout the period that sanctions were in effect through non-US subsidiaries, just as the company did with Iraq while UN sanctions were in place. [Halliburton Watch: http://www.halliburtonwatch.org/about_hal/libya.html]

[315] BBC News. 30 Jan. 2005. *"US oil companies return to Libya."* http://news.bbc.co.uk/go/pr/fr/-/2/hi/business/4219623.stm

[316] Titan Corporation (now L-3 Titan Group) is "a leading provider of comprehensive information and communications products, solutions, and services for National Security. Serving the Department of Defense, intelligence agencies, and other government customers" and its business focus includes "Homeland Security, supporting first responders, securing American borders and continuing to combat the War on Terrorism" as well as intelligence, surveillance, reconnaissance. See: http://www.titan.com/ AND: BBC News.

2 Mar. 2005. "US company admits Benin bribery." http://news.bbc.co.uk/2/hi/business/4310331.stm; AND: IRIN news. 2 Mar. 2005. "US firm admits guilt in bribery probe connected to Benin president." http://www.irin-news.org/report.asp?ReportID=45879&SelectRegion=West_Africa&Select Country=BENIN

[317] It is impossible to find one definition for "Green Revolution" that would be acceptable to all. While some define the Green Revolution as the "dramatic" increase in crop yields and agricultural productivity effected with the use of hybrid seed varieties, "advances in genetics and petrochemicals and machinery," chemical fertilizers and pesticides, this is generally the one adopted and used by proponents of this kind of agriculture, including many agrochemical and bio-technology firms and politicians they've helped into office with generous campaign donations. Others prefer to focus on what the Green Revolution entails in the way of technology, defining it as the modification of agriculture in the 1950s and 60s, which included new seed varieties, the chemical fertilizers and pesticides, and more mechanization, which may have been intended to bring higher yields, thereby leaving off the value judgement that the Green Revolution actually succeeded in improving farming around the world. The controversy surrounding the Green Revolution starts, therefore, with its definition.

[318] Mben, Paul. 2 Nov. 2004. "L'agence de Biotechnologies, un outil précieux de développement et de biosécurité." *L'Independent* (1095): 4; AND: Mben, Paul. 2004. "Les solutions préconisées par Syngenta." 2 Nov. 2004, *L'Independent* (1095): p 4

[319] Valenghi, Daniel; Traoré, Djibril and Merceron, Franck. 2004. *Programme coton biologique: rapport activités semestriel 1/2004.* Bamako, Mali: Helvetas Mali.

[320] Deen, Thalif. 6 July 2004. "Development: tied aid strangling nations, says UN." IPS. http://ipsnews.net/interna.asp?idnews=24509

[321] Bolton, 2007. p 78.

[322] The G7 brings together the finance ministers of Canada, France, Germany, Italy, Japan, the UK,and the US. The G8 is the annual meeting of heads of states of those seven countries, plus Russia. [ActionAid International. 2005. *Real Aid.* http://www.actionaidusa.org/Action Aid Real Aid.pdf]

[323] Syngenta Corporate Governance: http://www.syngenta.com/en/index.aspx

[324] Coalition Nationale Contre les OGM et pour la sauvegarde de patrimoine genetique du Mali. July 2004. *Manifeste: Le Mali face à la menace des O.G.M.*

[325] White, Pamela. 29 July 2004. Correspondence to CCA-ONG from Pamela White, Directrice au Mali USAID/Mali. Bamako, Mali

[326] Neither of these institutions to fight against corruption in Mali was independent of the president of the country. Neither had ever investigated any powerful figures in the country. Many African presidents obeyed donor requirements and set up committees to investigate corruption, and some

found them useful tools for investigating anyone in their government or outside it who might challenge them politically.

[327] Roundup is a Monsanto glyphosate-based herbicide, and Monsanto's Roundup Ready seeds are resistant to this herbicide.

[328] At a 2005 meeting in Thailand of the body that advises the UN Convention on Biological Diversity, Canadian negotiators attacked a UN report critical of "terminator" seeds, the most controversial of genetically modified seeds. Terminator crop varieties produce only infertile seeds, which ensures that farmers cannot plant them and must purchase new seeds each year. The Canadian negotiators pushed that the ban on such sterilization be lifted to allow testing and commercialization of Terminator technology that was patented in 1998 by the US Department of Agriculture (USDA) and the world's largest seed company, Delta & Pine Land Company (D&PL). In 1999, Monsanto said it would stop using the technology, and other companies followed suit because of concerns raised by its opponents that the terminator genes might spread to non-GM crops, and widespread outrage around the world that poor farmers would not be able to use seeds from their own crops. A ban was placed on the technology in 2000, which Canada along with Australia and New Zealand challenged – unsuccessfully – at the meeting in Thailand in February 2005. However, in October 2005, the USDA and D&PL applied for a patent for terminator technology in Canada, and obtained it. On 31 May 2007, a bill was introduced into Parliament in Canada by the agriculture critic of the New Democratic Party that, if passed, would ban research and testing of terminator technology in the country. On 1 June 2007, Monsanto took over D&PL, which holds a patent for terminator in Canada. [Forge, Frederic. 22 Mar. 2006. "The terminator technology." Ottawa: Library of Parliament. Parliamentary Research and Information Service. http://www.parl.gc.ca/information/library/ PRBpubs/prb0588-e.pdf; AND: Vidal, John. 9 Feb. 2005. "Canada backs terminator seeds." *The Guardian.* http://www.guardian.co.uk/science/2005/ feb/09/gm.food

14 Why do you bring your mistakes here?

[329] Greaves, Thomas. 1996. "Tribal rights," IN: Brush S and Stabinsky D (eds). *Valuing local knowledge – indigenous people and intellectual property rights.* Washington, DC: Island Press.

[330] BBC News. 11 Mar. 2008. "World warned on high food costs." http://news.bbc.co.uk/2/hi/in_depth/7288959.stm

[331] Ferrett, Grant. 27 Oct. 2007. "Biofuels 'crime against humanity'." BBC News. http://news.bbc.co.uk/2/hi/americas/7065061.stm

[332] For a list of some of those running the show at Davos 2008, see: World Economic Forum Annual Meeting 2008 http://www.weforum.org/en/ events/ArchivedEvents/AnnualMeeting2008/index.htm

[333] Caplan, 2008. p 83.

[334] Reuters. 25 Jan. 2008. "Gates gives 300 mln for African farming." http://www.reuters.com/article/gc07/idUSL2327163620080125

[335] Alliance for a Green Revolution in Africa. http://www.agra-alliance.org/

[336] BBC News. 25 Jan. 2008. "Boost for Africa's depleted soils." http://news.bbc.co.uk/2/hi/science/nature/7209608.stm

[337] Marsden, William. 2007. *Stupid to the Last Drop – how Alberta is bringing environmental Armageddon to Canada (and doesn't seem to care).* Toronto: Alfred A. Knopf. p 70.

[338] See: OXFAM Briefing Paper 76. 15 June 2005. A round for free: how rich countries are getting a free ride for subsidies at the WTO. http://www.oxfam.org/en/files/bp76_dumping_roundforfree_050615.pdf

[339] Patel, 2008. p 120.

[340] See: Pollan, Michael. 2006. *Omnivore's Dilemma – a natural history of four meals.* New York: Penguin Books; AND: Pollan, Michael. 2008. *In Defense of Food – an eater's manifesto.* New York: The Penguin Press; Schlosser, Eric. 2002. *Fast Food Nation – the dark side of the all-American meal.* New York: HarperCollins.

[341] See: Shiva, Vandana. 1997. *The Plunder of Nature and Knowledge.* Cambridge, MA: South End Press; Shiva, Vandana. 1999. *Stolen Harvest – the hijacking of the global food supply.* Cambridge, MA: South End Press; Shiva, Vandana. 1991. *The Violence of Green Revolution: Third World agriculture, ecology and politics.* Penang, Malaysia: Third World Network; AND: Tsiko, Sifelani. "Africa resists 'Green Revolution'." 28 Jan. 2008. *Black Star News.* http://blackstarnews.com/?c=122&a=4174

[342] Shiva, 1991. p 1.

[343] Patel, 2008. p 25; See: *India Today.* 29 Nov. 2004. available at http://www.undp.org.in/hdrc/pc/Dec03/GreenRevolution.pdf

[344] McNamara, Robert. 1973. *One Hundred Countries, Two Billion People: the dimensions of development.* London: Pall Mall Press.

[345] Shea butter is a high-quality oil from the shea nut *(Vitellaria paradoxa)*, and is also known by its French name, *karité.*

[346] Structural Adjustment Programs had suppressed or eliminated agricultural subsidies, including all those on farming inputs that modern agricultural experts had just spent a decade or so introducing to Africa, and on which African farmers had already become independent. In 1996, I interviewed Ismael Serageldin, then Vice President for Environmentally Sustainable Development at the World Bank. I asked him why, when there was so much concern about food security and hunger in Africa, the Bank and IMF had insisted on eliminating all subsidies on farm inputs. He denied that those subsidies had ever reached the poorest farmers who needed them. Challenged for evidence on this, he merely repeated the claim, which my interviews with farmers in half a dozen African countries contradicted.

[347] Dumont, Réné. 1988. *False Start in Africa.* London, UK: Earthscan Publications Limited (original English translation by André Deutsch Limited

in 1966). p 193. Originally published in 1962 as *L'Afrique noir est mal partie,* by Editions du Seuil.

[348] The International Council for Research in Agroforestry (ICRAF) was a modest organization established in Nairobi, Kenya, 1978 by Canada's International Development Research Centre (IDRC). ICRAF had a mandate limited to Africa, where it was intended to document agroforestry systems. In 1991, ICRAF joined the Consultative Group on International Agricultural Research (CGIAR) and became the International Centre for Research in Agroforestry, with a global mandate for scientific research. In 2002, ICRAF changed its name to the World Agroforestry Centre.

[349] Personal communication.

[350] In the mid-1990s, ICRAF researchers determined that phosphate, or the lack of it in African soils, is the greatest limiting factor to crop production in Africa, after water. They then carried out a survey of phosphate deposits on the continent, seeking sources that might be exploited for rock phosphate that would be far cheaper than imported fertilizers from multinational companies that produced and sold them. Their survey took them as far as Madagascar, where they used a boat to search remote coastal areas. They learned that while Africa was rich in phosphate deposits, they had nearly all been taken over as concessions by multinational companies, to produce inorganic fertilizers that Africa would have to import. It should also be noted that many subsistence farmers in Africa – from Zambia to Kenya – said to me that continuous use of inorganic fertilizers has a long-term negative impact on soils, reducing levels of organic matter and ultimately impoverishing the soils they are supposed to enrich, and further increasing the need for purchased fertilizer, creating a vicious circle.

[351] See: BBC News. 30 June 2005. "African sands 'set for upheaval'." http://news.bbc.co.uk/go/pr/fr/-/2/hi/science/nature/4634595.stm; AND: Thomas D, M Knight, and Wiggs GFS. 2005. "Remobilization of southern African desert dune by twenty-first century global warming." *Nature* 435: 1218-1221.

[352] De Wit, Maarten and Stankiewicz, Jacek. 2006. "Changes in surface water supply across Africa with predicted climate change." *Science* DOI: 10.1126/science.1119929.

[353] *Washington Post.* 25 July 2008. "Heavyweights to lobby for more biofuel." p D4. http://www.washingtonpost.com/wp-dyn/content/article/2008/07/24/AR2008072403703.html

[354] Land tenure in much of rural Africa is complex and intricate, governed still be traditional rulers who allocate land for use without any written property deeds denoting ownership. Some have seen this as a deterrent to improved land use, as those without fixed tenure may not wish to plant trees or invest in the land. But there are arguments to be made that this unwritten land tenure has also prevented the proliferation of massive plantations and protected smallholders. As agribusinesses begin to demand fixed land-tenure from governments and chiefs, smallholders risk losing

ancestral farmlands and forests that till now have provided them subsistence and independence.

[355] Marcotting, or air-layering, involves wounding the branch of a mother tree, selected in this case for a particularly quality or timing of its fruit or nut production, and then wrapping that wound with a plastic bag containing a rooting medium such as sawdust or soil, until shoots emerge from the wounded branch and form roots in the bag. Large trees can sustain up to seven of these wounds. The branches can then be lopped off with the resultant marcots, which are placed in a simple propagator of plastic over a frame. There they grow into small trees that can be transplanted, and mature rapidly.

[356] Fortin Daniel, LôModou and Maynart, Guy. *Plantes médicinales du Sahel.* 1997. Dakar: Enda-Editions. *Série Etudes et Recherches* no. 187-188-189. This book was produced with the support of two organizations that offer the kind of development assistance that enables Africans to develop their own continent with an African perspective – ENDA Tiers Monde and the Centre Canadien d'Etudes et de Cooperation Internationale (CECI).

[357] *Combretum micranthum* G. don. Seed Leaflet. No. 129, Dec. 2007. http://www.sl.life.ku.dk/upload/c_micranthum.pdf

[358] Cameroonian researchers told me that bio-prospectors often go to live with indigenous groups, posing as anthropologists. When they discover a particular plant with a huge potential market value, they either take it back to pharmaceutical labs to isolate and synthesize the active molecule, or if that fails, market the herbal treatment using its African origins as a marketing tool. A good example is the recent 'discovery' by Phytopharm of *Hoodia gordonii*, a cactus used by the Kung Bushmen in the Kalahari Desert to stave off hunger. This new anti-obesity remedy made headlines as the "dieter's dream" across the Western world, even coverage on Oprah Winfrey's television show. Phytopharm then sold the 'rights' to the US pharmaceutical giant Pfizer (maker of Viagra), shares of which rose as they took ownership of this plant knowledge. Fortunately, the Bushmen had a lawyer, South African Roger Chennelis, who was fighting for financial compensation for the true discoverers of this herbal medicine, and the true owners of rights to the knowledge. Meanwhile, bio-prospectors continue to experiment with 300 plants used regularly as medicines by the people of the Kalahari. [Barnett, Antony. 17 June 2001. "In Africa the Hoodia cactus keeps men alive; now its secret is 'stolen' to make us thin." *The Observer.*]

[359] Sceptics in Africa have suggested to me that these imported chemical strategies to fight malaria are "tied aid." They serve the interests of chemical and pharmaceutical lobbies more than they do the African population. The Global Fund for Malaria provides money to NGOs across Africa to promote the use of the insecticide-treated bed nets; one woman working on such a project told me that they were not permitted to promote the use of locally made mosquito nets, which can be found in the markets, and were instructed to promote only the imported nets. She also noted that many people in West Africa don't sleep on beds; they sleep on mats on the floor, and that the imported bed nets are simply not practical. I could find no

Africans working on the project to promote the use of treated bed nets who were willing to use one themselves. They said they had tried for a while, but that their children had developed coughs and felt sick. They also said they were concerned that by using the nets, they would reduce the number of mosquito bites they received but that they would never be able to eliminate them, and fewer bites might mean a lower tolerance for malaria. When I reminded them of the science that had gone into testing the treated nets, and evidence that their use had reduced deaths caused by malaria especially among vulnerable groups (small children, pregnant women), they shrugged and said they were simply not convinced. When I asked why they promoted something they would not use themselves or even believe in, they said they had no choice; they had no other job opportunities so they did what they were paid to do.

[360] The renewed push for and the eventual WHO approval in 2006 of indoor spraying of DDT to combat malaria in Africa, after many years during which it had been banned in some countries because of health and environmental risks, was interesting. In North America, right-wing columnists (and right-wing think tanks funded by large petrochemical and corporate interests), with no obvious knowledge of or compassion for Africans, overnight became champions of African people and wrote scathing commentaries about "environmentalists" who were labelled "racist" and blamed for millions of malaria deaths in Africa. The DDT spin job was orchestrated by the same groups with Orwellian names – "Junk Science, Tech Central Station" – that also deny climate change. The main DDT cheerleader was the Competitive Enterprise Institute (CEI) backed by enormous corporate sponsors such as ExxonMobil and Monsanto, pharmaceutical interests and foundations that fund the American Enterprise Institute, such as the John M. Olin Foundation (petrochemical wealth). The CEI, in turn, backed "Africa Fighting Malaria," established in 2000 in Washington, DC and South Africa. There were also pseudo-scientific publications such as *21st Century Science & Technology.* The ploy worked. In 2006, Dr. Arata Kochi, head of the WHO malaria control, issued a press release to announce the new WHO policy to promote DDT. This was done in Washington, DC, and not at WHO headquarters in Geneva, and Dr. Kochi was flanked by a right-wing US Senator. [See: Mourin, Jennifer. 26 Sept. 2006. "Why DDT? WHO's campaign promoting DDT greeted with condemnation at the IFCS." PAN AP. http://www.panna.org/files/panapWhyDdt20060926.pdf; AND: Pesticide Action Network North America (PANNA) "Who's promoting DDT?" http://www.panna.org/ddt/promoting; AND: Pesticide Action Network North America (PANNA) "DDT & malaria: setting the record straight." http://www.panna.org/files/ddtTruthSheetJuly06.pdf]

[361] 21 Apr. 2008. Executive Summary of the Synthesis Report of the International Assessment of Agricultural Knowledge, Science and Technology for Development (IAASTD) http://www.agassessment.org/docs/SR_Exec_Sum_210408_Final.pdf; AND: BBC News. 15 Apr. 2008. "UN calls for farming revolution." http://news.bbc.co.uk/2/hi/europe/7348728.stm; AND: 18 April 2008. "GM debate overshadows key UN agriculture report."

Farmers Guardian. http://www.farmersguardian.com/story.asp?section-code=1&storycode=17843

[362] Pearce, Fred. 29 Jan. 1994. France swaps debt for right to tropical timber. *New Scientist* 1910: 7.

[363] Simons T, Dawson IK, Duguma B and Tchoundjeu Z. 1998. "Passing problems: prostate and prunus – African team works to maintain sustainable supply of Pygeum bark." *HerbalGram* 43: 40-53.

[364] The French company, Fournier Pharma, was acquired by the Solvay Group in July 2005.

[365] Germany lost possession of Cameroon during World War I; in 1919 France and England assumed control and divided it into two separate colonies, which joined together as one country at independence.

[366] When I visited Cameroon in 2004, I learned that Plantecam had closed its doors and moved out. The pharmaceutical pickings had become a little slim and there had been too much pressure from local people and environmental groups in the country, notably bark harvesters themselves with support from British and German teams working with the Mount Cameroon Project, who together managed to convince the government to reduce quotas. Right to the end, Plantecam claimed it was promoting conservation and sustainable harvesting. Yet when it was actually ordered to do so, it slammed its doors closed and moved operations elsewhere.

[367] Leakey, Roger. June 1999. Editorial. "The evolution of agroforestry." *People and Plants Handbook* (5): Cultivating trees.

[368] The non-mist propagators make basic horticultural techniques accessible to Africa's rural people. They are simple and inexpensive to make locally, stretching plastic sheeting over a simple wooden frame to create a miniature greenhouse.

[369] In Cameroon, scientists pointed out to me that many common foods collected from the forest were also considered medicines when consumed in different doses. Many common chronic diseases common in the West were absent among peoples around the world before the introduction of Western diets and lifestyles. Using research compiled by a range of medical professionals working with native populations in Africa, Asia and Latin America, Michael Pollan lists these diseases that appear only when people adopt Western lifestyles – heart disease, diabetes, cancer, obesity, hypertension, strokes, appendicitis, diverticulitis, malformed dental arches, tooth decay, varicose veins, ulcers and hemorrhoids. [Pollan, 2008. pp 91-92.]

Part III: Everyone is waving at me

15 Lots to sing about

[370] SIL International http://www.sil.org/sil/

[371] Kershaw, Andy. 17 June 2005. "The myth of Saint Bob, saviour of Africa." *The Independent.* http://www.independent.co.uk/opinion/commentators/ andy-kershaw-the-myth-of-saint-bob-saviour-of-africa-494349.html

16 The library is burning

[372] "Sinankunya, quelle valeur culturelle?" *Donko: Magazine du Ministère de la Culture,* Mai 2003: 2-3.

[373] Africans were not passive victims to early European colonists and then later fought hard for their independence. Among the groups that fought against colonists were the Amhara in Ethiopia, the Shona in Zimbabwe, the Zulu in South Africa, Asante in Ghana. Up to 100 thousand Malagasies died fighting French colonialism in Madagascar, and Algerians fought an eight-year war of independence against the French. The Mau Mau fought the British in Kenya in the 1950s; as many as 20,000 Kenyans died in that uprising, while after four years, 32 white civilians had been killed. See: Caplan, 2008. p 27, 32.]

17 View from Timbuktu

[374] Côte d'Ivoire supplied companies such as Cadbury, Nestlé, Mars and The Hershey Company. Before the war broke out, there had been numerous studies revealing the extent of abuse of children labourers trafficked to the plantations from neighbouring countries, who were described as "slaves" by Save The Children Canada.

[375] France is the only non-African country that was actively involved in the conflict, sending 3,000 troops to guard a neutral zone between north and south, which were later subsumed into a UN force. But France was also accused by both sides of favouring the other, and did not engage as much support as it might have to try to force both sides to resolve the conflict, possibly because France did not feel it could afford to lose its dominant influence – and huge investments – in Côte d'Ivoire. Ivorian reggae star and peace advocate, Alpha Blondy, told me that the conflict had its roots in an unfair distribution of power and resources in the country, sanctioned for decades by former colonial power, France. He said that he feared it could escalate into genocide if both sides did not restrain their forces. On private FM stations, people close to President Gbagbo and also his wife – both self-declared born-again Christians – had called for an elimination of the northern Dioula people. To end the stalemate, in 2007, New Forces leader, Guillaume Soro, was made prime minister to rule with President Gbagbo, until new elections would allow Ivorians to vote. See: IRIN news. 8 Feb. 2006. "Côte d'Ivoire: profiles of three Ivorians facing UN sanctions." United Nations humanitarian news and information service (IRIN). http://www.irin-news.org/report.asp?ReportID=51619&SelectRegion=West_Africa; AND: United Nations Security Council SC/8631. Security Council Committee concerning Côte d'Ivoire issues list of individuals subject to measures imposed

by resolution 1572 (2004). http://www.un.org/News/Press/docs/2006/sc8631.doc.htm

[376] Kola nuts, of which there are several varieties from different trees indigenous to West and Central Africa, are extremely important culturally, and are chewed as a very mild stimulant to counter fatigue (much like a cup of coffee in the West). Marriages, naming ceremonies, visits and any discussions to appease tension between individuals or among groups are not complete without gifts of Kola nuts. They are a major commodity for regional trade.

[377] Gardner, Brian. 1968. *The quest for Timbuctoo.* London: Cassell & Co Ltd.

[378] Eltahir, E A B and Gong, C. 1996. "Dynamics of wet and dry years in West Africa." *Journal of Climate,* 9(5): 1030-1042.

[379] The acknowledged "father" of the foreign efforts to resurrect and study the manuscripts of Timbuktu is Professor John Hunwick of Northwestern University in Illinois, US, who has been working closely with Malian and European scholars for decades, to preserve, restore and translate some of the key manuscripts from Arabic into French and English. In Timbuktu, Malian historians are full of praise for Professor Hunwick, and call him their "father" or "grandfather."

[380] Monbiot, George. 2008. *Bring On the Apocolypse: essays on self-destruction.* Toronto: Anchor Canada. p 142.